I0112984

NBER International Seminar
on Macroeconomics 2005

NBER International Seminar
on Macroeconomics 2005

Jeffrey A. Frankel and Christopher A. Pissarides, editors

The MIT Press
Cambridge, Massachusetts
London, England

NBER/International Seminar on Macroeconomics 2005
ISSN: 1932-8796
ISBN-13: 978-0-262-06265-7 (hc.:alk.paper)—978-0-262-56229-4 (pbk.:alk.paper)
ISBN-10: 0-262-06265-8 (hc.:alk.paper)—0-262-56229-4 (pbk.:alk.paper)

Published annually by The MIT Press, Cambridge, Massachusetts 02142.

© 2007 by the National Bureau of Economic Research and the Massachusetts Institute of Technology.

All rights reserved. No part of this book may be reproduced in any form by any electronic or mechanical means (including photocopying, recording, or information storage and retrieval) without permission in writing from the publisher.

Standing orders/subscriptions are available. Inquiries, and changes to subscriptions and addresses should be addressed to Triliteral, Attention: Standing Orders, 100 Maple Ridge Drive, Cumberland, RI 02864, phone 1-800-366-6687 ext. 112 (U.S. and Canada), fax 1-800-406-9145 (U.S. and Canada).

In the United Kingdom, continental Europe, and the Middle East and Africa, send single copy and back volume orders to: The MIT Press, Ltd., Fitzroy House, 11 Chenies Street, London WC1E 7ET England, phone 44-020-7306-0603, fax 44-020-7306-0604, email info@hup-MITpress.co.uk, website http://mitpress.mit.edu.

In the United States and for all other countries, send single copy and back volume orders to: The MIT Press c/o Triliteral, 100 Maple Ridge Drive, Cumberland, RI 02864, phone 1-800-405-1619 (U.S. and Canada) or 401-658-4226, fax 1-800-406-9145 (U.S. and Canada) or 401-531-2801, email mitpress-orders@mit.edu, website http://mitpress.mit.edu.

This book was set in Palatino and was printed and bound in the United States of America.

NBER Board of Directors by Affiliation

Officers

Elizabeth E. Bailey, *Chairman*
John S. Clarkeson, *Vice Chairman*
Martin Feldstein, *President and Chief Executive Officer*
Susan Colligan, *Vice President for Administration and Budget and Corporate Secretary*
Robert Mednick, *Treasurer*
Kelly Horak, *Controller and Assistant Corporate Secretary*
Gerardine Johnson, *Assistant Corporate Secretary*

Directors at Large

Peter C. Aldrich	Jessica P. Einhorn	John Lipsky
Elizabeth E. Bailey	Martin Feldstein	Laurence H. Meyer
John H. Biggs	Roger W. Ferguson, Jr.	Michael H. Moskow
John S. Clarkeson	Jacob A. Frenkel	Alicia H. Munnell
Don R. Conlan	Judith M. Gueron	Rudolph A. Oswald
Kathleen B. Cooper	Robert S. Hamada	Robert T. Parry
Charles H. Dallara	Karen N. Horn	Marina v. N. Whitman
George C. Eads	Judy C. Lewent	Martin B. Zimmerman

Directors by University Appointment

George Akerlof, *California, Berkeley*
Jagdish Bhagwati, *Columbia*
Ray C. Fair, *Yale*
Michael J. Brennan, *California, Los Angeles*
Glen G. Cain, *Wisconsin*
Franklin Fisher, *Massachusetts Institute of Technology*
Saul H. Hymans, *Michigan*

Marjorie B. McElroy, *Duke*
Joel Mokyr, *Northwestern*
Andrew Postlewaite, *Pennsylvania*
Uwe E. Reinhardt, *Princeton*
Nathan Rosenberg, *Stanford*
Craig Swan, *Minnesota*
David B. Yoffie, *Harvard*
Arnold Zellner (Director Emeritus), *Chicago*

Directors by Appointment of Other Organizations

Richard B. Berner, *National Association For Business Economics*
Gail D. Fosler, *The Conference Board*
Martin Gruber, *American Finance Association*
Arthur B. Kennickell, *American Statistical Association*
Thea Lee, *American Federation of Labor and Congress of Industrial Organizations*
William W. Lewis, *Committee for Economic Development*

Robert Mednick, *American Institute of Certified Public Accountants*
Angelo Melino, *Canadian Economics Association*
Jeffrey M. Perloff, *American Agricultural Economics Association*
John J. Siegfried, *American Economic Association*
Gavin Wright, *Economic History Association*

Directors Emeriti

Andrew Brimmer	Franklin A. Lindsay	Richard N. Rosett
Carl F. Christ	Paul W. McCracken	Eli Shapiro
George Hatsopoulos	Peter G. Peterson	Arnold Zellner
Lawrence R. Klein		

Relation of the Directors to the Work and Publications of the NBER

1. The object of the NBER is to ascertain and present to the economics profession, and to the public more generally, important economic facts and their interpretation in a scientific manner without policy recommendations. The Board of Directors is charged with the responsibility of ensuring that the work of the NBER is carried on in strict conformity with this object.

2. The President shall establish an internal review process to ensure that book manuscripts proposed for publication DO NOT contain policy recommendations. This shall apply both to the proceedings of conferences and to manuscripts by a single author or by one or more co-authors but shall not apply to authors of comments at NBER conferences who are not NBER affiliates.

3. No book manuscript reporting research shall be published by the NBER until the President has sent to each member of the Board a notice that a manuscript is recommended for publication and that in the President's opinion it is suitable for publication in accordance with the above principles of the NBER. Such notification will include a table of contents and an abstract or summary of the manuscript's content, a list of contributors if applicable, and a response form for use by Directors who desire a copy of the manuscript for review. Each manuscript shall contain a summary drawing attention to the nature and treatment of the problem studied and the main conclusions reached.

4. No volume shall be published until forty-five days have elapsed from the above notification of intention to publish it. During this period a copy shall be sent to any Director requesting it, and if any Director objects to publication on the grounds that the manuscript contains policy recommendations, the objection will be presented to the author(s) or editor(s). In case of dispute, all members of the Board shall be noti-

fied, and the President shall appoint an ad hoc committee of the Board to decide the matter; thirty days additional shall be granted for this purpose.

5. The President shall present annually to the Board a report describing the internal manuscript review process, any objections made by Directors before publication or by anyone after publication, any disputes about such matters, and how they were handled.

6. Publications of the NBER issued for informational purposes concerning the work of the Bureau, or issued to inform the public of the activities at the Bureau, including but not limited to the NBER Digest and Reporter, shall be consistent with the object stated in paragraph 1. They shall contain a specific disclaimer noting that they have not passed through the review procedures required in this resolution. The Executive Committee of the Board is charged with the review of all such publications from time to time.

7. NBER working papers and manuscripts distributed on the Bureau's web site are not deemed to be publications for the purpose of this resolution, but they shall be consistent with the object stated in paragraph 1. Working papers shall contain a specific disclaimer noting that they have not passed through the review procedures required in this resolution. The NBER's web site shall contain a similar disclaimer. The President shall establish an internal review process to ensure that the working papers and the web site do not contain policy recommendations, and shall report annually to the Board on this process and any concerns raised in connection with it.

8. Unless otherwise determined by the Board or exempted by the terms of paragraphs 6 and 7, a copy of this resolution shall be printed in each NBER publication as described in paragraph 2 above.

Contents

Abstracts

1 Macroeconomic Derivatives: An Initial Analysis of Market-Based Macro Forecasts, Uncertainty, and Risk
Refet S. Gürkaynak and Justin Wolfers

In September 2002, a new market in "Economic Derivatives" was launched allowing traders to take positions on future values of several macroeconomic data releases. We provide an initial analysis of the prices of these options. We find that market-based measures of expectations are similar to survey-based forecasts although the market-based measures somewhat more accurately predict financial market responses to surprises in data. These markets also provide implied probabilities of the full range of specific outcomes, allowing us to measure uncertainty, assess its driving forces, and compare this measure of uncertainty with the dispersion of point-estimates among individual forecasters (a measure of disagreement). We also assess the accuracy of market-generated probability density forecasts. A consistent theme is that few of the behavioral anomalies present in surveys of professional forecasts survive in equilibrium, and that these markets are remarkably well calibrated. Finally we assess the role of risk, finding little evidence that risk-aversion drives a wedge between market prices and probabilities in this market.

2 The Roots of Low European Employment: Family Culture?
Yann Algan and Pierre Cahuc

OECD countries faced largely divergent employment rates during the last decades. However, the whole bulk of the cross-national and cross-temporal heterogeneity relies on specific demographic groups: prime-age women and younger and older individuals. This paper argues that family labor supply interactions and cross-country heterogeneity in family culture are key for explaining these stylized facts.

First we provide a simple labor supply model in which heterogeneity in family preferences can account for cross-country variations in both the level and the dynamics of employment rates of demographic groups. Second, we provide evidence based on international individual surveys that family attitudes do differ across countries and are largely shaped by national features. We also document that cross-country differences in family culture *cause* cross-national differences in family attitudes. Studying the correlation between employment rates and family attitudes, we then show that the stronger preferences for family activities in European countries may explain both their lower female employment rate and the fall in the employment rates of young and older people.

3   Shadow Sorting
Tito Boeri and Pietro Garibaldi

This paper investigates the border between formal employment, shadow employment, and unemployment in an equilibrium model of the labor market with market frictions. From the labor demand side, firms optimally create legal or shadow employment through a mechanism that is akin to tax evasion. From the labor supply side, heterogeneous workers sort across the two sectors, with high productivity workers entering the legal sector. Such worker sorting appears fully consistent with most empirical evidence on shadow employment. The model also sheds light on the "shadow puzzle," the increasing size of the shadow economy in OECD countries in spite of improvements in technologies detecting tax and social security evasion. Shadow employment is correlated with unemployment, and it is tolerated because the repression of shadow activity increases unemployment. The model implies that shadow wage gaps should be lower in depressed labor markets and that deregulation of labor markets is accompanied by a decline in the average skills of the workforce in both legal and shadow sectors. Based on micro data on two countries with a sizeable shadow economy, Italy and Brazil, we find empirical support for these implications of the model. The paper suggests also that policies aimed at reducing the shadow economy are likely to increase unemployment.

4 Globalization and Equilibrium Inflation-Output Tradeoffs
Assaf Razin and Prakash Loungani

The paper shows that capital account and trade account liberalizations affect the inefficiency of a New Keynesian open economy macro equilibrium by altering the relative weights attached to the output gap and inflation terms in the representative household's utility-based loss function. It is well known that with capital account liberalization the household is able to smooth fluctuations in consumption, while trade liberalization permits specialization in domestic production and diversification in domestic consumption. We show that an important implication of these features is that capital market and trade openness (i.e., "globalization") reduce the weight of the output gap term in the utility-based loss function. The paper provides a re-interpretation of evidence on the effect of openness on the inflation-output tradeoff, which supports the model's predictions.

5 Fiscal Externalities and Optimal Taxation in an Economic Community
Marianne Baxter and Robert G. King

The Stability and Growth Pact is a continuing source of economic controversy within Europe. The Pact recognizes that individual member states experience divergent business cycle conditions which may lead them to run deficits at certain points in time. However, the pact is designed to encourage member states to adopt fiscal policies that imply zero deficits on average and to limit their deficits to three percent of GDP at any point in time.

We study the nature of fiscal externalities within an economic community, such as Europe, which lacks explicit rules for fiscal policy coordination, assuming that each country chooses its tax rates optimally given the fiscal stance of other countries. Allowing for real shifts to country productivity and public expenditure, we find that the fiscal deficit can be a poor indicator of fiscal externalities: countries with different labor and consumption tax rates can exert exactly the same external effect but have very different fiscal deficit behavior. Trade deficits are, by contrast, much more informative about the effects that an individual country has on other members of the community.

6   Fiscal Divergence and Business Cycle Synchronization: Irresponsibility Is Idiosyncratic

Zsolt Darvas, Andrew K. Rose, and György Szapáry

Using a panel of 21 OECD countries and 40 years of annual data, we find that countries with similar government budget positions tend to have business cycles that fluctuate more closely. That is, fiscal convergence (in the form of persistently similar ratios of government surplus/deficit to GDP) is systematically associated with more synchronized business cycles. We also find evidence that reduced fiscal deficits increase business cycle synchronization. The Maastricht "convergence criteria," used to determine eligibility for EMU, encouraged fiscal convergence and deficit reduction. They may thus have indirectly moved Europe closer to an optimum currency area, by reducing countries' abilities to create idiosyncratic fiscal shocks. Our empirical results are economically and statistically significant, and robust.

7   Dual Inflation and the Real Exchange Rate in New Open Economy Macroeconomics

Balázs Világi

This paper studies how the models of the new open economy macroeconomics, which usually focus on the relationship between the nominal exchange rate and the external real exchange rate, can explain the coexistence of permanent dual inflation, namely diverging inflation rates for tradable and non-tradable goods, and appreciation of the CPI-based real exchange rate in emerging market economies.

It is shown that the impact of asymmetric sectoral productivity growth on the CPI-based real exchange rate depends heavily on the market structure, and that the models of new open economy macroeconomics can be reconciled with the Balassa-Samuelson effect only if pricing to market is added to models.

It is demonstrated that the presence of nominal and real rigidities helps to explain the slow and incomplete adjustment of the relative price of non-tradables to tradables.

8   Trade Invoicing in the Accession Countries: Are They Suited to the Euro?
Linda S. Goldberg

The accession countries to the euro area are increasingly binding their economic activity, external and internal, to the euro area countries. One aspect of this phenomenon concerns the currency invoicing of international trade transactions, where accession countries have reduced their use of the U.S. dollar in invoicing international trade transactions. Theory predicts that the optimal invoicing choices for accession countries depend on the composition of goods in exports and imports and on the macroeconomic fluctuations of trade partners, both bearing on the role of herding and hedging considerations within exporter profitability. These considerations yield country-specific estimates about the degree of euro-denominated invoicing of exports. I find that the exporters of some accession countries, even in their trade transactions with the euro zone and other European Union countries, might be pricing too much of their trade in euros rather than in dollars, thus taking on excessive risk in international markets.

Introduction

Jeffrey A. Frankel and Christopher A. Pissarides

The International Seminar on Macroeconomics (ISOM) meets every June in a different European city, bringing together American and European economists to study a variety of topics within "macroeconomics," defined very broadly. The tradition started in 1978, and during the first half of its life was popularly known as the "Gordon-deMenil seminar." Jeffrey A. Frankel is now overall co-director of ISOM, with Francesco Giavazzi as his European counterpart.

This volume contains a selection of the papers originally presented at the 28th International Seminar on Macroeconomics, which took place in Budapest on June 17–18, 2005. The meeting was kindly hosted by the Magyar Nemzeti Bank—the Central Bank of Hungary—and in particular by its Deputy Governor, György Szapáry, who took an active role in the proceedings. In 2005 the program was organized by Jeffrey A. Frankel and Christopher A. Pissarides. The papers published here have gone through the usual refereeing process for NBER Conference volumes.

Geographically, ISOM has been venturing farther afield than its origins in the major countries of Western Europe. The 2005 meeting was the first held in Central or Eastern Europe, and the first held in any of the ten countries that had officially acceded to the European Union the year before, in 2004. Subsequent ISOM meetings will continue to extend our interest in the east.

ISOM Tradition and Transition

From 1990 through 2003, the National Bureau of Economic Research organized ISOM jointly with the European Economic Association and a selection of the papers was published in the Association's journal. One goal, originally, was to help narrow what was perceived to be a gap between the two continents. European academic macroeconomists several decades ago were more insular than their American counterparts (notwithstanding that the United States may have been the more insular place, economically and politically). In any case, times have changed. Europe now turns out many fine macroeconomists, who are doing frontier research and are well-plugged in to what goes on outside the borders of the countries of their birth, in other European countries as well as across the oceans.

In 2004, both sponsoring parties decided that the collaboration had accomplished its mission. The NBER became the sole sponsor of ISOM. We continue to work with a local host in a different European country each summer, and to divide the authors and discussants equally between Americans and Europeans. But with the 27th annual ISOM proceedings, we inaugurated a new regime. Now the proceedings are published by MIT Press as the *NBER International Seminar on Macroeconomics*. The new proceedings, of which *NBER ISOM 2005* is the second annual installment, appear as a companion volume to the *NBER Macroeconomics Annual*. The *Macro Annual* has since its birth in 1986 established a genuinely unique reputation for must-read articles on a range of relevant macroeconomic topics, written by leaders of the field, mostly based in the United States. Thus both conference series have distinguished pedigrees, and the decision by MIT Press to bring the two together as parallel publications was inspired and auspicious.

Overview of the Volume

The eight papers published in the 28th volume of ISOM, as usual, cover quite a range of topics. While the subject matter of the papers ranges widely, one can weave some overarching themes.

The eight chapters fall into two categories. **Part I** deals with **Macroeconomic Policy and Labor Markets.** The first four of this year's papers explore relationships among macroeconomic aggregates that are of universal interest among advanced countries, one of them on macro derivatives, one on the implications of globalization, and two specifically regarding labor markets. **Part II** considers **Implications of an Expanding Monetary Union.** The four papers here are more relevant specifically to some of the topical questions associated with the Eastward expansion of the EU and EMU. Two concern fiscal policy in a region that has unified economically. Two deal with aspects of the mechanics of the process when a country such as Hungary joins the euro: the real exchange rate and the choice of invoice currency, respectively.

Part I: Macroeconomic Policy and Labor Markets

We now summarize the chapters in greater detail.

Refet S. Gürkaynak and Justin Wolfers lead off with "Macroeconomic Derivatives: An Initial Analysis of Market-Based Macro Forecasts, Uncertainty, and Risk." In September 2002, a new market in "Economic Derivatives" was launched allowing traders to take positions on future values of non-farm payroll employment, initial jobless claims, retail sales, and ISM business sentiment. The authors provide an initial analysis of these data (predictions regarding 153 data releases over the first 2 ½ years of the futures market). Previous researchers have used survey data to measure market expectations of official economic statistics. But economic derivatives have several major advantages over surveys in that they provide market-implied probabilities of specific outcomes, and they predict somewhat more accurately and less biasedly market reactions to new data releases. They also allow a measure of uncertainty in investors' forecasts, which is quite a different thing—both in principle and in practice—from the dispersion of views across market participants. Finally, the authors find no evidence of a risk premium, suggesting that the derivative prices can be used as a good measure of market expectations. Announcements of the payroll employment numbers—measured as deviations from the expectations embodied in the derivatives, are the ones that have the greatest impact, particularly on the stock and bond markets. Evidently a strong labor market is one of the best indicators of a strong overall economy.

Which leads us to the subject of the labor market. In "The Roots of Low European Employment: Family Culture?" Yann Algan and Pierre Cahuc take a fresh look at the cross-country differences in employment rates across advanced countries. As is well known, the biggest differences in employment rates across OECD countries are due mainly to female employment rates and to the employment of older man and women. Southern European countries have much lower employment rates than Scandinavian or Anglo-Saxon countries, essentially because fewer women come out to seek employment and more men retire early. The authors investigate the extent to which these differences are the result of cultural differences rooted in religion and in beliefs about the role of the individual in the family. They make use of international data sets on social attitudes and find strong evidence in favor of their hypothesis that in European countries there are beliefs about the role of the family that are instrumental in the explanation of cross-country employment differences.

In "Shadow Sorting," Tito Boeri and Pietro Garibaldi take a close look at the unreported activity in labor markets. A variety of taxes and regulations on labor market activity push many workers to the underground economy, foregoing some of the benefits of a legally registered and more secure job for a job that pays no taxes and minimizes paperwork. The authors look at evidence on the shadow economy drawn from Italy and Brazil and conclude that there are close substitutions between shadow activity and unemployment. Employers choose whether to offer legally registered jobs or unreported jobs by weighing the benefits of avoiding tax on the latter, against the bigger security of employment of the former. Workers weigh up a similar trade-off and sort themselves according to their skill. More skilled workers seek jobs in the legal economy whereas less skilled ones may consider taking an unregistered job rather than face the risk of more unemployment. As a result, there is a close relation between the shadow employment rate and unemployment. Governments avoid monitoring more closely unreported jobs and closing them down, because this can increase unemployment. The authors find indirect evidence consistent with this hypothesis from their two countries.

In "Globalization and Equilibrium Inflation-Output Tradeoffs," Assaf Razin and Prakash Loungani examine the implications of increased international economic integration, both with respect to trade and capital flows, for the way the monetary authorities manage the long-run inflation rate. In an open economy, the representative consumer's payoff to unanticipated monetary expansion, in terms of higher output for a given increase in inflation, is likely to be less than in a closed economy. The authors demonstrate theoretically that international integration reduces the relative weight of output in the utility-based objective function. Instead, people should and do put relatively more weight on price stability. The authors bring some evidence on the inflation-output tradeoffs that supports the claim that globalization increases the relative weight of inflation in the monetary authority's objective function. This helps explain why central bankers around the world have delivered lower levels of inflation over the last decade than in the preceding several decades (which supports arguments of David Romer and Ken Rogoff, among others).

Part II: Implications of an Expanding Monetary Union

Economists have for some time tried to figure out what was the rationale behind the original Maastricht criteria that required new aspirants to EMU first to reduce their budget deficits below 3 percent of GDP, as well as the Stability and Growth Pact (SGP), which required that EMU members keep the deficits there. After all, this sort of fiscal convergence was not on the list of the various textbook criteria that have long been thought to qualify countries to give up their individual monetary policies and join a currency union. A typical example of such a criterion, rather, is synchronization of their business cycles (known as the pattern of "symmetric shocks"), because it reduces the need for individual monetary policies at the national level. To the contrary, one might think that when giving up the instrument of an independent monetary policy, it is all the more important for a country to retain the instrument of an independent fiscal policy, so as to be able to respond to idiosyncratic shocks.

In "Fiscal Externalities and Optimal Taxation in an Economic Community," Marianne Baxter and Robert G. King examine a set of relevant issues. The fiscal policies of members of an economic union such as the EU create externalities for each other. A common rationale for the Maastricht criteria or SGP is that countries that get into trouble through large budget deficits could force the European Central Bank to bail them out. Baxter and King, however, emphasize in their model a different kind of externality in the setting of tax rates. They conclude that the trade deficit is a better indicator of the fiscal costs imposed on others than the fiscal deficit which is the traditional focus.

In "Fiscal Divergence and Business Cycle Synchronization: Irresponsibility is Idiosyncratic," Zsolt Darvas, Andrew K. Rose, and György Szapáry perform for fiscal links an exercise that had been formerly performed for trade links: to see if business cycle synchronization is endogenous with respect to convergence. Their empirical finding is that fiscal convergence, defined as persistently similar ratios of government deficit to GDP, is indeed systematically associated with more synchronized budget cycles. Synchronized budget cycles imply less need for separate monetary policies, so this finding supports the SGP. To understand the authors' rationale for this finding, forget the idea that governments use discretionary fiscal policy to respond intelligently and benevolently to shocks in such a way as to stabilize the economy. Rather, governments are instead sometimes irresponsible, using fiscal policy to maximize their own objectives, such as winning elections, or are incompetent, such as responding to a downturn after it is too late, or otherwise producing fiscal policies that are as likely to be procyclical as countercyclical. As a result, independent fiscal policies are perfectly capable of exacerbating cyclical fluctuations rather than dampening them. The question then becomes whether they do so in a way that is correlated across EMU members, so that they can be partially offset with a common monetary policy, or whether they instead vary independently from country to country. The authors' answer is "yes:" preventing countries from following idiosyncratic fiscal policies raises the cyclical correlation, and thereby makes EMU more workable. Some may wish to interpret this result as a rationale for the SGP.

Countries that aspire to join the euro, such as the ten new EU members, must worry about more than the inability to use monetary policy to respond to future shocks. They must also worry about going in at an exchange rate that leaves their currency neither overvalued nor undervalued. This can be tricky in a rapidly growing economy that has nontraded goods, due to the Balassa-Samuelson effect. In "Dual Inflation and the Real Exchange Rate in New Open Economy Macroeconomics," Balázs Világi shows that the outcome of different productivity growth rates in traded and non-traded goods sectors depends on both market structure and market frictions, such as nominal rigidities. He argues that the Balassa-Samuelson effect is consistent with the modern modeling approach in open economy macroeconomics, which assumes rigid prices, if firms price to the market. But if this is the case then small open economies such as the emerging economies of central and Eastern Europe will experience different inflation rates in tradable and non-tradable goods and an appreciating currency. This naturally has implications for the timing of entry into the euro and the need to have consistent price-setting mechanisms across the eurozone countries, since entering the eurozone binds the exchange rate against the main trading partners and requires the satisfaction of inflation targets.

In "Trade Invoicing in the Accession Countries: Are They Suited to the Euro?" Linda S. Goldberg investigates the extent to which the ten accession countries (plus Bulgaria, whose accession date is 2007) are adopting the euro as the currency in which they invoice their exports. She finds that they adopted the use of euros at a rapid rate, but have perhaps gone too far. Whereas Asian countries invoice in dollars to an extent that exceeds their trade with the U.S. and other trade transactions in homogeneous commodities, Eastern European countries do the reverse, making too little use of the dollar and too much of the euro, relative to their trade with the euro countries. Theory predicts that optimal invoicing choices depend on the composition of goods in exports and imports and on the macroeconomic fluctuations of trade partners. These considerations yield country-specific estimates of the desired degree of euro-denominated invoicing among the accession countries, which the actual degree of euro invoicing apparently exceeds.

But perhaps the explanation is that the newly acceding EU members have had their sights firmly fixed on a future of increased integration with the West.

Part I: Macroeconomic Policy and Labor Markets

1

Macroeconomic Derivatives: An Initial Analysis of Market-Based Macro Forecasts, Uncertainty, and Risk

Refet S. Gürkaynak, *Bilkent University and CEPR*
Justin Wolfers, *University of Pennsylvania, CEPR, IZA, and NBER*

1. Introduction

In 1993 Robert Shiller forcefully argued for the creation of a new set of securities tied to the future path of the macroeconomy. He argued that existing equity markets represent future claims on only a small fraction of future income, and that active "macro markets" would allow for more effective risk allocation, allowing individuals to insure themselves against many macroeconomic risks.

In October 2002, Goldman Sachs and Deutsche Bank set up the first markets tied directly to macroeconomic outcomes; they call these products "Economic Derivatives." These new markets allow investors to purchase options whose payoff depends on growth in non-farm payrolls, retail sales, levels of the Institute for Supply Management's manufacturing diffusion index, initial unemployment claims, and the Euro-area harmonized CPI. New U.S.-based markets have recently been created for GDP and the international trade balance, and plans are underway for securities on U.S. CPI.[1]

In this market "digital" or "binary" options are traded, allowing traders to take a position on whether economic data will fall in specified ranges, thereby providing market-based measures of investors' beliefs about the likelihoods of different outcomes. That is, the option prices can be used to construct a risk-neutral probability density function for each data release. Until the introduction of these Economic Derivatives such information was unavailable and probabilistic or density forecasts still remain quite rare.

We now have data for the first 2½ years of this market, and use these to provide an initial analysis. Given that we have only 153 data releases, many of our results will be suggestive. To preview our findings, in section 3 we find that central tendencies of market-based forecasts are very similar to, but more accurate than surveys. Further, financial market responses to data releases are also better captured by surprises measured with respect to market-based expectations than survey-based expectations, again suggesting that they better capture investor expectations. Some behavioral anomalies evident in survey-based expectations—such as forecastable forecast errors—are notably absent from market-based forecasts.

The Economic Derivatives market prices options on many different outcomes, allowing us to assess forecasts of a full probability distribution. In section 4 we compare the dispersion of the option- and survey-based distributions, and exploit the unique feature of our data that allows us to address the distinction between disagreement and uncertainty. Distributions of survey responses are measures of disagreement, or heterogeneity of beliefs, across respondents. Measuring uncertainty requires knowing how much probability agents attribute to outcomes away from the mean expectation and economic derivatives prices at different strikes provide exactly that information. Although there appears to be some correlation between disagreement and uncertainty, we find that on a release-by-release basis disagreement is not a good proxy for uncertainty. The time series of market-based measures of uncertainty also provides some evidence in favor of the view that (at least market participants believe that) non-farm payrolls and retail sales follow GARCH-like processes. In section 5 we move beyond the first and second moments of the distribution, analyzing the efficacy of these option prices as density forecasts.

While most of our analysis proceeds as if market-prices correspond one-for-one with probabilities, in section 6 we ask whether it is reasonable to expect risk aversion to drive a wedge between prices and probabilities. We find that the risk premium is in most cases sufficiently small that it can be ignored for many applications. Finally, we investigate the extent to which pricing of Economic Derivatives can provide an informative estimate of the degree of risk aversion of investors.

We view part of our contribution as simply introducing these fascinating data to the research community and thus in the next section we provide some institutional background on the details of the contracts traded, and on the market clearing mechanism.

2.   The Market for Economic Derivatives

The institutional features of these new macro markets are worthy of some comment. Economic Derivatives are securities with payoffs based on macroeconomic data releases. Non-farm payrolls options, for example, settle when the employment report is released and the payrolls number is known.

The standard instruments traded are a series of digital (binary) options. The digital call (put) options pay $1 if the release is above (below) the strike. Typically around 10–20 different options are traded, each at different strike prices. Both puts and calls are traded for each data release. For transparency we will focus on the price of a "digital range"—a contract paying $1 if the announced economic number lies between two adjacent strike prices. Other types of options, such as digital puts and calls, capped vanilla options and forwards, are also traded in these markets. Each of these can be expressed as portfolios of digital ranges and are priced as such.

Figure 1 shows the prices of digital ranges from the May 12, 2005 auction (more on auctions below) which traded on what the monthly percentage change in retail sales (excluding autos) in April 2005 would be. The data was released later in the same day. Assuming risk-neutrality (which we will assume and defend in section 6), this histogram corresponds to the forecast probability distribution of the possible outcomes of this release. The mean of the distribution, the market's expectation,

An Example: Price of Digital Options
Auction on Retail Trade Release for April 2005; Held May 12, 2005

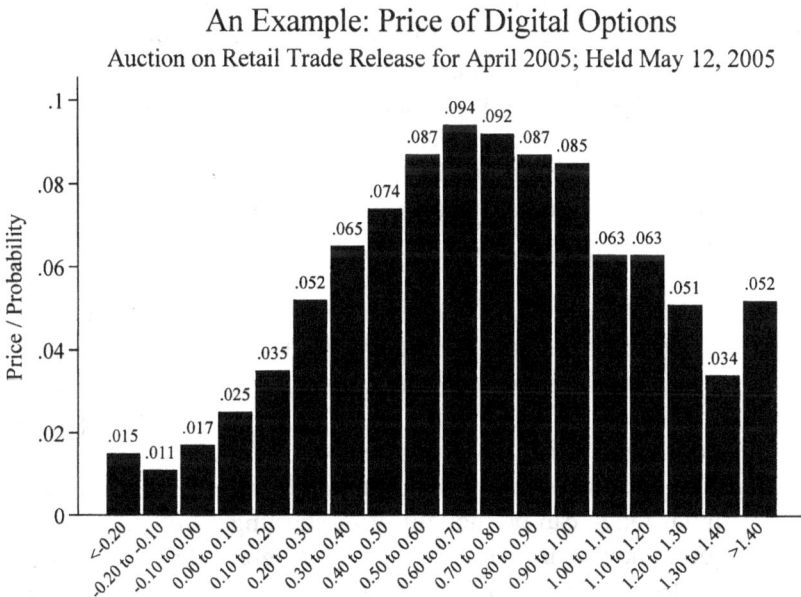

Figure 1
State-price distribution for the April 2005 retail sales release

was 0.72 percent, compared to the mean survey forecast of 0.5 percent. In the event, the released value came in at 1.07 percent, closer to the market-implied expectation. Assuming that probability is distributed uniformly within each bin, these market prices suggest that investors attributed about a 22 percent probability to the release coming in as high or higher. The major novelty of the economic derivatives market is that it allows the calculation of this implied probability.

While most financial markets operate as a continuous double auction, the market for economic derivatives is run as a series of occasional auctions, reflecting an attempt to maximize liquidity.[2] The auction mechanism is also noteworthy as it is a pari-mutuel system. That is, for a given strike price all "bets" (puts and calls) that the specified outcome either will or will not occur are pooled; this pool is then distributed to the winners in proportion to the size of their bet (the number of options purchased).[3] As such, the equilibrium price of these binary options is not known at the time the orders are made; indeed, it is only known when the last trade has occurred. Throughout the auction period (usually an hour) indicative price estimates are posted, reflecting what the price would be were no more orders to be made.

The use of pari-mutuel systems is unusual in financial markets, but common in horse race betting. Eisenberg and Gale (1959) provide useful results on the existence and uniqueness of equilibrium in such settings. The one important difference of this auction mechanism from horse race betting is that in the Economic Derivatives market it is possible to enter limit orders. This yields the possibility of multiple equilibria, which is resolved by an auction-clearing algorithm that chooses the equilibrium price vector that maximizes total trades.[4] As in traditional Dutch auctions, all trades (at a given strike) that take place are executed at the same price, regardless of the limit price.

This pari-mutuel mechanism is useful because it expands the number of ways to match buyers with sellers. While traders can be matched if one buyer's demand for calls matches another trader's demand for puts, the system does not require this. The horse track betting analogy is useful: even if nobody "sells" a given horse, as long as people bet on different horses the betting market clears. Similarly, buying a given digital range can be thought of as shorting all other outcomes and therefore having investors bidding at different strikes allows the pari-mutuel algorithm to clear the market and generate much greater volume.

In the economic derivatives market, option payoffs are determined with reference to a particular data release. Thus the payoff is based on, for example, the initial BLS estimate of growth in non-farm payrolls, rather than the best estimate of the statistical agencies (which will be subject to revision for years to come). In this sense these options provide hedges against event risk, where the events are data releases.

The events/auctions that are covered in the empirical analysis of this paper are growth of non-farm payrolls, the Institute for Supply Management manufacturing diffusion index (a measure of business confidence), change in retail sales ex-autos, and initial jobless claims. Options on GDP and trade balance releases commenced subsequent to our data collection efforts. Options on the Eurozone Harmonized Index of Consumer Prices also exist, but unfortunately we lack the high frequency financial market data for European securities required to analyze these data. Of the four markets that we do analyze, the non-farm payrolls market is the most liquid; business confidence and retail sales markets have liquidity comparable to each other but are less liquid. Initial claims options are the least liquid, however because this is a weekly release we have the largest number of observations in this market.[5]

Typically these auctions have taken place in the morning of the data release and they were sometimes preceded by another auction on the same release one or two days prior (non-farm payrolls auctions are held on both the morning the data are released and one day before).[6,7] Thus economic derivatives provide hedging opportunities against only very high frequency movements—event risk—and really cannot be said to provide the sorts of business cycle frequency risk-sharing opportunities envisioned by Shiller (1993). We return to a more careful assessment of the role of risk in these markets in section 6. But first we focus on the uses of market prices as forecasts.

3. The Accuracy of Market-based Forecasts

We begin by comparing forecasts generated by the Economic Derivatives market with an alternative information aggregator, the "survey forecast" released by Money Market Services (MMS) on the Friday before a data release.[8] Specifically, we compare the mean forecast from each mechanism, although our results are insensitive to the choice of mean versus median forecasts. For the MMS forecast, the "consensus" forecast typically averages across around 30 forecasters. For the market-based forecast, we aggregate across the distribution of outcomes and calculate the distribution's mean assuming that the probability distribution is uniform within each bin (boundaries of bins are defined by adjacent strikes).[9] As such, we implicitly assume that the price of a digital option is equal to the average belief that the specified outcome occurs. Wolfers and Zitzewitz (2005) discuss the relationship between prediction market prices and beliefs. We return to this issue in later sections, showing that ignoring risk aversion does very little violence to the data.

Figure 2 shows the relative forecasting performance of the survey- and market-based forecasts. Visual inspection suggests that the market-based forecast mildly dominates the survey forecast, a fact verified formally in Table 1.

Table 1 examines two specific measures of forecast accuracy: the mean absolute error and the root mean squared error, contrasting the performance of the Economic Derivatives market and the survey respondents. Each column reports these summary statistics for a different data series. In order to provide some comparability of magnitudes across columns we normalize the scale of each by dividing our measures of forecast errors by the historical standard deviation of survey forecast

Comparing Forecast Performance

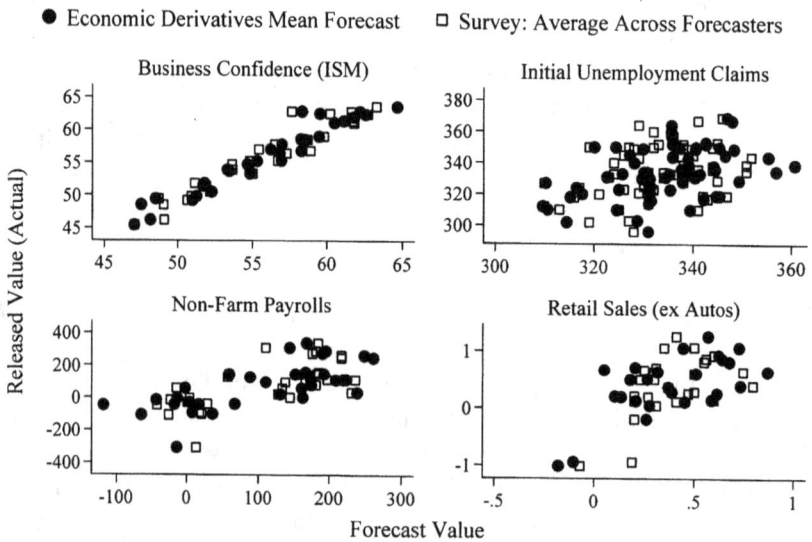

Figure 2
Comparing forecast performance

Table 1
Comparing the accuracy of mean forecasts

	Non-farm payrolls	Business confidence (ISM)	Retail sales (ex autos)	Initial unemployment claims	Pooled data
	Panel A: Mean Absolute Error				
Economic derivatives	0.723	0.498	0.919	0.645	0.680
	(.097)	(.090)	(.123)	(.061)	(.044)
Survey	0.743	0.585	0.972	0.665	0.719
	(.098)	(.093)	(.151)	(.063)	(.046)
	Panel B: Root Mean Squared Error				
Economic derivatives	0.907	0.694	1.106	0.808	0.868
	(.240)	(.257)	(.262)	(.126)	(.102)
Survey	0.929	0.770	1.229	0.831	0.921
	(.268)	(.296)	(.364)	(.130)	(.124)
	Panel C: Correlation of Forecast with Actual Outcomes				
Economic derivatives	0.700	0.968	0.653	0.433	0.631
	(.126)	(.047)	(.151)	(.114)	(.063)
Survey	0.677	0.961	0.544	0.361	0.576
	(.130)	(.052)	(.168)	(.117)	(.066)
	Panel D: Horse Race Regression (Fair-Shiller)				
	$Actual_t = \alpha + \beta * Economic\ Derivatives_t + \gamma * Survey\ Forecast_t$ (+survey fixed effects)				
Economic derivatives	1.06	0.91**	1.99**	1.64***	1.25***
	(0.78)	(.37)	(.79)	(.60)	(.29)
Survey	−0.14	0.17	−1.03	−1.21*	−0.24
	(0.89)	(.38)	(1.10)	(.68)	(.30)
Adjusted R^2	0.46	0.93	0.40	.20	.99
Sample size (Oct. 2002–Jul. 2005)	33	30	26	64	153

Notes: Forecast errors normalized by historical standard error of survey-based forecasts. (Standard errors in parentheses.) ***, **, and * denote statistically significant regression coefficients at 1 percent, 5 percent, and 10 percent, respectively.

errors over an earlier period.[10] Thus, the units in the table can be read as measures of forecast errors relative to an historical norm. This scaling makes the magnitudes sufficiently comparable that we can pool our observations across data series in the final column.

Comparing the two rows of Panel A shows that the market-based forecasts errors were on average smaller than the survey forecasts for all four data series. To interpret the magnitudes, start by noting that in all cases the estimates are less than one, implying that both sets of forecasts were more accurate than the survey forecast had been over the pre-2002 period. Beyond this, the improvements in forecast accuracy are meaningful, if not huge. For instance, pooling all of the data shows that relying on market-based forecasts rather than survey forecasts would have reduced the size of forecast errors by 0.04, which by virtue of the scaling is equivalent to 5½ percent of the average forecast error over the preceding decade. While meaningful, this reduction is not statistically significant. Panel B shows that analyzing the root mean squared error yields roughly similar results. In Panel C we compare the correlation of each forecast with actual outcomes. (Naturally these correlations can also be interpreted as the coefficient from a regression of standardized values of the outcome on standardized values of the forecast.) Each of these coefficients is statistically significant, suggesting that each forecast has substantial unconditional forecasting power. Even so, the market-based forecast is more highly correlated with outcomes than the consensus forecast for all four data series.

Panel D turns to a regression-based test of the information content of each forecast following Fair and Shiller (1990). Naturally there is substantial collinearity, as the market- and consensus-based forecasts are quite similar. Even so, we find rather compelling results. A coefficient of unity for the market-based forecast cannot be rejected for any of the indicators. By contrast, conditioning on the market-based forecast renders the survey forecast uninformative, and in three of four cases the survey-based forecast is not statistically different from zero and in the one case in which it is significant, it has a perverse negative coefficient. In the final column we pool the forecasts to obtain more precise estimates and again the market-based forecast dominates, and this difference is both statistically and economically significant.

These findings are probably partly due to the fact that the economic derivatives auction occurs on the morning of the data release, while the survey takes place up to a week before. Thus, option prices incorporate more information than was available to survey respondents. In an attempt to partly ameliorate this information advantage, we also reran our regressions in Panel D, controlling for two indicators of recent economic news: the change in equity prices and bond yields between the market close on the night prior to the release of the survey data to the night before the economic derivatives auction. These indicators for the release of relevant news were typically insignificant, and our main conclusions were not much altered by this control.

It seems likely that the improved performance is due to the market effectively weighting a greater number of opinions, or more effective information aggregation as market participants are likely more careful when putting their money where their mouth is.

We next ask which forecast aggregator better predicts the financial market reactions to the release of economic statistics. Or alternatively phrased, we ask: which forecast best embeds the forecasts of the equity and bond markets? In Figures 3A and 3B we show the short-term change in the S&P 500 and the 10-year Treasury note yield that result from the release of economic news. The solid dots measure the innovation as the deviation of the announced economic statistic from the economic derivatives forecast, while the hollow squares represent the innovation as the deviation from the consensus forecast.

Table 2 formalizes the comparisons in Figures 3A and 3B. Specifically, we run regressions of the form:

$$\Delta Financial\ variable_t = \alpha + \beta^* \left(Actual_t - Forecast_t^{Economic\ Derivs} \right)$$

$$+ \gamma^* \left(Actual_t - Forecast_t^{Survey} \right).$$

We measure changes in stock and Treasury markets around a tight window, comparing financial market quotes five minutes prior to the data release to 25 minutes after the event.[11] We analyze changes in implied Treasury yields, rather than changes in their prices, and report these changes in basis points; the stock market response is reported as percentage change. As before, we rescale our forecast error variables so that the estimates can be interpreted as the effect of a one-standard deviation forecast error.

Several patterns emerge in these data. First, comparing columns suggests that the non-farm payrolls release has the largest effect on financial markets; retail trade and business confidence are also important, but the weekly initial claims data rarely moves markets by much. Comparing panels shows that the yields on longer-dated securities more reliably and more forcefully respond to the release of these economic statistics than do yields on short-term Treasury bills. It is likely that short-term interest rate expectations have been strongly anchored by Federal Reserve statements recently, reducing the sensitivity of short-term yields to data release surprises. The stock market also responds quite vigorously to non-farm payrolls.[12] Lastly, comparing rows within each panel, financial markets appear to respond to economic data to the extent that they differ from the Economic Derivatives forecast; conditioning on this, the survey forecast has no statistically significant explanatory power in any individual regression.

Equity Market Responses to Economic Statistics

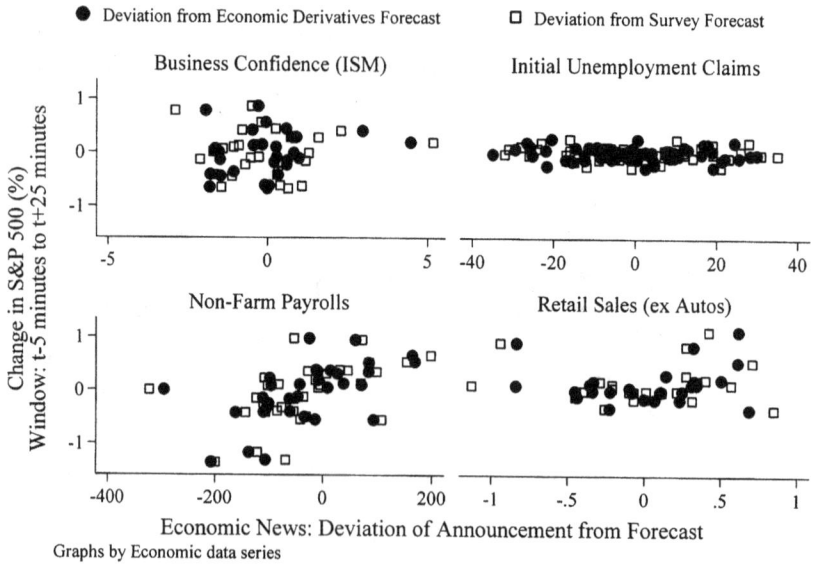

Figure 3A
Equity market responses to surprises

Bond Market Responses to Economic Statistics

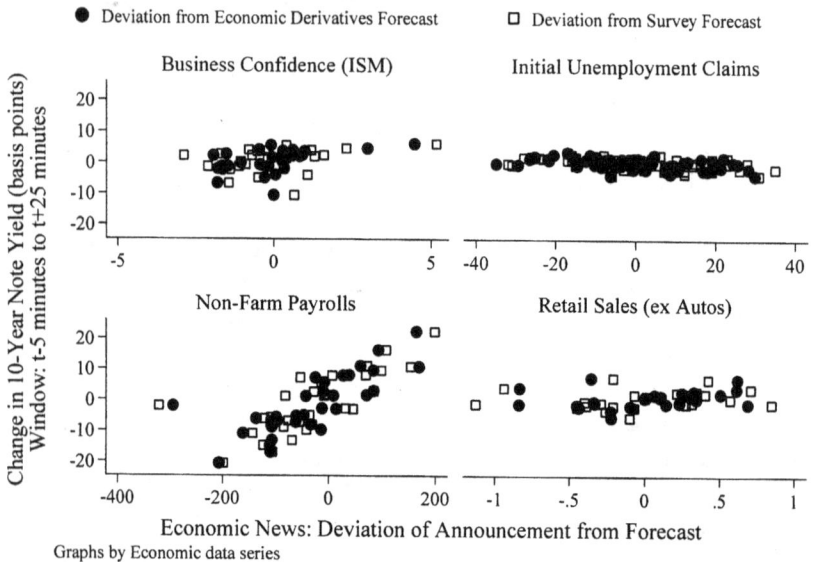

Figure 3B
Bond market responses to surprises

To maximize our ability to test the joint significance across columns, we pool our data across all four economic series and run:

$$\Delta Financial\ variable_t = \sum_{s \in Economic\ series} \alpha_s + \beta_s*\left(Actual_{s,t} - Forecast_{s,t}^{Consensus}\right)$$

$$+ \gamma_s*\left(Actual_{s,t} - Forecast_{s,t}^{Survey}\right).$$

The final column of Table 2 reports the joint statistical significance of the β's and the γ's, respectively. These joint tests clearly show that financial markets respond to the innovation as measured relative to the Economic Derivatives forecast and conditional on this, appear not to respond to the deviation of the data from the survey forecast.

In sum, Tables 1 and 2 establish that the Economic Derivatives forecast dominates the survey forecast (although survey forecasts perform quite well) both in predicting outcomes and in predicting market responses to economic news. Many previous papers have demonstrated that professional forecasters exhibit a range of predictable pathologies. For instance, Mankiw, Reis, and Wolfers (2003) analyze data on inflation expectations from the Survey of Professional Forecasters and the Livingstone Survey, finding that the median forecast yielded errors that were predictable based on recent economic developments, past forecast errors, or even the forecast itself. Were similar results to persist in the Economic Derivatives market, these predictable forecast errors would yield profitable trading opportunities.

In Table 3 we repeat many of the tests in that earlier literature, asking whether forecast errors are predictable based on a long-run bias (Panel A), on information in the forecast itself (Panel B), on previous forecast errors (Panel C), or on recent economic news (Panel D). We test the efficiency of the survey forecast and the Economic Derivatives forecasts separately, thus each cell in the table represents a separate regression. As before, we rescale the forecast errors by the historical standard deviation of the survey forecast errors for each indicator.

Each regression in Table 3 asks whether forecast errors are predictable; each panel tests different sets of predictors, and each column performs the test for a different economic indicator. The final column provides a joint F-test that the forecast errors are not predictable, aggregating across all four economic indicators in each row. In each succeeding panel we ask whether each forecast yields predictable on the basis of a simple constant term (Panel A), information in the forecast itself (Panel B), based on the forecast error from the previous month (Panel C), or based on recent economic information (Panel D).[13] Only

Table 2
Predicting market responses to economic statistics

	Non-farm payrolls	Business confidence (ISM)	Retail sales (ex autos)	Initial unemployment claims	Joint significance (F-test)
$\Delta Financial\ variable_t = \alpha + \beta * (Actual_t - Forecast_t^{Economic\ Derivs}) + \gamma * (Actual_t - Forecast_t^{Survey})$					
Panel A: 3 Month Treasury Bill					
Economic derivatives	4.41**	0.428	–0.094	–0.087	p=.0006
	(1.71)	(.434)	(.491)	(.601)	
Survey	–2.50	–0.166	0.067	–0.123	p=.1374
	(1.66)	(.396)	(.442)	(.585)	
Panel B: 6 Month Treasury Bill					
Economic derivatives	6.21**	1.034	0.221	–1.294	p=.0004
	(2.40)	(.786)	(.751)	(.785)	
Survey	–3.47	–0.483	–0.054	0.976	p=.1184
	(2.33)	(.769)	(.675)	(.764)	
Panel C: 2 Year Treasury Note					
Economic derivatives	12.61**	3.96*	2.60	–1.40	p=.0016
	(6.04)	(1.98)	(2.16)	(1.15)	
Survey	–2.50	–1.71	–1.73	0.42	p=.7841
	(5.87)	(1.79)	(1.94)	(1.11)	
Panel D: 5 Year Treasury Note					
Economic derivatives	14.94**	5.54**	3.66	–3.17**	p=.0001
	(6.39)	(2.07)	(2.44)	(1.22)	
Survey	–3.90	–2.56	–2.53	2.06*	p=.4254
	(6.21)	(1.86)	(2.19)	(1.19)	
Panel E: 10 Year Treasury Note					
Economic derivatives	10.40*	5.09**	3.37	–2.12*	p=.0007
	(5.22)	(1.90)	(2.04)	(1.12)	
Survey	–1.64	–2.53	–2.36	1.22	p=.4955
	(5.07)	(1.71)	(1.83)	(1.09)	
Panel F: S&P 500					
Economic derivatives	0.888**	0.575**	0.434*	–.106	p=.0001
	(.386)	(.226)	(.252)	(.084)	
Survey	–0.514	–0.466**	–0.367	0.092	p=.0058
	(.375)	(.204)	(.227)	(.082)	

Notes: Dependent variables normalized by historical standard error of survey-based forecasts. (Standard errors in parentheses) ***, **, and * denote statistically significant at 1 percent, 5 percent, and 10 percent.
For sample size, see Table 1.

Table 3
Tests of forecast efficiency

	Non-farm payrolls	Business confidence (ISM)	Retail sales (ex autos)	Initial unemployment claims	Joint significance (F-test)
		Panel A: Bias			
		$Forecast\ error_t = \alpha$			
Economic derivatives	−0.29*	−0.03	0.04	−0.04	p=.419
	(.15)	(.13)	(.22)	(.10)	
Survey	−0.29*	−0.06	0.03	0.05	p=.371
	(.16)	(.14)	(.25)	(.10)	
		Panel B: Internal Efficiency			
		$Forecast\ error_t = \alpha + \beta * Forecast_t$			
		[Square brackets shows test $\alpha=\beta=0$]			
Economic derivatives	−0.049	−0.078	−0.309	−0.371**	p=.182
	(.174)	(.053)	(.310)	(.167)	
	[p=.161]	[p=.345]	[p=.604]	[p=.031]	
Survey	0.043	0.095	0.512	−0.398**	p=.173
	(.204)	(.059)	(.476)	(.197)	
	[p=.196]	[p=.273]	[p=.564]	[p=.127]	
		Panel C: Autocorrelation			
		$Forecast\ error_t = \alpha + \rho * Forecast\ error_{t-1}$			
Economic derivatives	−0.091	−0.008	−0.383*	0.002	p=.186
	(.183)	(.191)	(.188)	(.128)	
Survey	−0.078	0.142	−0.500**	−0.074	p=.016
	(.183)	(.190)	(.180)	(.128)	
		Panel D: Information Efficiency			
		$Forecast\ error_t = \alpha + \beta * Slope\ of\ yield\ curve_{t-1} + \gamma * \Delta S\&P\ 500_{t-1,t-10}$			
		[Square brackets shows test $\beta=\gamma=0$]			
Economic derivatives	β=−0.100	β=0.287	β=0.078	β=0.102	p=.800
	(.229)	(.186)	(.322)	(.121)	
	γ=0.051	γ=−0.039	γ=−0.073	γ=−0.012	
	(.060)	(.054)	(.094)	(.053)	
	[p=.640]	[p=.241]	[p=.735]	[p=.677]	
Survey	β=−0.031	β=0.390*	β=0.132	β=0.137	p=.672
	(.237)	(.201)	(.359)	(.123)	
	γ=0.046	γ=−0.043	γ=−0.076	γ=−0.018	
	(.063)	(.059)	(.105)	(.054)	
	[p=.759]	[p=.127]	[p=.737]	[p=.502]	
		Panel E: Joint Test of All Predictors (p-value of joint significance)			
		$Forecast\ error_t = \alpha + \beta * Survey\ Forecast_t + \beta_2 * Market\ Forecast_t + \beta_3 * Forecast\ error_{t-1}$			
		$+ \beta_4 * Slope\ of\ yield\ curve_{t-1} + \beta_5 * \Delta S\&P\ 500_{t-1,t-10}$			
Economic derivatives	p=.900	p=.129	p=.228	p=.015	p=.0664
Survey	p=.625	p=.036	p=.017	p=.004	p=.0003

Notes: Each cell represents a separate regression.
Dependent variables normalized by historical standard deviation of survey-based forecasts.
(Standard errors in parentheses) ***, ** and * denote statistically significant at 1 percent, 5 percent, and 10 percent.

Panel C seems to show evidence of behavioral biases, with the survey-based forecast yielding significantly negatively autocorrelated forecast errors, particularly for retail sales. Equally we should not overstate this result: while we cannot reject a null that market-based forecasts are efficient, we also cannot reject a null that they show the same pattern of predictable forecast errors as the survey-based forecasts.

Finally in Panel E we combine each of the above tests, testing whether forecast errors are predictable based on the full set of possible predictors (including both the market- and survey-based forecasts themselves). On this score the superior performance of the market-based forecasts is much more evident. The survey-based forecasts yield predictable forecast errors for three of the four statistical series; not surprisingly, the survey does best on non-farm payrolls, which is the most closely watched of these numbers. The market-based forecasts show no such anomalies except in the case of initial claims, which is easily the least liquid of these markets. Overall these results confirm the results in the earlier behavioral literature documenting anomalies in survey-based forecasts. Equally, they suggest that such inefficiencies are either absent, or harder to find in market-based forecasts.

This section compared the mean forecast from surveys and economic derivatives, with the basic finding that while surveys do well (despite some behavioral anomalies), markets do somewhat better in forecasting. If one is only interested in forecasting the mean, using surveys might suffice; however, Economic Derivatives provide a lot more information than just the mean forecast. Observing that the mean of the market-based probability distribution "works" the way it should is comforting and holds promise for the information content of the higher moments of the distribution, the subject of the next section.

4.   Disagreement and Uncertainty

We now turn to analyzing the standard deviation of the state-price distribution. We will refer to this standard deviation as "uncertainty," reflecting the fact that this is the implied standard error of the mean forecast. Table 4 compares the market's average assessment of uncertainty with the realized root-mean-squared error of both the market- and survey-based forecasts over the same period. These results suggest that the market-based measure of uncertainty is reasonably well calibrated. We also include a third comparison: estimates by the official statistical agencies of the standard error of their measurements of these

Table 4
Expectations and realizations of forecast accuracy

RMSE of Forecasts (or standard deviation of forecast error)	Non-farm payrolls	Business confidence (ISM)	Retail sales (ex autos)	Initial unemployment claims
Expectations				
Market-implied standard deviation	96.1	2.01	0.44	12.5
Realizations				
SD of market forecast errors	100.7	1.40	0.42	15.1
SD of survey forecast errors	103.7	1.55	0.46	15.5
Sampling error				
Standard error of official estimate	81.5	n.a.	0.5	n.a.

Note: For estimates of the standard errors of the official estimates, see Wolfers and Zitzewitz (2004, p. 115).

economic statistics, where available. Market expectations of the RMSE of forecast errors are only slightly larger than sampling error in the case of non-farm payrolls, and slightly smaller in the case of retail sales.

Explicit measures of uncertainty are rare in macroeconomics, so we compare this market-based measure with the standard deviation of point forecasts across forecasters, and following Mankiw, Reis, and Wolfers (2003), we refer to the latter as "disagreement." The (previous) absence of useful data on uncertainty had led many researchers to analyze data on disagreement as a proxy for uncertainty. To date there has been very little research validating this approach, and indeed the only other measure of uncertainty we are aware of (from the Survey of Professional Forecasters) shows only weak comovement with measures of disagreement (Llambros and Zarnowitz 1987).

Figure 4 shows results consistent with Llambros and Zarnowitz: disagreement and uncertainty comove, but the correlation is not strong. The obvious difference in the levels is due to the fact that central expectations of respondents are close to each other even when each respondent is uncertain of their estimate.

In Table 5 we analyze these relationships a little more formally, regressing uncertainty against disagreement. Panel A shows that there is a statistically significant positive correlation between disagreement

Disagreement and Uncertainty

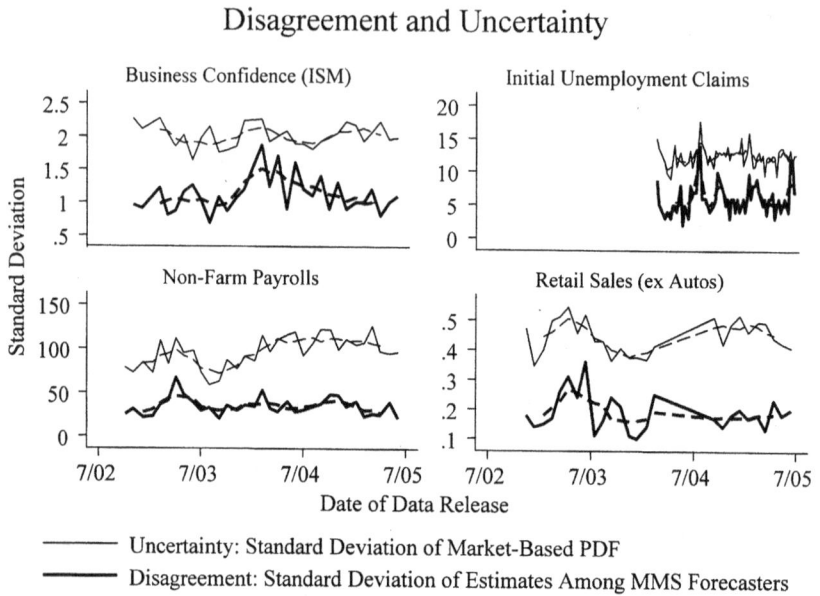

Uncertainty: Standard Deviation of Market-Based PDF
Disagreement: Standard Deviation of Estimates Among MMS Forecasters

Dashed lines show 5-period centered moving averages

Figure 4
Disagreement and uncertainty

and uncertainty for all series except ISM. The final column shows the joint significance of the coefficients on disagreement, suggesting that the contemporaneous relationship is quite strong. Indeed, Chris Carroll has suggested that one can interpret these regressions as the first stage of a split-sample IV strategy, allowing researchers to employ disagreement as a proxy for uncertainty in another dataset. This, of course, depends on how high an R^2 one views as sufficient in the first stage regression.

Panel B of this table carries out a similar exercise focusing on lower-frequency variation. In this case, disagreement and uncertainty are still correlated but this correlation is substantially weaker. The 5-period moving average of disagreement is a significant explanator of the 5-period moving average of uncertainty only for retail sales and initial claims. (Even this overstates the strength of the relationship, as we do not correct the standard errors for the autocorrelation generated by smoothing.) Jointly testing the significance across all four indicators we find that the relationship between low frequency variation in disagreement and uncertainty is not statistically significant, and the R^2s

Table 5
Disagreement and uncertainty

	Non-farm payrolls	Business confidence (ISM)	Retail sales (ex autos)	Initial unemployment claims	Joint Significance (F-test)
	Panel A: Contemporaneous Relationship				
	$Uncertainty_t = \alpha + \beta^*Disagreement_t$				
Disagreement	0.66**	−0.03	0.44**	0.27***	p=.0002
	(.29)	(.12)	(.16)	(.07)	
Constant	73.6	2.04	0.36	10.86	
	(10.39)	(.134)	(.03)	(.47)	
Adjusted R^2	0.11	−0.03	0.20	0.17	
	Panel B: Low Frequency – 5 Period Centered Moving Averages				
	Smoothed Uncertainty_t = $\alpha + \beta^*$Smoothed Disagreement_t				
Disagreement	0.55	0.10	0.65**	0.32***	p=.1498
	(.47)	(.10)	(.24)	(.06)	
Constant	77.7	1.89	0.32	10.5	
	(16.8)	(.11)	(.05)	(.37)	
Adjusted R^2	0.01	−0.002	0.23	0.32	

Notes: (Standard errors in parentheses) ***, **, and * denote statistically significant at 1 percent, 5 percent, and 10 percent.

of these regressions are again sufficiently low and varied as to caution that disagreement might be a poor proxy for uncertainty in empirical applications.

Having demonstrated fairly substantial time series variation in uncertainty (albeit over a short period) naturally raises the question: What drives movements in uncertainty?

In Panel A of Table 6 we look to see whether any of the variation is explained by movements in expected volatility of equity markets. That is, our regressors include the closing price of CBOE's VIX index on the day prior to the economic derivatives auction, as well as the closing price one and two months prior (for the initial claims, these lags refer to one and two weeks earlier). As in Tables 1–3, we rescale the uncertainty measure by the standard deviation of historical forecast errors to allow some comparability across columns. Panel A shows that for all four indicators the contemporaneous values of the implied volatility index is uncorrelated with uncertainty about forthcoming economic data. While a couple of specific lags are statistically significant, they suggest a somewhat perverse negative correlation between

Table 6
Modeling uncertainty

	Non-farm payrolls	Business confidence (ISM)	Retail sales (ex autos)	Initial claims
	Panel A: Uncertainty and Expected Volatility			
	$Uncertainty_t = \alpha + \beta_1{}^*VIX_t + \beta_2{}^*VIX_{t-1} + \beta_3{}^*VIX_{t-2}$			
VIX_t	0.76	0.41	0.04	0.10
	(.95)	(.72)	(1.07)	(.86)
VIX_{t-1}	−1.93**	0.79	1.15	−0.44
	(.86)	(.69)	(1.27)	(1.04)
VIX_{t-2}	0.23	−1.01*	−0.93	−0.22
	(.80)	(.57)	(.98)	(.85)
Joint sig?	p=0.02	p=0.31	p=0.73	p=0.80
Adjusted R^2	0.21	0.02	−0.07	−0.03
	Panel B: Persistence			
	$Uncertainty_t = \alpha + \beta_1{}^*Uncertainty_{t-1} + \beta_2{}^*Uncertainty_{t-2} + \beta_3{}^*Uncertainty_{t-3}$			
$Uncertainty_{t-1}$	0.34*	0.24	0.43*	0.20
	(.19)	(.19)	(.23)	(.13)
$Uncertainty_{t-2}$	0.37*	−0.26	0.14	0.01
	(.19)	(.20)	(.23)	(.13)
$Uncertainty_{t-3}$	−0.12	0.11	−0.13	−0.24*
	(.19)	(.19)	(.21)	(.13)
Joint sig?	p=0.02	p=0.45	p=0.14	p=0.10
Adjusted R^2	0.24	−0.01	0.12	0.06
	Panel C: Pseudo-GARCH Model			
	$Uncertainty_t = \alpha + \beta_1{}^*Uncertainty_{t-1} + \beta_2{}^*Uncertainty_{t-2} + \beta_3{}^*Uncertainty_{t-3}$ $+ \gamma_1{}^*Forecast\ Error_{t-1}^2 + \gamma_2{}^*Forecast\ Error_{t-2}^2 + \gamma_3{}^*Forecast\ Error_{t-3}^2$			
$Uncertainty_{t-1}$	0.37*	0.21	0.47*	0.16
	(.21)	(.22)	(.25)	(.13)
$Uncertainty_{t-2}$	0.38	−0.12	−0.10	0.02
	(.22)	(.23)	(.25)	(.13)
$Uncertainty_{t-3}$	−0.13	0.05	0.12	−0.20
	(.19)	(.20)	(.24)	(.12)
Joint sig?	p=0.01	p=0.82	p=0.28	p=0.26
F'cast error$_{t-1}^2$	0.05**	0.02	0.05**	0.03**
	(.02)	(.02)	(.03)	(.01)
F'cast error$_{t-2}^2$	0.02	−0.02	−0.03	0.01
	(.02)	(.02)	(.03)	(.01)
F'cast error$_{t-3}^2$	−0.01	−0.00	−0.00	−0.00
	(.02)	(0.02)	(.02)	(.01)
Joint sig?	p=0.05	p=0.41	p=0.21	p=0.11
Adjusted R^2	0.38	−0.009	0.21	0.11
n [Panel A, B/C]	[33,30]	[30,27]	[26,23]	[64,61]

Notes: (Standard errors in parentheses) ***, **, and * denote statistically significant at 1 percent, 5 percent, and 10 percent. VIX_t refers to the close of CBOE's VIX index on the day prior to the auction. VIX_{t-1} refers to the day prior to the previous data release. $Uncertainty_{t-1}$ refers to the standard deviation of the state price distribution for the previous data release in that series. All of the uncertainty measures are rescaled by the historical standard deviation of forecast errors for that series.

uncertainty and expected volatility in the stock market. This lack of correlation likely suggests that uncertainty is usually not about the fundamental state of the economy but about the particular data release— perhaps because the seasonal factors are sometimes more difficult to forecast.

Panel B also examines the persistence of uncertainty, and uncertainty about non-farm payrolls and retail sales appears to show some degree of persistence. Finally Panel C jointly tests whether uncertainty is a product of both past uncertainty and past realizations, as posited in GARCH models. Market assessments of the uncertainty in non-farm payrolls, retail sales, and initial claims appears to be well-described by these variables, although we find no such evidence for ISM.[14] Finally we ask whether these market-based measures of uncertainty actually predict the extent of forecast errors.

Figure 5 seems to suggest that uncertainty is not strongly related to larger (absolute) forecast errors (note that these forecast errors are standardized by their historical standard errors). We perform a more formal test in Table 7. If the uncertainty measure is appropriately calibrated, we should expect to see a coefficient of one in the regression of absolute forecast errors on uncertainty.

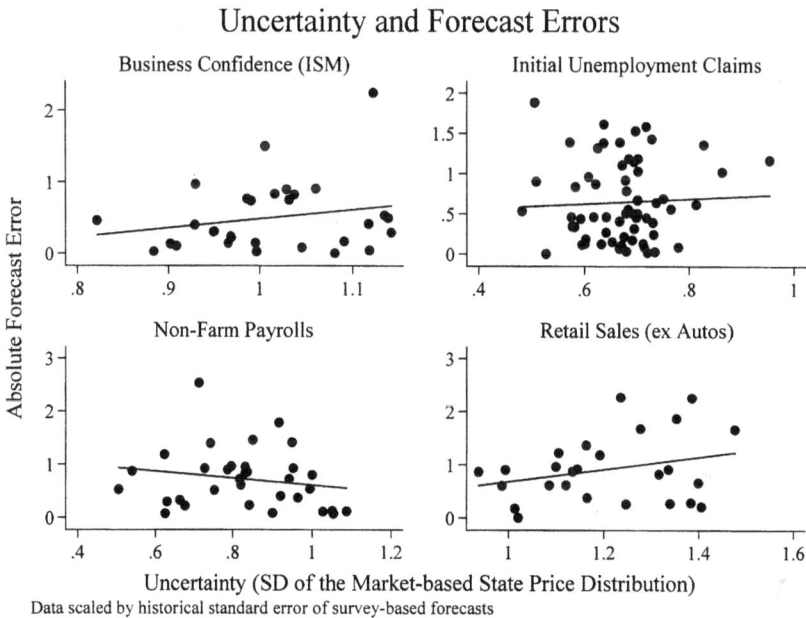

Figure 5
Uncertainty and forecast errors

Table 7
Uncertainty and forecast errors

	Non-farm payrolls	Business confidence	Retail trade (ex autos)	Initial claims	Joint Significance (F-test)
	Absolute Forecast Error$_t$ = α + β*Uncertainty$_t$				
Uncertainty (β)	−0.65	1.27	1.16	0.31	p=0.26
	(0.64)	(1.08)	(0.80)	(.77)	
Test: β=0 (No information)	p=0.32	p=0.25	p=0.16	p=0.69	
Test: β=1 (Efficient forecast)	p=0.02	p=0.81	p=0.84	p=0.37	p=0.09

Notes: (Standard errors in parentheses)
***, **, and * denote statistically significant at 1 percent, 5 percent, and 10 percent, respectively.
Forecast errors normalized by historical standard error of survey-based forecasts.

Overall Table 7 suggests that these tests have very little power. In no individual case is the absolute forecast error significantly correlated with the market-based measure of uncertainty. The final column pools the data, again finding no evidence of a significant correlation. That is, the data cannot reject the null that there is no information in the time series variation in market-based uncertainty that helps predict time series variation in forecast errors. On the other hand, the estimates are imprecise enough that, as the second row shows, we cannot reject a coefficient of unity for three out of the four series either.

Of course the object of interest in these regressions—the standard deviation of the state price distribution—is a summary statistic from a much richer set of digital options or density forecasts, and so we will obtain greater power in the next section as we turn to analyzing these density forecasts more directly.

5.   Full Distribution Implications

A particularly interesting feature of the Economic Derivatives market is that it yields not only a point estimate, but also a full probability distribution across the range of plausible outcomes. Exploiting this, we can expand our tests beyond section 3, which asked whether the mean forecast is efficient, to also ask whether the prices of these options yield efficient forecasts of the likelihood of an economic statistic falling in a given range.

Figure 6 provides an initial analysis, pooling data from all 2,235 digital call options (contracts that pay $1 if the announced economic statistic is above the strike price) across our 153 auctions. We grouped these options according to their prices, and for each group we show the proportion of the time that the economic statistic actually is above the strike price. These data yield a fairly close connection, and in no case do we see an economically or statistically significant divergence between prices and probabilities.

While the evidence in Figure 6 suggests that the Economic Derivatives prices are unbiased, it does not speak to the efficiency of these estimates, an issue we now turn to. Because density estimates are hard to come by (see Diebold, Tay, and Wallis 1999 for an example), the forecast evaluation literature has focused on evaluating point forecasts rather than densities. An intermediate step between point and density estimate evaluation is interval forecast evaluation. An interval forecast is a confidence interval such as "non-farm payrolls will be between 100,000 and 180,000 with 95 percent probability." Christoffersen (1998) shows that a correctly conditionally calibrated interval forecast will provide a hit sequence (a sequence of correct and incorrect predictions) that is independently and identically Bernoulli distributed with the desired coverage probability. A

Auction Prices and Probabilities: Digital Calls
Aggregating data across all auctions into 20 call price bins

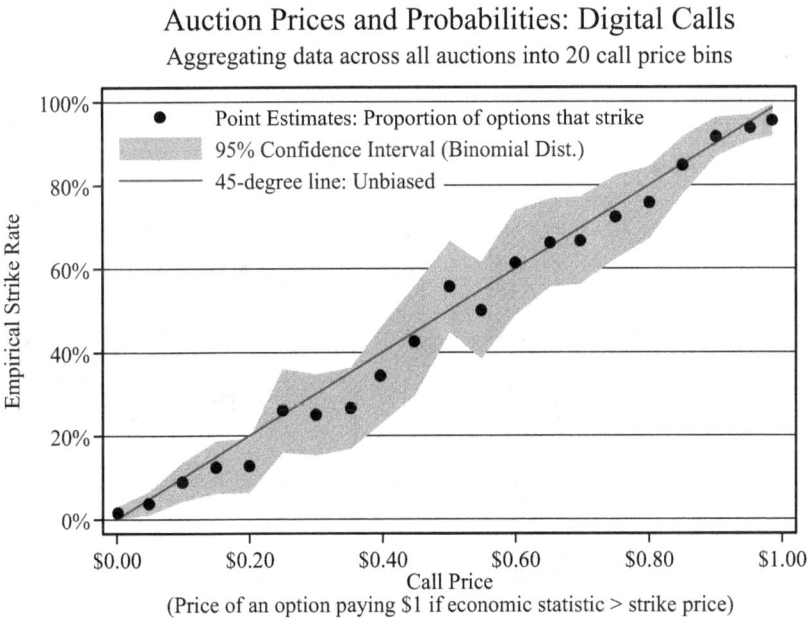

Figure 6
Prices and probabilities – digital call options

density forecast can be thought of as a collection of interval forecasts, and Diebold, Gunther, and Tay (1998) show that the i.i.d. Bernoulli property of individual interval forecasts translates into the i.i.d. uniform (0,1) distribution of the probability integral transform, z_t, defined as

$$z_t = \int_{-\infty}^{y_t} \pi(x)dx \overset{iid}{\sim} Uniform(0,1)$$

where $\pi(x)$ denotes the price of an option paying \$1 if the realized economic statistic takes on the value x, and y_t is the actual realized value of economic statistic. Thus z_t can be thought of as the "realized quantile," and the implication that this should be uniformly distributed essentially formalizes the argument that if the prediction density is correct, the "x" percent probability event should be happening "x" percent of the time. In the data we do not observe exact state-prices $\pi(x)$, but rather digital ranges, $\int_a^b \pi(x)dx$; to estimate the realized quantile we simply assume that $\pi(x)$ is uniformly distributed within each strike-price range.

In Figure 7 we calculate the realized quantile for each auction, pool the estimates across different economic statistics, and plot the relevant

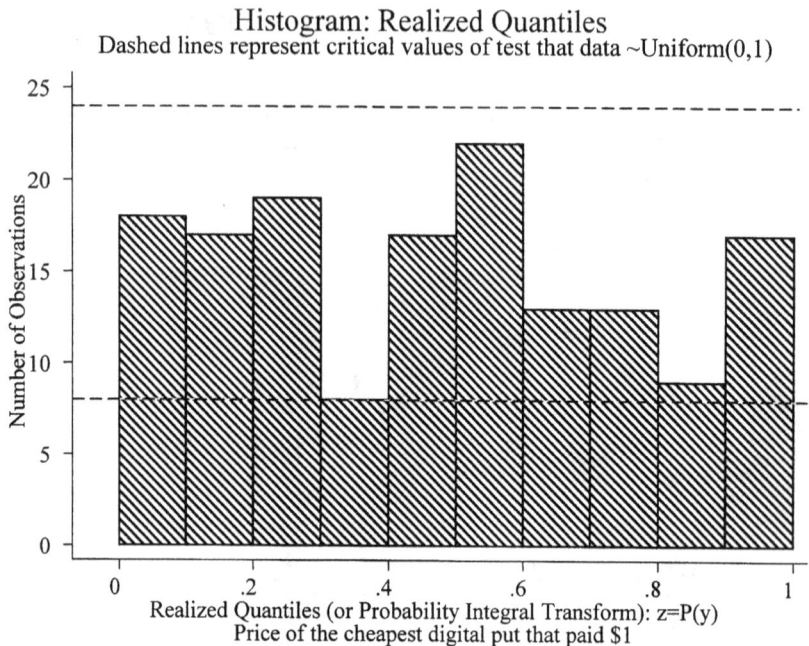

Figure 7
Histogram of realized quantiles

histogram. A simple way to test for deviations from uniformity derives from inverting the earlier logic: if the distribution is uniform, then the probability that any given realization is in any given bin should follow a Bernoulli distribution with the hit probability equal to the width of the bin, and hence the number of realizations in each bin should follow a binomial distribution. Thus in Figure 7 we show the relevant 95 percent critical values under the assumption of i.i.d. uniformity.

Figure 7 shows that the distribution is generally close to uniform, albeit with a peak around 0.5, which is suggestive of excess realizations close to the median forecast. That said, this distribution is statistically indistinguishable from a uniform distribution.[15]

The inference in this figure is partly shaped by the specific bin widths chosen for the histogram. Figure 8 shows an alternative representation, mapping both the entire cumulative distribution function of the probability integral transform and the uniform distribution. The figure also shows the deviations from uniformity that would be required for a Kolmogorov-Smirnov test to reject a null that the realized quantiles are drawn from a uniform distribution. As seen, this suggests that the data are fairly close to an idealized uniform (0,1) distribution, and that these data yield no statistically significant evidence falsifying this null.

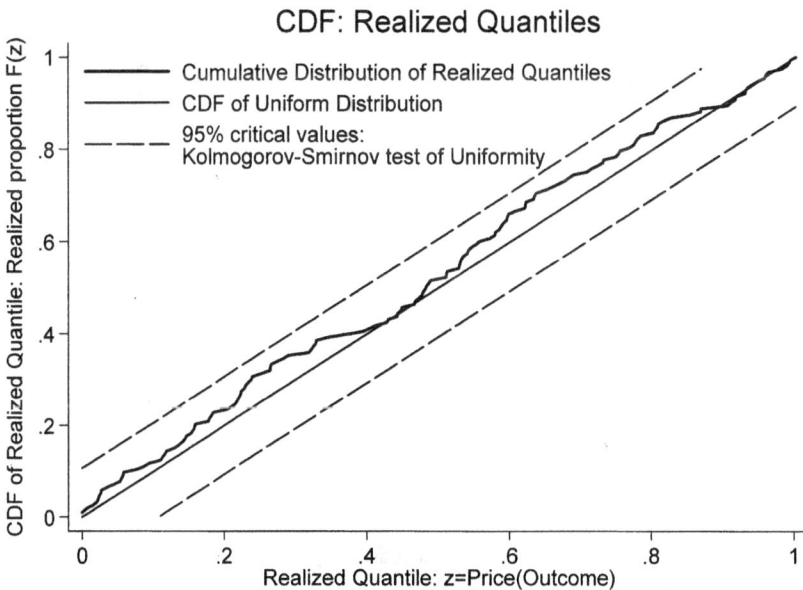

Figure 8
Cumulative distribution function of realized quantiles

Delving deeper, Figure 9 plots the same transformed variable for each data series separately.

Disaggregating the realized quantile by data series confirms that there is little evidence of non-uniformity of these distributions although there are some interesting hints of small miscalibrations in density forecasts. In particular, the ISM CDF is too steep in the central section, suggesting that too few realizations fall in the tails of the forecast distribution. The non-farm payrolls probability integral transform series is also very close to the upper critical value, suggesting too many realizations in the left tail. Neither of these leads to a rejection of the uniform distribution null hypothesis, however.

Figures 8 and 9 show that the economic derivatives based density forecasts have correct coverage. Efficient density forecasts also require independence of the probability integral transform variables over time. We therefore now turn to examining the time series of the probability integral transforms in Figure 10.

The time series plots do not suggest any clear time series correlation. To be sure, we have run simple AR(3) models, and found no statistically significant evidence of autocorrelation.

CDF: Realized Quantiles

Dashed lines show 95% Kolmogorov-Smirnov critical values under null z~U(0,1

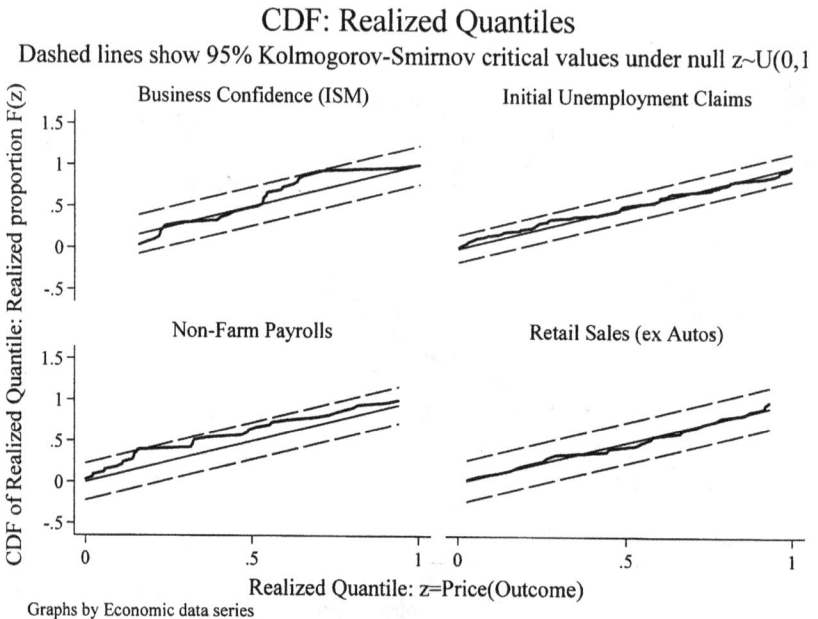

Graphs by Economic data series

Figure 9
Cumulative distribution function of realized quantiles, by data release

Time Series: Realized Quantiles

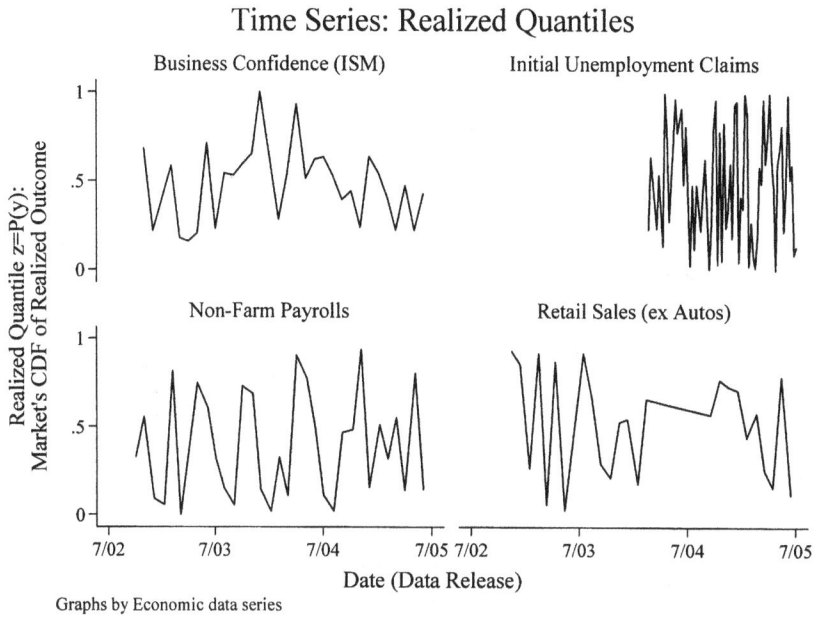

Figure 10
Time series of probability integral transforms

Finally we turn to a test that allows us to test jointly for both serial independence and uniformity of the realized quantile, maximizing our statistical power. Berkowitz (2001) notes that there exist more powerful tests for deviations from normality than from uniformity, particularly in small samples. He suggests analyzing a normally-distributed transformation of the probability integral transform. Specifically, he advocates analyzing:

$$n_t = \Phi^{-1}(z_t) = \Phi^{-1}\left(\int_{-\infty}^{y_t} \pi(x)dx\right)$$

where $\Phi^{-1}(z_t)$ is the inverse of the standard normal distribution function. Thus, if z_t is i.i.d.~U(0,1), then this implies that n_t is i.i.d.~N(0,1). We can thus test this null against a first-order autoregressive alternative allowing the mean and variance to differ from (0,1) by estimating:

$$n_t - \mu = \rho(n_{t-1} - \mu) + \varepsilon_t.$$

We estimate this regression by maximum likelihood. Berkowitz shows the exact log-likelihood function for the univariate case; it is simple to adapt this to the case of an unbalanced panel as in the present case:

$$L = \sum_{t=1}^{Unobs.\ Lag} \left[-\frac{1}{2}\log(2\pi) - \frac{1}{2}\log\left(\frac{\sigma^2}{1-\rho^2}\right) - \frac{\left(n_{s,t} - \mu/(1-\rho)\right)^2}{2\sigma^2/(1-\rho^2)} \right]$$

$$+ \sum_{t=1}^{Observe\ Lag} \left[-\frac{1}{2}\log(2\pi) - \frac{1}{2}\log(\sigma^2) - \frac{\left(n_{s,t} - \mu - \rho n_{s,t-1}\right)^2}{2\sigma^2} \right]$$

where the first term aggregates over observations where the lagged dependent variable is not observed, and the second term aggregates over all others.

Table 8 reports our estimation results. Estimating 3 parameters across each of 4 data series we find only two coefficients that are individually statistically distinguishable from the efficiency null. For each series we perform a likelihood ratio test that jointly tests whether the estimated models significantly deviate from the efficiency null. For none of our series is there significant evidence that the realized quantiles violate the i.i.d. uniform requirement. Finally, in order to maximize our statistical

Table 8
Testing for autocorrelation in the probability integral transform

	Non-farm payrolls	Business confidence	Retail trade (ex autos)	Initial claims	Pooled data
	$n_t - \mu = \rho(n_{t-1} - \mu) + \varepsilon$, where $n_t = \Phi^{-1}\left(\int_{-\infty}^{Outcome_t} - \pi(x)dx\right)$				
Mean (μ)	−0.46**	0.03	0.04	−0.04	−0.10
	(.19)	(.15)	(.17)	(.15)	(.09)
Variance (σ^2)	1.05	0.70	0.76	1.46*	1.16
	(.26)	(.18)	(.21)	(.26)	(.13)
Autocorrelation (ρ)	−0.11	0.23	−0.31	0.05	0.001
	(.17)	(.26)	(.19)	(.13)	(.09)
$LL(\hat{\mu}, \hat{\sigma}^2, \hat{\rho})$	−18.20	−12.59	−11.45	−51.45	−100.42
$LL(0,1,0)$	−21.34	−13.65	−12.82	−54.19	−101.99
LR test	6.27	2.12	2.73	5.48	3.16
	(p=0.10)	(p=0.55)	(p=0.44)	(p=0.14)	(p=0.37)
Sample size	33	30	26	64	153

Notes: (Standard errors in parentheses)
***, **, and * denote statistically significant deviations from the null at 1 percent, 5 percent, and 10 percent, respectively.
Forecast errors normalized by historical standard error of survey-based forecasts.

power we pool the estimates across all four indicators, and once again the test suggests that these density forecasts are efficient.

The evidence presented in this section shows that economic derivatives option prices are accurate and efficient predictors of the densities of underlying events. This finding is surprising in the sense that asset prices usually embed a risk premium due to risk aversion and for this reason tend to be systematically biased—a bias that does not seem to be present in this market. The implications of risk and risk aversion in the pricing of economic derivatives are the subjects of the next section.

6. The Role of Risk

Thus far we have interpreted the prices of digital options as density forecasts—an approach that would be warranted if investors were risk-neutral. Yet options and option markets exist precisely because there is risk, and it seems plausible that agents willingly pay a risk premium for the hedge offered by macroeconomic derivatives. We now turn to assessing the magnitude of this risk premium. To preview, we find that for an investor who holds the S&P 500 portfolio the aggregate risks that are hedged in these markets are sufficiently small that for standard assumptions about risk aversion the premium should be close to zero. Further, we show that option prices are typically quite close to the empirical distribution of outcomes. We then explore the corollary of these results, investigating what the pricing of these options implies about risk aversion.

Using option prices to make inference about risk and risk aversion is not a new idea, but is seldom attempted in the literature due to the complications arising from properties of standard options—complications that are not present in the economic derivatives market. In important papers, Jackwerth (2000) and Aït-Sahalia and Lo (2000) analyzed options on the S&P 500 to derive measures of risk aversion. Using economic derivatives to measure perceived risk and risk attitudes is far easier for several reasons. First of all, the options in these markets provide direct readings of state-prices; these do not have to be constructed from portfolios of vanilla options. More importantly, since the options expire within the same day of the auction, time discounting is not an issue and the discount factor can be set to zero. Similarly none of the concerns arising from the presence of dividends are present here.

To illustrate the relationship between risk aversion and the pricing of economic derivatives, we start by considering a representative investor who is subject to some risk that with probability p will change her wealth to β percent of its current value, w. The investor can buy or sell economic derivatives to protect herself against this shock. We consider the purchase of a derivative that pays \$1 per option purchased if the event occurs. Thus, the investor chooses how many derivatives to purchase (x) at a price π to maximize her expected utility:

$$\underset{\{x\}}{\text{Max}}\ EU(w) = pU\big(\beta w + (1-\pi)x\big) + (1-p)U(w - \pi x).$$

The first-order condition yields an optimal quantity of options, x^*:

$$\frac{U'(\beta w + (1-\pi)x^*)}{U'(w - \pi x^*)} = \frac{\pi(1-p)}{p(1-\pi)}.$$

That is, the investor purchases options until the marginal rate of substituting an additional dollar between each state is equated with the ratio of the marginal cost of transferring a dollar between states.

Because these economic derivatives are in zero net supply, in a representative agent model equilibrium requires that $x^* = 0$, yielding the equilibrium price:

$$\pi = \frac{p}{p + (1-p)\dfrac{U'(w)}{U'(\beta w)}}.$$

This expression yields some very simple intuitions. If β is unity then the probability and the state price are the same regardless of the degree of risk aversion. Indeed, such an option would be redundant because there is no risk to be hedged. Alternatively if agents are risk-neutral ($U'(w) = U'(\beta w)$), then again the option price represents the probability that the event will occur. If investors are risk averse and the option pays off following a negative shock to wealth ($\beta < 1$) then the state price is higher than the true probability. If the option pays off following a positive wealth shock ($\beta > 1$) then the risk-averse investors will price it at a value lower than its probability. Alternatively phrased, risk aversion leads the state-price distribution to shift to the left of the probability distribution, and this shift is larger the smaller the ratio $U'(w)/U'(\beta w)$; that is, distribution shifts further left for more risk-averse investors, and for larger adverse shocks.

Extending this logic to the case where the investor is subject to many possible shocks, and where there are markets available for her to hedge each risk is somewhat cumbersome, but yields only a minor modification. Specifically, the investor may face a variety of shocks where each specific shock, indexed by i, changes wealth to β_i percent of baseline and occurs with probability p_i. Investors hedge these risks so as to maximize expected utility by purchasing x_i options at price π_i, and each such option pays \$1 if the specified shock occurs. We refer to π_i as a state-price, and the distribution as the state-price distribution. The representative consumer's problem is:

$$\underset{\{x_i\}}{Max}\ E[U(w)] = \sum_i p_i U\left(\beta_i w + x_i - \sum_j \pi_j x_j\right).$$

We combine the first-order condition with the pari-mutuel mechanism constraint that total premiums paid should cover total payoffs in all states of the world ($\forall i : x_i = \sum_j \pi_j x_j$), to derive the following fairly intuitive expression for the risk premium:

$$\frac{\pi_i}{p_i} = \frac{U'(\beta_i w)}{\sum_j p_j U'(\beta_j w)}.$$

In Figure 11 we use this equilibrium relationship to assess the relationship between state prices and probabilities at different levels of risk aversion. Specifically, to make this exercise relevant to assessing the pricing of economic derivatives, we solve for the entire state-price distribution when the investor risks being hit by wealth shocks that are drawn from a normal distribution. In this example a one-standard deviation negative shock causes wealth to decline by 1 percent (That is, $\beta = 1 + 0.01z$ where $z \sim N(0,1)$). We calculate option prices for the log-utility case ($\gamma = 1$), a substantially more risk averse case ($\gamma = 5$) at the upper end of values usually assumed to be plausible by macroeconomists, and for a level of risk aversion typically thought implausible, but required to generate the observed equity premium ($\gamma = 20$).

As can be seen fairly clearly, for standard levels of risk aversion, the price distribution closely resembles the risk-neutral distribution. Increasing risk-aversion shifts the distribution to the left and the higher the risk aversion the more the state-price and data generating distributions are different.

More generally, our option pricing formula allows us to utilize data on two objects of the utility function, the distribution of shocks and the state prices, to make inferences about the third, the risk premium. In order to assess the likely magnitude of the risk premium, we begin by

State Price Distributions

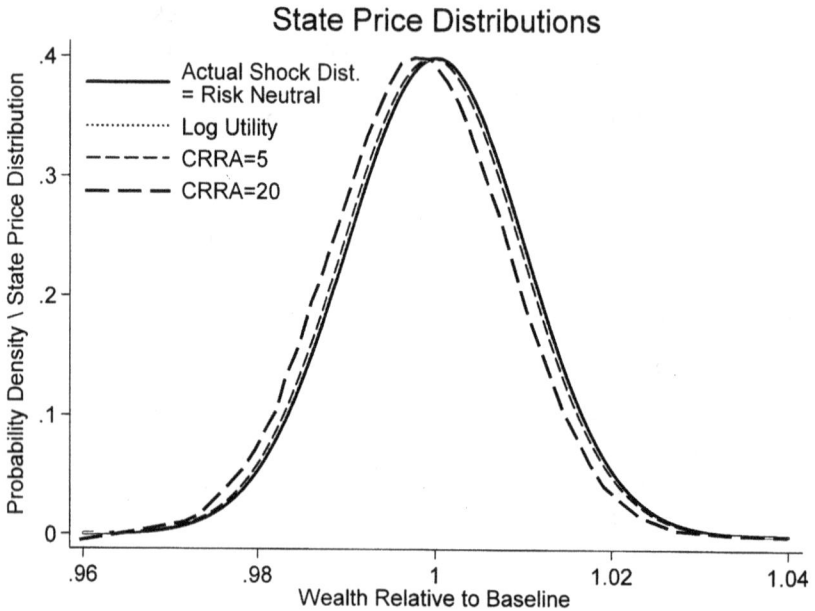

Figure 11
Risk aversion and state-price distributions

analyzing the divergence between the state-price distribution and the shock distribution that would be implied by specific utility functions and the economic shocks we see in our data. This requires us first to map the relationship between economic shocks and changes in wealth, then to map the empirical distribution of such economic shocks, before plugging these data into the above equation to back out the risk premium suggested by the theory.

Our analysis in section 3 (and specifically Figure 2) shows that the economic statistics have important effects on equity and bond markets. Backing out the implications of these shocks for wealth requires us to be more precise about a specific model of the economy. We assume complete markets, which imply the existence of a representative investor (Constantinides 1982). Following Jackwerth (2000) and Ait-Sahalia and Lo (2000) we assume that movements in the S&P 500 are representative of shocks to the entire stock of wealth. While one might be concerned that news about the economy affects different sectors differently, these are diversifiable risks, and so with complete markets should not affect wealth. Thus to recover the shock to wealth that macroeconomic derivatives allow one to hedge, we analyze the stock-market response to economic shocks in Table 9. That is, we run:

$$\Delta S\&P\ 500_t = \alpha + \beta^*\left(Actual_t - Forecast_t^{Economic\ Derivs}\right).$$

As before, we examine changes in the 30-minute window around the announcement, and we scale the forecast error by the historical standard deviation of forecast errors for that series.

As expected, we find that positive shocks to non-farm payrolls, business confidence and retail trade are positive shocks to wealth, while higher initial claims is a negative shock. Comparing columns, it is clear that the non-farm payrolls surprise is easily the most important shock. The coefficient is also directly interpretable: a one standard deviation shock to non-farm payrolls raises wealth by 0.37 percent and the 95 percent confidence interval extends from +0.17 percent to +0.54 percent. These magnitudes are all much smaller than those used to construct Figure 11, suggesting that the relationship between prices and probabilities is even closer than that figure suggested. More to the point, these coefficient estimates correspond to $\beta - 1$ in the simple model presented above, allowing us to calculate the risk premium directly.

Rather than make specific parametric assumptions, we simply observe the distribution of different sized economic shocks in our data, and use a kernel density smoother to recover the shock distribution, using the estimates in Table 9 to rescale forecast errors into the corresponding wealth shocks. In this framework the frequency of specific shocks, their effects on wealth, and assumptions about risk aversion are sufficient to yield an estimate of the expected risk premium embedded

Table 9
Effects of economic news on the S&P 500

Dependent variable: %ΔS&P 500	Non-farm payrolls	ISM	Retail sales (ex autos)	Initial claims
$Actual_t - Forecast_t^{Economic\ Derivs}$ (Normalized by historical SD)	+0.37%*** (.10)	+0.11% (.11)	+0.04% (.06)	−0.01% (.02)
Adjusted R^2	0.31	0.005	−0.03	−0.006
n	33	30	26	64

Notes: Forecast errors normalized by historical standard error of survey-based forecasts. (Standard errors in parentheses)
***, **, and * denote statistically significant at 1 percent, 5 percent, and 10 percent, respectively.

in any particular strike price. Consequently in Figure 12 we show the state price distribution that the theory implies, based on the empirical shock distribution and assumptions about risk aversion. The risk-premium is simply the difference between the state price distribution, and the risk-neutral or empirical shock distribution.

Clearly for most plausible utility functions the risk premium is extremely small. Indeed, for log utility the risk premium is less than 1 percent of the price even for very extreme outcomes. Even with rates of constant relative risk aversion as high as five, the risk premium is still essentially ignorable; the only real exception to this is the non-farm payrolls release, which constitutes a much larger shock to wealth. In that instance, the price of an option with a strike price two standard deviations from the mean may be inflated by around 4 percent (and hence a call option would be priced at $0.026 instead of $0.025). If the relevant relative risk aversion parameter is as high as 20, then the data suggest that option prices might be somewhat more biased.

Of course, for many applications, the mean forecast implicit in the state price distribution is the object of interest. Thus in Table 10 we compute

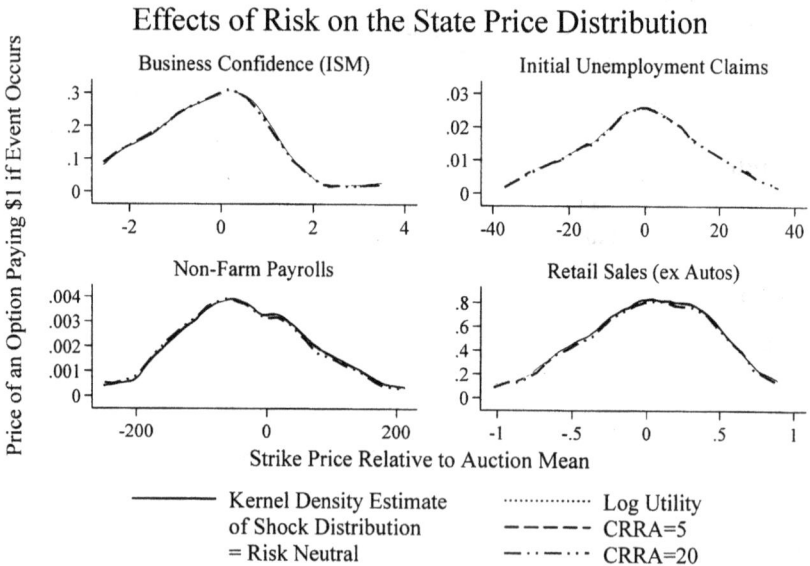

Effects of Risk on the State Price Distribution

Graphs by Economic data series

Figure 12
Effects of risk on the state price distribution

Table 10
Measures of central tendency of the probability and state-price distribution

	Non-farm payrolls	ISM	Retail sales (ex autos)	Initial claims
	Panel A: Risk Premium:			
	Mean of probability distribution less mean of state-price distribution			
Risk-neutral (γ=0)	0	0	0	0
Log utility (γ=1)	−0.32	−0.001	−0.0002	0.002
Risk-averse (γ=5)	−1.60	−0.005	−0.0009	0.008
Extremely risk averse (γ=20)	−6.40	−0.021	−0.0034	0.033
	Panel B: Risk Premium			
	Measured relative to historical standard deviation of forecast error			
Risk-neutral (γ=0)	0	0	0	0
Log utility (γ=1)	−0.0028	−0.0005	−0.0005	0.0001
Risk-averse (γ=5)	−0.0137	−0.0028	−0.0023	0.0004
Extremely risk averse (γ=20)	−0.0553	−0.0107	−0.0094	0.0018

Notes: In panel A, the units are thousands of non-farm payroll jobs, points on the ISM index, percentage growth in retail sales, and thousands of initial claims. Panel B measurements are relative to a one standard deviation shock.

the difference between the mean of the state price distribution and the mean of the underlying probability distribution for different values of assumed risk aversion. Again these numbers are based on the empirical distribution of shocks, although assuming normally distributed shocks yields similar magnitudes. Our aim is simply to provide a rule-of-thumb adjustment for calculating the mean of the probability distribution from the widely reported mean of the auction price distribution.

Panel A shows that, under risk aversion, the mean of the state price distribution will under-estimate the mean of the risk-neutral ("true") distribution for the three pro-cyclical series, but will lead to a minor overstatement of initial claims, which is countercyclical. The adjustments in Panel A are in the same underlying units as the statistics are reported in, and hence suggests, for instance, that if the relative risk aversion of investors is five, then the mean of the state price distribution understates the mean forecast by about 1600 jobs. Panel B presents these same results in a metric that better shows that these magnitudes are small, scaling the risk-premium adjustment by the standard error of the forecast. In each case the bias from simply assuming risk-neutrality is less than one-tenth of a standard error, and in most cases, it is orders of magnitude smaller.

While Table 10 suggests that risk *should* lead the market-based forecast to be only slightly lower than the risk-neutral forecast, we can take advantage of the time series movement in uncertainty to test this.[16] In Figure 13 we show forecast errors and uncertainty for each data series. In no case is the regression line statistically significant, suggesting that the data do not falsify the implications in Table 10 that the slope should be approximately zero. Notice that this exercise is slightly different from the one in Table 10 as here we look at the consequences of time-variance in the amount of risk, while in Table 10 the amount of risk is implicitly taken as invariant but the price of risk changes.

In sum, Figure 12 and Table 10 imply that under standard assumptions about risk, the state price distribution is a reasonable approximation to the true underlying probability distribution, and this conclusion holds even when we make fairly extreme assumptions about risk aversion. Indeed, Figure 13 and our analysis of the probability integral transform in the previous section confirmed precisely this point and in most cases market prices provided quite successful estimates of empirical realizations.

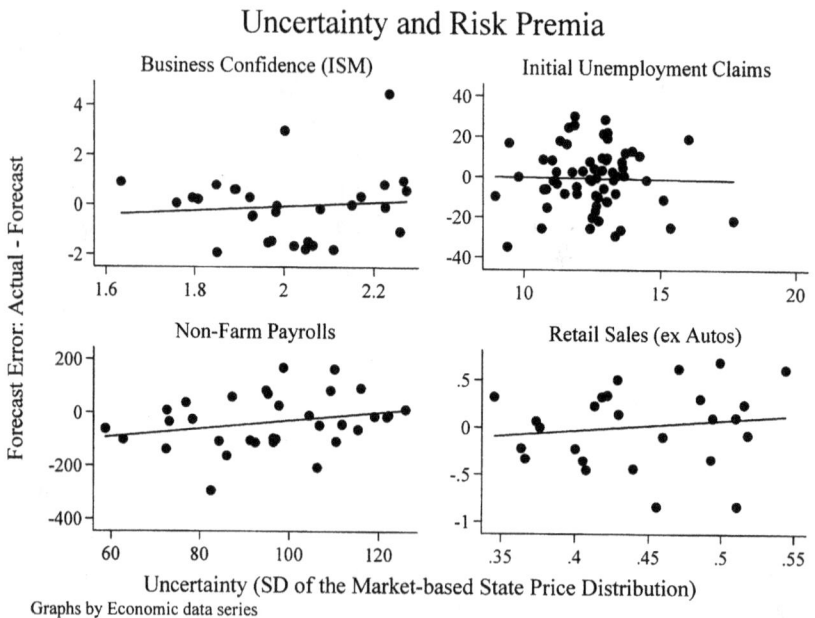

Figure 13
Uncertainty and risk premia

Figure 14 makes this point in an alternative manner, pooling the data across all auctions within each data series to map both the empirical shock distribution and the average state price distribution. The two appear remarkably close given the limited number of observations identifying the distribution of outcomes.

Our option-pricing formula also suggests that we can compare option prices and observed outcomes to back out an estimate of risk aversion. Indeed, under the assumption of constant relative risk aversion of γ, our option pricing formula directly yields a log-likelihood function:

$$L = \sum_{a}^{Auctions} \left[log\left(\pi_a^*\right) + \gamma \, log\left(\beta_a^*\right) - log\left(\sum_{s}^{Strikes_a} \pi_{s,a}\beta_{s,a}^{-\gamma} \right) \right]$$

where auctions are indexed by a and digital options within each auction are further indexed by s, the asterisk indexes the winning digital option, and thus π^* and $\pi_{s,a}$ come from the data, while estimates of the wealth impacts of shocks, β_i are taken from Table 8, and β^* is the relative wealth position given the observed shock.

We pooled all of our data to estimate the coefficient of relative risk aversion (γ), but these data do not yield much power: the 95 percent confidence interval around our estimate of γ extends from –182 to +27, with a central estimate that suggests risk-loving behavior. This is readily apparent in Figure 13, which shows that the state price distribution is to the right of the outcome distribution for non-farm payrolls, and to the left of the outcome distribution for the counter-cyclical initial claims data. (As Figure 12 shows, risk aversion would suggest the opposite pattern.)

However, rather than highlight our point estimate, we regard its enormous imprecision as arguably more interesting.[17] This imprecision derives from the fact that under our complete market assumptions the economic risks that can be hedged in this market are sufficiently small that alternative views about risk aversion do not affect all that much how one would price options tied to these risks. From an estimation standpoint this implies small amounts of noise in the option prices potentially yield very different implications for point estimates of implied risk aversion. Again, Figure 12 is instructive: essentially our estimates suggest that the data cannot distinguish between any of the state price distributions drawn on that figure, and given how close they are, this is not particularly surprising.

State Price Distribution and the Outcome Distribution

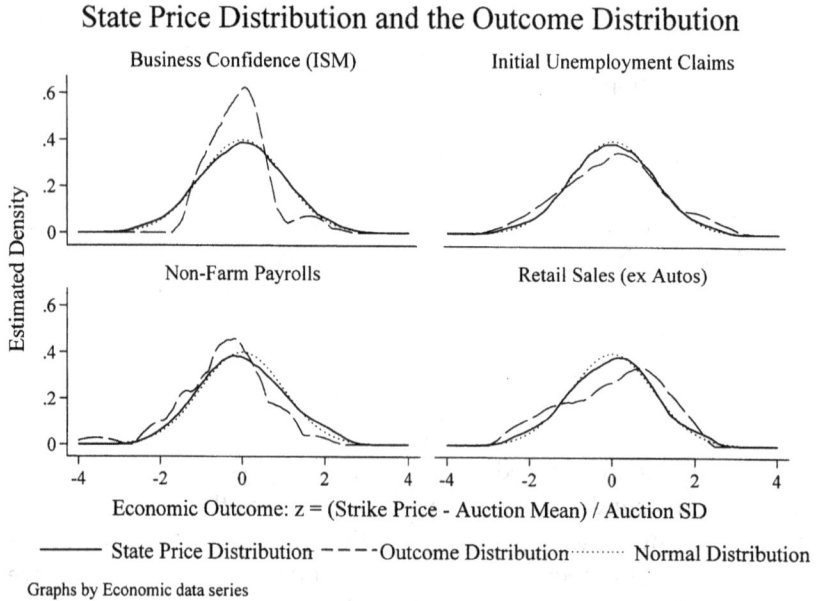

Figure 14
State price distribution and the distribution of outcomes

Thus while this market does not yield particularly useful estimates of risk aversion, the flipside is that this is driven by the fact that option prices are relatively insensitive to assumptions about risk aversion. From a practical perspective this is good news: the option prices that we observe in this market are a reasonable approximation to the risk-neutral distribution.

7. Conclusions

In this paper we provided a first analysis of the option prices from the new economic derivatives market. Economic derivatives (which have an interesting, pari-mutuel, market clearing mechanism) are novel because these binary options are written on economic data releases and state-prices of different strikes provide information not only about markets' central belief but also about implied probabilities of outcomes away from the mean. This information is not available from surveys.

We dwelled on several aspects of the economic derivatives, starting with their predictive performance. These options appear to yield efficient *density* forecasts, a rarity. Knowing that event probabilities are correctly priced in this market makes inference using the dispersion statistics convincing. In particular, this justifies using the option-based standard deviation to measure uncertainty about a data release. Comparing uncertainty with disagreement, the standard deviation of survey responses, showed that these two measures of dispersion do not have a high degree of correlation. It may not be advisable to use disagreement as a proxy for uncertainty.

The density forecast efficiency tests, when applied to market-based measures, are joint tests of efficient pricing and absence of risk premia. Our finding that economic derivatives based densities are efficient therefore indicate that risk premia in this market are unlikely to be sizable. We exploited the institutional structure of economic derivatives to study risk and risk aversion. This is quite straightforward when options from this market are used, compared to using S&P 500 options, which require taking into account time discounting and dividends. We believe economic derivatives are promising instruments for economists who would like to use asset prices to learn about agents' beliefs and preferences.

We should emphasize that we view this paper as an initial exploration. We showed that economic derivatives correctly capture subjective beliefs and provided some applications of this information. Having these subjective probabilities will facilitate future research to study how expectations are formed and how they relate to actions, as well as to analyze agents' responses to occurrence of events of different prior subjective probabilities.

Acknowledgements

The authors would like to thank Jeffrey Crilley and Banu Demir for excellent research assistance. Thanks also to Chris Carroll, Frank Diebold, John Fernald, Jeffrey Frankel, Jose Lopez, Glenn Rudebusch, Betsey Stevenson, Adam Szeidl, Jonathan Wright, and Eric Zitzewitz for useful discussions and to Bill Cassano and Kevin Keating of Goldman Sachs for helping us with institutional detail. This paper was partly written while Gürkaynak was at the Federal Reserve Board. He thanks that institution for the outstanding research environment it provided. Wolfers gratefully acknowledges the support of a Hirtle, Callaghan and Co. – Arthur D. Miltenberger Research Fellowship, Microsoft Research, the Zell/Lurie Real Estate Center, and the Mack Center for Technological Innovation.

Notes

1. Beyond these markets, the Chicago Board of Trade is offering federal funds rate futures and options and the Chicago Mercantile Exchange has a thinly traded CPI futures contract. Online markets such as Hedgestreet and Tradesports also offer an array of economic derivatives to retail investors.

2. Currently every order must go through Goldman Sachs, Deutsche Bank, or ICAP (an interdealer broker). As of the writing of this paper (September 2005) an agreement was in place to involve the CME in the auction process.

3. The transaction cost—the fee paid to Goldman Sachs and Deutsche Bank—is 1 percent of the notional amount (one cent per digital option) capped at 10 percent of the price of the option.

4. The auction clearing pari-mutuel algorithm, called "Parimutuel Derivative Call Auction technology" is patented by Longitude Inc., who also license their product to create markets in mortgage prepayment speeds and natural gas and crude oil inventories (see Baron and Lange, 2003, for more on this algorithm).

5. Auctions of initial claims options are not held for the releases that immediately precede the employment report. Our data set consists of 33 non-farm payrolls auctions, 30 business confidence auctions, 26 retail trade auctions, and 64 initial claims auctions.

6. Some auctions on European inflation take place two months prior to the data release.

7. When more than one auction was held for a single data release, we analyze data from the latest auction.

8. MMS was acquired by Informa in 2003 and no longer exists; Action Economics is now providing the same survey service. We use the MMS numbers for most of our sample and the Action Economics survey for the more recent period. Bloomberg survey numbers were used to fill some gaps. Despite using more than one source, we call our survey numbers "the MMS survey" as most of our data is from this source. The MMS survey sample consists mainly of professional economists working in financial markets, and many of the firms surveyed are probably also participants in the economic derivatives market.

9. More specifically, throughout the paper we treat the distribution as discrete, assuming that all probability mass occurs at the midpoint of the relevant bin. For the tails we impute an upper- and lower-bound so that the midpoint would be equal to the mean of that bin if the pdf were normal. Our results are invariant to different treatments of tail probabilities.

10. In order to maintain a non-overlapping sample, we calculated the standard deviation of the survey-based forecast errors for samples ending in October 2002. The "historical" sample begins in January 1990 for non-farm payrolls and retail sales, in July 1991 for ISM, and in July 1997 for initial claims. The historical standard errors of these forecasts are 115,600 non-farm payroll jobs, 18,500 initial unemployment claims, 0.37 percent growth in retail sales and 1.99 points of the ISM index.

11. The intraday data we use help us isolate the market reaction to the data release in question with minimum noise. The yields we use are yields of on-the-run Treasury securities. The stock price changes are from S&P futures contracts as the stock market is not open at 8.30 a.m. (EST), when the three of the four macroeconomic data series we are interested in are released (ISM is a 10.00 a.m. release). In taking the market snapshots, if

there is no trade in a given security five minutes before the event, we search back in time until we find a trade or a settlement price. If there is no trade exactly 25 minutes after the event we again search back in time, until the data release moment. If there are no trades in this 25 minute interval we mark a zero change, assuming that if there was a surprise in the data release that changed the shadow price of a security there would have been a trade over this time period. We do not search for a trade forward in time so as to ensure that the price change we observe is not due to another event that took place later in the same day. The data set is described in detail in Gürkaynak, Sack, and Swanson (2005).

12. Note that while a strong data release for an important statistic should unambiguously push yields up, the effect on stock prices is not as clear. The news that the state of the business cycle is better than expected will lift the S&P index, but the associated increase in interest rates has a dampening effect on equities.

13. Panel D controls for the slope of the yield curve (measured as the difference between the ten year and 3-month yields), and the change in the S&P 500 over the preceding ten trading days as regressors.

14. While Table 6 provides useful descriptive detail, it is silent on the issue of driving forces. There are potentially three important influences that may be driving variation in uncertainty about a particular economic statistic: fundamental uncertainty about the true underlying state of the economy, data-driven uncertainty whereby other data series have not spoken clearly about the state of the economy, and uncertainty about the extent of possible measurement error in the underlying economic statistic. Financial market responses to economic news can potentially help sort out which driving forces are important as economic news has its largest impact on beliefs (and hence on financial markets) when there is greater uncertainty about the true state of the economy. By contrast, traders will be more likely to discount the same sized shock if their uncertainty reflects concerns about measurement. Our statistical tests for these produced very imprecise estimates that we do not report, but we note this potential use of economic derivates based information.

15. Note that the critical values are appropriate for each bin separately, but they are inappropriate for jointly testing that the heights of all bins are drawn from a binomial distribution.

16. We thank Jeffrey Frankel for suggesting this test to us.

17. Note that when estimating implied risk aversion in this fashion, we treated the β_i as known. The confidence interval would have been even wider had we accounted for the variance imparted by having the β's estimated.

References

Aït-Sahalia, Yacine, and Andrew W. Lo. 2000. "Nonparametric Risk Management and Implied Risk Aversion." *Journal of Econometrics* 94: 9–51.

Baron, Ken, and Jeffrey Lange. 2003. "From Horses to Hedging." *Risk* 16(2): 73–77.

Berkowitz, Jeremy. 2001. "Testing Density Forecasts, with Applications to Risk Management." *Journal of Business and Economic Statistics* 19(4): 465–474.

Christoffersen, Peter. 1998. "Evaluating Interval Forecasts." *International Economic Review* 39: 841–862.

Constantinides, George. 1982. "Intertemporal Asset Pricing with Heterogeneous Consumers and without Demand Aggregation." *Journal of Business* 55(2): 253–276.

Diebold, Frank X., Todd Gunther, and Anthony S. Tay. 1998. "Evaluating Density Forecasts, with Applications to Financial Risk Management." *International Economic Review* 39: 863–883.

Diebold, Frank X., Anthony S. Tay, and Kenneth F. Wallis. 1999. "Evaluating Density Forecasts of Inflation: The Survey of Professional Forecasters." In R. Engle and H. White (eds.), *Festschrift in Honor of C.W.J. Cranger.* Oxford: Oxford University Press, 76–90.

Eisenberg, Edmund, and David Gale. 1959. "Consensus of Subjective Probabilities: The Pari-Mutuel Method." *Annals of Mathematical Statistics* 30: 165–168.

Fair, Ray C., and Robert J. Shiller. 1990. "Comparing Information in Forecasts from Econometric Models." *American Economic Review* 80(3): 375–389.

Gürkaynak, Refet S., Brian Sack, and Eric Swanson. 2005. "Did Financial Markets Think Disinflation Was Opportunistic?" Manuscript, Federal Reserve Board.

Jackwerth, Jens Carten. 2000. "Recovering Risk Aversion from Option Prices and Realized Returns." *The Review of Financial Studies* 13(2): 433–451.

Llambros, Louis, and Victor Zarnowitz. 1987. "Consensus and Uncertainty in Economic Prediction." *Journal of Political Economy* 95(3): 591–562.

Mankiw, N. Gregory, Ricardo Reis, and Justin Wolfers. 2003. "Disagreement about Inflation Expectations." *NBER Macroeconomics Annual* 18: 209–248.

Shiller, Robert. 1993. *Macro Markets.* Oxford: Oxford University Press.

Wolfers, Justin, and Eric Zitzewitz. 2004. "Prediction Markets." *Journal of Economic Perspectives* 18(2): 107–126.

Wolfers, Justin, and Eric Zitzewitz. 2005. "Interpreting Prediction Market Prices as Probabilities." *Mimeo*, University of Pennsylvania.

Comment

Christopher D. Carroll, *Johns Hopkins University and NBER*

This paper opens up what promises to be a whole new approach to macroeconomic research. Market-based forecasts of macroeconomic variables provide a promising way to neatly sidestep the intractable, insoluble, and semi-theological debates about how expectations are formed that have plagued macroeconomics since Keynes first speculated that "animal spirits" were a driving force in business cycles.

So you might say I'm a fan.

In fact, the first part of my discussion will argue that the results of the paper are even more important than one might conclude from the authors' own analysis, because they focus on the (microscopic) differences between survey-based forecasts and market-based forecasts, rather than on the impressive similarities between them. The brief latter part of the discussion raises some reasons for caution about the institutional design and operation of these markets.

1. Comparing Survey and Auction Based Expectations

A substantial part of the paper (Tables 1–3) compares expectations as revealed by the auction market to the mean forecasts of a survey of professional forecasters. An incautious reader might get the impression that these results suggest the market-based expectations are notably better than those of the survey. In fact, I think the opposite interpretation is the right one: When used to measure the same thing, survey-based expectations are, for analytical purposes, indistinguishable from market-based expectations.

Consider, for example, the non-farm payrolls data, which are for most purposes the most important single U.S. data release.[1] The authors present the following comparative statistics about the two. (These are taken from their Table 1).

Table 1
Prediction errors from auction and survey (non-farm payrolls)

	Mean absolute error (AbsErr)	Root mean squared error (RMSE)	Correlation with actual outcome
Auction	0.723	0.907	0.700
Survey	0.743	0.929	0.677

The table speaks for itself.

The authors emphasize the results for their other data series, which could be described as providing a smidgen of evidence that the market forecasts are more accurate than the survey forecasts. I will shortly express some quibbles with this interpretation. But before doing so, I would like to point out that even under the authors' interpretation, the superiority of the auction forecast is generally small.

This is important because the macroeconomic derivatives markets have been operating only for a short time. Since, according to the NBER Business Cycle Dating Committee, the average postwar business cycle in the U.S. has had a duration of about eight years, the usefulness of these data for macroeconomic analysis will arguably be modest for at least a decade. If instead we draw the conclusion that the macroeconomic derivatives markets have definitively revealed the impressive qualities of survey-based expectations, the scope of the paper's usefulness is vastly expanded, since various kinds of survey-based expectations have been collected for a very long time (for example, the Survey of Professional Forecasters has been conducted since 1968).

1.1 Quibbles

As the authors note, the auctions they analyze do not provide any real opportunity for hedging macroeconomic risks in the sense Shiller (1993) originally proposed because they are generally conducted only a few hours (or at most a few days) before the data are released.

This timing, however, means that participants in the auctions have more recent information than survey participants, whose views are collected every Friday. In the case of a data series released on a Thursday, the auction participants' information set could incorporate nearly a week's worth of extra knowledge about the state of the economy.

This problem is particularly serious for initial claims for unemployment insurance, since this is a weekly series released on Thursday mornings. Indeed, it is remarkable that the almost week-old surveys do almost as well as the previous-day auctions in forecasting this weekly series.

An alternative way of analyzing the authors' data (and one that is fairer to the forecasters) would be to hypothesize that both forecasters' and auction participants' views are rational; in that case, Hall (1978) taught us that the auction results should equal the survey results plus a random expectational error that reflects the forecasters' extra information:

$$A_t = S_{t-1} + \varepsilon_t, \tag{1}$$

which can be tested by estimating a regression

$$A_t = z_0 + z_1 S_{t-1} \tag{2}$$

and testing $z_0 = 0$ and $z_1 = 1$.

To test this proposition as an overall characterization of the authors' data, it is necessary to put the various statistics on a common footing in the sense of having comparable means and measures of variability. I did so by subtracting, for each series, the mean realized value over the sample period, and dividing by the gap between the maximum and minimum realized sample values.[2]

Results are plotted in Figure 1. As the figure illustrates, there is a very strong association between the survey and the auction predictions.

The point is illustrated statistically by Table 2, which reports the results of a regression like the one contemplated in equation (2). The hypotheses that $z_0 = 0$ and $z_1 = 1$ cannot be rejected at standard significance levels, and the $\bar{R}^2$ for the regression is over 90 percent. When the sample is restricted to the crucial non-farm payrolls data, similar results obtain.

One way of testing whether the more up-to-date information held by auction market participants could plausibly explain a modest superiority in their forecasts is to see whether auctions that are held closer to the date of the data release produce forecasts that are more accurate. Unfortunately, the authors' dataset contains only a few auctions that were held earlier than the day on which a data series was released. Most of these were for the ISM data. Table 3 calculates the size of the absolute error for the 21 auctions that were held on the morning of the data release, the four auctions that were held one day before, and the three auctions that were held three days before. (There seem to be no examples of auctions conducted two days before the release). The mean absolute error is notably larger for the auctions conducted rela-

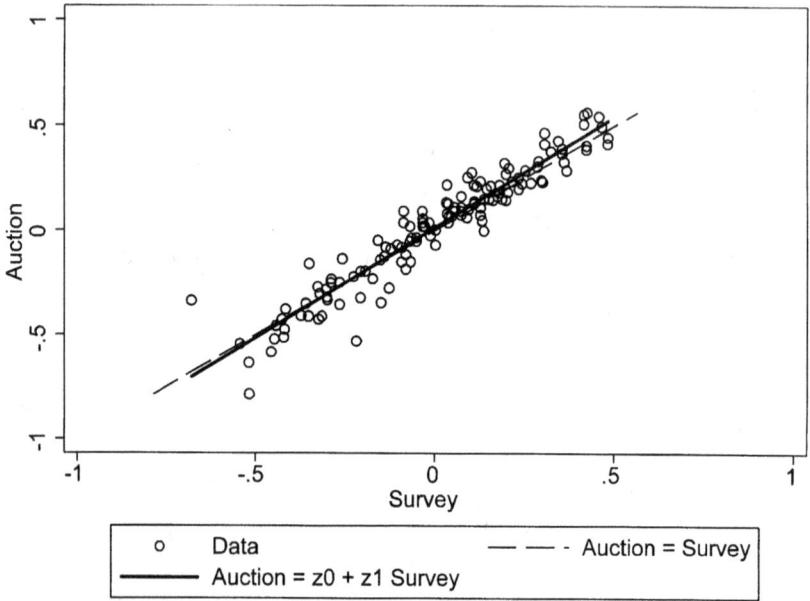

Figure 1
Survey expectations versus auction expectations

Table 2
Regression of auction on survey expectations

Data series	z0	z1	$\bar{R}^2$
	Auction = z0 + z1 Survey		
All	0.013	1.055	0.91
	(0.007)	(0.039)	
Payrolls	0.001	1.096	0.95
	(0.014)	(0.052)	

Robust standard errors in parentheses.

Table 3
Absolute error for different ISM auction horizons

Days between auction and data release	Number of auctions	Mean absolute error
0	21	0.48
1	4	0.57
3	3	0.56

tively earlier, as would be true if significant news generally arrives in the period leading up to the release (though separate tests (not shown) indicate that these differences are not statistically significant).

The authors emphasize the results of a final horse race (in Table 2) between the two series. They show (convincingly) that financial market reactions to the actual data release are stronger when the "surprise" is measured as the deviation from the auction forecast than when it is measured as the deviation from the survey forecast, at least for the payrolls data.

Again a possible explanation is the later date of the auction than the survey. Another possibility that the authors suggest is that the participants in the auctions are precisely the same people whose financial transactions, post-release, will determine the market reaction. If this is true, it would be puzzling if their opinions did *not* have more influence on financial market outcomes than the opinions of bystanders like the economists participating in the surveys.

None of this is meant to dispute the proposition that the auction based forecasts are a superior source of information, when both auction and survey data exist. As the authors show, the auction data paint a much richer picture of expectations than is available from the surveys, particularly with respect to the probability distribution over possible outcomes, which can be condensed (as the authors show) in any of several ways to measure uncertainty. In 30 years there may be no reason to use survey data at all because a sufficient amount of auction data will be available. But for the time being, the authors' results provide compelling evidence that surveys capture an enormous amount of useful information.

This richness is used in section 4 of the paper to examine a question that heretofore has been a matter of speculation: whether disagreement among survey participants can be interpreted as a measure of uncertainty.

On the whole their conclusion is that such an interpretation is problematic. Table 4 reproduces the key results from their analysis of this question, in which they regress measures of uncertainty on measures of disagreement. The absolute magnitudes of the coefficients are not meaningful, because there is no obvious mapping between the cross-forecaster standard deviation of forecasts of the mean value of the release, and the standard deviation of the released data itself. The right questions are the degree of statistical significance of the relationship

Table 4
Uncertainty versus disagreement

	Uncertainty = $\alpha + \beta$ Disagreement	
Series	β	$\bar{R}^2$
Payrolls	0.66**	0.11
	(0.29)	
Retail sales	0.44**	0.20
	(0.16)	
Initial claims	0.27***	0.17
	(0.07)	
ISM	−0.03	−0.03
	(0.12)	

between uncertainty and disagreement, and the total proportion of uncertainty that can be measured by disagreement. Except for the ISM series, the authors find a highly statistically significant relationship between disagreement and uncertainty.

They tend to emphasize, however, the finding that the $\bar{R}^2$ is well below one in all cases. But there is clearly sampling error in the survey of forecasters; how to think about this is not entirely obvious, since there are forecasters who exist but are not in the survey and the survey participants vary over time. By itself this would be enough to prevent an $\bar{R}^2$ equal to one even if the authors' measures of uncertainty were perfect.

My own sense is that the more important question is whether disagreement can be interpreted as a statistically reliable indicator of the degree of uncertainty, rather than a direct measure. One way to make the question concrete is to ask whether the regression the authors report can be thought of as the first stage of a two-stage least squares regression of uncertainty on disagreement. One could then use the prediction of the estimated equation as a contemporaneous measure of appropriately calibrated uncertainty. Judged in this way, the $\bar{R}^{2}$'s for the first stage regressions and the high statistical significance of the coefficients are plenty good enough to interpret the prediction of the model as an (instrumented) measure of uncertainty. (Of course, careful econometrics would have to make sure that this cross-section disagreement is not perfectly correlated with some other macro variable (like the inflation rate).)

2. Caveats about Macro Markets

Despite their many attractive properties, it is worth worrying a little bit (at this early stage) about the longer term consequences of the creation of macro markets, especially for the data collection process.

I have the fullest faith in the integrity and objectivity of the staff at the agencies that produce economic data. But there can be no doubt that the creation of macro markets will increase both the pressure on the staff and the ease with which an unscrupulous employee could exploit inside information. Data security procedures need not only to be objectively rigorous but also to be transparently seen to be rigorous. Possibly there should be a systematic ongoing program (by the Securities and Exchange Commission?) to monitor trading in macro markets for any signs of insider trading.

Another concern is that if macro markets become sufficiently popular (and lucrative), the economic agencies may have a problem of retaining senior staff. If senior officials were regularly lured away from their posts by the offer of salaries many times higher than the government can provide, it might be difficult to preserve the institutional memory and expertise necessary for guaranteeing the consistency and high quality of U.S. statistics. Probably the only appropriate measure that could be taken to prevent this (in addition to paying appropriately high salaries to the senior staff) would be to impose strict ethics rules that require a substantial waiting period (say, five years) between the time of departure from a statistical agency and any employment that exploits that expertise in the context of macro markets.

Finally, and perhaps most significantly, the existence of macro markets could influence the data collection procedures themselves. Although the currently existing auction markets probably do not pose much risk in this dimension, when markets are created for longer-term forecasts (as they inevitably will be), the holders of those auction contracts will have the incentive to become lobbying groups for or against changes in the methods of data collection. Imagine, for example, that macro markets had existed at the time of the Boskin Commission on reform of the CPI in the mid-1990s, or the redefinition of the unemployment rate in the early 1990s. If each decision a commission announces results in immediate capital gains or losses of billions of dollars for holders of contingent securities, there will be extraordinary incentives to subvert the objectivity of the decision makers. Good institutional design could certainly circumvent these pressures, but if data collection procedures are perceived to be able to be influenced by the appointment of ad hoc committees nominated by politicians there is reason to worry.

This risk could perhaps be alleviated if the agencies that produce the data were to create standing committees of scientific advisors associated with each of the major statistical releases for which macro markets exist or are in contemplation. For example, a panel of distinguished labor economists might be recruited to monitor proposed changes to the non-farm payrolls survey. These committees might borrow the model of the NBER Business Cycle Dating Committee: Meetings only when warranted by some event, but a committee that is always well defined. This would provide some transparent insulation against the political forces that might otherwise mobilize to have commissions appointed whose members would be picked to reach preordained conclusions.

It is important to resolve these issues early, because the whole superstructure of macro markets will be undermined if the integrity of the data collection process comes into question. But if addressed early, these problems should not be serious.

3. Conclusions

All quibbles aside, this paper, and the macro markets that it is the first to explore, represent a tremendous innovation in macroeconomic analysis. I look forward with great anticipation to the literature that will undoubtedly flow from them.

Notes

1. Like the authors, Fleming and Remolona 1997 find that this data release moves the bond market more than any other, and more recently Faust et. al. 2003 have found that this data release moves exchange rates even more than monetary policy surprises.

2. Results were similar when the data were scaled, following the authors, by the presample standard error; the resulting figure is slightly more legible using my scaling method.

References

Faust, Jon, John H. Rogers, Eric Swanson, and Jonathan H. Wright. 2003. "Identifying the Effects of Monetary Policy Shocks on Exchange Rates Using High Frequency Data." *Journal of the European Economic Association* 1: 1031–1057.

Fleming, Michael, and Eli Remolona. 1997. "What Moves the Bond Market?" *Federal Reserve Bank of New York Economic Policy Review* 3: 31–50.

Hall, Robert E. 1978. "Stochastic Implications of the Life-Cycle/Permanent Income Hypothesis: Theory and Evidence." *Journal of Political Economy* 96: 971–987.

Shiller, Robert J. 1993. *Macro Markets: Creating Institutions for Managing Society's Largest Economic Risks.* Oxford: Oxford University Press.

Comment

Adam Szeidl, University of California, Berkeley

1. Introduction

This is an interesting and informative paper that explores pricing behavior in a new market for macroeconomic derivatives. Asset markets where risk associated with future macroeconomic events can be traded are a recent financial innovation. These markets may allow more efficient sharing of macro risks and increase economic welfare. To assess their potential, it is important to understand how well existing economic derivatives markets function. Analyzing data from one such market where claims on macroeconomic indicators including non-farm payrolls are traded, this paper argues that (1) Expectations derived from market prices are more accurate than survey-based forecasts and less subject to behavioral biases; (2) The market predicts the probability distribution of outcomes remarkably well; (3) Risk aversion plays at most a small role in determining prices in this market.

I begin by discussing potential theoretical foundations for the empirical findings. Then I briefly discuss features of the market mechanism, and finally turn to the role of risk aversion. My comments suggest additional empirical tests that can sharpen our understanding of how markets for economic derivatives function.

2. Theory

Perhaps surprisingly, it is not easy to come up with plausible microfoundations for findings (1) and (2). Why are prices accurate predictors of outcomes? And why are prices more accurate than survey-based forecasts, when in many economic models, prices are functions of the beliefs that forecasts measure? To answer these questions, I begin by exploring the mechanism through which markets may aggregate information. A large theoretical literature (e.g., Grossman 1976 or more recently Reny and Perry 2003) argues that markets correctly aggregate heterogeneous information in the presence of common prior beliefs. In practice, however, the common prior assumption appears to be at odds with often-observed disagreement in survey forecasts among professional forecasters, because different individuals with common priors cannot agree to disagree (Aumann 1976). A plausible alternative in this context is to assume that disagreement is due to heterogeneous prior beliefs.

However, with heterogeneous beliefs, as argued for example by Manski (2004), it is not a-priori clear that predictive markets should correctly aggregate information. To see the logic, note that in principle, a wealthy individual with incorrect beliefs may be able to push prices away from fundamental values by the sheer size of her investment. More formally, Wolfers and Zitzewitz (2005) show that with risk-averse investors and a competitive market, the price will equal the wealth-weighted average belief in the population. This result confirms that market prices can depart from true expectations if the distribution of beliefs is correlated with wealth. On the other hand, in this model, accurate market prices obtain if the average belief in the population correctly predicts outcomes. This suggests that the reason why predictive markets function so well is that the average belief of investors is correct.

To test this proposition, one can look for alternative empirical measures of beliefs. A natural candidate, used for example by Mankiw, Reis, and Wolfers (2003), is survey-based forecasts. If one accepts that such surveys are a good measure of beliefs, then the Wolfers-Zitzewitz model predicts that surveys will forecast outcomes at least as well as market prices. However, this prediction contradicts finding (1) of this paper. How can prices be more accurate than surveys, when surveys are a direct measure of investors' beliefs?

To resolve this contradiction, one has to relax one of the assumptions of the previous argument. It must be that either (a) prices are not more accurate than survey-based forecasts; or (b) surveys do not reflect true beliefs; or (c) prices are accurate not because they reflect average beliefs, but for some different reason. Distinguishing between these alternatives would be useful to better understand the workings of predictive markets.

Let us address each possibility in turn. Case (a) suggests that finding (1) in the paper is due to other differences between the survey and market data. Timing is one such difference: while the predictive market meets on the morning of the data release, the survey is collected up to a week earlier. Given such differences in timing, information that becomes available after the survey is collected may be reflected in the market price. This explanation suggests that surveys are good measures of expectations. From a practical perspective, this would be useful, because survey data is more widely available than data from predictive markets. Using the data of the current paper, this explanation can be tested by comparing the differential accuracy between surveys and forecasts depending on the difference in timing. When this explanation is correct, surveys that take place later should be closer in accuracy to market prices.

Case (b) may hold for example if survey respondents have little to lose from making incorrect predictions, while market participants have money at stake. In this case, earlier work where beliefs are measured using survey based forecasts is potentially misleading. While there is little doubt that predictions do improve when the stakes are higher, the question is quantitative. How much does precision increase when the stakes go up? A preliminary empirical approach to explore this question is to compare the accuracy of predictions across markets with different stakes, as measured perhaps by total investment in short and long positions. In markets with higher total investment, we should find that prices are better predictors of outcomes.

In my view, case (c) is the least likely. If prices do not reflect average beliefs, then we are back to the original puzzle: Why do prices in predictive markets forecast outcomes so accurately?

To summarize, the most plausible theory raises the question of whether finding (1) is caused by the different nature of surveys versus markets or their differential timing, and suggests additional empirical tests to help sort out whether markets are just as accurate as surveys or more accurate because the stakes are small for survey participants.

3.   The Pari-Mutuel Mechanism

Understanding the logic of information aggregation in predictive markets is further complicated by the fact that the market mechanism is not competitive. The market is a modified version of the pari-mutuel mechanism often used in horse race betting. Eisenberg and Gale (1959) explore Nash equilibrium in a simple version of the basic pari-mutuel model. They establish existence and uniqueness of equilibrium; however, the equilibrium they find need not involve prices that correctly predict outcomes. To quote the last sentence in their paper: "In the case of two bettors with equal budgets if the first bettor's subjective probability distribution on two horses is ((1/2),(1/2)) then the equilibrium probabilities will be ((1/2),(1/2)) regardless of the subjective probabilities of the second bettor, as the reader will easily verify." Therefore, in the special case discussed in the quote, the price will be independent of the beliefs of the second bettor. This example suggests that exploring the actual market mechanism in more detail can lead to useful insights about the logic of information aggregation.

4.   Risk Aversion

My final topic is the role of risk aversion. Using a simple model with power utility investors, the paper shows that for reasonable coefficients of relative risk aversion the risk premium of holding economic derivatives should be very small. Based on this argument, the authors conclude that risk is unlikely to affect asset prices in predictive markets.

One problem with this logic is that the same calibration argument, if applied to the aggregate stock market, would imply that risk plays at most a minor role in determining expected stock returns, and that the equity risk premium should be very small. As it is well known, this implication of the model is robustly contradicted in the data (e.g., Mehra and Prescott 1985). This equity premium puzzle suggests that the standard power utility model should not be used to assess the effect of risk in influencing asset prices. An alternative approach to gauge the impact of risk on prices is to note that for most investors, investing in predictive markets is likely to be a relatively small risk. There are studies suggesting that decision making in the presence of small risk is well-described by loss-aversion preferences that have a kink at the status quo level of wealth (see for example, Thaler, Tversky, Kahneman, and Schwartz 1997). Calibrating a model with such loss-averse investors would be an empirically more plausible way to assess the role of risk in affecting predictive market prices.

To conclude, this is an interesting paper that documents useful facts about the functioning of economic derivatives' markets. I hope that my discussion helps in suggesting additional empirical tests to sharpen our understanding of the mechanism through which these markets aggregate information.

References

Aumann, Robert. 1976. "Agreeing to Disagree." *The Annals of Statistics* 4: 1236-1239.

Eisenberg, Edmund, and David Gale. 1959. "Consensus of Subjective Probabilities: The Pari-mutuel Method." *Annals of Mathematical Statistics* 30: 165–168.

Grossman, Sanford. 1976. "On the Efficiency of Competitive Stock Markets Where Trades Have Diverse Information." *Journal of Finance* 31: 573–585.

Mankiew, Gregory N., Ricardo Reis, and Justin Wolfers. 2003. "Disagreement about Inflation Expectations." *NBER Macroeconomics Annual.*

Manksi, Charles F. 2004. "Interpreting the Predictions of Prediction Markets." Working Paper no. 10359. Cambridge, MA: National Bureau of Economic Research.

Mehra, Rajnish, and Edward C. Prescott. 1985. "The Equity Premium: A Puzzle." *Journal of Monetary Economics* 15: 145–161.

Reny, Philip J., and Perry, Motty. 2003. "Toward a Strategic Foundation for Rational Expectations Equilibrium." Working Paper. University of Chicago and Hebrew University.

Thaler, Richard H., Amos Tversky, Daniel Kahneman, and Alan Schwartz. 1997. "The Effect of Myopia and Loss Aversion on Risk Taking: An Experimental Test." *Quarterly Journal of Economics* 112: 647–661.

Wolfers, Justin, and Eric Zitzewitz. 2005. "Interpreting Prediction Market Prices as Probabilities." Working Paper. University of Pennsylvania and Stanford University.

2

The Roots of Low European Employment: Family Culture?

Yann Algan, *Marne la Vallée University OEP, Paris School of Economics, IZA*

Pierre Cahuc, *Université Paris 1, CREST-INSEE, IZA, CEPR*

1. Introduction

OECD countries faced highly contrasted employment patterns over the last three decades. However, this cross-national heterogeneity is mainly concentrated on particular demographic groups. Actually, Figure 1 shows that the employment rate of prime-age men has been quite similar across countries since 1970.[1] In contrast, the employment rates of younger people, prime-age women, and older people display significant cross-country variations. Moreover, Figure 1 shows that OECD countries also differ in the evolution pattern of the employment rates of demographic groups. All OECD countries have undergone the same steady rise in female employment rates and a slight decrease in prime-age male employment rates. But while the employment rates of younger and older individuals have remained quite stable in Anglo-Saxon and Scandinavian countries, they both have dramatically fallen in Continental and Mediterranean countries.

To the best of our knowledge, there is still no framework that explains such stylized facts which lie at the heart of the cross-country differences in aggregate employment rates over the last decades. The aim of this paper is to fill this gap. We argue that the key to understanding these stylized facts lies in family attitudes and labor supply interactions between the different generations of family members.

To that end, we provide a simple labor supply model that accounts for relations within the nuclear family and the extended family. In this framework, stronger preferences for nuclear and extended family relations lower the labor supply of women, younger and older people. Moreover, we show that an exogenous shock to the household production of women—such as the observed fall in the price of household durable goods—may have differential impact on the labor supply of

Employment rates by demographic groups

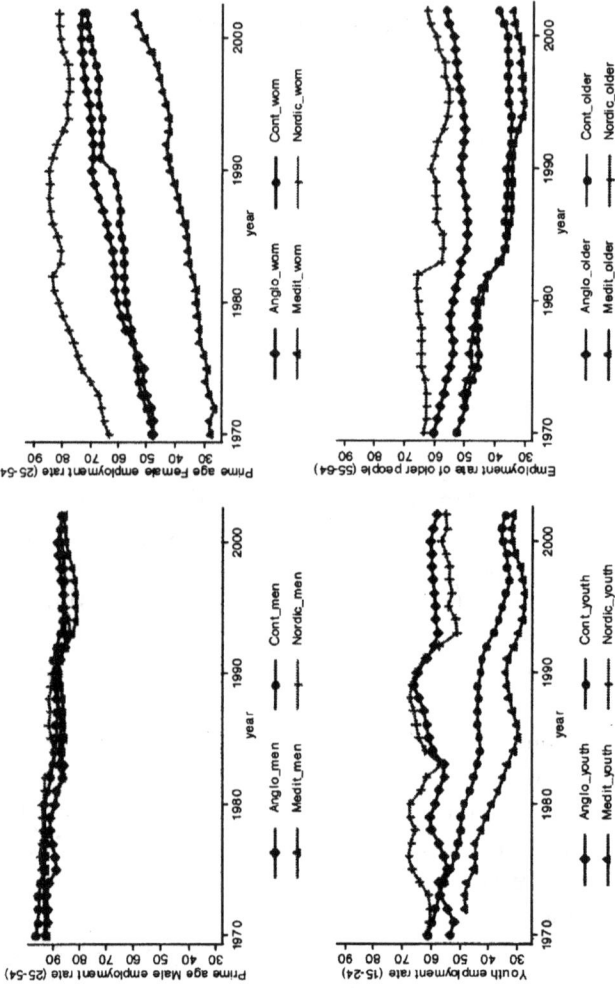

Anglo: UK_US   Continental: Fra_Germ   Mediterranean : Ita_Sp   Nordic: Dk_Swd

Figure 1
OECD employment rates by demographic groups over the period 1970–2003
Source: OECD.

each family member that depends on the extent of family relations. Following Greenwood et al. (2005), we relate the rise in female participation observed in all OECD economies to an exogenous decline in the price of durable goods used in household production. Specifically, this drop in the price of household durable goods allows women to substitute waged work to home production. The decline in the price of household durable goods also increases home production. Then, assuming that family activities[2] are complementary to home production, all the members of the family have incentives to spend more time in family activities. This latter effect is more important when individuals are strongly attached to family activities. Therefore, the higher the weight put on family relations, the higher is the decline in the labor supply of younger and older individuals when prime-age female labor supply rises.

The empirical relevance of the model is then tested on international micro and macro data. We first document that people living in different OECD countries do significantly differ with respect to their family attitudes. To that end, we use international social surveys on family values and relations (the *World Value Survey* and the *International Social Survey Program*) which cover the main OECD countries over the last two decades. These surveys allow us to disentangle the role played by individual characteristics and country specific effects on family attitudes. Second, we show that these specific national family attitudes are highly correlated with the employment rates of the different demographic groups by running estimations on aggregate OECD data over the last two decades. This correlation pattern is generally robust to the inclusion of traditional time-varying labor market institutions and other country dummies which could account for other cross-country differences in institutions.[3] We also stress that accounting for family attitudes is promising for understanding the dynamics of employment rates. By gathering a new database on the prices of household durable goods for an extensive set of OECD countries over the last two decades and controlling for labor market institutions, we find that the drop in the price of household durable goods has had stringent differential impacts on demographic groups across countries. This fall has been significantly correlated with the rise in female employment rates in all countries, consistently with Greenwood et al. (2005) results. But this effect goes beyond the nuclear family and significantly reduces the labor supply of younger and older individuals in Mediterranean and Continental countries while there is no evidence of such an interaction in Nordic or Anglo-Saxon countries.

This finding suggests that labor supply interactions within the nuclear and the extended family are a key element for understanding the evolution pattern of employment rates.[4] From this perspective, if low employment in Europe originates in a specific family culture[5] widely shared by a majority of the population, the European employment strategy,[6] which aims at increasing the employment rate of women, younger, and older people, may be inadequate as it might try to market services (such as child care or Sunday family meals) that people prefer to produce at home. Accordingly, it is important to know whether the correlation between family attitudes and employment outcome can be interpreted as a relation where family culture *causes* employment outcomes.

The last contribution of the paper is thus an attempt at uncovering the causal link at work in the correlation between country specific family attitudes and employment patterns. It may be argued that heterogeneity in national family attitudes only mirrors heterogeneity in national institutions. To that regard, traditional explanations putting the emphasis on labor market rigidities and competition between demographic groups on the labor market may explain both employment rates[7] and family attitudes.[8] In other words, the causality could go only from institutions to employment rates and family attitudes. We thus go one step further by providing some empirical evidence that national family attitudes are shaped by cultural primitives. In particular, we show that people facing *a priori* the same economic environment by living in the same country—but who differ by the national origin of their ancestors—do have significantly different family attitudes, even after controlling for all their relevant socioeconomic individual characteristics.[9] Moreover, their family attitudes are perfectly in lines with those currently expressed in their country of origin.

The paper is organized as follows. Section 2 displays some stylized facts about the employment rates of different demographic groups for 19 OECD countries over the period 1970–2003. The labor supply model used to explain the employment participation of prime age men, prime age women, young, and old people is presented in section 3. Empirical evidence on the relation between family attitudes and employment rates are analyzed in section 4. Section 5 offers some concluding comments.

2. Stylized Facts

We begin by examining the main stylized facts concerning the employment rates of OECD countries over the last decades. The analysis covers the period 1970–2003 for 19 countries: Australia, Austria, Belgium, Canada, Denmark, Finland, France, Germany, Greece, Ireland, Italy, Japan, Netherlands, Norway, Portugal, Spain, Sweden, the UK, and the US. In this realm, it is well known that Nordic and Anglo-Saxon countries are nowadays good performers whereas Continental European and Mediterranean countries are much less efficient. As of 2003, the employment rate of the 15–64 years old population reaches 73.2 percent in Nordic countries, 71.4 percent in Anglo-Saxon countries, but only 64.8 percent and 55.1 percent in Continental-European and Mediterranean countries, respectively.[10] Yet we show that the main cross-country and cross-temporal variations are concentrated on specific demographic groups.

2.1 Dispersion of Employment Rates

Table 1 indicates that the cross-national dispersion of prime-age male employment rates is much smaller than differences in the employment rates of other demographic groups, such as prime-age women and younger and older people. Row 2 in Table 1 indicates that the coefficient of variation (equals to the standard deviation over the mean) of prime age male employment rate over the whole period 1970–2003 is very small. It is about 20 times as small as the coefficient of variation at stakes for the other demographic groups, whose dispersion of employment rates is very close during this period.

The third and fifth rows of Table 1 show that global employment rate increased by about 3 percentage points between 1970 and 2003.

Table 1
Employment rates in 19 OECD countries over the period 1970–2003

Employment rate	15–64	Male 25–54	Female 25–54	15–24	55–64
(1) Mean 1970–2003 (%)	64.16	88.81	59.12	48.94	46.59
(2) Coefficient of variation 1970–2003 (%)	1.57	0.33	6.87	6.44	6.86
(3) Mean 1970 (%)	64.65	94.57	50.36	56.88	53.94
(4) Coefficient of variation 1970 (%)	1.01	0.05	6.62	2.83	5.11
(5) Mean 2003 (%)	67.38	86.76	70.36	44.88	49.43
(6) Coefficient of variation 2003 (%)	0.83	0.06	1.34	8.35	5.93

Source: OECD.

However, this global rise hides very different time-series employment patterns for the different demographic groups. On average, the relative employment incidence of prime-age women rose steadily by 20 percentage points. Meanwhile, all the other demographic groups faced employment drops: 8 percentage points for prime-age men, 12 percentage points for younger people, and 4 percentage points for older people.

It is also clear from rows 4 and 6 in Table 1 that the cross-country variation in prime-age male employment rates is much smaller than that of the other groups. In 2003, the coefficient of variation for the 25–54 years old men is more than 20 times as small as the coefficient of variation of prime-age women, 140 times as low as that of younger people, and 98 times as low as the coefficient of variation for older people. Looking at the cross-temporal evolution in employment rates, it turns out that the coefficient of variation has decreased for women but has significantly increased for younger people (and to a lesser extent for older individuals) during the last decades. This evolution suggests a convergence in prime-age female employment rate concomitant to a divergence in the employment rates of younger and older individuals.

Accordingly, Table 1 makes plain that the whole differences in global employment rates across OECD countries stem from differences in the employment rates of specific demographic groups, namely prime-age women, and younger and older people. Moreover, the broad picture displayed by Table 1 suggests that the employment rates of these demographic groups evolved very differently: women participate more and more in the labor market while the other groups tend to be less and less employed.

2.2   The Universal Rise in Female Employment Rates

Not only did the female employment rate increase on average over the period 1970–2003 but it increased everywhere. Figure 2 displays the annual growth rate of female prime-age employment rate for each of the 19 OECD countries. It appears that this growth rate has been positive on average in each country, the rise being sharper in Ireland and Mediterranean countries. Yet cross-country comparison in level reveals that prime-age female employment rate remained much lower in Mediterranean countries than in Nordic and Continental European countries all over the period. Figure 3 illustrates this point for the year 2003. On average, 80 percent of prime-age women are employed in Nordic coun-

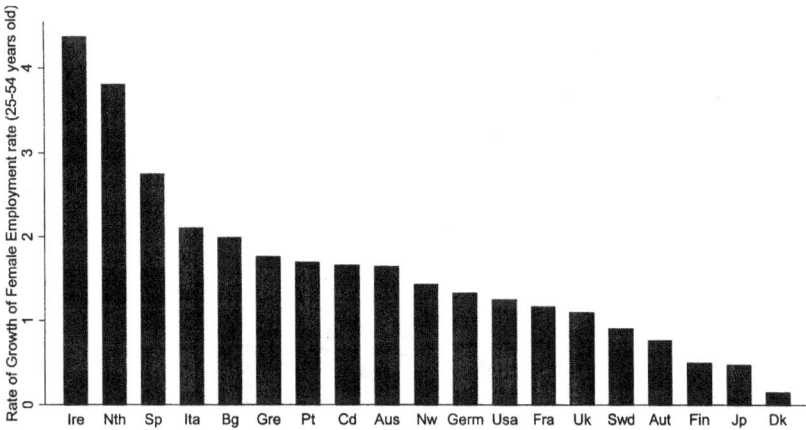

Figure 2
Annual rate of growth of prime age female employment rate in 19 OECD countries over the period 1970–2003

tries. This rate falls to approximately 70 percent in Continental European and Anglo-Saxon countries. And Mediterranean countries lag far behind with a prime-age female employment rate no higher than 60 percent.

Thus when looking at female employment rate, two stylized facts emerge: (1) a common rise in female employment rates in all countries over the last decades; (2) a persistent cross-country heterogeneity in the level of employment rates. Most researches on female labor-market participation generally focus on the second stylized fact and put the blame on detrimental labor market or family policies. But this explanation is hardly compatible with the first stylized fact. The rise in female labor supply has been sharper precisely in Mediterranean and European Continental countries where institutions are usually said to be the most detrimental to female participation (Bertola, Blau, and Kahn 2002).

2.3 Diverse Experiences for Prime Age Men, Younger and Older People

Whereas the female employment rate increased in all OECD countries, this is far from being the case for the other demographic groups.

Looking at prime-age men first, Figure 4 shows that their employment rates decreased almost everywhere. A comparison of Figures

Algan & Cahuc

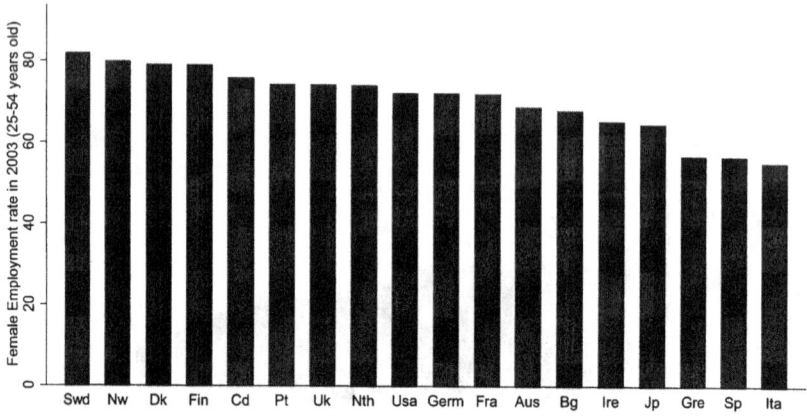

Figure 3
Prime age female employment rate in 2003
Source: OECD.

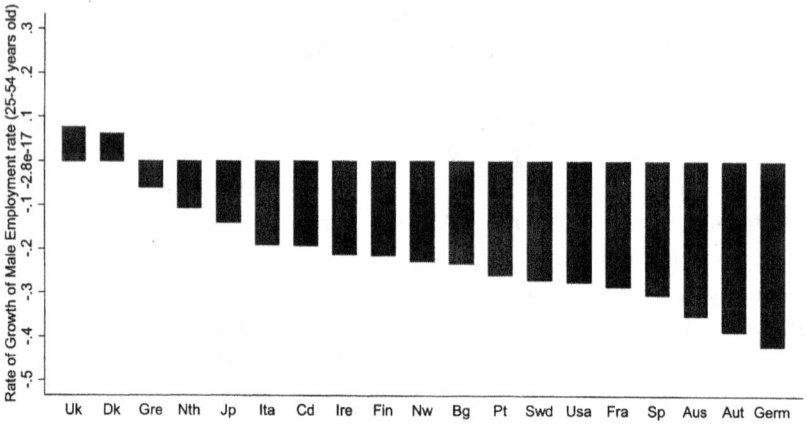

Figure 4
Annual rate of growth of prime age male employment rate in 19 OECD countries over
the period 1970–2003

2 and 4, however, also reveals that cross-national differences in the growth rate of prime-age male employment rates are much smaller than that of women.

This picture contrasts with the labor market outcomes of younger individuals. Figure 5 shows that OECD countries faced very different changes in youth employment rates, the annual growth rate varying from –2 percent to 0.7 percent. This heterogeneity has had sizeable effects in the long-run. Let us compare France and the U.S. as a textbook example to illustrate this point. The two countries started from approximately the same youth employment rate in 1970, around 52 percent. But while the youth employment rate slightly increased over the period at an annual rate of .02 percent in the U.S., it dramatically fell at an annual rate of 1.4 percent in France. As a consequence, French youth employment rate lagged far behind its American counterpart with a level of 30 percent against 53 percent in the U.S. in 2003. More generally, the youth employment rate has decreased sharply in almost all European Continental and European countries while it has remained quite stable or has slightly increased in Anglo-Saxon and Nordic countries.

The employment patterns of older individuals offer a mirror image to that of the young generation. Figure 6 shows that OECD countries also faced very different changes in the employment incidence of older people. While their employment rates rose in almost all Anglo-Saxon and Nordic countries such as Denmark and the United Kingdom,

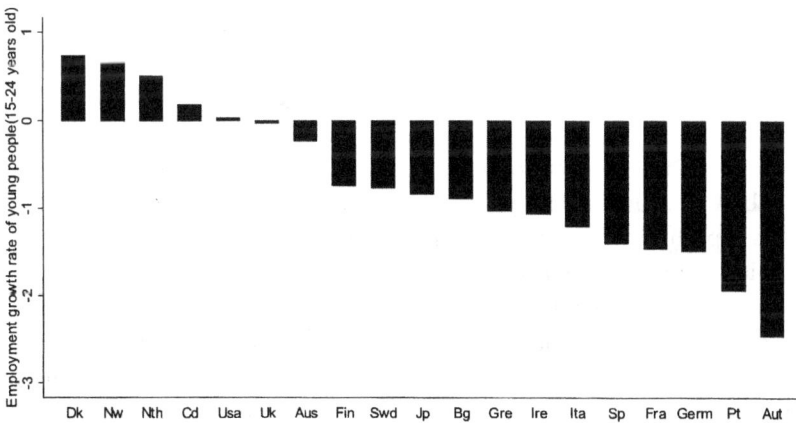

Figure 5
Annual growth rate of youth employment rate in 19 OECD countries over the period 1970–2003

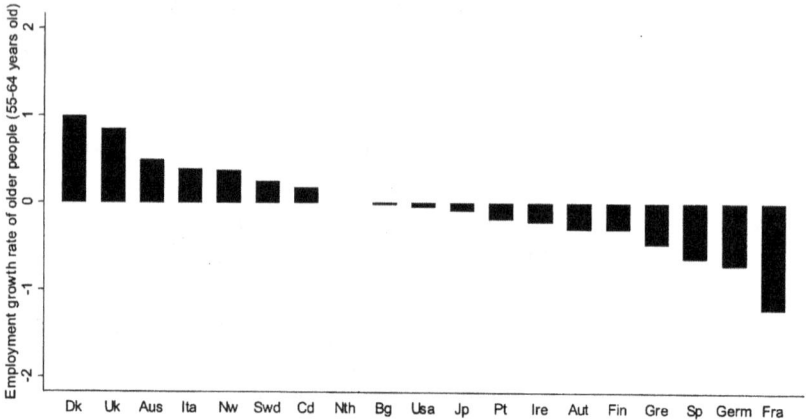

Figure 6
Annual growth rate of employment of older people in 19 OECD countries over the period 1970–2003

they dramatically decreased in Continental European and Mediterranean countries such as France, Germany, Spain, Italy, and Greece. Once again the comparison France–U.S. is quite instructive. The employment gap for individuals aged between 55 and 64 years old has sharply widened from 5 percentage points to 25 percentage points over the period.

These stylized facts suggest that countries which have been able to keep high employment rates for younger people are also those that had good performances for older people. Figure 7 provides evidence on this strong positive cross country-correlation between the growth rate of the employment rates of young and older people. Countries like Denmark and Norway managed to increase employment for both the young and the old generations, whereas France, Germany, and Spain had bad records for both populations.

As a preliminary conclusion, it appears that the evolution of OECD employment rates over the last 30 years is characterized by a universal increase in female employment rates and much more diverse experiences concerning the other demographic groups. As of 2003, countries with low aggregate employment rates have been unable to sufficiently raise the entry of women into the labor market to catch up to the high female employment rate of Nordic countries. Moreover, countries that faced low female employment rates also suffered from the exit of younger and older people out of employment. Accordingly, the two

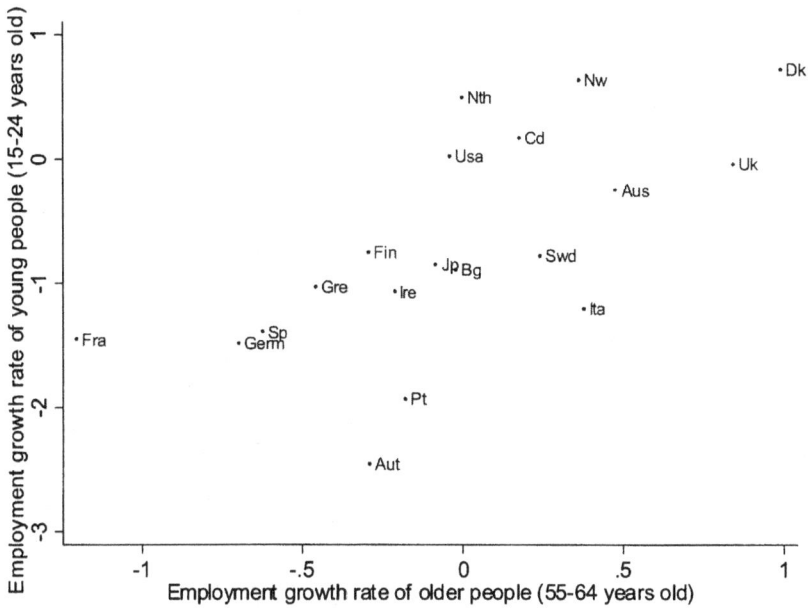

Figure 7
Correlation between the employment annual growth rates of young and older people
Source: OECD 1970–2003.

questions that have to be addressed in order to explain the cross-country differences in employment rates over the last 30 years are:

(1) Why is the prime-age female employment rate still low in some countries despite its rise common to all countries?

(2) Why did the employment rate of younger and older people decrease in some countries and not in others?

3.   The Model

In this section, we provide a simple theoretical framework that allows us to explain the universal increase in the labor supply of prime-age women and the declining participation of other demographic groups in some countries over the last 30 years.

This framework highlights the differential impact of the observed decline in the relative price of household durable goods on the labor supply of the different demographic groups observed over the last decades. Such a decline has allowed women to substitute household durable goods to housework in the production of home goods. Accordingly, women have been able to enter into the labor market and to devote more time to leisure. Moreover, the drop in the household durable goods price influences the labor supply of other demographic groups through its impact on the production of home goods. Assuming that family activities and home production are complementary, increased home production triggered by the decline in the price of household durable goods creates incentives to devote more time to family activities, this effect being more important in economies in which individuals are strongly attached to family values.

This model allows us to incorporate in a simple framework the interactions between technology and family preferences. These two elements are generally considered as the main determinants of the increase in female labor market participation but are treated separately in the literature. Galor and Weil (1996) and Greenwood, Seshadri, and Yorukoglu (2005) argue that the rise in female labor force participation is due to technological shocks either on waged labor, with a change in the nature of jobs, or in the home sector, with the emergence of engines of liberation for female housework. But this technological explanation could not account by itself for cross-national differences in the level of female employment unless it assumes that such a technological shock has been restricted to specific OECD countries. Other explanations stress changes in social norms and family preferences as more and more women worked (Fernandez, Fogli, and Olivetti 2004). This line of inquiry generally puts the emphasis on within country evolution of family preferences. We rather stress potential cross-country differences in family preferences at one point in time to document the differential impact of common shocks on national employment rates.

3.1   The Nuclear Family

We consider the relations between spouses within the nuclear family in a simple standard model of the family (Bergstrom 1997) in which we make the distinction between time devoted to home production, to family activities, to personal leisure, and to waged work. The preferences of the nuclear family are represented by the utility function

$$u(c, l_m, l_f, f) = \ln c + \lambda_f \ln l_f + \lambda_m \ln l_m + \phi \ln F,$$

where c stands for consumption of a numeraire good purchased in the market; l_f and l_m denote female and male personal leisure respectively, and F represents a "family good." The parameters λ_i $(i = f, m)$ and ϕ reflect the weight put on individual leisure and the family good respectively $(\lambda_i > 0, \phi > 0)$.

The family good is a composite of a good produced at home in quantity c_H, and leisure time that spouses spend together in family activities. Specifically

$$F = \min(c_H, \mu_f s_f, \mu_m s_m),$$ (1)

where s_f and s_m denote respectively the amount of time devoted by women and men to joint family activities. $\mu_f > 0$ and $\mu_m > 0$ are two parameters.

This formulation captures in a simple way the idea that there is a complementarity between home production and time that spouses devote together to family activities. Typically the time spent cooking at home is only valuable to the extent that the two spouses spend time to enjoy the resulting meal. Moreover this formulation allows us to extend the traditional literature by distinguishing personal leisure from family activities. This point might be key for understanding the EU-U.S. employment gap. By ignoring this distinction, recent researches assume that the widening of the EU-U.S. employment gap is only due to a shock in the preference for leisure (see Blanchard 2004). Yet this shift towards non-work time could hide different non-market activities such as family activities. Naturally, this distinction is not neutral in terms of policy recommendations.[11]

Goods are produced in the home thanks to household durables k and to female labor h_f. The production function reads

$$c_H = \left[\eta h_f^{\frac{\sigma-1}{\sigma}} + (1-\eta)k^{\frac{\sigma-1}{\sigma}} \right]^{\frac{\sigma}{\sigma-1}}, \quad \eta \in [0,1],$$ (2)

where $\sigma > 0$ is the elasticity of substitution between female time spent to housework and household durable goods.

Total time is normalized to unity for each individual. Female leisure equals total time, minus hours worked in the market, denoted by m_f, minus hours worked in the home, denoted by h_f, and minus hours spent with the spouse, denoted by s_f. That is

$$l_f = 1 - m_f - h_f - s_f.$$ (3)

Male leisure equals total time minus hours worked in the market and hours spent with the spouse

$$l_m = 1 - m_m - s_m. \tag{4}$$

The budget constraint of the nuclear family reads

$$c + pk + w_m(l_m + s_m) + w_f(l_f + h_f + s_f) \le w_f + w_m + R \equiv W, \tag{5}$$

where p is the price of the household durable good and R stands for non-labor income.

The maximization problem of the nuclear family reads

$$\max_{\{c,k,h_f,s_f,s_m,l_f,l_m\}} \ln c + \lambda_f \ln l_f + \lambda_m \ln l_m + \phi \ln F,$$

subject to (1), (2), (5), and $h_f \ge 0$, $s_f + h_f + l_f \le 1$, $s_m + l_m \le 1$, $k \ge 0$.[12]

The first-order conditions for interior solutions can be written as

$$l_i = \frac{\lambda_i}{1 + \lambda_f + \lambda_m + \phi} \frac{W}{w_i}, \quad i = f, m,$$

$$h_f = \frac{W\phi(1 + \lambda_f + \lambda_m + \phi)^{-1}}{p^{1-\sigma}\left(\dfrac{(1-\eta)}{\eta}w_f\right)^{\sigma} + w_f + \left(\dfrac{w_f}{\mu_f} + \dfrac{w_m}{\mu_m}\right)\left[\eta\left(\dfrac{w_f}{p}\right)^{\sigma-1} + (1-\eta)\right]^{\frac{\sigma}{\sigma-1}}},$$

$$s_i = \frac{W\phi\mu_i^{-1}(1 + \lambda_f + \lambda_m + \phi)^{-1}}{[(1-\eta)^{\sigma}p^{1-\sigma} + \eta^{\sigma}w_f^{1-\sigma}]^{\frac{\sigma}{\sigma-1}} + \left(\dfrac{w_f}{\mu_f} + \dfrac{w_m}{\mu_m}\right)}, \quad i = f, m.$$

According to these equations, our model yields the following main predictions. First, female housework h_f increases with the price of the durable household good p if the elasticity of substitution between female housework and durable household good is sufficiently high. More precisely, it turns out that female housework increases with p if $\sigma > 1$. Next, time devoted to family activity s_i always decreases with the price of durable household goods. This result is due to the complementarity between home production and family activity. The higher the price of household durable goods p, the lower is the household production c_H, and the lower the time devoted by the two spouses to family activities.

As a consequence, the effect of household durable prices on the female time devoted to home production and family activity $(h_f + s_f)$ is *a priori* ambiguous. But it can be checked that there exists a threshold value of the elasticity of substitution, denoted by $\bar{\sigma}$, above which total time spend by women for family increases with p. Eventually, leisure, $l_{\prime}$ does not depend on the price of the durable household good in this simple setting.

Accordingly, this model shows that the drop in the price of durable household goods p that occurred in the OECD countries may explain the rise in female labor supply and the decrease in male labor supply in a framework in which (1) the elasticity of substitution between durable household goods and female homework is higher than $\bar{\sigma}$ and (2) family activity and the good produced in the home are complementary.

The model also predicts that more inclination for the "family good" (corresponding to higher values of ϕ) decreases the labor supply of both women and men. However, the impact on the labor supply of women is bigger because they devote more time to housework and to family activities whereas men spend more of their time in family activities only. Moreover, the absolute value of the derivative of female labor supply with respect to the price of household goods increases with ϕ. This property may explain that women work less but that their labor supply is more responsive to changes in the prices of the durable household goods in countries in which individuals have stronger preferences for family activities.

3.2   The Extended Family

The members of the extended family are young adults and older people. They benefit from interactions with the nuclear family which allow them to consume a share $\varepsilon \in [0, 1]$ of the good produced in the home of the nuclear family.[13] We assume that nuclear family members derive the same utility from their own consumption as from the consumption of the extended family members up to the share ε. Thus this share enters into the utility of the nuclear family in the same way as the other part of the consumption. From this point of view, the parameter ε can be interpreted as the intensity of the extended family ties.

Preferences of young adults and older people are represented by the utility function[14]

$$v(c_{\varepsilon}, l_{\varepsilon}, f_{\varepsilon}) = \ln c_{\varepsilon} + \lambda_{\varepsilon} \ln l_{\varepsilon} + \phi_{\varepsilon} \ln F_{\varepsilon}$$

where c_{ε} denotes the consumption of the marketable good, l_{ε} stands for leisure and F_{ε} is the "family good." The parameters $\lambda_{\varepsilon} > 0$ and

$\phi_\varepsilon > 0$ capture the weight put on individual leisure and the family good respectively. The definition of the family good is similar to that of the nuclear family. Specifically

$$F_\varepsilon = \min(\varepsilon c_H, \mu_\varepsilon s_\varepsilon), \tag{6}$$

where c_H is the consumption of the good produced at the nuclear family's home and s_ε is the time devoted to family activities. To keep the model simple, we neglect potential home production by the members of the extended family.

The maximization problem of a member of the extended family reads

$$\max_{\{c_\varepsilon, l_\varepsilon, s_\varepsilon\}} \ln c_\varepsilon + \lambda_\varepsilon \ln l_\varepsilon + \phi_\varepsilon \ln F_\varepsilon,$$

subject to the budget constraint

$$c_\varepsilon + w_\varepsilon(l_\varepsilon + s_\varepsilon) \leq w_\varepsilon + R_\varepsilon \equiv W_\varepsilon,$$

and to the constraints (6) and $s_\varepsilon + l_\varepsilon + m_\varepsilon \leq 1$.[15] The parameters w_ε and R_ε denote the wage and the non-labor income of the extended family members respectively.

The labor supply of the members of the extended family is given by the following first-order conditions

$$m_\varepsilon = \begin{cases} \max\left\{1 - \dfrac{(\lambda_\varepsilon + \phi_\varepsilon)}{1 + \lambda_\varepsilon + \phi_\varepsilon} \dfrac{W_\varepsilon}{w_\varepsilon}, 0\right\} & \text{if } \dfrac{\mu_\varepsilon \phi_\varepsilon}{1 + \lambda_\varepsilon + \phi_\varepsilon} \dfrac{W_\varepsilon}{w_\varepsilon} \leq \varepsilon c_H, \\[4mm] \max\left\{1 - \dfrac{\lambda_\varepsilon}{1 + \lambda_\varepsilon} \dfrac{W_\varepsilon}{w_\varepsilon} - \dfrac{\varepsilon c_H}{(1 + \lambda_\varepsilon)\mu_\varepsilon}, 0\right\} & \text{otherwise.} \end{cases}$$

It follows that the labor supply of young adults and older individuals decreases with the share ε of the home production they can get. Moreover, a drop in the price of the durable household good also decreases their labor supply since home production increases and they can devote more time to family activities.

The predictions of the model can be illustrated by simple calibration exercises reported in Figures 8 and 9. The values of the parameters are chosen as follows: $w_f = 1$, $w_m = 1.2$, $w_\varepsilon = 1$, $\lambda_m = \lambda_f = 0.1$, $\lambda_\varepsilon = 1$, $R = R_\varepsilon = 0$, $\mu_m = \mu_f = 10$, $\mu_\varepsilon = 2$, $\sigma = 3$, $\eta = 0.7$, $\phi_\varepsilon = .3$, $\varepsilon = .5$. Wage values have been chosen to reproduce the average wage gap between men, on one hand, and women and members of the extended family, on the other hand, observed in OECD countries, which is about 20 percent.

Labor supply for $\phi = 0.5$

0.85
0.8
0.75
0.7
0.65
0.6
0.55
p

0.5   0.6   0.7   0.8   0.9

Labor supply for $\phi = 0.1$

0.84
0.82
p

0.5   0.6   0.7   0.8   0.9

0.78
0.76

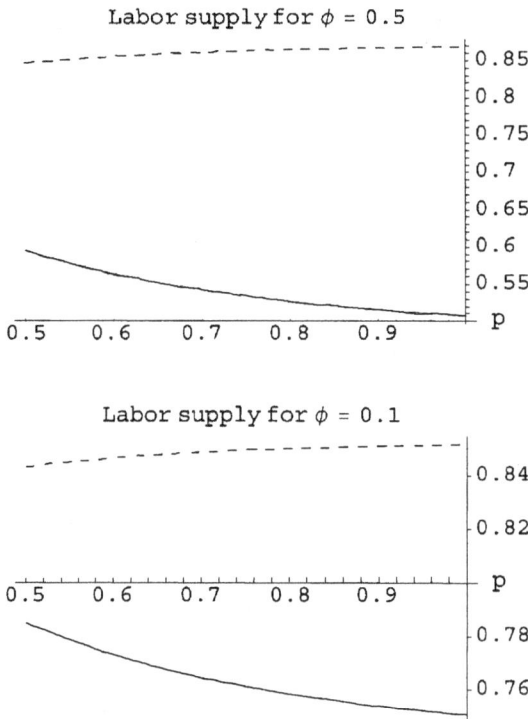

Figure 8
Female (continuous lines) and male (dotted lines) labor supply with strong (left-hand side panel) and weak (right-hand side panel) preferences for the family good

The non-labor incomes are assumed to be equal to zero for the sake of simplicity. The values of λ_i, μ_i, and η allow us to reproduce the average OECD participation rates of the different demographic groups and the share of household durable goods in total household expenditures in 2003 (which is about 8 percent in OECD countries according to Eurostat) for an intermediate value of $\phi = 0.3$. Then, we choose a plausible value of the elasticity of substitution σ that allows us to reproduce the typical changes in male and female labor market participation for a 50 percent drop in the price of the household durable good p in countries with strong ($\phi = 0.5$) and weak ($\phi = 0.1$) preferences for the family good. Last, the values of ϕ_ε and ε allow us to match the evolution of the market participation of younger and older people as members of the extended family.

Figure 8 displays the consequence of a decline in the price of the durable household goods on prime-age female and prime-age male

Labor supply extended family

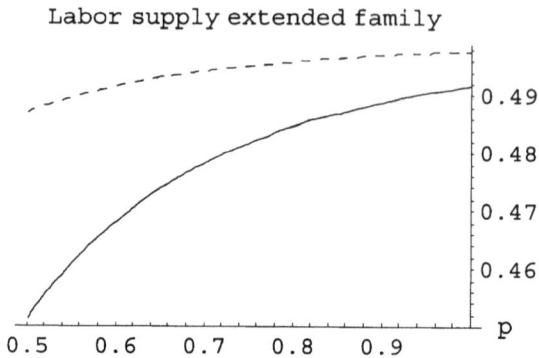

Figure 9
Labor supply of the members of the extended family with strong (continuous line) and weak (dotted line) preferences for the family good ($\phi = 0.5$ and $\phi = 0.1$ respectively)

labor supplies as a function of preferences for family activities. It entails a small decrease in prime-age male labor market participation (ranging between 86 percent and 84 percent) whatever the preference for family activities. However, the change in female labor supply is much more contrasted. The implied rise in prime-age female labor supply is much steeper when there is a strong preference for family activities ($\phi = 0.5$), going from 51 percent to 60 percent. In contrast, the increase in prime-age female labor supply is largely softened by weak family preferences ($\phi = 0.1$), ranging from 75 percent to 78.5 percent.

Figure 9 looks at the effects of a similar decline in the price of the household durable goods on the labor supply of the extended family. While the labor supply of the extended family members remains quite stable in economies with low preferences for family, it dramatically falls in economies putting a high weight on family.

Figure 10 shows that our model can also account for similar changes in female employment rates concomitant to different changes in the employment rates of younger and older people. This can be seen by looking at the influence of family ties on the response of the labor supply of the extended family members to the decline in the price of durable household goods. When family ties are strong ($\varepsilon = 0.9$, the value of ϕ_ε being equal to 0.3 in both cases considered in Figure 10), the right-hand side panel of Figure 10 shows that the rise in female labor supply is compatible with is a 6 percentage points drop in the labor supply of the members of the extended family. By contrast, when family ties are weak ($\varepsilon = 0.1$), the same rise in female labor supply is concomitant to

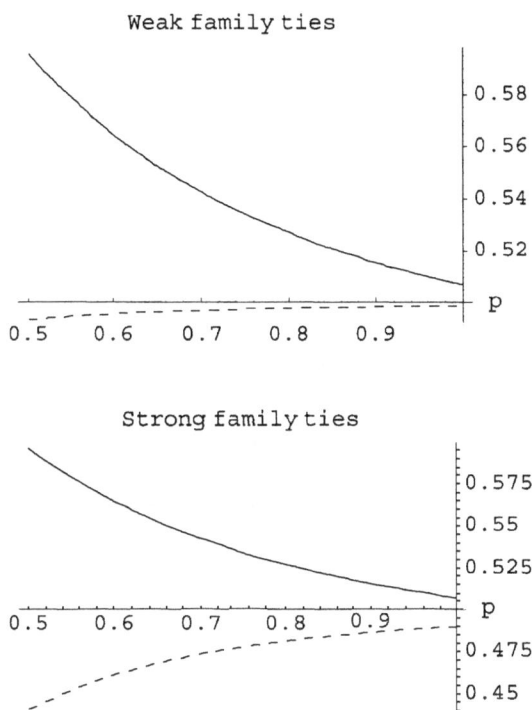

Weak family ties

Strong family ties

Figure 10
Female labor supply (continuous lines) and labor supply of the members of the extended family with strong family ties ($\varepsilon = 0.9$) and weak family ties ($\varepsilon = 0.1$)

a 0.6 percentage point drop in the labor supply of the members of the extended family. From this point of view, our model allows us to explain why the U.S. on one hand, and some Continental European countries such a Germany and France, on the other hand, had similar changes in female employment rate over the three last decades and very contrasted changes in employment rates of younger and older workers.

As a conclusion, this model predicts three main effects of a fall in durable good prices on the family labor supply: (1) female labor supply increases, (2) male labor supply decreases, and (3) the labor supply of young adult and senior decreases. Moreover, the size of the variations in labor supply depends on (1) the preference ϕ for family and (2) the strength of family ties between the nuclear family and the members of the extended family measured by ε. If the nuclear family members put a higher weight on the family good (ϕ large), a fall in the price of durable household goods entails a stronger increase in female labor supply and in household production. This rise in home production leads to a larger reduction in the labor supply of the extended family members, this effect being amplified by the importance of the extended family ties measured by the parameter ε.

The following part of the paper provides some empirical evidence which support these predictions.

4. Empirical Evidence

This section assesses the link between family attitudes and employment patterns of OECD countries over the last three decades. First, we stress that individuals living in different countries highly differ regarding attitudes towards prime-age people and younger and older individuals, within the family and on the labor market. We also provide some elements indicating that cross-country differences in family perceptions originate in cross-country differences in family culture.[16] We then show that national family attitudes are highly correlated with the employment rates of the different demographic groups over the period, even after controlling for other potential country specific effects and time-period shocks. Eventually and consistently with the predictions of the labor supply model, we show that differences in national family attitudes are significantly correlated with the cross-national variation in the responses of the demographic employment rates following a common drop in the price of household durable goods.

4.1 International Heterogeneity in Family Culture

This section documents to what extent people living in different OECD countries differ in their family perceptions. We then provide some evidence that these cross-national differences in family perceptions are deeply rooted in national family cultures.

First, we probe into attitudes towards the role of young individuals, old individuals, and prime-age men and women within the family and on the labor market.[17] To that end, we use international surveys on individual values: the *World Value Survey* (WVS) and the *International Social Survey Programme* (ISSP). The WVS covers four waves (1981–1984, 1990–93, 1995–1997, 1999–2002) and provides key questions on family attitudes. The *ISSP* complements this information with specific surveys on gender roles and family relations since the mid-eighties. For the sake of comparison, our analysis will be restricted to the same 19

OECD countries: Australia, Austria, Belgium, Canada, Denmark, Finland, France, Germany, Greece, Ireland, Italy, Japan, Netherlands, Norway, Portugal, Spain, Sweden, UK, and USA.

This first step allows us to show that there is a strong cross-country heterogeneity in family attitudes, even after controlling for observed individual heterogeneity. This finding raises the issue of the interpretation of such an heterogeneity. It can be the case that individuals express a traditional perception of family, according to which women should stay at home to raise children for instance, because they live in countries in which institutions are detrimental to female waged labor. In other words, does cross-country heterogeneity in family attitudes originate in cross-country heterogeneity in economic environments only? Or is this cross-country heterogeneity also ingrained in different national family culture, namely in heterogeneity in preferences for family ties and/or in household skills for home production? We shed some light on this issue by using direct information on the attitude of individuals living in the same country but whose ancestors came from different countries.

4.1.1 Attitudes Towards Nuclear Family

We examine attitudes towards the nuclear family by looking at the perception of gender roles and parenthood.

Gender Roles

We first consider the cross-national heterogeneity in the perception of gender roles on the labor market and within the family. Our primary interest lies in attitudes towards gender division of labor captured by the following questions: *"When jobs are scarce, men should have more rights to a job than women"* (WVS) and *"Family life suffers if women wok full time"* (ISSP).[18] The first question is followed by the scale: *"agree, neither, disagree."* The answers to the other question are ranged between: *"strongly agree, agree, disagree, strongly disagree."*

To evaluate potential cross-national specificities in family attitudes, we make use of two indicators. The first one is based on average national preferences by reporting the mean reply to each question. Yet this naive indicator might capture heterogeneity in individual characteristics rather than national features. To overcome this flaw, we run ordered probit estimation for each question by controlling for the main individual characteristics and by including country-fixed effects which capture the role of specific national features. Regarding individual characteristics, we take into account the age and age squared, the level of education measured as the number of years in school, the marital status, the number of children, the family income coded by the surveys between low, middle and high incomes, and the employment status. Moreover, we control for the political affiliation coded by the surveys between left, center and right wings. We also include the religious affiliation by distinguishing the following main categories: Catholic, Protestant, Buddhist, Muslim, Jews, other religions, and without any religion. All the estimations are based on the working age population between 16 and 64 years old.

Results are reported in Figure 11 for the available surveys in the nineties. The x-axis shows the mean reply at the country-level to each question. The basic picture is that of a great deal of heterogeneity across countries. On average Mediterranean countries, Japan, and to a lesser extent Continental European countries, put a much higher weight on gender division of labor within the family compared to Scandinavian and Anglo-Saxon countries. To give a hint of such variation, we re-scale

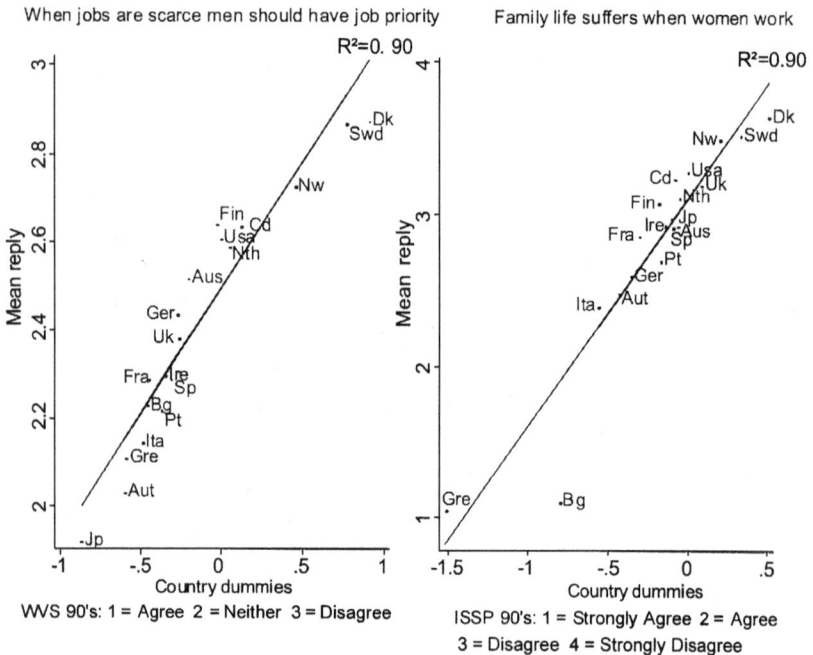

Figure 11
Gender roles in OECD countries

the former question between 0-1 for (strongly) disagree and (strongly) agree. It turns out that in Japan, a majority of 57.1 percent of people do agree with job priority for men. The Mediterranean countries (Greece, Italy, Portugal, and Spain) and the Continental European countries (Austria, Belgium, France, Germany, Netherlands) come next with 41.2 percent and 39.3 percent of agreement respectively. In the other Anglo-Saxon countries (Australia, Canada, United Kingdom, United States) and Nordic countries, this share of agreement sharply falls to 21.2 percent and 11.5 percent.

The y-axis reports the contribution of country dummies to individual answers. The figure suggests that individual attitudes towards gender role are overwhelmingly shaped by national specificities. The correlation between the mean-reply and country dummies is almost perfect, yielding a coefficient of determination equal to 0.9. Moreover, Table 2 reports that all country-fixed effects are statistically significant at the 1 percent level in explaining attitudes towards gender roles. Regarding individual characteristics, the male breadwinner values are highly positively correlated with the number of children and the fact to be a man, to be married, to lean to the right wing and to belong to Catholic or Muslim denominations. In contrast, traditional gender role values are significantly negatively correlated with the level of education and to a lesser extent with the level of income.

Parenthood

A second important issue is whether differences in attitudes towards the nuclear family are driven by the representation of motherhood. This point is critical in as much as it could be linked to the observed cross-country heterogeneity in family policies and in the gender employment gap (Jaumotte 2003). We address this issue by using the two following questions: *"A child needs both a mother and a father at home to grow up happily" (WVS), "A preschool child suffers if the mother works" (ISPP)*. The former question is available for the four waves of the *WVS*. The latter one is provided by *ISPP* for two specific waves on family attitudes in 1994 and 2002.

Figure 12 replicates the same exercise as before by plotting the mean response against the country-fixed effects concerning the two latter questions in the 1990s and early 2000s. The picture is still that of a great cross-country heterogeneity mainly driven by national specificities, the correlation between the mean-reply and the fixed effects being close to one. To give a hint of such national variation, we group the answers

Table 2
Estimations of family attitudes: Ordered probit estimates

	Job priority for men over women (1)	Preschool child suffers if mother works (2)	Older people should be forced to retire early (3)	Children should be taught to be independent (4)
Male	−.222**	−.264***	−.048**	−.135***
	(.024)	(.012)	(.023)	(.019)
Age	−.018**	−.011***	−.013	.043***
	(.008)	(.002)	(.008)	(.006)
Age2	.000	.000	.000	−.000***
	(.000)	(.000)	(.000)	(.000)
Education (in years)	.029***	.028***	.026***	.025***
	(.003)	(.001)	(.002)	(.002)
Number of child	−.046***	−.019***	.001	−.042***
	(.010)	(.005)	(.010)	(.008)
Partner	−.184***	−.023	−.074**	−.074**
	(.040)	(.015)	(.035)	(.029)
Employed	.163***	.199***	.025	.085***
	(.020)	(.015)	(.025)	(.021)
Income class: Middle		Reference		
Lower income	−.124***	.029	−.079***	.016
	(.030)	(.016)	(.029)	(.025)
Upper income	.126***	.141***	.047	.032
	(.030)	(.017)	(.029)	(.029)
Political orientation: Center		Reference		
Left	.108***	.161***	−.024	.159***
	(.029)	(.015)	(.027)	(.023)
Right	−.168***	−.066**	−.005	−.089***
	(.027)	(.016)	(.026)	(.022)
Religious affiliation: No _ religion		Reference		
Catholic	−.166	−.088***	−.144***	−.293***
	(.036)	(.021)	(.035)	(.031)
Protestant	−.128	−.055***	−.010	−.242**
	(.042)	(.021)	(.040)	(.034)
Buddhist	−.118	.107**	−.072	−.245***
	(.079)	(.049)	(.090)	(.069)
Muslim	−.790***	−.656***	.103	−.991***
	(.208)	(.111)	(.222)	(.204)
Jews	.717**	−.037	.181	−.176
	(.286)	(.129)	(.215)	(.133)
Other_religion	−.200***	−.242***	−.111*	−.348***
	(.064)	(.036)	(.063)	(.050)
Country dummies	Yes***	Yes***	Yes***	Yes***
Adj- R^2	.0934	.0610	.078	.118
Observations	13244	28544	13266	19942

A negative sign increases the likelihood that individuals agree with the statement ***:1 percent, **: 5 percent, *: 10 percent

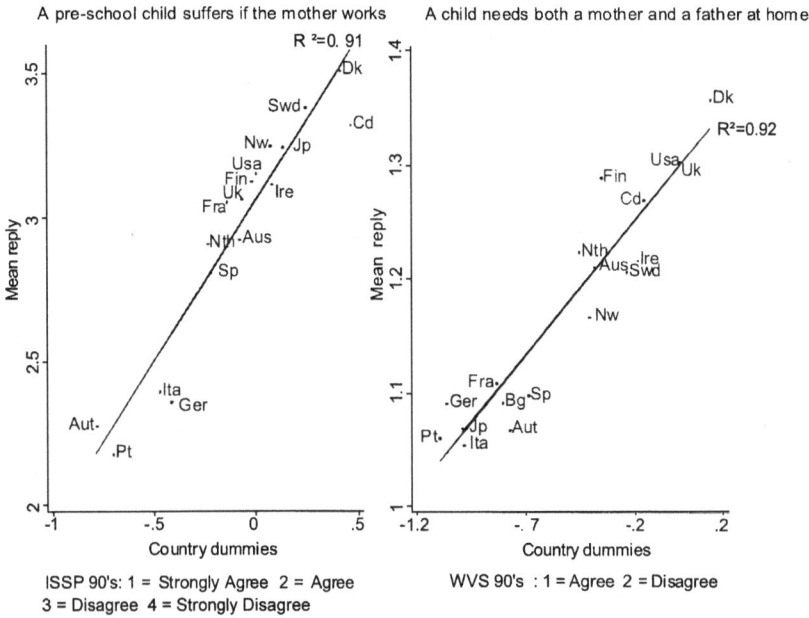

Figure 12
Parenthood in OECD countries

into two categories: agree and disagree and use the same regional clusters as before. On average, the group of Mediterranean and Continental countries do agree at 90 percent with the statement *"A child needs both a mother and a father at home to grow up happily."* This share is reduced by 20 percent when looking at Anglo-Saxon and Nordic countries. This difference becomes even sharper concerning the second statement *"A preschool child suffers if the mother works."* In typical Mediterranean and Continental European countries like Italy and Germany, 72 percent and 68 percent of people, respectively, share this traditional perception of motherhood. By contrast, they are no more than 38.3 percent in the United States and 30.4 percent in Sweden to back this statement. Obviously, such discrepancies may have strong links with female employment rates as documented in the next section.

4.1.2 Attitudes Towards Extended Family Relations

We extend our investigation on family attitudes to the role of young and elderly people within the extended family. A number of contributions (Fogli 2004, Bentolila and Ichino 2000) have stressed the cross-national variations in family arrangements between generations, in particular regarding the leaving age of children from parental household. In the following, we complement this line of inquiry on two grounds in order to uncover the two key parameters of the extended family model: that is, the preference for family activities and the strength of family ties. First, we directly look at individual attitudes towards the extended family rather than family arrangement outcomes. Second we provide new evidence on the extent to which family members share household activities between each other.

Let us first focus on attitudes towards the extended family. We start by looking at potential international differences in the perceptions of older people. The *WVS* first provides some evidence regarding their role on the labor market by asking the following question: *"When jobs are scarce, older people should be forced to retire from work early."* Figure 13 reports the mean-reply against country dummies which still capture national values. The sample is made up of people between 18 years old and 64 years old and is taken from the two waves 1990–1993 and 1995–1997. On average, Mediterranean countries and to a lesser extent Continental European countries are much more prone to support this statement than Nordic and Anglo-Saxon countries. But remarkably enough, this ordering is less clear-cut than before. In particular, Finland is much closer to Mediterranean countries than its Nordic counterparts in this realm. By contrast, Japan has the same stand on this issue as

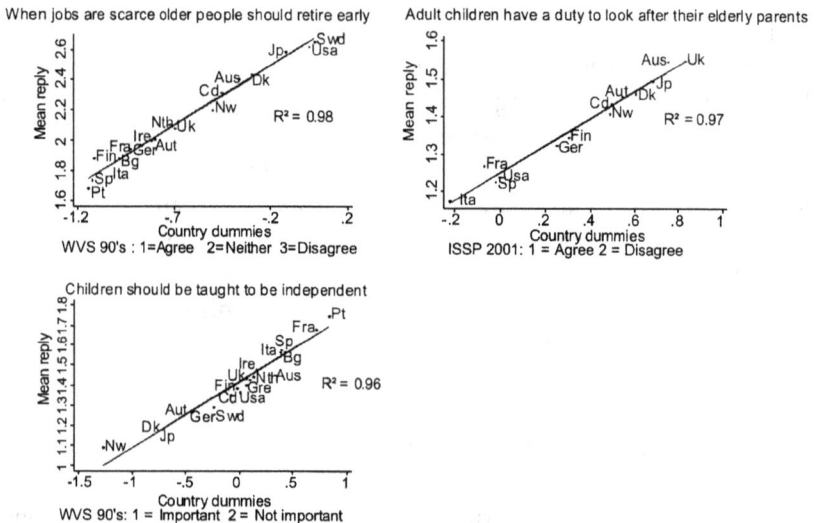

Figure 13
Family attitudes towards older and young people in OECD countries

Nordic countries or the United States. This point is all the more remarkable that the Finnish employment rate of older workers is precisely close to the Mediterranean one while that of Japan is one of the highest among OECD countries with Sweden and the U.S. The Probit estimates of the other individual characteristics are reported in Table 2, col. 3. The probability to agree with early retirement is positively correlated with the fact to be a man, to have a partner or to have a low level of education.

Figure 13 also reports the family relations between prime age and older individuals captured by the following question: *"Adult children have a duty to look after their elderly Parents."* The answers are scaled between *"Agree, Disagree."* Once again, there is a distinct cluster of Mediterranean countries (Italy, Spain) alongside France which back such support within the family. In contrast, Nordic countries and Anglo-Saxon countries (with the exception of the U.S.) seem much less concerned by such generational links.

Regarding attitudes towards young people, the most relevant available question for our issue is related to their independence and is provided by the *WVS* question: *"Here is a list of qualities that children can be encouraged to learn at home. Which if any do you consider to be really important: Independence?"* The answers are scaled between *"Important, Not important."* Following our previous strategy, Figure 13 reports the mean-reply on the x-axis against the proxy for family attitudes yielded by country dummies on the y-axis. The sample is still made up of the working age population on the two waves 1990–1993 and 1995–1997. On average, child independence appears to be a top quality for 75.1 percent of people in Nordic countries. This figure is twice as high as that of Mediterranean countries in which this quality is stressed by only 38.2 percent of the population. This opposition pattern also holds between Anglo-Saxon and Continental European countries. While 62 percent of Americans put the emphasis on child's independence, no more than 29 percent in France follow this stand. This heterogeneity is largely shaped by national specificities. Even by controlling for standard characteristics and cultural features such as religious affiliation, the correlation between the mean-reply and country dummies remains very high, the coefficient of determination being equal to 0.96. The effects of the other individual characteristics are reported in Table 2, col. 4. Promotion of child independence is negatively correlated with the fact to be a man, to belong to the right wing, and to be either Catholic or Muslim.

Let us now turn to the relationships within the extended family. We address this issue by using a specific *ISSP* wave on social networks run in 2001. Due to the lack of data, we focus on four main countries representative of the main OECD clusters, namely Denmark, Germany, Spain, and the United States. We first provide evidence that countries strongly differ in the strength of the contacts between the different family members. Figure 14-bottom left shows the share of children between 15 and 24 years old reporting to have at least daily physical contacts with their mother and conversely the share of elderly people having at least daily contacts with their adult daughter. Daily contacts include living in the same home. It turns out that contacts across generations are two times as high in Spain—and to a lesser extent in Germany— as in Denmark and the United Sates. But countries also highly differ regarding the way the different family generations share home activities. Figure 14-bottom right provides evidence on such discrepancies by reporting the mean reply for the question: *"Suppose you had to stay in bed for a few days and needed help around the house, with shopping and so on. Who would you turn to first for help?"* The answers involve relatives (husband, mother, father, daughter, son), social relations (from

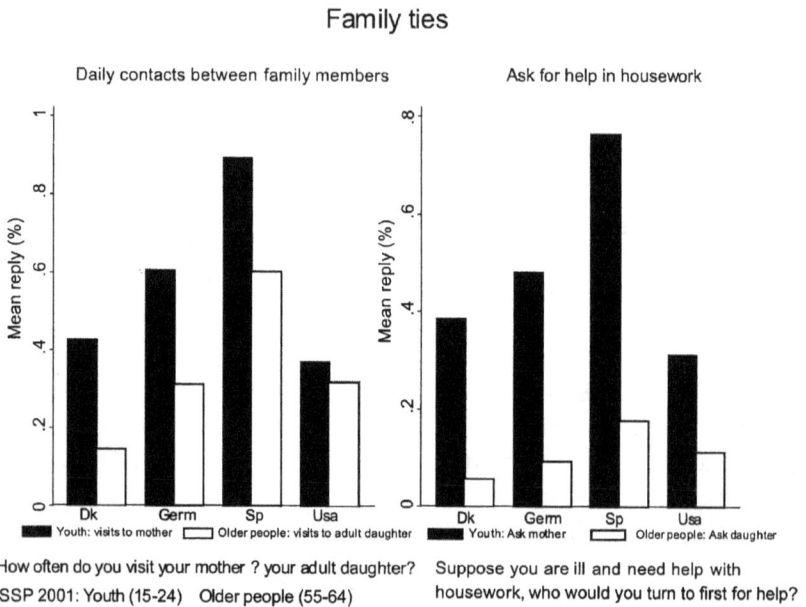

Family ties

How often do you visit your mother ? your adult daughter?
ISSP 2001: Youth (15-24)   Older people (55-64)

Suppose you are ill and need help with housework, who would you turn to first for help?

Figure 14
Family networks in OECD countries in 2001

workplace, neighbors, friends), and private services. An overwhelming majority of young people would turn first to their mother in Spain and in Germany while they are no more than one-third to share this reaction in the United States. If the differences are less sizeable regarding the answers given by older people, the same cross-country opposition pattern holds. These pictures suggest much stronger links between prime-age women and the other members of the family in Continental and Mediterranean European countries. Accordingly, one should expect much stronger interactions between female labor supply and that of the other demographic groups in these latter countries.

4.1.3 Cultural Foundations of Family Attitudes

The observation of cross-country heterogeneity in family attitudes and family relations does not necessarily mean that individuals living in the same country share a common culture—i.e., common preferences for family ties or common skills in household production. Living in a specific country can influence one's own family perception and family relations through the channel of the relative economic returns of family and market activities. For instance, it is well known that child-care subsidies, paid maternity and parental leaves are more favorable to female waged work in Nordic countries than in Mediterranean countries (Jaumotte 2003). This situation may lead individuals living in Mediterranean countries to declare more frequently that *"preschool child suffers if the mother works."* But it might be the case that individuals living in Mediterranean countries also share a common culture which makes them more prone to traditional family attitudes. In this case family policies would be the outcome rather than the cause of the family attitudes.

In order to investigate this issue, we look at the reactions of people who come from different national origins but face the same economic environment because they live in the same country. To that end, we use information provided by the *ISSP* on the ethnic or cultural backgrounds of the respondents *"From what country or part of the world did your ancestor come from? If there is more than one country, which one of these countries do you feel closer."*[19] Answers to these questions are essentially provided for countries with a rich history of immigration and in particular for the United States on which our analysis is based.[20] In order to use the maximum number of observations, we group the different countries of origins into the following clusters: European Continental countries (Austria, France, Germany, Netherlands), Mediterranean countries

(Italy, Spain), and European Anglo countries (UK and Ireland). We also include people whose ancestors come from Latin American (overwhelmingly made up of Mexican) since they represent a substantial amount of the sample and can be used as a benchmark for comparing the other clusters (they display the most traditional perception of the family). We then assess to what extent the country of origins do matter by using dummies for each cluster. We also control for the main sociodemographic characteristics (age, sex, education, marital status, number of children, political orientation, religion) and the main economic variables captured by the employment status.

Table 3 shows the estimation results for the question *"A preschool child suffers if the mother works."*[21] This question is available for the two specific surveys run by the *ISSP* on gender roles in 1994 and 2002. The sample is made up of the working age population. Table 3, col. 1 shows that individuals whose ancestors come from European Continental and Mediterranean countries or Latin America agree more frequently than those who originate from Nordic and English countries with the statement *"A preschool child suffers if the mother works."* Table 3, col. 2 reports the cross-country estimates run on the different countries belonging to the previous clusters. The comparison of columns 1 and 2 indicates that the ordering of country dummies associated with the country of the ancestors of people living in the U.S. is the same as the ordering of country dummies associated with the country where people currently live. This suggests that individuals living in the U.S. share some common family culture with people living in the countries of their ancestors. Accordingly, the perception of family is not only shaped by economic features that influence the relative economic returns of family and market activities: To some extent, the cross-country heterogeneity in family attitudes is shaped by cross country heterogeneity in family culture. From this perspective, it is worth analyzing the link between cross-country heterogeneity in family attitudes and cross-country heterogeneity in employment rates.

4.2   Labor Market Outcomes of Family Attitudes

This section shows that family attitudes are highly correlated with the employment rates of the different demographic groups in OECD countries over the period 1970–2003. We first stress that the cross-national heterogeneity in family attitudes identified previously is significantly correlated with the cross-country dispersion in the level of employment rates. We then show that family perception displays a

Table 3
Cultural roots of family attitudes: Ordered probit estimates

	Estimations on the US Country of origins (1)	Cross-country estimations Country of residency (2)
Latin America	Reference	
Mediterranean	.133	.331***
	(.140)	(.042)
European Continental	.215*	.478***
	(.122)	(.039)
European Anglo	.291***	.937***
	(.110)	(.039)
Nordic	.512***	1.084***
	(.202)	(.043)
Men	−.339***	−.238***
	(.065)	(.016)
Age	−.021	−.004
	(.011)	(.003)
Age2	.000	−.000*
	(.000)	(.000)
Education (in years)	.015	.029***
	(.012)	(.001)
Number of child	.003	−.009
	(.027)	(.006)
Partner	−.066	−.043**
	(.073)	(.019)
Employed	.186**	.178***
	(.077)	(.019)
Political orientation: Center	Reference	
Left	.205***	.190***
	(.077)	(.019)
Right	−.128*	−.034*
	(.076)	(.020)
Religion: Protestant	Reference	
Catholic	.038	−.045*
	(.030)	(.025)
No religion	.030	.084***
	(.098)	(.026)
Other_religion	.095	−.328***
	(.160)	(.048)
Income_class: Center	Reference	
Low	.103	.022
	(.075)	(.020)
High	.128	.174***
	(.083)	(.021)
Adj- R²	.0343	.0802
Nb of informations	1185	18438

A negative sign increases the likelihood that individuals agree with the statement ***:1 percent, **: 5 percent, *: 10 percent steady correlation with the dynamics of employment rates of the different demographic groups. Moreover, in accordance with the model, we find that a common exogenous shock on the price of household durable goods is correlated with contrasted changes in the labor supply of the demographic groups depending on family attitudes. Actually, the drop in the price of durable household goods over the last decades is significantly correlated with the rise in female labor supply in all countries. But this drop only displays a significant correlation with the labor supply of young and older people in countries with strong extended family ties.

4.2.1 Family Attitudes and Employment Rate Levels

We start by gauging the correlation between family attitudes and the level of employment rates of the different demographic groups. This issue is part of an emerging literature dealing with the link between family perception and labor market participation (see Neumark and Postlewaite 1998, Fernandez, Fogli, and Olivetti 2004). However, the current literature generally focuses on individual labor supplies within the same country. We extend the analysis by looking at the cross-country aggregate outcomes of such family attitudes. To the best of our knowledge, no attempt has been made so far to quantify the relation between employment rates and family values in cross-country time series. This caveat is partly due to the lack of suitable data. Indeed, we need both cross-national and cross-temporal evidence on family attitudes to disentangle the role of family perception from other specific country effects. We try to fill this gap by using the three main waves of the *World Value Survey* (1981–1983, 1990–1992, 1999–2002).[22]

In line with the previous section, we capture national family attitudes by the remaining country-fixed effects in the ordered probit estimates of individual attitudes towards family. But we run these estimates on each specific wave, which yields us different time observations for the family perception. The key issue is to relate these family attitudes to the employment rates at stakes during the corresponding periods. To compare stationary levels, we regress the five-year average value of the employment rate in the early '80s (1981–1984), the early '90s (1990–1994) and the late '90s (1995–1999) on the country dummies obtained from the estimations of family attitudes (see Table 2) over the three corresponding waves.

Figure 15 provides a first hint on the raw correlations between national family attitudes and employment rates in the early '90s. It first reports a

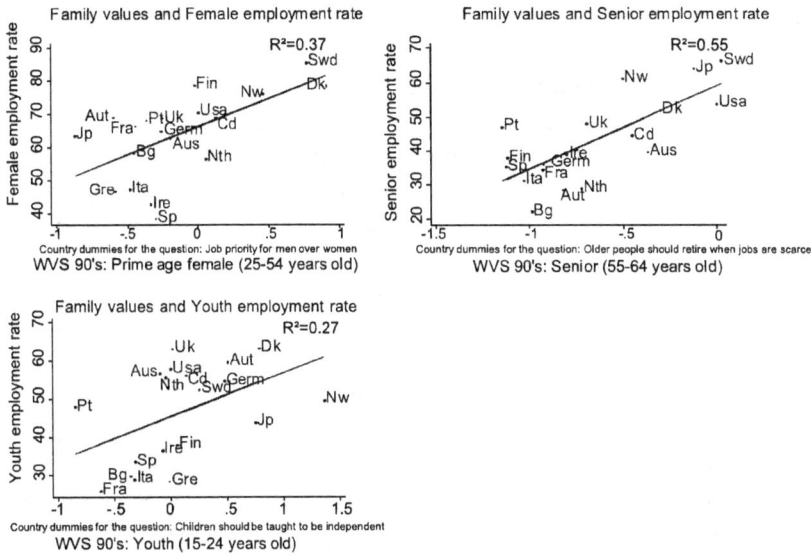

Figure 15
Correlation between national family attitudes and employment rates in OECD countries

significant positive correlation between prime-age female employment rate and the preferences over gender division of labor proxied by the country dummies for the question *"When jobs are scarce, men should have more rights to a job than women."* (WVS). Three main groups appear. The Nordic countries are the most opposed to male job priority and display the highest female employment rates. Anglo-Saxon and European Continental countries seem to share both the same attitudes towards gender roles and the same average female employment rates. Interestingly enough, a Mediterranean country like Portugal has preferences towards gender roles much closer to Anglo-Saxon and Continental countries and displays accordingly a pretty high female employment rate. The last group is made up of countries with both low employment rates and a positive bias in favor of male job priority. Typical countries belonging to this group are Italy, Greece, Ireland, Spain, or Belgium and Japan.

Figure 15 also reports a significant correlation between the employment rate of older people and national attitudes over their role on the labor market as proxied by the fixed effects for the question *"When jobs are scarce, older people should be forced to retire from work early."* The coefficient of determination amounts to 0.46. But interestingly enough, this correlation does not square into the traditional opposition of countries. In particular Japan, the United States, and some Nordic countries like Sweden are strongly at odds with a forced retirement and do have approximately the same employment rate of older people. By contrast, Finland, which is as favorable as Continental and Mediterranean countries to early retirement, displays the same employment rate pattern as these countries. Eventually, Figure 15 shows that the same significant correlation holds between youth employment rate and national family values over their independence proxied by the country dummies for the question: *"Here is a list of qualities that children can be encouraged to learn at home. Which if any do you consider to be really important: Independence?"* The same opposition pattern emerges between Mediterranean and European Continental countries characterized by both low youth employment rate and low concern for youth independence and at the other extreme Anglo-Saxon and Nordic countries which display the exact inverse picture.

This basic picture suggests a strong cross-country correlation between national perception of the role of each family member and their corresponding employment rates. Yet there may be alternative reasons for the above positive partial correlation such as labor market institutions or family policies.

In what follows, we attempt to quantify the specific contribution of family attitudes by taking account of the main variables used in the current labor market literature. We first control for the most relevant time-varying institutions accounted for by Nickell et al. (2001) and Bertola, Blau, and Kahn (2002). Therefore, we include trade-union density, employment protection, trade-union coordination and the level of unemployment benefits in the employment rate estimations of all demographic groups. Regarding female employment rate, we follow Jaumotte (2003) by including family policies—proxied by the share of public spending in child care—and socio-demographic variables captured by the Barro-Lee index of the number of years of education of women aged between 25 and 55 years old and the share of child per women. In order to understand youth employment, we also need to take into account the number of years of education and subsidized education. Due to the availability of data, we focus on the level of education by using the Barro-Lee index on the average years of school of people aged between 15 and 25 years old. Eventually, the employment rate of older workers is likely to be affected by fiscal incentives to retire and the official age of retirement. We control for these characteristics by using Blondal and Scarpetta (1997) data.[23]

Obviously, the employment rates of the different demographic groups are potentially influenced by a number of other country specific variables. We control as far as we can for these specific features by including country dummies. Potential aggregate macroeconomic shocks are accounted for by including time period dummies. The prime age male unemployment rate is also included as a proxy for national labor market conditions.

Both the previous indicators and the employment rates by demographic groups are taken as five-year average. The sub-periods correspond to that of the national family attitudes indicators: the early '80s (1980–1984), the early '90s (1990–1994) and the late '90s (1995–1999).

The GLS estimates are reported in Table 4. Each demographic employment rate is regressed on the corresponding family perception indicator; that is national attitudes towards (1) gender roles in the case of prime-age female employment rate (25–54), (2) child independence for youth employment rate (16–24), and (3) early retirement for the employment rate of older people (55–64). Recall that the family indicator is made up of the coefficients associated with the country-fixed effects in the previous estimates of family attitudes. For each question, the country of reference is chosen as the one displaying the highest average answer in favor of male job priority over women (Japan), early retirement of older individuals (Portugal), and low independence for children (France). Thus a positive coefficient associated with the national family indicator indicates a relative increase compared to the most "traditionalist" country in the probability to oppose job priority for men, to oppose early retirement for older workers, and to promote child independence.

Table 4 shows that for all demographic groups the corresponding national family indicator has a statistically highly significant impact on employment rates. Col. 2 and col. 3 report that the fact to be at odds with job priority for men or to oppose early retirement for older people is significantly positively correlated with the employment rates of women and older individuals respectively. Besides, col. 4 in Table 4 shows that national family attitudes relatively more favorable to child independence are positively correlated with youth employment rate. Strikingly enough, these national family indicators display a higher statistical power of explanation than most of the standard labor market institutions used in the current literature.

Table 4
Family attitudes and employment rate levels: GLS estimates

	Employment rate Women (1)	Employment rate Older people (2)	Employment rate Young people (3)
Family attitudes	.077***	.019**	.076***
	(.002)	(.008)	(.015)
Employment protection	.005	−.048**	.036
	(.005)	(.022)	(.029)
Union coordination	.034	−.003	−.019
	(.021)	(.014)	(.013)
Union density	−.065	−.228***	.476***
	(.123)	(.039)	(.078)
Unemployment benefit	−.024	−.125***	.317***
	(.071)	(.034)	(.045)
Unemployment rate Prime-age men	−.922***	−.040	−.240***
	(.242)	(.112)	(.018)
Children per women	−.084		
	(.095)		
Education	.032**	−.005	−.006
	(.013)	(.005)	(.006)
Family policy	.006***		
	(.001)		
Off. age retirement		.007***	
		(.001)	
Time dummies		Yes***	
Country dummies		Yes***	
Number of observations	49	53	53

Notes: GLS estimates with heteroskedastic errors.
National family attitudes proxied by:
(1) Country dummies in "When jobs are scarce, men should have job priority over women."
(2) Country dummies in "When jobs are scarce, older people should retire earlier."
(3) Country dummies in "Children should be taught to become independent."

It is also instructive to try to quantify the economic meaning of the coefficients at stakes. Actually the previous coefficients are hardly interpretable by themselves since the family indicators consist of country dummies associated with answers coded in multiple values. To cope with this flaw, we have recoded the answers to the previous questions into agree-disagree (1-0) and run probit estimates with marginal effects. In this case, the national family perception indicators capture in each country the relative change in the probability of agreement with the related family statements compared to the most "traditionalist" country. We then estimate the impact of these new indicators on the employment rate of each demographic group by taking into account the previous labor market and family policies. It turns out that a relative decrease in national family preferences in favor of job priority for men or early retirement for older individuals is associated with an increase in female employment rate of 13 percent and a rise by 4.3 percent in the employment rate of older people respectively. Conversely, an increase in national family attitudes in favor of child independence relatively to the country which is the most opposed to this statement would be associated with an increase of 29.5 percent in youth employment rate. As a conclusion national family attitudes display a statistically significant and economically sizeable correlation with the employment rates of the different demographic groups in OECD countries.

4.2.2 Family Attitudes and the Dynamics of Employment Rates

This section shows that national family attitudes are also highly correlated with the dynamic evolution of employment rates. We examine to what extent the decline in the price of household durable goods is correlated not only to the labor supply of women but also to the labor supply of the extended family members. The theoretical model predicts that the rise in home production triggered by the decline in the price of household durable goods should create incentives for younger and older individuals to devote more time to family activities and to decrease their labor supply. But this effect is expected to be significant in countries which have been previously found to have strong national attachment to family relations only.

To test this correlation pattern, we use cross-national evidence on the evolution of household durable goods prices over the last decades. This dataset—constructed by Eurostat—provides yearly information on the price index of home appliances for a sample of OECD countries since 1975.[24] The index only includes household appliances intended to save labor in household cleaning and maintenance such as vacuums, washing machines, clothes dryers, dishwasher, microwave ovens; it excludes furniture and audiovisual appliances.[25] The relative price of home appliances is computed as the ratio of the home appliance price index to consumer price index by taking 1985 as the reference year. The countries with enough reliable data are: Denmark, France, Germany, Italy, Spain, United Kingdom, and the United States. In all countries, the relative price of home appliances has dramatically fallen, with an average yearly drop of 1 percent.

Table 5 reports the GLS estimates of the correlation pattern between household good durable prices and the employment rate of young and older people. To evaluate the differential impact of the price of household durable goods depending on family relations, we group the countries into the main four clusters identified in the previous analysis of national family attitudes: Anglo-Saxon countries, European continental countries (France and Germany), Mediterranean countries (Italy and Spain), and Scandinavian countries (Denmark). To identify the specific

Table 5
Household durable good prices and employment rates: GLS estimates

Variables	Employment rate Young people (1)	Employment rate Older people (2)
Household durable goods prices		
Anglo countries	−.114	−.187
	(.073)	(.092)
Mediterranean countries	.377***	.242**
	(.127)	(.102)
Continental countries	.368***	.029***
	(.151)	(.001)
Scandinavian countries	−.156	−.273
	(.335)	(.309)
Employment protection	−.204***	−.042***
	(.030)	(.004)
Unemployment benefit	.120***	−.042
	(.037)	(.044)
Union coordination	−.018	.002
	(.015)	(.024)
Union density	−.031	−.162
	(.062)	(.106)
Unemployment rate prime-age men	−.894***	−.001
	(.104)	(.001)
Constant	.311*	.973**
	(.179)	(.308)
Country dummies	Yes***	
Time dummies	Yes***	
Nb observ.	127	

GLS estimates with heteroskedastic standard errors.
*** : 1 percent, ** : 5 percent , *:10 percent.

role of household durable good price on the employment rate of young and older people, we also include the same time-varying labor market institutions (Nickell et al. 2001) as the previous estimations. Yet, we do not include the average level of education and the tax incentives for retirement for which we do not have yearly information. We try to partly overcome this lack of data by including both country dummies and time period dummies. The regressions are based on the period 1975–1995.

Column 1 in Table 5 first shows a high discrepancy in the correlation pattern between youth employment rates and durable goods prices. There is a robust positive correlation in Mediterranean and Continental countries, an increase in the home appliance price being associated with a 0.37 percent decrease in youth employment in these groups of countries. By contrast, the correlation between these two variables becomes negative and is no longer statistically significant in Anglo-Saxon and Scandinavian countries. As to the effects of traditional labor institutions, employment protection and unemployment benefits have a significant negative impact. Column 2 in Table 5 provides a mirror image regarding the correlation between the employment rate of older worker and the price of household durable goods. The most noticeable result is the sizeable positive correlation between the employment rate of this demographic group and the relative appliance price index in Mediterranean and Continental countries. The correlation is statistically significant at the 5 percent level. By contrast, the correlation turns out to be negative in Anglo-Saxon and in Denmark and is no longer statistically significant. This finding suggests that the same technological shock to home production may have led to significant cross-national differences in the employment path of younger and older individuals depending on national family attitudes.

5. Conclusion

Is the low European employment rate rooted in specific European family culture? Although this paper is far from providing a definitive stand on this issue, we show converging evidence in favor of a positive answer to this question. First, the European employment gap is overwhelmingly concentrated on demographic groups for which the European dominant family perception is precisely unfavorable to their labor market participation. Second, the evolution of the employment rates of the different demographic groups over the last decades has been highly

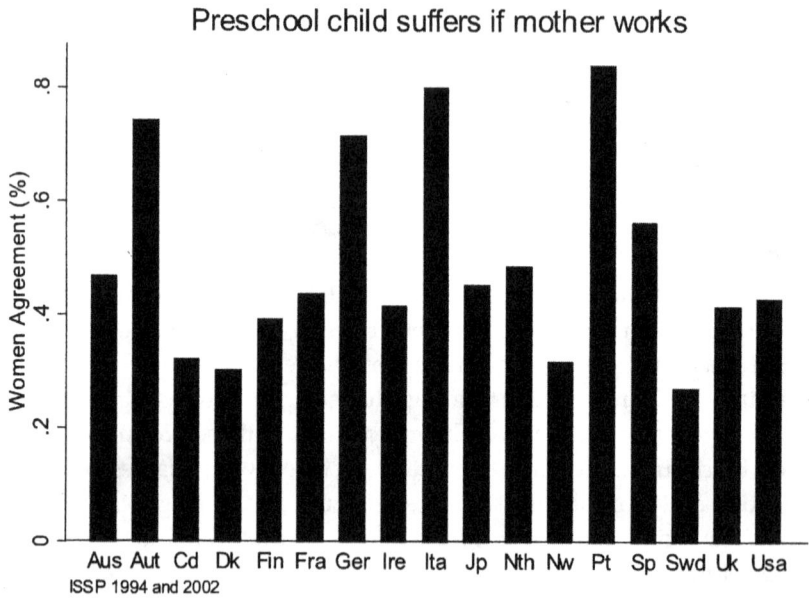

Figure 16
Share of women who agree or strongly agree with the statement "A preschool child suffers if mother works"

correlated in countries displaying strong preferences for family relations, the upward trend in female labor supply having led to a dramatic
fall in youth and senior employment rates in European countries only.
This evolution pattern suggests strong labor supply composition effects
within the family in countries which are found to be more attached to
family ties. Eventually, we have shown that family attitudes are influenced by cultural factors in as much as people sharing the same backgrounds as their ancestors but facing a different economic environment
tend to react identically on family issues.

Naturally, the identification of cultural factors remains a complex
issue since culture may deeply interact with institutions and evolve
with the economic environment.[26] As preferences are likely to be influenced by labor market experience, culture cannot be considered as an
exogenous variable out of reach from labor market institutions. Conversely, institutions also depend on family preferences[27] as far as they
are shaped by individuals.

Yet we argue that deepening the cultural roots of low European
employment rates remains a top agenda issue for both positive and nor-

mative analysis of labor market outcomes. For instance, let us consider the current European policy recommendations to promote the employment rates of mothers in European Continental and Mediterranean countries. Actually, Figure 16 shows that an overwhelming majority of women in these countries do agree (or strongly agree) with the statement *"A preschool child suffers if the mother works."* And it has been shown in the core paper that this response is likely to be linked to cultural perception of motherhood rather independently of policy incentives. To that regard, the implementation of the European recommendations of the Lisbon strategy might well not be welfare improving.

Acknowledgements

We thank Tito Boeri, Alessandra Fogli, Francis Kramarz, Alan Manning, Christopher Pissarides, Claudia Sénik, and participants at the International Seminar on Macroeconomics in Budapest and at the PSE seminar for very helpful comments.

Notes

1. This paper is focused on employment rates, but our results still hold for participation rates.

2. We distinguish home production from family activities made up of leisure time that family members spend together.

3. Our approach does not aim at dismissing the influence of institutions on employment. We rather stress the influence of family attitudes that has been much less analyzed by economists. We view our paper as a step towards a more complete analysis that accounts for interactions between institutions, family attitudes and employment.

4. According to Rogerson (2003) and Freeman and Schettkat (2005), the deterioration of the European employment rates relatively to the U.S. comes from the higher weight put on home production in European countries. Blanchard (2004) provides a similar argument based on higher preference for leisure in European countries. But these explanations leave unexplained why only youth and elderly employment rates have dramatically fallen while female employment rates have steadily increased in European Continental and Mediterranean countries.

5. By family culture, we mean common preferences for family rules, roles, habits, activities, and/or common household skills for home production.

6. The European employment strategy is avaliable at http://europa.eu.int/index_ en.htm.

7. Bertola et al. (2002) and Wasmer (2001) argue that labor market rigidities hinder the employment of outsider groups (younger, women, and older individuals) or lead to more stringent crowding out effects between demographic groups. Yet this line of inquiry

leaves unexplained the dynamics of employment rates. Over the last three decades, female employment rate has risen more in Mediterranean countries whose institutions are the most detrimental to outsiders. Inversely, male employment rates have decreased everywhere whatever their level of protection. Moreover the crowding out effects raised by a demographic shock such as the rise in female labor supply could be relevant in the short-run but are unlikely to persist over more than 30 years.

8. Some papers have shown that family ties are influenced by the economic environment. Becker et al. (2004) and Fogli (2004) analyze the influence of job insecurity on youth emancipation decisions. Ermisch (1999), Martinez-Granados and Ruis-Castillo (2002), Gianelli and Monfardini (2003), and Diaz and Guillo (2004) stress the importance of the access to housing.

9. This type of empirical strategy has been used by Reimers (1985), Blau (1992), Carroll, Rhee, and Rhee (1999), Antecol (2000), Guinnane, Moehling, and Grada (2002), Giuliano (2004) and Fernandez and Fogli (2005). Blau (1992) and Guinnane, Moehling, and Grada (2002) examine whether the fertility of immigrants differs from that of the native born in the U.S. Reimers (1985) and Antecol (2000) study the effect of the country of origin on the labor force participation of immigrants. Using the same approach, Giuliano (2004) focuses on family leaving arrangements and Fernandez and Fogli (2005) analyze female labor participation and fertility. Caroll, Rhee, and Rhee (1999) use this approach for the analysis of saving behavior. All these studies find some significant influence of the cultural background on behaviors and economic outcomes.

10. The countries belonging to each cluster are: Anglo-Saxon (Australia, Canada, UK, and U.S.), European continental (Austria, Belgium, France, Germany, Netherlands), Mediterranean (Greece, Italy, Portugal, Spain), and Nordic (Finland, Norway, Denmark, Sweden).

11. Freeman and Schettkat (2005) have stressed the empirical relevance of the distinction of non-market activities for understanding the EU-U.S. employment gap. They distinguish four categories: market work, household work, leisure, and personal time. They show that countries differ much more on household work rather than leisure.

12. The utility function implies that the constraints $c \geq 0$, $l_m \geq 0$, $l_f \geq 0$, $s_f \geq 0$, $s_m \geq 0$ are never binding.

13. Introducing the possibility that members of the extended family also benefit from a share of the marketable good purchased by the nuclear family would keep unchanged the results obtained below.

14. For the sake of simplicity, we do not distinguish potential differences in the valuation of leisure derived by the family members.

15. The utility function implies that the constraints $c_e \geq 0$, $l_e \geq 0$, $s_e \geq 0$ are never binding.

16. Some papers have also documented that there are differences in attitudes within countries. Azmat, Güell, and Manning (2004) found an effect on female unemployment rates of attitudes to female work at regional level even when including country fixed effects.

17. Recent studies have stressed cross-national variation in the allocation of time between market and home activities (Freeman and Schettkat 2004). We complement this line of inquiry by laying stress directly on preferences and distinguishing the role played by each demographic group in this realm.

18. We checked that answers to other related questions yield similar results. These questions are: "If a woman earns more money than her husband, it is almost certain to cause problems" (WVS), "A university education is more important for a boy than a girl" (WVS), "Man's job is to earn money, wife's job is look after home and family" (ISSP).

19. Unfortunately we cannot use the WVS questions on family attitudes in as much as this survey does not document the country of origins of the ancestors.

20. The ISSP also provides some information about the ancestors' countries of people living in Canada. The same opposition pattern emerges between people with French and Anglo-Saxon origins. Yet this comparison may be more biased with specific regional policies.

21. The other questions on gender roles—such as "Family life suffers when women works" or "A man's job is to earn money: a women's job is to look after home and family"—yield quantitatively similar results.

22. The wave 1995–1997 displays a high number of missing data and is less exploitable. Note that the questions are not reported for all countries at each wave. The estimates are based on unbalanced samples.

23. We only report the estimations for the legal age of retirement for which we have enough information for the period 1980–2000. Tax incentives are proxied by the expected increase in old-age pensions for a 55 year-old male by working for ten years more. This indicator yields consistent results by increasing the participation of older worker but only covers two periods 1967 and 1995.

24. This database has been used by Cavalcanti and Tavares (2004) for assessing the role of durable price on female labor supply. We extend this analysis to other demographic groups and stress the key interactions between prices and preferences.

25. Cavalcanti and Tavares (2004) used this dataset to show the significant impact of the price of household durable goods on female labor supply. We thus directly focus on the labor supply of extended family members and their contrasted evolution by groups of countries.

26. See Bisin and Verdier (2001) for an analysis of the dynamics of preference and cultural evolution.

27. See Algan and Cahuc (2006) for a political economy analysis of job protection based on male breadwinner values.

References

Algan, Y., and P. Cahuc. 2006. "Job Protection: The Macho Hypothesis." *Oxford Review of Economic Policy* 22(3): 390–410.

Antecol, H. 2000. "An Examination of Cross-Country Differences in the Gender Gap in Labor Force Participation Rates." *Labour Economics* 7: 409–426.

Azmat, G., M. Güell, and A. Manning. 2004. "Gender Gaps in Unemployment Rates in OECD Countries." CEP Working Paper no. 607. London School of Economics.

Becker, S. O., S. Bentolila, A. Fernandes, and A. Ichino. 2004. "Job Insecurity and Children's Emancipation." Mimeo, CEMFI.

Bentolila, S. A., and Ichino. 2000. "Unemployment and Consumption: Are Job Losses Less Painful near the Mediterranean?" CEPR Working Paper no. 2539.

Bertola, G., F.D. Blau, and L. Kahn. 2002. "Labor Market Institutions and Demographic Employment Patterns." CEPR Working Paper no. 3348.

Bergstrom, T.C. 1997. *A Survey of the Theory of the Family, Handbook of Population and Family Economics*. M.R. Rosenzweig and O. Stark, (eds.), chap 2: 22–79.

Bisin, A., and T. Verdier. 2001. "The Economics of Cultural Transmission and the Dynamics of Preferences." *Journal of Economic Theory* 97: 298–319.

Blanchard, O. 2004. "The Economic Future of Europe." MIT Working Paper no. 0404.

Blau, F. 1992. "The Fertility of Immigrant Women: Evidence from High Fertility Source Countries." In: G.J. Borjas and R. Freeman, eds., *Immigration and the Workforce: Economic Consequences for the United States and Source Areas.* Chicago: The University of Chicago Press: 93–133.

Blondal, S. and S. Scarpetta. 1997. "Early Retirement in OECD Countries: The Role of Social Security Systems." OECD Economic Studies no. 29.

Carroll, C.D., C. Rhee, and B. Rhee. 1999. "Does Cultural Origin Affect Saving Behavior? Evidence from Immigrants." *Economic Development and Cultural Change* 48(1): 33–50.

Cavalcanti, T., and J. Tavares. 2004. "Women Prefer Larger Governments: Female Labor Supply and Public Spending." Lisbon University Working Paper.

Diaz, A., and D. Guillo. 2004. "Family Ties and Labor Supply." Working Paper, Department of Economics, Universidad Carlos III.

Ermisch, J. 1999. "Price, Parents, and Young People's Household Formation." *Journal of Urban Economics* 45: 47–71.

Fernandez, R., A. Fogli, and C. Olivetti. 2004. "Mother and Sons: Preference Formation and Female Labor Force Dynamics." *Quarterly Journal of Economics* 119: 1249–1299.

Fernandez, R., and A. Fogli. 2005. "Culture: An Empirical Investigation of Beliefs, Work, and Fertility. Federal Reserve Bank of Minneapolis, Research Department Staff Report 361.

Fogli, A. 2004. "Endogenous Market Rigidities and Family Ties." New York University Working Paper.

Freeman, R.B., and R. Schettkat. 2005. "Marketization of Household Production and the EU–US Gap in Work." *Economic Policy* 41: 5–50.

Galor, O., and D. Weil. 1996. "The Gender Gap, Fertility and Growth." *American Economic Review* 86: 374–387.

Gianelli, G. C., and C. Monfardini. 2003. "Joint Decisions of Household Membership and Human Capital Accumulation of Youths: The Role of Expected Earnings and Local Markets." *Journal of Population Economics* 16: 265–285.

Giuliano, P. 2004. "On the Determinants of Living Arrangements in Western Europe: Does Cultural Origin Matter?" Mimeo, U.C. Berkeley.

Greenwood, J., A. Seshadri, and M. Yorukoglu. 2005 "Engine of Liberalization." *Review of Economic Studies* 72: 109–133.

Guinnane, T., C. Moehling, and C. Grada. 2002. "The Fertility of the Irish in America in 1910." Mimeo, Yale University.

Jaumotte, F. 2003. "Female Labour Force Participation: Past Trends and Main Determinants in OECD Countries." OECD Working Paper no. 30.

Martınez-Granados, M., and J. Ruiz-Castillo. 2002 "The Decisions of Spanish Youth: A Cross Section Study." *Journal of Population Economics* 15: 305–330.

Neumark, D., and A. Postlewaite. 1998 "Relative Income Concerns and the Rise in Married Women's Employment." *Journal of Public Economics*: 157–183.

Nickell, S., L. Nunziata, W. Ochel, and G. Quintini. 2001. "The Beveridge Curve, Unemployment and Wages in OECD from the 1960s to the 1990s." LSE Working Paper no. 0502.

Reimers, C.W. 1985. "Cultural Differences in Labor Force Participation among Married Women." *American Economic Review*, Papers and Proceedings 75: 251–255.

Rogerson, R. 2003. "Structural Transformation and the Deterioration of European Labor Market Outcomes." Arizona State University Working Paper.

Wasmer, E. 2001. "The Causes of the Youth Employment Problem: A Labor Supply Side View." In D. Cohen, T. Piketty, and G. Saint–Paul, eds., *The New Economics of Rising Inequalities*.

Comment

Tito Boeri, Bocconi University, IGIER, and CEPR

1. Introduction

This is a very interesting and ambitious paper. To my knowledge, it is the first attempt to address within a unified framework adjustment along many different and relevant extensive margins. It covers interactions between labor market participation of women, youth unemployment and non-employment among those closer to the official retirement age. The goal is to explain the wide cross-country variation in employment rates of these "marginal groups" of the labor force and their interactions, notably the reasons why the womenisation of the workforce only in a subset of countries has gone hand in hand with a decline of participation among the other groups. The key message offered by the paper is that social customs *by themselves* play a crucial role in determining these interactions between, on the one hand, employment of prime-aged women, and, on the other hand, participation of young and old people. Social customs indeed affect the size of the family in different countries and the way in which the different components care about the joint household product. Thus, the intensity of family ties is crucial in creating a link between participation decisions of women and decisions of other members of the extended households to be working or involved in home production.

The paper draws very much on the new anthropological literature on participation, fertility, and wage formation. It is very much in the spirit of this literature the idea that (1) culture causes labor market behavior rather than being the other way round, and (2) culture matters not only indirectly—i.e., by shaping institutions affecting economic behavior—but also directly, altering preferences of individuals, hence their behavior per given institutions. The distinction between direct and indirect effects of social customs is important also from a normative standpoint. Let me try to clarify this with reference to a specific example. A key implication of this paper is that the employment targets of the EU, defining threshold employment rates for all these marginal groups, have two major shortcomings: (1) they ignore the relevant interactions between the various targets, and (2) they do not take into account that more employment for all of these groups may reduce welfare of households. If culture is affecting labor market behavior mainly via institutions, then one could still argue in favor of the EU employment targets, provided that there is some sluggishness (e.g., driven by political-economic constraints) in the adjustment of institutions to preferences.

The issue is that unless we can characterize and detect a direct causal effect of culture on preferences and constraints of individuals, we can see the role of culture mainly in the cultural dimensions which are behind the different institutional configurations.

My main criticism to this very insightful paper is that institutional explanations are too readily dismissed. I am, in other words, not yet convinced of the fact that this paper isolates the direct effect of culture rather than an effect of, inter alia, social customs intermediated by institutions. In particular, I have three remarks: (1) family size is not only related to family values, but has to do also with institutions, (2) some relevant institutions are not included in the regressions which are supposed to isolate national cultural identities, and (3) there may be more stringent ways to test the implications of the model, which are based on micro data, actually on microwave data.

2. Family Size Matters

As the Figure 1 suggests, there is significant cross-country variation in Europe as to the incidence of large families. While in Denmark less than one household out of five has more than four members, in Ireland there is one large family out of three.

The difference in the size of families cannot be entirely attributed to social customs. It is quite likely that the presence of large families has to do with the housing market, fertility rates, labor market conditions, pension rules, availability of childcare, gaps in the welfare system filled by the extended family, etc. While it is not accurate to associate the size of families to social customs only, there is no reason to believe that home production technologies or the substitutability between women

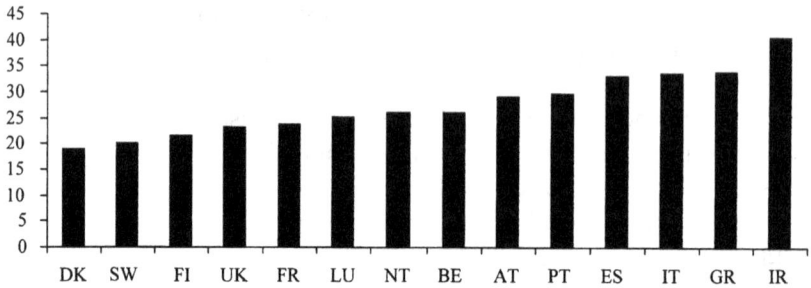

Figure 1
Percentage of households with more than four members

and other members of the family is independent of size. For instance, large scale production may involve a lower substitutability of women with other household members, e.g., grandparents may not be in a condition to take care of a large number of children. The asymmetric effects of the decline in the price of household durable goods on nuclear versus extended families, which play a crucial role in the explanation provided by Algan and Cahuc, may therefore capture a pure scale effect: a single dishwasher frees time for work for many persons. Technological change in home production may also be more gender-biased when it takes place at larger production levels. In other words, scale matters and scale is not the same thing as family values.

3.   The Missing Institutions

A number of institutions are very important in affecting the substitutability between women and other members of the household. The usual suspect is clearly legislation on part-time employment, but the whole battery of so-called "family friendly" policies (e.g., measures encouraging a better sharing of family responsibilities between men and women, extended maternity leave, working-time flexibility synchronized between husbands and wives, etc.) are likewise important in affecting the way in which higher participation of women could interact with labor market choices of other groups of the labor force. These institutions are not in the regressions displayed in Table 4 of the paper and cannot be captured by country dummies, since they have been subject to many reforms in recent years. By the way, the fact that institutions are being changed so frequently may suggest that we are out of the equilibrium in the relationship between social customs and institutions. In other words, there may be sluggishness in the adjustment of institutions to changes in social customs.

4.   A Microwave Test?

Finally, I believe that a more direct test of the theory would require using micro-level data on participation choices of different household members depending on the household durable goods consumption. The European Commission Household Panel (ECHP) survey has a battery of questions on durable good consumption and labor market participation along intensive and extensive margins. It therefore offers a good empirical basis to test the theory of the authors. Unfortunately the ECHP does not have questions eliciting values of individuals, so that we cannot look at the relevant interactions between culture and the decline in the price of household durable goods. Yet we can use the cross-sectional variation in the use of these appliances to detect the effects of this shock on hours of work under different institutional-cultural configurations. For illustrative purposes, I tabulate below the results of a simple linear regression of hours of work against individual characteristics (age, educational attainments, etc.) plus dummies capturing the presence in the house of a microwave (dmw) or a dishwasher (ddw) as well as interactions of the above variables with household size, in order to control for the size effects outlined above. I run this regression for two countries located at the extremes of the distribution of household size (see Table 1) and deemed to correspond to much different attitudes towards family ties. What I find in the data is that ownership of a dishwasher or microwave frees time for work only for Italian women. It has no effect on men labor supply in Italy and no effect whatsoever in Denmark. Importantly, as documented by insignificant interaction dummies, the size of the family does not appear to be relevant: there is no difference in the reaction to shocks in nuclear or large families.

Summarizing, this is a very intriguing and stimulating paper pointing out the relevant interactions between participation rates by gender and age groups. While I am not entirely persuaded that it is social customs per se to drive the results exhibited by the authors, I do believe that this paper paves the way for a very promising avenue of research on interactions between employment rates, household size, and institutions.

Table 1
Testing the micro(wave) foundations: Dependent variable: hours of work

	Coef	std. err.	t
Italy			
Italian men			
Dmw	.452	.894	0.51
Ddw	−.226	.827	−0.27
Compdmw	.1703	.221	0.77
Compddw	.120	.202	0.59
Italian women			
Dmw	1.360	.685	1.98
Ddw	1.080	.621	1.74
Compdmw	.250	.171	−1.46
Compddw	−.279	.153	−1.82
Denmark			
Danish men			
Dmw	−1.594	1.083	−1.47
Ddw	1.250	1.154	1.08
Compdmw	.402	.341	1.18
Compddw	−.0538	.373	−0.14
Danish women			
Dmw	.411	1.129	0.36
Ddw	−.726	1.204	−0.60
Compdmw	−.1798	.347	−0.52
Compddw	.214	.375	0.57

Note: dmw = dummy possession of micro wave; ddw = dummy possession of dish-washer; compdmw = interaction between number of household members and dummy possession of micro wave; compddw = interaction between number of household members and dummy possession of dishwasher.
Regressors include controls for age (linear and quadratic), years of education (linear and quadratic), and previous work experience.
Source: Echp, 1994–2001.

Comment

Alessandra Fogli, New York University

1. Introduction

This paper offers a new interpretation of the patterns of European employment rates over the last 30 years that is based on the crucial role of the family. It presents some interesting evidence on the evolution of the employment rates of the different demographic groups and develops a model based on the interaction between technology and family preferences that is able to capture the main features of the data.

While the employment rate of prime age males decreased slightly everywhere and that of prime age females rose in all European countries, the dynamics of the employment rates of younger and older individuals were very different across countries: these rates remained quite stable in Anglo-Saxon and Scandinavian countries while they dramatically decreased in Continental and Mediterranean countries.

The authors explain this phenomenon by means of a model in which a common shock, the decline in the price of durables, interacts with cross country heterogeneity in family preferences. In this original framework, the decision making unit is the family, which derives utility not only from consumption of a market good and from female and male leisure, but also from a different activity, called family activity, which requires as inputs a household good and family members' time. The most intuitive example of family activity is a family dinner, which requires the presence of a meal to consume and some time of each member of the family to consume it. Meals are produced using female housework and appliances. A key assumption is that, while the meal and family members' time are complements in the production of the family dinner, female time and appliances are substitutes in the production of the meal. It follows that, as the price of appliances drops, women devote less time to housework (so their labor supply in the market increases) but also more meals are produced. Because meals and family members' time are complements in the production of the family dinner, old and young members of the family will increase the time spent around the family table and consequently decrease their labor supply on the market. This effect will be stronger the larger the weight on the family activity in the family's utility function.

In the empirical section of the paper, the authors provide three types of evidence in support of their story. They first show that an individual's attitudes toward gender roles, as well as an individual's attitudes toward the proper role of young and old people in the economy, are significantly affected by the country of residence, after controlling for several individual characteristics. They then provide evidence that this cross-country heterogeneity in attitudes are significant in explaining differences across countries in the employment rates of different demographic groups, after controlling for labor market institutions. So, for example, the country fixed effects estimated in the individual regression of attitudes toward gender roles are significant in explaining cross-country differences in the employment rates of prime age women, while the country fixed effects estimated in the regression of attitudes toward youth independence are significant in explaining differences in youth employment rates, after controlling for several labor market institutions. The last piece of evidence concerns the relationship between the decline in the price of household durables and the dynamic evolution of employment rates. The theoretical model predicts that a decline in the price of household goods should induce old and young people to devote more time to family activities, and therefore to a reduction in their employment rates. This effect is expected to be larger the stronger the preferences for family activities. In the data the correlation over time between employment rates of young and old people and price of household durables is positive and significant for Mediterranean and Continental countries, while is negative and insignificant for Anglo-Saxon and Scandinavian counties. The authors interpret these results as evidence that the same technological shock has induced very different employment rate dynamics among young and old people in different European countries depending on the national attitudes toward family relations.

The assumption that individuals in different countries are endowed with different preferences over the family good is crucial to the story and I will explore its implications in this comment. In particular, the kind of preference heterogeneity the authors assume in their model delivers implications for the patterns of expenditures across countries and for the relationship between female and youth employment rates. These implications are discussed in the following section. Next, I discuss the empirical evidence presented in the paper and make some comments on the link between theoretical model and data.

1.1. Preferences for the Family Good: Implications from the Theory

The model developed in this paper has an important implication for the share of expenditures on household appliances across countries.

The model predicts that a decrease in the price of household appliances implies an increase in women's labor force participation rates together with a decline in the employment rates of young and old people, these effects being larger in magnitude for countries with stronger preferences for the family good. However, given the price of the household appliances, the model also delivers implications for how families that only differ in their preference over the family activity, allocate their expenditures among different goods. In the model families purchase on the market two types of goods: a numeraire consumption good c, and the household appliance k at the price p, used in the production of the family activity. The first order conditions imply:

$$\frac{c}{pk+c}=\frac{1}{q\left(\frac{1-\eta}{p}\right)\frac{\varphi}{z}p} \tag{1}$$

where the left hand side in (1) is the share of total expenditures that goes in the consumption of the market good. Given the unit price of the household good, q, the unit price of the family activity, z, and the price of the household good, which are the same across countries, the way families allocate their expenditures between market good and household appliances depends on the preference parameter φ, which captures cross country heterogeneity in families' taste for the family activity. In particular, since household appliances are used in the production of the family activity, the stronger the preference for the family activity, the larger the expenditure share in household appliances.

Given the difference in the preference parameter φ assumed in the paper, the model generates large differences in the share of expenditures in household appliances. Assuming, as the authors do, that the price of household appliances has declined uniformly across European countries at a rate of about 1 percent a year, Figure 1 plots the implied evolution of the expenditure share in household appliances for Mediterranean countries ($\varphi = 0.5$) and Anglo-Saxon countries ($\varphi = 0.1$) starting in 1975 with the price normalized to 1 and letting the price drop to 0.6. For these parameter values, the model predicts a share of expenditures in household appliances for Mediterranean countries well above 30 percent for all values of the price, and a share for Anglo-Saxon countries between 5 and 7 percent.

Is this implication in accordance with the empirical evidence?

Eurostat has data on the overall structure of consumption expenditure for most European countries by detailed COICOP level. These data are based on household budget surveys, conducted in different countries in 1988, 1994, and 1999. The countries identified as Mediterranean in the empirical section of the paper are Italy and Spain, while the Anglo-Saxon ones correspond to United Kingdom and United States. Accordingly, Figure 1 reports, together with the prediction of the model, data on the average expenditure shares in "Furnishings, household equip-

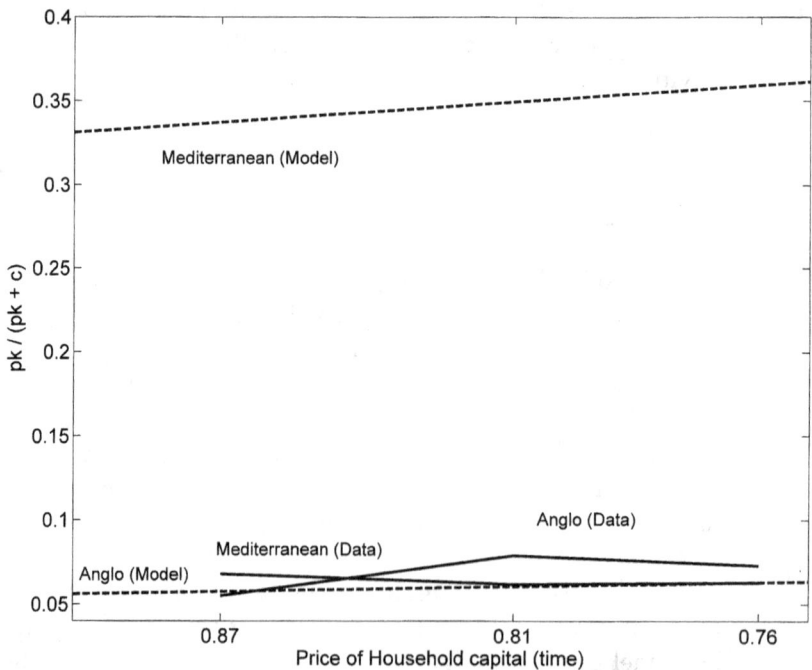

Figure 1
Expenditure shares in household appliances

ment and routine maintenance of the house" for Italy and Spain against that of United Kingdom for the years in which the data are available, which correspond, given the assumption of a drop in price of 1 percent a year starting in 1975 with the price normalized to 1, to a price of 0.87, 0.81, and 0.76. This category of expenditures includes "Household Appliances" together with other types of expenditures such as household textiles, tools and equipment for the house and garden, etc. In Italy the share of expenditures in this broad category was around 7 percent over the entire period while the share of expenditures in "Household Appliances" alone has never reached 1 percent. Similarly in Spain, the expenditure share in the broader category has never even reached 6 percent, with no more that 0.9 percent spent in household appliances. Therefore, the implied expenditure shares in household appliances seem to be way too large for Mediterranean countries, even when we consider the broader definition.

However, the more problematic assumption is not the level of φ for the Mediterranean countries, but rather the difference in the value of φ between Mediterranean and Anglo-Saxon countries.

If we look at the United Kingdom, the average expenditure share in the broader category of household goods is about 7 percent over the period, with the portion spent in household appliances equal to about 1.1 percent. These shares are remarkably similar to those observed for Mediterranean countries.

Given this evidence, the data seem to suggest that any difference in the parameter φ should be negligible, so that a theory based on differences across countries in the taste for household goods will never deliver differences across countries in employment rates which are quantitatively relevant.

The model also delivers predictions on the relationship between female and youth employment rates. Countries where the employment rates of young people drop the most are the countries where female employment rates increase the most, and are those characterized by strong preferences for the family activity (left panel, Figure 2). The opposite should be true for countries with weak preferences over the family good (right panel, Figure 2).

However, in the data presented by the authors and reproduced in Figure 3, the series for the female employment rate in Continental countries (strong preferences for family good) displays identical behavior to that of the Anglo-Saxon countries (weak preferences for family good), while the series for the youth employment rates are very different, with

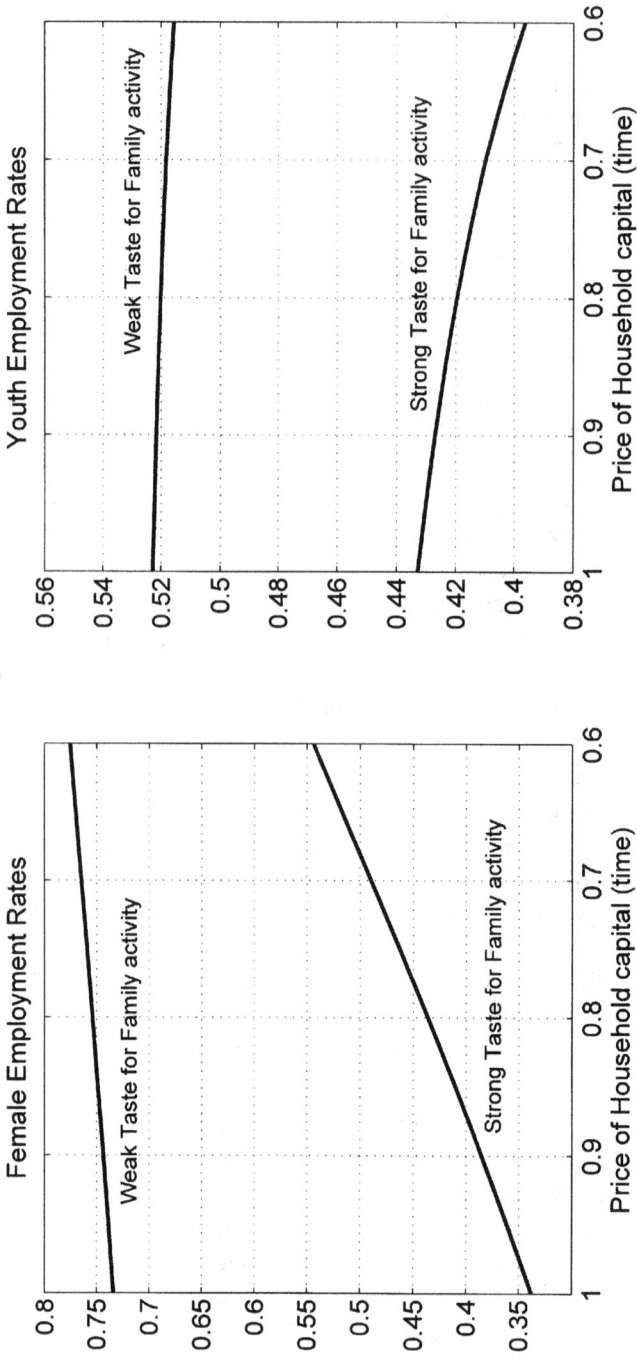

Figure 2
Female and youth employment rates

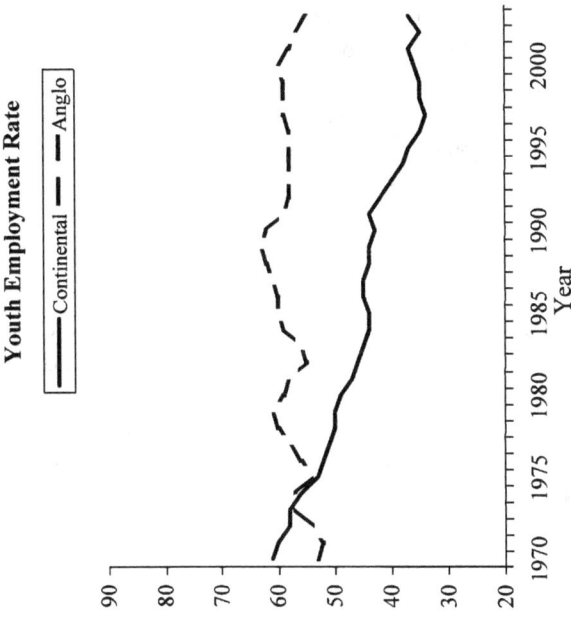

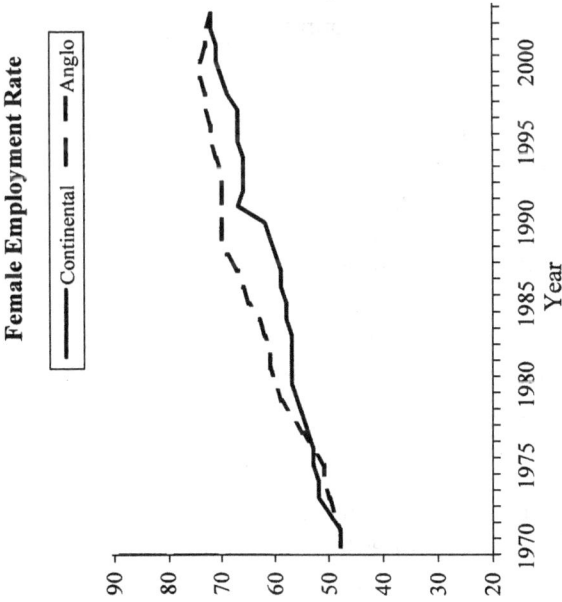

Figure 3
Youth and female employment rates

the one in Continental countries strongly decreasing and that in Anglo-Saxon countries pretty much constant over the period.

This evidence suggests that differences in family activities might not be very large, and even if they were they could not explain, for example, the observed differences in youth employment rates between Continental Europe and Anglo-Saxon countries.

1.2. *Preferences for the Family Good: The Empirical Evidence*

In the empirical section of the paper, the authors show that country fixed effects are significant in explaining differences across individuals in attitudes toward gender roles, living arrangements and role in society of young and old individuals. However, in the model, the authors assume away all these differences and consider an environment in which the household good can only be produced using female time, while no direct or indirect evidence is produced on the assumed cross-country differences in preferences for the family good.

Also, the authors show that these differences matter to explain cross country differences in employment rates. However, somewhat surprisingly, they do not include in their analysis some obvious variables that are directly related to youth and senior employment and largely differ across countries, like differences in school systems, school to work programs, part time work, flexible contracts for young individuals and pension and tax systems for old ones.

Finally, the evidence on the differential impact of a decline in the price of durables on the employment rates of different countries is suggestive but not convincing: while it is true that A causes B in the model, i.e., that a decline in the price of durables affects employment rates only in countries with strong preferences over the family good, there are many reasons why this may be the case which have nothing to do with the particular story told in this paper. In other words, the empirical evidence presented in the paper is too reduced form to be considered convincing and alternative hypothesis need to be explored.

2. Conclusion

This provocative paper suggests that the employment rate of young people in Mediterranean countries has dramatically fallen over the last few decades because individuals in these countries have strong preferences for family activities and optimally chose to spend more time around the dinner table after a drop in the price of household appliances made family meals cheaper and more readily available. The evidence presented in this comment suggests that this is probably not the whole story, and that likely other factors are important to explain employment patterns in Southern Europe. Yet this paper raises some important issues: to understand the evolution of the employment rates of different demographic groups it is necessary to analyze them jointly and in such analysis the family should have a primary role.

This paper also makes another important point: a theory based on purely technological differences across countries would have a hard time in explaining the large amount of heterogeneity observed in employment rates across European countries. In this respect, it is important to explore the role played by differences in preferences.

3

Shadow Sorting

Tito Boeri, *Bocconi University, IGIER, and CEPR*
Pietro Garibaldi, *University of Turin, IGIER and CEPR*

1. Introduction

Modern information technologies allowing information cross-checking coming from different administrative sources and to quickly buildup and update inventories of bank accounts, make it relatively easy to detect and repress shadow activity. However, this is not done and Governments' statements of "tolerance zero" vis-à-vis the informal sector do not seem to be taken too seriously by firms and workers who continue to go underground. Indeed, the informal sector is flourishing: available estimates point to an upward trend in the size of shadow economy in OECD countries from high levels. The shadow share of GDP ranges from a low 10 percent of GDP in the Nordics, UK, and Switzerland to peaks of 20 to 30 percent in Southern Europe and Ireland and 40 percent in transitional economies of Eastern Europe and Asia.

Why is the informal sector so tolerated? How do borders between shadow employment, legal employment, and unemployment evolve under different macroeconomic conditions and institutional configurations? What does the reduction of the shadow sector imply in terms of labor productivity?

In this paper we address these issues theoretically and empirically, and we offer a simple explanation of the "shadow puzzle": shadow employment and unemployment are two faces of the same coin. Shadow employment is indeed correlated with unemployment. Based on macro, regional as well as microdata in Italy and Brazil we find clear evidence for this claim. Following this result, we argue that shadow employment is tolerated because its repression increases unemployment, with undesirable political consequences.

Our theory endogenizes the choice of both, workers *and* firms, to go idle in an equilibrium model of the labor market with market frictions.

From the labor demand side, firms optimally create legal or shadow employment through a mechanism that is akin to tax evasion. Being shadow means not paying taxes (including social security contributions) and not being liable to severance pay in case of a breakup of the employment relationship. However, there is a positive probability that irregular employment is detected, in which case the match is immediately dissolved. From the labor supply side, heterogeneous workers sort across the two sectors, with high productivity workers entering the legal sector. Such worker sorting appears fully consistent with most empirical evidence on shadow employment.

Repressing shadow employment, that is, increasing the detection probability, means increasing job destruction and reducing job creation in the shadow segment. While this repression tends to increase total employment in the legal sector, it also increases unemployment. Available theories of the informal sector—recently reviewed by Schneider and Enste (2000)—do not capture these trade-offs. This is because such theories take a partial equilibrium approach, focus either on labor demand or on labor supply, and do not consider sorting of workers with varying productivity levels in the two pools. Another distinguishing feature of our model is indeed that it self-selects workers in the two pools endogenously, by determining the productivity threshold demarcating the two pools.

The model implies a positive correlation between unemployment and shadow employment that is evident in cross country data as well as in regional data from Brazil and Italy, two countries with large shadow employment. To ensure that such correlation is not a statistical artifact we use a unique Brazilian data set where unemployment and shadow employment are two mutually exclusive states, and we find strong support for the positive correlation.

The model also implies that shadow wage gaps should be lower in depressed labor markets. We find empirical support also for this implication.

The paper proceeds as follows. Section 1 presents a few empirical regularities on shadow employment. Section 2 introduces and solves the model, obtaining the various equilibrium configurations. Section 3 evaluates the comparative static properties of the equilibria and provides some numerical simulations of the model. Section 4 assesses the empirical relevance of the model, drawing on micro data from two countries with a large shadow pool, namely Brazil and Italy. Finally, section 5 briefly summarizes and concludes.

2. Shadow Facts

The consensus definition of the shadow economy is "all economic activities which contribute to the officially calculated (or observed) gross national product, but escape detection in the official estimates of GDP" (Feige 1989 and 1994; Lubell 1991; and Schneider 1994). This definition encompasses not only legal, but also illegal activities, such as trade in stolen goods, drug dealing, gambling, smuggling, etc. In this paper we confine our attention to a subset of the shadow economy, namely to legal activities. As is apparent from the above, our notion of shadow employment is one of a lawful activity were it reported to tax authorities and subject to work regulations. We focus on this (large) subset of the shadow economy as our aim is to contribute to the literature on the enforcement of labor regulations and to complement research on tax evasion, which has so far overlooked the effects of tax evasion and shadow employment on unemployment.[1]

Unfortunately, available estimates of the shadow economy do *not* disentangle legal from illegal shadow economy and rarely provide measures of shadow employment. The methods being used to measure the shadow economy either draw from *direct* inferences, that is surveys trying to elicit involvement of respondents in unregistered activities or estimates based on tax audits, or from *indirect* methods, which basically draw on the inconsistencies between different statistical sources in order to gauge the size of the underground economy. Among the latter methods, discrepancies between national income and expenditure statistics or between physical input (mainly electricity consumption) indicators of economic activity and official GDP statistics or between changes in the volumes of transactions and official GDP-GNP growth or in terms of "excess" currency demand (basically the residuals of a standard currency demand function), are the most frequently used. All the above methods have pros and cons, and the wide variance of estimates being provided is an indication of the limitations of these techniques. With these caveats in mind, let us briefly review the evidence on the size of the shadow economy, as also repeatedly summarized by Schneider (2002, 2003, 2004).

There are two key findings which are confirmed by all studies of which we are aware. The first common denominator of these "*consensus guesses*" is a marked upward trend in the size of the shadow economy. Figure 1 reproduces the (unweighted) average "shadow share" of GDP in all OECD countries for which estimates, *based on the same*

**Size of the Shadow Economy (% of GDP)
Unweighted Average over 21 OECD countries**

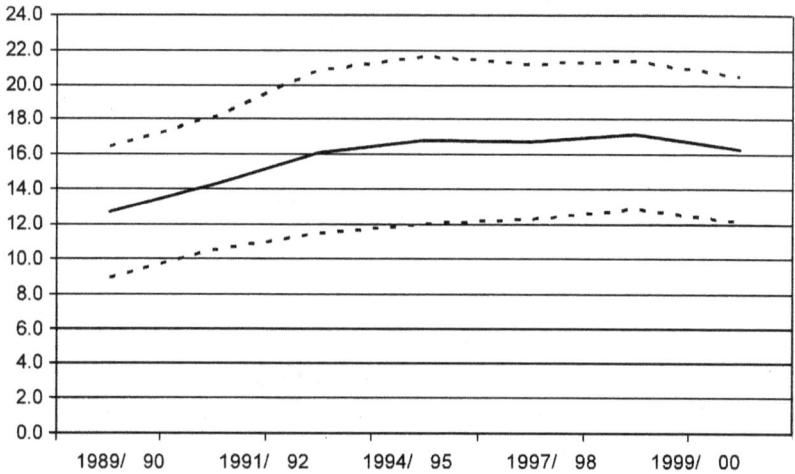

Countries: Australia, Austria, Belgium, Canada, Denmark, Finland, France, Germany, Great
Britain, Greece, Ireland, Italy, Japan, Netherlands, New Zealand, Norway, Portugal, Spain,
Sweden, Switzerland, USA
Sources: Currency demand approach, Friedrich Schneider

Figure 1
The upward trend of the shadow economy

methodology, are available for a relatively long-series. As revealed by
the dotted lines (plotting one standard deviation above and below
the unweighted cross-country average), there is no sign that this
trend has increased the cross-country dispersion in the size of the
shadow economy. The coefficient of variation of the shadow shares
actually decreased from 1989–2000 to 2002–2003 and there is not a
single country with a declining shadow share. The upward trend in
the shadow share is consistent across methods: it is found to hold
not only in estimates based on currency demand, but also on the so-
called DYMIMIC method (dynamic multiple indicators multiple
causes, Giles 1999) which estimates a set of structural equations within
which the size of the shadow economy cannot be measured directly
and then uses this predicted structural dependence in estimating the
size of the shadow economy. Also estimates of the shadow economy
in terms of headcounts point to an upward trend: Schneider (2000)
estimated that in the European area the number of persons working in

the unofficial economy doubled within the two decades from 1978 to 1998.

The second fact is the relatively low productivity of shadow jobs documented by studies relying on micro-level data. In particular, Gonzaga (2003), Almeida and Carneiro (2005), drawing on data on the informal sector in Brazil, Lacko (2000), and Commander and Rodionova (2005), focusing on transitional economies, as well as Boeri and Garibaldi (2002) and Brandolini and D'Alessio (2002), drawing on Italian data consistently document that workers engaged in shadow employment have, on average, lower educational attainments than regular workers and/or hold jobs requiring unskilled workers. The way in which shadow jobs are identified in these studies may not be neutral with respect to the productivity content of jobs in the two pools. However, the fact that low-skilled workers (or occupations) are represented in shadow employment is consistent across alternative measures of shadow employment.

Figure 2 displays the distribution of employment by educational attainment for shadow and non-shadow segments of the labor force in Italy, according to different data sources and definitions. In particular, the top panel draws on Bank of Italy data and identifies shadow employment by looking at self-reported social security records: shadow employees are those who either reported to have never paid social security contributions throughout their career (definition 1) or who report the same number of months of contributions (definition 2) during the same employment spell two years apart (which implies that they have not been paying contributions in between the two interviews).[2] Clearly definition 1 is more restrictive than definition 2. The mid-panel of Figure 2 draws on Labor Force Survey data and identifies as shadow employees those individuals who are employed according to internationally agreed, objective, definitions, but who define themselves as non-employed. Finally, the bottom panel draws on data collected by an ad-hoc Istat-Fondazione Curella survey carried out in Sicily in 1995 (Busetta and Giovannini 1998). In this context, shadow employment is identified in the individuals reporting to hold an irregular job, where irregular means not paying social security contributions, understating the actual pay in order to pay lower taxes and contributions or being altogether without a labor contract.

All data sources and measures of shadow employment suggest that workers with lower educational attainments are over-represented in the shadow pool.

Shadow Employment by Educational Attainment of the Workforce
a) Bank of Italy survey, average 1995-2002

Education	Shadow (Def.1)	Shadow (Def. 2)	Control (Def.1 and 2)	Shadow (Def. 3)	Control (Def.3)
	Δcontrib=0	Δcontrib=0 + Δcontrib <0	Δcontrib=2	No contribution at all	At least 1 year of contribution
Primary or lower	13.5	14.7	7.5	32.1	30.5
Lower secondary	35.4	33.6	27.8	31.5	27.7
Lower vocational (3 years)	6.8	6.5	9.1	4.0	6.3
Secondary school	33.8	32.0	40.8	23.9	26.4
Tertiary education	10.5	13.1	14.8	8.5	9.1

b)LFS data, Italy average 1995-2002

Education	Shadow	Regular employment
Primary or lower	38.4	15.0
Lower secondary	25.6	36.1
Lower vocational (3 years)	4.3	7.8
Secondary school	24.5	29.9
Tertiary education	7.2	11.2

c) Istat-Fondazione Curella, Sicily 1995

Education	Main job		Secondary job	
	Shadow	Regular employment	Shadow employment	Regular employment
Primary or lower	24.0	13.5	19.5	8.8
Lower secondary	27.3	26.1	20.7	17.6
Secondary school	40.3	41.9	39.0	44.1
Tertiary education	8.4	18.4	20.7	29.4

Figure 2
Shadow employment by educational attainment of the labor force

Overall, shadow employment has mainly the characteristics of "marginal shadow employment," that is, employment in low productivity jobs, rather than "development shadow employment," i.e., new jobs having the potential to become highly productive after some gestation period. In other words, "infant industry" arguments cannot be applied to justify tolerance vis-á-vis the informal sector. We are looking for deeper and empirically more relevant ("development shadow employment" seems to involve a tiny fraction of unregistered employment) explanations for the weak repression of shadow employment.

3.   A Two Sectors Model with Sorting

3.1   *Shadow Employment and Worker's Sorting*

We consider an economy with a measure one of heterogenous workers
and two sectors. The worker type is indicated by x, where x refers to
labor market productivity and its value is drawn from a continuous
cumulative distribution function F with support $[x_{min}, x_{max}]$. x is a fixed
time invariant worker characteristic, with $x_{min} > 0$.

There are two sectors in the labor market: the regular sector and the
shadow sector. The gross value of production of each worker is indicated with px where p is a productivity component common to all jobs
and x is an idiosyncratic component. To keep the notation simple, we
initially assume that $p = 1$, and we consider changes in p in the numerical simulations. In the regular sector firms pay a production tax τ in
every period in which they employ a worker. In the shadow sector the
tax is evaded and there is an instantaneous monitoring rate equal to ρ.
Conditional on being monitored in the shadow sector, the shadow job
is destroyed. Both regular and shadow jobs are exogenously destroyed
at rate λ.[3]

Firms can freely post a vacancy in either sector. We focus on single
jobs, and each firm is made of one job. Posting a vacancy in the regular
sector costs k_g per period while in the shadow sector costs k_b. There
is free entry of firms in both sectors and the equilibrium value of a
vacancy is driven down to zero. Job creation characterizes the labor
demand side of the model.

The labor supply is governed by the workers' sorting behavior.
Workers are endowed with a unit of time and freely decide whether it
is optimal to search and work in the shadow sector or in the legal sector.
Entering a sector is a full time activity, and workers cannot simultaneously work and/or search in both sectors. In the legal sector there is a
specific unemployed income (the unemployment benefits) which is not
available in the shadow sector.

Labor markets are imperfect, and there are market frictions in each
sector. We follow the main matching literature (Pissarides 2000) and
assume that the meeting of vacant jobs and unemployed workers is
regulated by a matching function with constant returns to scale. Different matching functions exist in different sectors. In what follows we
let with v_g and v_b the number of vacancies in both sectors, and u_g and u_b

the number of unemployed job seekers. The matching function in each sector is indicated with

$$m^i(u^i, v^i) \qquad i = g, b$$

with positive first derivative and negative second derivative. As in the traditional matching models with constant returns to scale, the transition rate depends on the relative number of traders and it is indicated with $\theta^i = v^i/u^i$. Specifically, the transition rate for firms is indicated with $q^i(\theta^i) = m(u^i, v^i)/v^i$ with $q'(\theta^i) < 0$, while the transition rate for workers is indicated with $\alpha'^i(\theta^i) = \theta^i q(\theta^i)$ with $\alpha' > 0$.

Successful matches in each sector enjoy a pure economic rent, and we let wages be the outcome of a Nash bargaining problem, with workers getting a fraction β of the total surplus. We assume, for simplicity, that β is identical in the two sectors.

We solve the model in three steps. First we present the value functions and the asset equations, and define the key equilibrium conditions. Next, we solve the workers' sorting behavior in partial equilibrium, taking as given job creation (the labor demand side of the model) and the transition rate in each market. We then focus on job creation taking worker behavior as given. Finally we discuss the general equilibrium of the model, and we perform a set of numerical simulations.

3.2 Discussion

Before proceeding to the solution of the model, a few important issues need to be discussed. Our theory does not deal with the optimal enforcement of legal activity. Within the model, enforcement takes place through the combination of random detection (the monitoring rate ρ) and finite punishment (in the form of job destruction). The influential analysis of Becker (1968) has shown that, from the social welfare standpoint, it is always optimal to substitute a higher fine for a lower probability of detection, and that fines should be optimally set at their maximum level. In such optimal enforcement setting, shadow employment would not be observed in equilibrium. While the Becker argument is clear and convincing, we rarely observe such harsh punishment, possibly because important market imperfections reduce the size of the optimal fine. Davidson, Martin, and Wilson (2004) have recently shown that with capital market imperfections and/or asymmetric information, the optimal fine lies below the maximum level. Even though we do not explicitly take into account these features, we believe that our realistic enforcement rule can be rationalized in such more complex models, which are nevertheless left to further research.

The difference between legal and shadow jobs considered in the model focuses only on tax compliance, and does not consider the possibility that jobs in the two sectors differ along other important dimensions, such as capital intensity, health insurance, and firm sponsored training. In reality, workers' sorting decision probably takes into account various job characteristics, and there is evidence that legal jobs provide more training. We believe that it is technically possible to provide such key extensions, without affecting the main results of the paper.

Our model considers shadow employment as a full-time activity and does not allow workers to hold multiple jobs (i.e., a regular job alongside a shadow job). In terms of flows, the model ignores on the job search and direct transitions from shadow to legal employment without intervening unemployment spells. Some of these features were considered by Boeri and Garibaldi (2002) in a matching model with fixed labor supply, without any scope for worker sorting, the key feature of this paper.

3.3   Value Functions

The value of a filled job in the legal sector with productivity x reads

$$rJ^g(x) = x - w^g(x) - \tau + \lambda[V^g - J^g(x)]$$

where τ is the tax rate, V^g is the value of a vacancy and r is the pure discount rate. Jobs are destroyed at the exogenous rate λ, and $w_g(x)$ is the wage rate.

Unemployment is a full time activity, and workers cannot work in the shadow sector during an unemployment spell. The value of unemployment in the legal sector for a worker of type x is

$$rU^g(x) = b + \alpha^g(\theta)[W^g(x) - U^g(x)]$$

where b is the specific unemployed income (the unemployment benefits), and $W^g(x)$ is the value of the job for a type x. The value of a job in the legal sector is

$$rW^g(x) = w^g(x) + \lambda[U^g(x) - W^g(x)].$$

Posting vacancies in the legal sector is costly, and yields a per period return equal to $-k_g$. Conditional on meeting a worker, at rate $q^g(\theta^g)$, the firms gets the expected value of a job. In formula, its expression reads

$$rV = -k_g + q^g(\theta^g) \, [E \, [J(z) \mid z \in \Omega] - V]$$

where the expectation is taken with respect to the productivity of workers who search in the legal sector. The expression Ω refers to the support of workers who search in the legal sector.

The value functions for jobs in the shadow sector are similarly defined. The main differences is that in the shadow sectors firms do not pay the production tax τ and the job is monitored and destroyed at rate ρ. Further, there is no specific unemployed income b. The four value functions read

$$rJ^b(x) = x - w^b(x) + (\lambda + \rho)[V^b - J^b(x)]$$

$$rW^b(x) = w^b(x) + (\lambda + \rho)[U^b(x) - W^b(x)]$$

$$rU^b(x) = \alpha^b(\theta^b)[W^b(x) - U^b(x)]$$

$$rV^b = -k_b + q^b(\theta^b) \, [E \, [J^b(z) \mid z \in \Omega^c] - V^b]$$

where Ω^c is the support of workers who search in the shadow sector.

Wages in each sector and in each job are the outcome of a bilateral matching problem and workers get a fraction β of the total surplus so that

$$[W^i(x) - U^i(x)] = \beta \, [W^i(x) - U^i(x) + J^i(x) - V^i] \qquad i = b, g.$$

For simplicity we have assumed that the fraction of the surplus is the same in both sectors.

3.4 Equilibrium Conditions

There are three key equilibrium conditions.

• Free entry and job creation in the legal sector (JC^g), which implies that the value of a vacancy be zero.

$$V^g = 0$$

This equation will determine market tightness in the legal sector θ^g.

• Free entry and job creation in the shadow sector (JC^b), which implies that the value of a vacancy be zero.

$$V^b = 0$$

This equation will determine market tightness in the shadow sector θ^b.

• Workers' sorting (*Sort*). If we assume that workers' sorting satisfies the reservation property, (a feature that holds in equilibrium) the labor supply is described by the marginal worker with productivity R, where R is the productivity level for which the worker is indifferent between the two sectors, so that

$U^g(R) = U^b(R)$.

Using the reservation property, the three key conditions are

$$\alpha^b(\theta^b)[W^b(R) - U^b(R)] = b + \alpha^g(\theta^g)[W^g(R) - U^g(R)] \qquad \text{(Sort)}$$

$$\frac{k_g}{q^b(\theta^b)} = \frac{\int_R^{x^u} J^g(z)dF(z)}{1 - F(R)} \qquad \text{(JC}^g\text{)}$$

and

$$\frac{k_b}{q^b(\theta^b)} = \frac{\int_{x_l}^R J^b(z)dF(z)}{F(R)} \qquad \text{(JC}^b\text{)}$$

The first condition says that the marginal worker is indifferent between searching for a job in the legal or the shadow sector. The second condition says that the total search costs in the legal sector are identical to the expected value of a job. The last condition has a similar interpretation, but refers to the shadow sector. The system determines the three endogenous variables θ^g, θ^b, and R.

3.5 Stocks

The model is closed by determining the stock of workers into the four possible labor market states: unemployment and employment in each of the two sectors. If we indicate with u^i the stock of unemployed in each sector and with n^i the stock of employed, we have

$u^g + u^b + n^g + n^b = 1$.

Workers' sorting implies that the share of workers in the shadow sectors is $F(R)$ while the remaining $1 - F(R)$ workers search in the legal sector. Employed workers in the shadow sector lose their job at rate $\lambda + \rho$ while they find jobs at a rate $\alpha^b(\theta^b)$ so that the balance flow condition for unemployment in the shadow sector is

$\alpha^b(\theta^b)u^b = (\lambda + \rho)(F(R) - u^b)$

where $n^b = F(R) - u^b$. Unemployment and employment in the shadow sector read respectively

$$u^b = \frac{(\lambda + \rho)F(R)}{\lambda + \rho + \alpha^b(\theta^b)}$$

$$n^b = \frac{\alpha^b(\theta^b)F(R)}{\lambda + \rho + \alpha^b(\theta^b)}$$

In the legal sector, the unemployment and the employment rate are respectively

$$u^g = \frac{\lambda(1 - F(R))}{\lambda + \alpha^b(\theta^b)}$$

$$n^g = \frac{\alpha^b(\theta^b)(1 - F(R))}{\lambda + \alpha^b(\theta^b)}$$

We are now in a position to formally define the equilibrium of the model.

Definition 1 *Equilibrium. The equilibrium is obtained by a triple R, θ^g, and θ^b and a vector of stock variables that satisfy the value functions J^i, W^i, U^i, V^i (i = g, b), Nash Bargaining, and (1) Workers' sorting, (2) Job Creation in the legal sector, (3) Job Creation in the shadow sector, (4) Balance flow conditions.*

3.6   Solving the Workers' Sorting Behavior

The surplus of a job in each sector is defined as the sum of the worker's and firm value of being on the job, net of the respective outside options, so that

$$S^i(x) = J^i(x) - V^i + W^i(x) - U^i(x).$$

Using the value functions previously defined, as well as the free entry condition (which drives the value of a vacancy down to zero), the surplus of a match for a legal job with productivity x is

$$(r + \lambda)S^g(x) = x - \tau - b - \alpha^g(\theta^g)[W^g(x) - U^g(x)].$$

Recalling that wages get a fraction β of the total surplus, the previous expression reads

$$S^g(x)=\frac{x-\tau-b}{r+\lambda+\beta\alpha^g(\theta^g)}$$

with $S' = 1/r + \lambda + \beta\theta q(\theta)$. Proceeding similarly, the surplus in the shadow sector is

$$S^b(x)=\frac{x}{r+\lambda+\rho+\beta\alpha^b(\theta^b)}.$$

In partial equilibrium, the job finding rates a^i are constant, and the surplus from the job is an increasing linear function of the match specific productivity x.

The surplus from the job can be used to obtain an expression for the value of unemployment, whose expression is given by

$$U^b(x)=\frac{\alpha^b(\theta^b)\beta x}{r+\lambda+\rho+\beta\alpha^b(\theta^b)}$$

$$U^g(x)=b+\frac{\alpha^g(\theta^g)\beta[x-\tau-b]}{r+\lambda+\beta\alpha^g(\theta^g)}.$$

Figure 3 shows the two value functions in partial equilibrium. The differences in the two curves are driven by the intercept (which is negative in the legal sector) and the slope. We make two key assumptions in this respect:

• **Taxation is large enough relative to unemployment benefits.** We formally assume that $b(r + \lambda) < \tau\alpha^g\beta$. This implies that the intercept of U^g is negative in Figure 3.

• **Monitoring is large enough.** We formally assume that $\alpha^g\rho\beta + (r + \lambda)\beta(\alpha^g - \alpha^b) > 0$. This implies that the value function of U^g is steeper than U^b.

From the value functions, we can get an expression for the reservation productivity. The reservation value R, if it exists, is the crossing point of the two lines. Its formal expression, when considering α^g and α^b exogenous and constant is

$$R=\frac{[\tau\alpha^g\beta-b(r+\lambda)](r+\lambda+\rho+\beta\alpha^b)}{\alpha^g\rho\beta+(r+\lambda)\beta(\alpha^g-\alpha^b)}.$$

Existence in partial equilibrium requires $R > 0$, and the two key assumptions above ensure that R is positive. The equilibrium we are

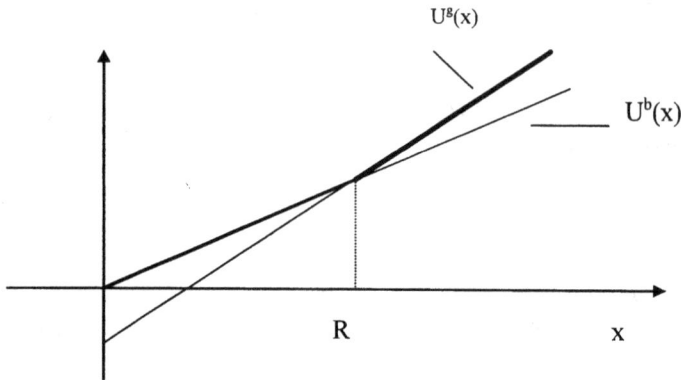

Figure 3
Workers' sorting in partial equilibrium (with constant job finding rate)

considering implies that shadow jobs are occupied by workers with low skills, in line with the evidence discussed in section 2 of this paper. This is a key premise of our theoretical analysis

Remark 2 *Shadow jobs are occupied by relatively low skilled workers.*

There are several results in the partial equilibrium setting, and are graphically obtained by shifts and movements of the two lines

• An *increase in unemployment benefits* reduces the reservation productivity R, so that more people search in the legal market. At given job finding rates, an increase in unemployment benefits increases legal employment. This is the standard entitlement effects of unemployment benefits, a labor supply phenomenon that was first noted by Burdett and Mortensen (1982) and Atkinson (1991) and recently received a lot of attention (Boeri 2000; Fredrikson and Holmlund 2001; Garibaldi and Wasmer 2005). Formally, it is obtained by noting that

$$\frac{\partial R}{\partial b} = -\frac{(r+\lambda)(r+\lambda+\rho+\beta\alpha^b)}{\alpha^g \rho\beta + (r+\lambda)\beta(\alpha^g - \alpha^b)} < 0.$$

• An *increase in taxation* increases shadow employment. This is the standard mechanism that taxation moves people away from the regular sector into the shadow employment, as noted by the work of Schneider (2002) and recently by Davis and Henrekson (2004). Formally, it is obtained by observing that

$$\frac{\partial R}{\partial \tau} = \frac{\alpha^g \beta (r + \lambda + \rho + \beta \alpha^b)}{\alpha^g \rho \beta + (r + \lambda)\beta(\alpha^g - \alpha^b)} > 0.$$

- An *increase in the monitoring rate* reduces shadow employment. An increase in the monitoring rate reduces the return from shadow employment and induces people to search in the legal market. Formally, this result is obtained by noting that

$$\frac{\partial R}{\partial \rho} = \frac{[b(r+\lambda) - \tau\alpha^g \beta]\alpha^b \beta(r+\lambda+\beta\alpha^g)}{[(r+\lambda)\beta(\alpha^b - \alpha^g) - \alpha^g \rho \beta]^2} < 0 \ .$$

3.7 Labor Demand and Job Creation

To solve for job creation we need to evaluate the expected value of a job. We first focus on legal jobs. After an integration by parts, and making use of the sharing rule, the integral in equation JC^g can be written as

$$\int_R^{x^u} S(z)dF(z) = S(x^u) - S(R) + (1 - F(R))S(R) - S'(R)\int_R^{x^u} F(z)dz$$

$$\frac{\int_R^{x^u}(1 - F(z))dz}{r + \lambda + \beta\theta^g q(\theta^g)} + \frac{(1 - F(z))[R - \tau - b]}{r + \lambda + \beta\theta^g q(\theta^g)}$$

so that the job creation condition is

$$\frac{k_g[r + \lambda + \beta\alpha^g(\theta^g)]}{q(\theta^g)(1 - \beta)} = \frac{\int_R^{x^u}(1 - F(z))dz}{1 - F(R)} + [R - \tau - b] \ . \tag{1}$$

Proceeding similarly for the expected value of bad jobs, the free entry condition reads

$$\frac{k_b[r + \lambda + \beta\alpha^h(\theta^b)]}{q(\theta^b)(1 - \beta)} = R - \frac{\int_{x_l}^{R} F(z)dz}{F(R)} \ . \tag{2}$$

Market tightness θ^i and the associated job finding rates α_i depend on the various parameters, as well as on the workers' sorting behavior. Most parameters have a direct effect on job creation, plus an indirect effect via the reservation productivity R. Formally, we can write

$\alpha^g(\theta^g) = \alpha^g(R(.), b, r, \lambda, \beta))$

$\alpha^b(\theta^b) = \alpha^b(R(.), \rho, \lambda, \beta))$

where the symbol $R()$ suggests that R is itself an endogenous variable. Some important comparative static results follow.

• *An increase in the reservation productivity R increases market tightness and the job finding rates in both sectors.* An increase in R increases the average quality of the workforce in both sectors, so that firms naturally respond by posting more vacancies per unemployed. This result is important, and shows how sorting affects job creation. Formally, it is obtained by noting that $\partial\theta^g/\partial R > 0$ and $\partial\theta b/\partial R > 0$ since

$$\frac{k_g}{(1-\beta)} \frac{\beta\alpha'^g(\theta^g)q^g(\theta^g) - q'^g(\theta^g)(r+\lambda+\beta\alpha^g(\theta^g))}{q^g(\theta^g)^2} \frac{\partial\theta^g}{\partial R} = \frac{f(R)\int_R^{x^u} F(z)dz}{(1-F(R))^2}$$

$$\frac{k_b}{(1-\beta)} \frac{\beta\alpha'^b(\theta^b)q^b(\theta^b) - q'^b(\theta^b)(r+\lambda+\beta\alpha^b(\theta^b))}{q^b(\theta^b)^2} \frac{\partial\theta^b}{\partial R} = \frac{f(R)\int_{x^l}^R F(z)dz}{F(R)^2}$$

where the LHS is positive since $q' < 0$.

• *An increase in unemployment benefits b,* at given reservation productivity R, reduces job creation in the legal sector. This is the standard adverse effect of unemployment income on job creation, an effect that works mainly through the wage rule.

• *An increase in taxation,* at given reservation productivity R, reduces job creation in the legal sector. This is also a textbook adverse labor demand effect of taxation.

• *An increase in the monitoring rate ρ,* at given reservation productivity R, reduces job creation in the shadow sector. Higher monitoring rate acts as an increase in the destruction rate on shadow jobs.

3.8   General Equilibrium

The general equilibrium of the model is obtained by solving for the triple R, θ^g, θ^b that simultaneously satisfy Sort JC^b and JC^g. One way to solve for the general equilibrium result is to consider the workers' sorting condition by explicitly considering the relationship between the job finding rates and the reservation productivity. This is equivalent to solving

$$\frac{\alpha^b(R,.)\beta R}{r+\lambda+\rho+\beta\alpha^b(R,.)} = b + \frac{\alpha^g(R,.)\beta[R-\tau-b]}{r+\lambda+\beta\alpha^g(R,.)} \tag{3}$$

where the expression $\alpha^b(R, .)$ and $\alpha^g(R, .)$ are consistent with the job creation conditions. Both sides of the expression are increasing functions of R. The difference with respect to the partial equilibrium result is that the expressions for the value of unemployment in equation (3) are no longer simple linear function, but they are both increasing functions of R. To understand this, consider the effects of an increase in R on the value of unemployment in both sectors; there are two effects at work.

• First, there is a positive *surplus effect*. This is analogous to the effect analyzed in partial equilibrium. An increase in R increases the value of unemployment in both sectors, but has a larger effect on the legal sector in light of the difference in the slope and the presence of ρ in the shadow sector.

• Second, there is a *job creation* effect. An increase in R increases the job finding rate in both sectors, since the average value of the workforce increases.

As both effects reinforce each other in a non-linear fashion, multiple equilibria cannot be ruled out ex-ante. This should not be surprising, since multiple equilibria in matching models with double heterogeneity are a standard feature (Albrecht and Vroman 2002).

Remark 3 *Multiple equilibria cannot be ruled out, and depend on the distribution of productivity.*

Since both sides are increasing and non-linear functions of R, there is no guarantee that the equilibrium is unique.

In the simulations that follow, where we use a distribution for the productivity x that is negative exponential, there is a unique equilibrium. In any case, if there were two equilibria, there would be different implications for the distribution of skills across the two sectors, with a perverse equilibrium that implies that high productivity workers enter the shadow sector. In Figure 4, the equilibrium of point A is consistent with the skilled distribution that we highlighted in the comparative static section. The feature of such an equilibrium can be described as follows

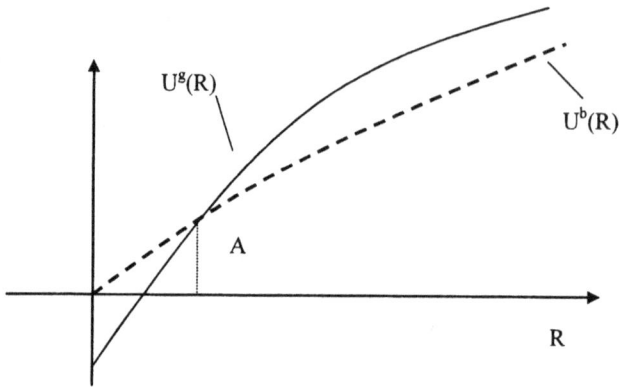

Figure 4
The general equilibrium

$$U^g(R^*) = U^b(R^*)$$

$$U'^g(R^*) > U'^b(R^*)$$

where the second condition ensures that the value function of the legal sector is the steepest one in the equilibrium point.

4. Simulations and Comparative Static

The comparative static results in the general equilibrium are not straightforward, since they combine the effect of each parameter on the labor demand and the labor supply of the model.

Consider the effects of taxation. An increase in taxes tend to push jobs into the shadow sector, and to decrease the value of each job. This is a standard result that reduces job creation. Yet, the resulting increase in R improves the average quality of the workforce in the legal sector, with a positive effect on job creation. As a result, the total effect on job creation may be ambiguous.

Consider an increase in the monitoring rate. On the one hand, it reduces R from the labor supply standpoint and reduces job creation in the shadow sector. Both effects reinforce each other, and tend to reduce R. On the other hand, the reduction in R, by increasing the average productivity of workers in the legal sector, feeds back on job creation in the legal sector, and tends to reduce R. This suggests that an increase in the monitoring rate can reduce job creation in the good sector.

Similar logical arguments follow for the other comparative static exercise. The increase in unemployment benefits reduces (in partial equilibrium) the number of people in the shadow sector by reducing R. The fall in R induces a feed back effect on the average quality of the workforce in the legal sector and, from the labor demand side, a reduction in job creation.

4.1   Baseline Specification

The baseline specification of the model is described in Table 1. With respect to the model presented in the equations, the empirical specification of the productivity is px, where x is the idiosyncratic component of productivity and p is an aggregate component. Further, in addition

Table 1
Calibration

Parameters	Notation	Legal	Shadow
Discount rate	r	0.03	
Separation rate	λ	0.15	0.15
Unemployed income	b	0.10	0.00
Firing tax	F	0.10	0.00
Matching elasticity	η^i	0.50	0.50
Monitoring rate	ρ	0.00	0.06
Production tax	τ	0.20	0.00
Matching function constant	A^i	0.50	0.50
Workers' surplus share	β	0.50	0.50
Common productivity	p	1.50	1.50
Search costs	k^i	0.40	0.40
Equilibrium values			
Sorting productivity	R	0.24	
Market tightness	θ^i	2.70	0.16
Job finding rate	α^i	0.82	0.28
Aggregate statistics			
Unemployment	u^i	12.10	7.52
Employment	n^i	66.23	14.15
Shadow rate	s	17.60	
Average wage	w^i	1.37	0.12

(a) Distribution is exponential with parameter $B = 1.00$.
Source: Authors' calculation.

to a production tax τ, the simulations consider also a firing tax T, to be paid only in the legal sector conditionally on a job separation (when the shock λ strikes).

The distribution is negative exponential. Figure 5 reports the difference between $U^g(R) - U^b(R)$ for different values of the reservation productivity. The general equilibrium is described by the crossing of such difference with the zero line. The figure clearly shows that there is a single crossing and that the equilibrium is unique. The baseline parameterization is described and reported in Table 1. Most parameters are standard in the literature (notably a 0.5 value for the bargaining share and the matching elasticity). The search costs correspond to 25 percent of the value of the labor product, a value that is roughly consistent with the structural estimates provided by Yashiv (2000).

The shadow rate, defined as the ratio between employment in the shadow sector and total employment (including both n^g and n^b at the denominator) is around 14 percent. We perform various comparative static exercises.

4.2   Changes in Aggregate Conditions

We study the effects of the increase in p on the general equilibrium of the model. The results are reported in Table 2. With the exception of p, all the other parameters are identical to those of Table 1.

An increase in aggregate productivity increases employment and reduces unemployment in the legal sector. Further, it reduces employment in the shadow sector. This is one of the key macroeconomic results of the paper. Unemployment and shadow employment are positively correlated across different states of the macroeconomy.

Remark 4 *Unemployment and shadow employment are two faces of the same coin. Worse aggregate conditions induce an increase in both unemployment and shadow employment (as well as its shadow rate).*

The logic of this result can be expressed as follows. The increase in p tends to increase job creation and market tightness. Simultaneously, the increase in p induces a fall in the marginal productivity R, so that average quality worsens in both sectors. This tends to reduce job creation. The second effect appears to be quantitatively more important in the legal sector, since the productivity is proportional to x.

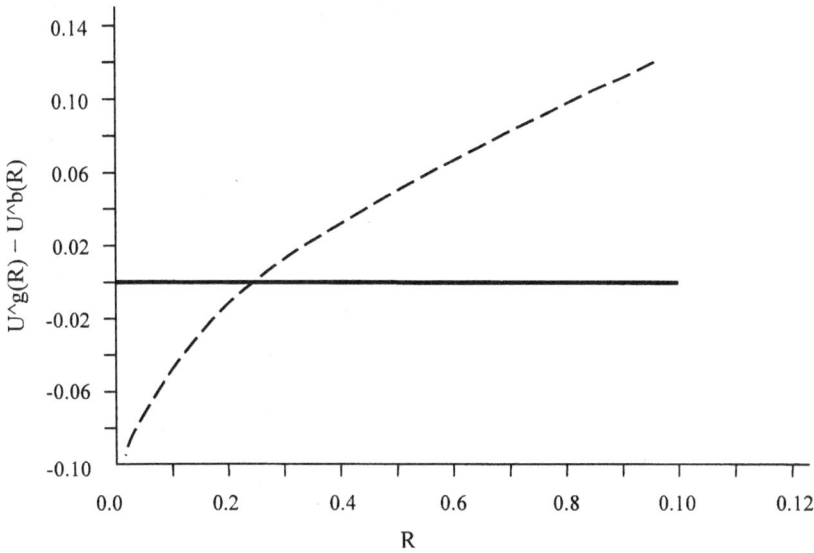

Figure 5
General equilibrium with exponential distribution

Table 2 shows that wage differentials between the legal and the shadow sector (the shadow wage gap) are quantitatively more important when aggregate business conditions are good.

Remark 5 *Wage differentials should be larger in less depressed regions.*

There are two adjustment mechanisms behind this result. First, a larger p directly affects match productivity inducing an increase in wages per any given x. Second, the rise in aggregate productivity involves a reduction of the productivity threshold so that the average quality of matches in both sectors decline. This tends to depress average wages in both sectors. As the aggregate shock is multiplicative, its direct (positive) effects on wages are quantitatively more important in the legal sector than in the shadow sector, whilst the indirect effects are nearly symmetric due to the common threshold, R.

4.3 Changes in Taxation and Regulations

We study the effects of the increase in τ on the general equilibrium of the model. The results are reported in Table 3. All the other parameters

Table 2
Changes in aggregate conditions

p	R	θ_b	θ_g	u_b	u_g	n_b	n_g	s	x_g	x_b	$\bar{w}_g$	$\bar{w}_b$
1.50	0.24	0.16	2.70	7.52	12.10	14.15	66.23	17.60	1.24	0.12	1.37	0.12
1.61	0.23	0.16	2.92	7.03	11.90	13.22	67.85	16.31	1.23	0.11	1.46	0.12
1.73	0.21	0.16	3.15	6.60	11.70	12.40	69.30	15.18	1.21	0.10	1.55	0.12
1.84	0.20	0.16	3.39	6.22	11.51	11.68	70.60	14.19	1.20	0.10	1.64	0.12
1.95	0.19	0.16	3.62	5.88	11.32	11.03	71.77	13.33	1.19	0.09	1.73	0.12

u_g and u_b are the unemployment rates respectively in the legal and shadow sector.
n_g, E_{n_b} are respectively legal and shadow employment.
x_g and x_b are the average idyosincratic productivity in the legal and shadow employment.
$\bar{w}_g$ and $\bar{w}_b$ are the average wages legal and shadow employment.
Source: Authors' calculation.

Table 3
Changes in total taxation conditions

τ	R	e_b	θ_g	u_b	u_g	n_b	n_g	s	x_g	x_b	$\bar{w}_g$	$\bar{w}_b$
0.200	0.24	0.16	2.70	7.52	12.10	14.15	66.23	17.60	1.24	0.12	1.366	0.120
0.205	0.26	0.18	2.73	7.70	11.87	15.08	65.35	18.75	1.26	0.12	1.380	0.128
0.210	0.27	0.19	2.77	7.83	11.62	16.05	64.44	19.94	1.27	0.13	1.395	0.136
0.215	0.29	0.21	2.80	8.06	11.38	17.06	63.50	21.18	1.29	0.14	1.411	0.144
0.220	0.31	0.22	2.84	8.24	11.12	18.10	62.53	22.45	1.31	0.15	1.427	0.153

u_g and u_b are the unemployment rates respectively in the legal and shadow sector.
n_g, E_{n_b} are respectively legal and shadow employment.
$\bar{w}_g$ and $\bar{w}_b$ are the average wages legal and shadow employment.
Source: Authors' calculation.

are identical to those of Table 1. More taxes and regulations (see Table 4) increase shadow employment and reduce legal employment. This is the standard result of Schneider (2002). It is also consistent with the work of Davis and Henrekson (2005).

The effect of taxation on unemployment is quantitatively very modest, since there are two countervailing effects at work. There is the indirect effect on job creation via the increase in the reservation productivity (reducing unemployment) plus the direct effect of taxes on market tightness in the legal sector (increasing unemployment).

Changes in regulation (through the firing tax) are qualitatively analogous to the effects of taxation.

4.4   Changes in the Monitoring Rate

We study the effects of the increase in ρ on the general equilibrium of the model. The results are reported in Table 5. An increase in monitoring intensity reduces the shadow rate, but it increases unemployment.

We view this result as extremely important, since it highlights one of the key reasons why governments may be reluctant to repress the shadow sector. The associated increase in unemployment is politically costly and thus avoided by utility maximizing politicians.

4.5   Changes in Unemployed Income

We now consider the effects of an increase in b (see Table 6). An increase in unemployed income reduces the shadow rate, and increases unemployment. Yet, the increase in participation in the legal sector increases legal employment and reduces shadow employment. Note that market tightness falls in both sectors.

The increase in unemployed income can be considered as a policy for uncovering (as opposed to repressing) shadow activities. Various difficulties are likely to exist in reality in enforcing this policy (unemployment income requires larger taxation and very good monitoring). Yet, it can be quite effective.

5.   Empirical Relevance

Our model implies: (1) a positive cross-sectional and time-series correlation between the size of the shadow sector and unemployment (the two phenomena are just two faces of the same coin), (2) a "shadow

Table 4
Changes in firing taxes

T	R	θ_b	θ_g	u_b	u_g	n_b	n_g	s	x_g	x_b	$\bar{w}_g$	$\bar{w}_b$
0.100	0.24	0.16	2.70	7.52	12.10	14.15	66.23	17.60	1.24	0.12	1.366	0.120
0.113	0.25	0.17	2.71	7.59	12.01	14.50	65.90	18.03	1.25	0.12	1.372	0.123
0.125	0.25	0.17	2.72	7.66	11.92	14.85	65.57	18.46	1.25	0.12	1.378	0.126
0.138	0.26	0.18	2.73	7.72	11.84	15.20	65.24	18.90	1.26	0.12	1.384	0.129
0.150	0.27	0.18	2.75	7.79	11.75	15.56	64.90	19.34	1.27	0.13	1.390	0.132

u_g and u_b are the unemployment rates respectively in the legal and shadow sector.
n_g, E_{n_b}, are respectively legal and shadow employment.
$\bar{w}_g$ and $\bar{w}_b$ are the average wages legal and shadow employment.
Source: Authors' calculation.

Table 5
Changes in monitoring intensity

ρ	R	θ_b	θ_g	u_b	u_g	n_b	n_g	s	x_g	x_b	$\bar{w}_g$	$\bar{w}_b$
0.06	0.24	0.16	2.70	7.52	12.10	14.15	66.23	17.60	1.24	0.12	1.37	0.12
0.07	0.22	0.13	2.62	7.31	12.53	12.48	67.67	15.57	1.22	0.11	1.33	0.11
0.09	0.20	0.11	2.57	7.17	12.86	11.24	68.73	14.05	1.20	0.10	1.31	0.10
0.10	0.19	0.10	2.53	7.08	13.11	10.27	69.54	12.87	1.19	0.09	1.29	0.09
0.11	0.18	0.08	2.50	7.01	13.31	9.50	70.18	11.92	1.18	0.09	1.28	0.08

u_g and u_b are the unemployment rates respectively in the legal and shadow sector.
n_g, E_{nb}, are respectively legal and shadow employment.
$\bar{w}_g$ and $\bar{w}_b$ are the average wages legal and shadow employment.
Source: Authors' calculation.

Table 6
Changes in unemployed income

b	R	θ_b	θ_g	u_b	u_g	n_b	n_g	s	x_g	x_b	$\bar{w}_g$	$\bar{w}_b$
0.100	0.24	0.16	2.70	7.52	12.10	14.15	66.23	17.60	1.24	0.12	1.366	0.120
0.104	0.24	0.16	2.67	7.46	12.20	13.85	66.49	17.24	1.24	0.12	1.360	0.118
0.108	0.24	0.15	2.65	7.40	12.29	13.56	66.75	16.88	1.24	0.11	1.355	0.116
0.111	0.23	0.15	2.63	7.34	12.39	13.27	67.01	16.53	1.23	0.11	1.349	0.113
0.115	0.23	0.15	2.61	7.27	12.49	12.97	67.27	16.17	1.23	0.11	1.343	0.111

u_g and u_b are the unemployment rates respectively in the legal and shadow sector.
n_g, E_{n_b}, are respectively legal and shadow employment.
$\bar{w}_g$ and $\bar{w}_b$, are the average wages legal and shadow employment.
Source: Authors' calculation.

wage gap" that is larger in countries-regions and years in which unemployment is lower, (3) a shadow employment that is increasing in taxation and labor market regulations, and (4) that tighter monitoring increases unemployment. From a political economy perspective, the latter result implies a lax enforcement of regulations in high-unemployment regions.

The purpose of this section is to evaluate the empirical relevance of (1), (2) and (4). Implication (3) is common to other models of the shadow economy and holds in many cross-sectional studies, as reviewed by Schneider (2002).

5.1 Two Faces of the Same Coin?

Figure 6 documents the correlation between the size of the shadow economy and the non-employment rate across countries and Figure 7 across Italian regions, in both cases over average period data. In particular, Figure 6 displays, on the vertical axis, the cross-country comparable estimates of the shadow economy over GDP provided by Schneider (2004) and, on the horizontal axis, non-employment rates (unemployed and inactive as a fraction of the working age population) obtained from harmonized Labour Force Survey (LFS) data. Regional non-employment rates are also obtained from the (Italian) LFS, while the regional estimates of shadow employment are drawn from Istat. The latter are provided in terms of full-time equivalents (ULA, "unità di lavoro equivalenti") and are estimated building on the difference between survey-based employment and employment levels, as computed on the basis of administrative (social security records) as well as estimates of illegal employment of foreign workers.[4]

The correlation is striking in both cases: the cross-country correlation is .7 with a t-statistic of 4.76; the cross-regional correlation is .94 with a t-statistic of 11.79. It holds also when shadow employment is broken down by broad sectors, e.g., it is not a byproduct of the specialization of Southern regions in sectors (e.g., agriculture) where shadow employment is larger. There is also no tendency over time to a reduction in regional differentials in shadow rates: they were in 1995 roughly as large as ten years earlier.

Unfortunately, there are no long series of shadow employment and unemployment from which to assess their pairwise correlation over time. Figure 8 hints at comovements between the shadow rate and unemployment in Italy. The shadow rate initially rose with unemployment and then, more recently declined together with unemployment.

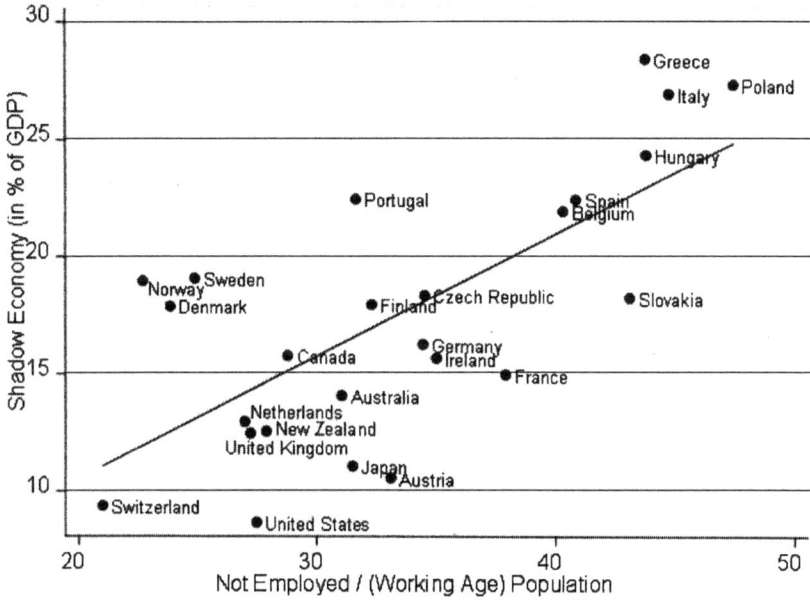

Figure 6
The size of the shadow economy and non-employment

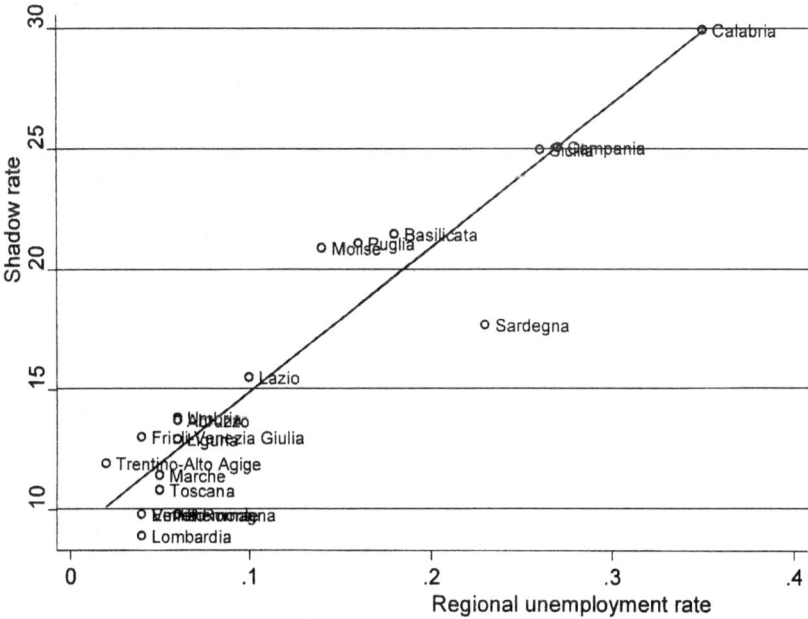

Figure 7
Shadow employment and unemployment across Italian regions

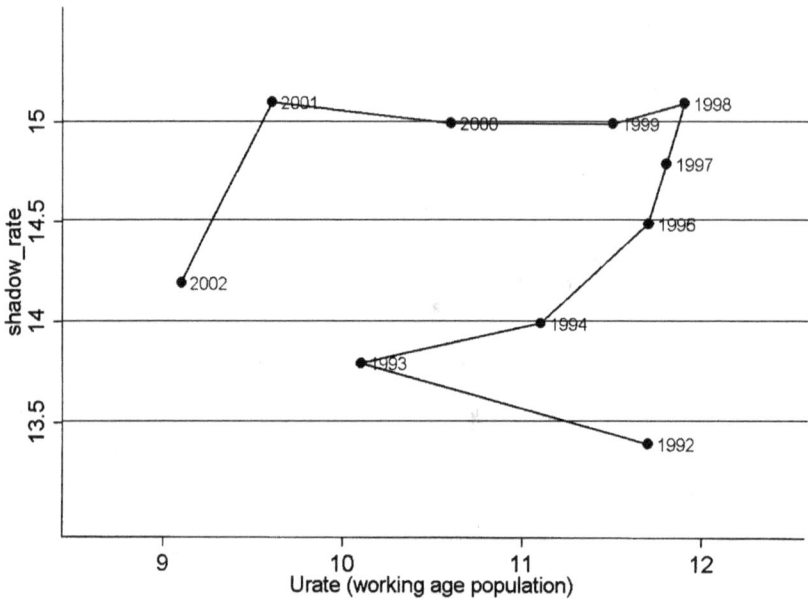

Figure 8
Unemployment and shadow employment over time in Italy

All these correlations are consistent with the implications of our model and can be rationalized by the fact that positive macroeconomic shocks or greater efficiency in a region increases job creation and reduces the reservation productivity level at which jobs turn into formal jobs. However, given the size and statistical significance of correlations, one may think that they are a mere statistical artifact, related to the way in which the two measures are defined. As discussed in the Annex, a spurious correlation may be induced between shadow employment and the unemployment rate, when shadow employment is wrongly classified as unemployment by Labor Force Statistics. The large unemployment rates observed also among prime-age men in Southern Italian regions suggest that LFS data may indeed mis-classify jobs in the shadow sector. Unfortunately, estimates of the shadow economy generally come from statistical sources which are silent on labor market aggregates. When LFS data are used to measure shadow employment (e.g., as done in Table 2), they either just scrap the surface of the phenomenon (the number are too small to achieve regional representation) or concentrate only on the subset of shadow employment which is not mis-classified by LFS statistics. Hence, there is no way to map shadow employment into the different LFS aggregates.

An important exception is the PME (Monthly Employment) survey carried out in six Brazilian metropolitan areas since 1982. The survey design is similar to the CPS in the U.S. and includes a question on the payment of social security contributions. Following Almeida and Carneiro (2005) and Gonzaga (2003), we identify shadow workers as those individuals reporting to work but stating that they do not have a social security card. It is a relatively large component of the labor force: the shadow rate can be as high as roughly one-third. By construction, these shadow workers cannot be classified as unemployed. Figure 9 displays the yearly shadow and unemployment rates in six Brazilian metropolitan areas since the inception of the survey. There is a remarkable positive correlation (ranging from .31 in Rio to .82 in Salvador with t-statistics in the range 3.4 to 6.1). This correlation cannot be a statistical artifact, and provides genuine evidence of our empirical implications.

5.2   The Shadow Wage Gap

Our model predicts that improvements in aggregate conditions increase the shadow wage gap.

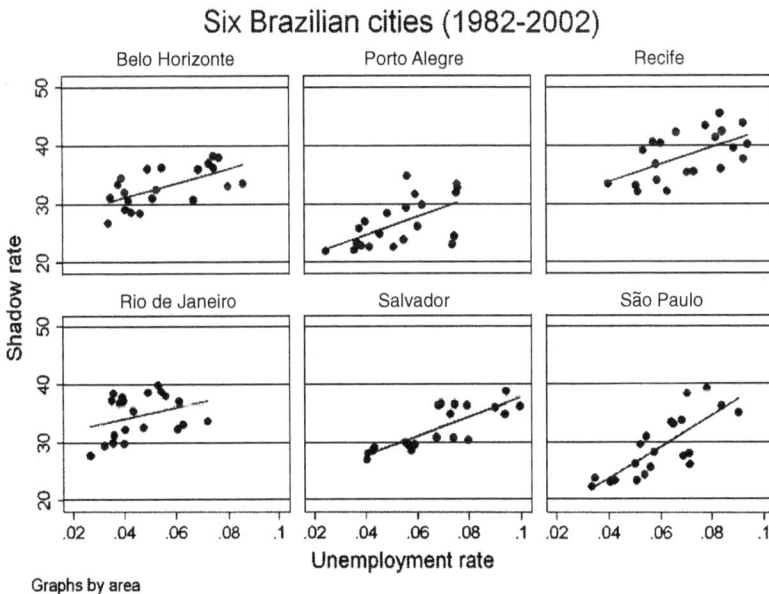

Figure 9
Shadow employment and unemployment in six Brazilian cities

Figure 10 displays the shadow wage gap and a simple Oaxaca decomposition of this gap in Italy over time and across two macro-regions characterized by very different aggregate conditions, such as the North and the Mezzogiorno. In particular, drawing on the Bank of Italy SHIW we run two standard wage regressions for the legal and the shadow sector (individuals stating that they are working but they never paid social security contributions)

$$\bar{w}^s = \bar{X}^s \beta^s$$

and

$$\bar{w}^b = \bar{X}^b \beta^b$$

where $\bar{X}^i$ denotes average "personal-demographic" characteristics (educational attainments, gender, age, family status, etc.) of sector "i" and β^i the returns to these characteristics. Then we can decompose the shadow wage gap as the sum of a difference in quantities (explained part) and differences in returns (unexplained part), e.g.,:

$$\bar{w}^s - \bar{w}^b = (\bar{X}^s - \bar{X}^b)\frac{1}{2}(\beta^s + \beta^b) + (\beta^s - \beta^b)\frac{1}{2}(\bar{X}^s + \bar{X}^b). \tag{4}$$

An advantage of this decomposition is that it isolates the component which drives the changes in the shadow wage gap according to our model: it is the unexplained (or difference in returns) component, that is, the second term in equation (4). The decomposition is akin to the partial equilibrium comparative static exercise above, in that it assumes that differences in returns are uncorrelated with changes in the characteristics of the two pools. It should be interpreted as an approximation of the first-round effects of changes in the aggregate shock. Our

| | | Oaxaca Decomposition of the Shadow Wage Gap | | |
		Shadow wage gap	Explained	Unexplained
All sample	1995	0.94	0.24	0.70
	1998	0.79	0.40	0.39
	2000	0.92	0.26	0.66
	2002	1.04	0.23	0.81
North	all years	0.95	0.30	0.65
South	all years	0.78	0.31	0.48

Notes: Controls include age, gender, family status and educational attainments
Source: Bank of Italy SHIW various years

Figure 10
Oaxaca decomposition of the shadow wage gap

exercise suggests that the shadow gap has been widening since 1998, at times in which unemployment was declining, and that it is larger in the dynamic North than in the depressed Southern labor markets. The key factor behind these differences is the unexplained (returns) component of the gap.

5.3   Enforcement

Modern information technologies allow tax administrations to easily collect and cross-check information from a variety of sources. For instance, the Spanish tax administration built-up an inventory of bank accounts which is particularly useful in tracking the shadow sector. The Italian "Agenzie delle Entrate" is developing an inventory of electricity, gas, telephone, and water bills of contributors, which can be readily cross-checked with tax records.

There are plenty of anecdotes about poor enforcement in high-unemployment regions, although it is very hard to document this. There are documents of the Italian Agenzia delle Entrate stating that enforcement should be milder in small units and in agriculture, where shadow employment is over-represented. Almeida and Carneiro (2005) report a negative correlation between unemployment and worksite inspections in Brazil. Broadly similar is the conclusions of the Osservatorio Veneto, although shadow employment in Veneto is very much related to immigration. A negative relationship between shadow employment and monitoring is driven in our model by the effects of controls on job creation in the shadow sector. But there can also be political economy arguments for observing less repression of the shadow sector in high unemployment regions.

6.   Final Remarks

An equilibrium search model of the labor market, with workers' sorting, attempts to explain the "shadow puzzle," the increasing size of the shadow economy in OECD countries in spite of improvements in technologies detecting tax and social security evasion. Our model has implications which are broadly supported by the, admittedly scant, evidence on shadow labor markets. In particular, we consistently find a positive cross-sectional and time-series correlation between the shadow rate and unemployment, and this correlation cannot be attributed to a statistical artifact.

Our model delivers also some policy implications. The most important is quite simple: *in order to reduce shadow employment, it is necessary to deregulate the labor market. Deregulation reduces unemployment, and shadow employment is reduced as a by-product.* In this context, the model confirms the traditional wisdom on labor market reforms, and suggests that any policy that fosters job creation and enhances aggregate productivity will induce a reduction in shadow employment. What about specific policies, aimed at discouraging the emergence of shadow activity? Our simple theory suggests that a very cautious approach in this area is warranted, since an increase in the monitoring rate may backfire: in equilibrium, higher monitoring reduces job creation, and increase unemployment. Tight enforcement of entitlement rules to unemployment benefits can be a better option acting on the supply side (when unemployment benefits are collected only by workers with a regular employment history, and cannot be cumulated to income from shadow jobs, the workers' incentive to enter the shadow sector are reduced) and hence has better job creation properties.

In further work we plan to investigate combinations of shadow and regular jobs, both in labor demand and supply. Although this extension will significantly increase the complexity of our model, we are aware that the choice to go shadow is not merely a dichotomic choice. Multiple job holding allows workers, for instance, to allocate hours across the two sectors. And firms can react to idiosyncratic productivity shocks by crossing borders between shadow and regular jobs.

Acknowledgements

Paper presented at the NBER Macroeconomic Conference held in Budapest in June 2005. We are indebted to Chris Pissarides and Bob Hall for their comments and to Paola Monti for excellent research assistance. We thank Rita Almeida, Jaspar Hoeke, and Sara Lemos for helping us in gathering Brazil data. Email: tito.boeri@unibocconi.it, pietro.garibaldi@unito.it.

Notes

1. See Burdett, Lagos, and Wright (2000) for an analysis of the relationship between crime and unemployment.

2. Clearly this second definition requires exploiting the longitudinal features of the Bank of Italy Survey. For a description see Boeri and Brandolini (2004).

3. In the simulations we also assume that conditional on striking, regular jobs need to pay a firing tax T.

4. See Calzaroni and Pascarella (1998) for details on the estimates of shadow employment in Italian macro-regions.

References

Albrecht J., and S. Vroman. 2002. "A Matching Model with Endogenous Skill Requirements." *International Economic Review* 43(1): 283–305.

Almeida, R., and P. Carneiro. 2005. "Does Labor Flexibility affect Firm Performance? Evidence from Brazil," mimeo, University College London. London, England.

Atkinson, A.B. 1991. "Comparing Poverty Rates Internationally: Lessons from Recent Studies in Developed Countries." *World Bank Economic Review* 5(1): 3–21.

Becker, Gary. 1968. "Crime and Punishment: An Economic Approach." *Journal of Political Economy* 76: 169–217.

Bernabe, S. 1999. "A Profile of Informal Employment: The Case of Georgia." ILO, Geneva.

Boeri, T. 2000. *Structural Change, Welfare Systems and Labour Reallocation*. Oxford: Oxford University Press.

Boeri, T., and A. Brandolini. 2004. "The Age of Discontent: Italian Households at the Beginning of the Decade." *Giornale degli Economisti e Annali di Economia* 3-4.

Boeri, T., and P. Garibaldi. 2002. "Shadow Employment and Unemployment in a Depressed Labor Market." CEPR Working Paper.

Brandolini, A., G. D'Alessio. 2002. "Evidenze sul lavoro sommerso nell'indagine della Banca d'Italia sui bilanci delle famiglie italiane," mimeo, Banca d'Italia, Roma.

Burdett, K, R. Lagos, and R. Wright. 2000. "*Crime and Unemployment*." Mimeo, New York University.

Burdett K., and D. Mortensen. 1982. "Labor Supply Under Uncertainty." In R.G. Ehrenberg, ed., *Research in Labor Economics*.

Busetta, P. and Giovannini, E. 1998. *Capire il Sommerso*, Fondazione Curella, Liguori editore, Napoli.

Calzaroni, M. 2000. "*L'occupazione come strumento per la stima esaustiva del PIL e la misura del sommerso*." Mimeo, Istat.

Calzaroni, M., and C. Pascarella. 1998. *Le unità di osservazione del processo produttivo nella nuova contabilità nazionale*, Atti della XXXIX Riunione della Società Italiana di statistica, Sorrento, aprile.

Commander, S., and Y. Rodionova. 2005. "A Model of Informal Economy with an Application to Ukraine," mimeo, European Bank for Reconstruction and Development (EBRD) and London Business School.

Davidson, Carl, Lawrence Martin, and John Wilson. 2004. "The Optimal Fine for Risk Neutral Offenders: Conquering the Becker Conundrum." Mimeo, University of Michigan.

Davis, S.J., and M. Henrekson. 2004. "Tax Effects on Work Activity, Industry Mix and Shadow Economy Size: Evidence from Rich-Country Comparisons." National Bureau of Economic Research Working Paper no. W10509.

Davis, S., and M. Henrekson. 2005. "Tax Effects on Work Activity, Industry Mix and Shadow Economy Size: Evidence from Rich Country Comparisons." Mimeo, University of Chicago.

Feige, E. 1989. *The Underground Economies. Tax Evasion and Information Distortion.* Cambridge: Cambridge University Press.

Feige, E. 1994. "The Underground Economies and Currency Enigma." *Supplement to Public Finance/Finances Publiques* 49: 119–36.

Fredrikson, P., and B. Holmlund. 2001. "Optimal Unemployment Insurance in Search Equilibrium." *Journal of Labor Economics* 19(2): 370–399.

Garibaldi, P., and E. Wasmer. 2005. "Equilibrium Search Unemployment, Endogenous Participation and Labor Market Flows." *Journal of the European Economic Association* 3(4): 851–882 (MIT Press).

Giles, D. 1999. "Measuring the Hidden Economy: Implications for Econometric Modelling." *Economic Journal* 109: 370–380.

Gonzaga, G. 2003. "Labor Turnover and Labor Legislation in Brazil." *Economìa* 4(1): 165–222.

Hirschman, Albert O. 1970. *Exit, Voice and Loyalty.* Cambridge: Harvard University Press.

Lackò, M. 2000. "Hidden Economy. An Unknown Quantity?" *Economics of Transition* 8(1): 17–33.

Lubell, H. 1991. *The Informal Sector in the 1980s and 1990s.* Paris: OECD.

Meldolesi, L. 2000. *Occupazione ed emersione: Nuove proposte per il Mezzogiorno d'Italia,* Carocci editore, Roma.

Meldolesi, L., and V. Aniello, eds. 1998. Un'Italia che non c'è: quant'è, dov'è, com'è, *Rivista di Politica Economica,* settembre-ottobre.

Pissarides, C. 2000. *Equilibrium Unemployment Theory.* Cambridge, MA: The MIT Press.

Saint-Paul, G. 1995. "The High Unemployment Trap." *Quarterly Journal of Economics* 110(2): 527–550 (MIT Press).

Schneider, F. 1994. "Measuring the Size and Development of the Shadow Economy: Can the Causes be Found and the Obstacles be Overcome?" In Hermann Brandstaetter and Werner Guth, eds., *Essay on Economic Psychology.* Berlin: Springer, 193–212.

Schneider, F. 2000. "The Increase of the Size of the Shadow Economy of 18 OECD Countries: Some Preliminary Explanations." CESifo Working Paper no. 306.

Schneider, F. 2002. "The Size and the Development of the Shadow Economies of 22 Transition and 21 OECD Countries." IZA DP no. 514.

Schneider, F. 2003. "The Shadow Economy." In C. Rowley and F. Schneider, eds. *Encyclopedia of Public Choice.* Dordrecht: Kluwer Academic Publishers.

Schneider, F. 2004. "The Size of the Shadow Economies of 145 Countries All over the World: First Results over the Period 1999 to 2003." IZA DP no. 1431.

Schneider, F., and D. Enste. 2000. "Shadow Economies: Size, Causes, and Consequences." *Journal of Economic Literature* 38(1): 77–114.

SNA. 1993. *System of National Accounts.* Commission of European Communities-INF-OECD-UN-WB.

Yashiv, Eran. 2000. "The Determinants of Equilibrium Unemployment." *American Economic Review* 90(5): 1297–1322.

Annex

A Statistical Artifact?

According to the labor force statistics, the working age population is classified as E^{lf}, U^{lf}, and N^{lf} where the values refer respectively to labor force employment, unemployment, and out of the labor force. If the labor force is indicated with *wap* the function reads

$E^{lf} + U^{lf} + N^{lf} = wap.$

The unemployment rate is than defined as

$$u^{lf} = \frac{U^{lf}}{E^{lf} + U^{lf}}.$$

The official istat definition of the shadow rate, s, is given by the estimate of shadow employment (lavoro irregolare) over the sum of regular employment E^r, and shadow employment E^s

$$s = \frac{E^r}{E^s + E^r}.$$

The key issue concerns the relationship between E^s and E^{lf} or whether shadow employment is part of the labor force employment. The answer depends on various assumptions regarding the position of shadow employment in the labor force statistics.

Assumption 1: *Shadow employment within the employment measured in the labor force surveys.*

This implies that

$E^{lf} = E^s + E^r.$

Therefore

$$u^{lf} = \frac{U^{lf}}{E^s + E^r + U^{lf}}$$

from which it follows that

$$\frac{\partial u^{lf}}{\partial E^s} < 0$$

$$\frac{\partial s}{\partial E^s} > 0.$$

In other words, an increase in shadow employment E^s leads to an increase in the shadow rate and to a decrease in the unemployment rate. The empirical correlation, in this case is *not* a statistical artifact.

Remark 6 *If shadow employment is part of labor force employment, the correlation between s and u is not a statistical artifact.*

Assumption 2: *Shadow employment is within the out of the labor force measured in the labor force surveys.*

This implies that

$$N^{lf} = \tilde{N} + E^s$$

where $\tilde{N}$ is a pure measure of out of the labor force (not observed in labor force statistics).

Therefore

$$u^{lf} = \frac{U^{lf}}{E^{lf} + U^{lf}}$$

from which it follows that

$$\frac{\partial u^{lf}}{\partial E^s} = 0$$

$$\frac{\partial s}{\partial E^s} > 0.$$

In other words, an increase in shadow employment leads to an increase in the shadow rate and has no impact on the unemployment rate. Also in this case, the empirical correlation is *not* a statistical artifact.

Remark 7 *If shadow employment is part of out of the labor force in labor force surveys, the correlation between s and u is not a statistical artifact.*

Assumption 3: *Shadow employment is within unemployment measured in labor force surveys.*

This implies that

$$U^{lf} = \tilde{U} + E^s$$

where $\tilde{U}$ is a pure unemployment rate while E^s is shadow employment. In this case the unemployment rate derived from labor force statistics is

$$u^{lf} = \frac{\tilde{U} + E^s}{E^{lf} + \tilde{U} + E^s}$$

from which it follows that

$$\frac{\partial u^{lf}}{\partial E^s} > 0$$

$$\frac{\partial s}{\partial E^s} > 0.$$

Remark 8 *If shadow employment is part of labor force unemployment, the correlation between s and u is a statistical artifact.*

In this latter scenario one should try to correct the official unemployment statistics. Is there a fraction of unemployed people that looks suspicious? Unfortunately there is no mapping from estimates of shadow employment to LFS definitions of employment, unemployment and inactivity. In order to devise some method to track the labor market status of shadow employment we need to introduce some identifying restrictions. This requires some theoretical guidance.

Comment

Robert E. Hall, Stanford University and NBER

Boeri and Garibaldi's paper combines two of my main current research interests: unemployment and the financing of social benefits, health in particular. Although the United States is not the main focus of discussions of the shadow economy, the issues raised in this interesting paper will become highly relevant if the expected high levels of health spending in future decades are financed by taxes.

Edward Prescott (2004) has attracted a good deal of attention for his claim that rising tax rates and corresponding benefits in Europe in comparison to the United States explain the decline in European work effort relative to the United States. As in his earlier work, Prescott considers a two-activity model, work and leisure (any activity out of the labor market, including work at home). Unemployment is not an explicit feature of the model or Prescott's analysis of variations in work effort across countries.

Mortensen and Pissarides (1994) launched the other main active branch of macroeconomic analysis of labor markets. Their model also has two activities, work and unemployment. Variations in participation or in hours of work are not part of their model, although they are not hard to add. Boeri and Garibaldi build a four-activity model in the tradition of Mortensen and Pissarides. Work and search occur in the legal sector and the shadow sector. Workers make a decision about where to search and thus where to work. This decision adds an important new dimension to the analysis.

The model has two important wedges. First, the legal sector pays taxes, which drive the usual wedge between the incentive to work and the reward to work. Second, the shadow sector faces law-enforcement monitoring. A key assumption of the model is that the authorities will shut down a shadow firm if detected. If, on the other hand, the authorities just start taxing shadow firms when they are found, all firms will launch in the shadow sector and then switch to the legal sector if detected (possibly shutting down at that point). Shut-down is inefficient within the economic theory of law enforcement, because it dissipates the search capital in a shadow firm. Theory would favor a monetary penalty in place of shut-down.

Another important assumption is that the value of search rises faster with skill in the legal sector. This assumption implies a cutoff level of skill, above which workers choose to search for jobs in the legal sector. This assumption seems realistic and the implication in line with the fact—firms employing high-wage workers are likely to be legitimate and workers in the shadow sector earn relatively little.

Table 1 summarizes how the various influences affect employment and unemployment in the two sectors.

The most important surprise is that raising unemployment benefits in the legal sector raises employment in that sector—the effect of attracting workers to search in the sector outweighs the shift toward more unemployment in the sector.

The model explains the rise in European unemployment in terms of higher taxes and higher unemployment benefits. Because it does not consider the participation margin, it cannot explain the entire decline in employment, and does not claim to.

The central issue for future policy in all countries, including emphatically the United States, is the effect of the growth of taxes on the division of activity between legal and shadow sectors. Hall and Jones (2005) project that socially optimal health spending in the United States will rise to half of GDP sometime late in the century. Though Europe trails

Table 1

	Legal sector		Shadow sector	
	Employment	Unemployment	Employment	Unemployment
Aggregate productivity	+	–	–	–
Taxation of legal sector	–	–	+	+
Monitoring of shadow sector	+	+	–	–
Unemployment benefits in legal sector	+	+	–	–

the United States in the level of health spending, growth is inevitable in Europe as well. Retirement benefits will also grow on both sides of the Atlantic, though not nearly as much as health spending. It's close to a certainty that health spending will be channeled through the government in Europe and highly likely that the government will have a growing role in financing health spending in the United States.

It is hard to see how the future holds anything other than dramatic increases in tax rates or government-mandated contributions to government-supervised health plans. The shrinkage of the legal sector, which will bear the burden of all of these taxes and contributions, and the corresponding rise in the shadow sector, will be substantial. Boeri and Garibaldi's analysis will be a central topic of public finance in coming decades. European governments will need to start taking law enforcement seriously—the paper suggests that benign neglect of the shadow sector has been the primary principle in Europe. The U.S. federal government enforces wage taxes quite effectively at present. But marginal rates in the U.S. counting income taxes and social-insurance contributions are only at about half the European level. As U.S. rates rise, the law enforcement efforts needed to control the social sector and prevent the complete collapse of the legal sector will be enormous.

The primary source of the potential collapse of the legal sector in all advanced countries is that people in the shadow sector will receive benefits even if they do not contribute to health and retirement programs. No civilized country will exclude older people from these benefits. Hence all of the effort needs to go into squeezing the shadow sector. Tensions in this area will be huge.

Boeri and Garibaldi have advanced the study of the shadow sector in an important way in this paper. I suspect that their work will be seen as pioneering in an area of economic analysis that will become absolutely central in social debates in coming decades.

References

Hall, Robert E., and Charles I. Jones. 2005. "The Value of Life and the Rise in Health Spending." Available at <http://emlab.berkeley.edu/users/chad/hx300.pdf>.

Mortensen, Dale T., and Christopher Pissarides. 1994. "Job Creation and Job Destruction in the Theory of Unemployment." *Review of Economic Studies* 61(3): 397–415.

Prescott, Edward C. "Why Do Americans Work So Much More than Europeans?" *Federal Reserve Bank of Minneapolis Quarterly Review* 28(1): 2–13.

Comment

Christopher A. Pissarides, Centre for Economic Performance, London School of Economics

The authors of this paper set themselves a challenging task. They ask, why is shadow employment in Europe increasing, when detection methods by the authorities must be improving? The answer they give is plausible—maybe because governments know that suppressing shadow employment would increase unemployment. Of course, there is another solution to the problem, the deregulation of legal employment. But if there are obstacles to deregulation, legal, political or ones likely to lead to economic disruption by trade unions and other vested interests, then governments can circumvent to some extent the measures by turning a blind eye to activity that does not comply.

The hypothesis put forward is not tested directly by the authors. Instead they set out to show that in an equilibrium with regulation there is a negative correlation between shadow employment and unemployment. In their model production efficiency is the same in the legal and underground economy, and the difference between them is that in the legal economy employers pay taxes and unemployed workers receive compensation. In the shadow sector no transfers take place. When shadow activity is detected the job is closed down.

The main result of the theoretical model is the demonstration that there is a cut-off skill level that sorts workers into the legal and shadow sectors. Shadow employment is associated with more labor turnover because of detection, and this discourages more skilled workers. Employment taxes and unemployment benefits are independent of income and high income workers lose more from turnover if UI benefits are low enough. So they avoid going to the shadow sector. Given that low-skill workers are willing to enter shadow employment it is easy to see how closing down this employment outlet will increase unemployment. The low-skilled will then apply for legal jobs and increase the unemployment queue.

But is the real reason that low-skill workers sort into shadow employment the fact that unemployment benefits are not generous enough to attract high-skill workers? It is certainly true that the opportunity cost of employment is higher for more skilled workers, so more frequent unemployment spells in the shadow sector may be a factor. To make the point more convincing the authors need to demonstrate that unemployment spells are indeed more frequent in the shadow sector. But this is not the main point. Usually, shadow employment is criticized for its low capital intensity and low commitment to training. The cost of a large shadow sector to the economy is both the output cost due to low investments in capital and training and the loss of tax revenue. I will show here that a modification to the authors' model delivers sorting along the lines discussed by the authors, but one that does not have to rely on the cost of unemployment. It also delivers a richer framework for thinking about shadow employment and, needless to add, the correlation between shadow employment and unemployment.

Firms offer training at some level z when a job match first takes place. We can think of this as either training for the worker or as capital investment, the theoretical results are not affected. Assuming that workers are distinguished by their skill x and the firm may choose different training levels in each sector, we can write $px(1 - \tau)f(z_g)$ for the output from a legal job and $pxf(z_b)$ for the output from a shadow job. The key assumption is that the skill level x and the returns to training are complementary.

The value of a legal job that is destroyed at rate λ is

$$(r + \lambda)J^g(x) = px(1 - \tau)f(z_g) - w_g(x).$$

The firm chooses z_g to maximize the value of its job,

$$\max_{z^g} J^g(z_g) - pz_g(1 - \tau).$$

I have implicitly assumed that the firm gets a tax rebate on money spent on training. Assume that the training choice is efficient, i.e., that $w_g(x)$ is taken as given when training choices are made, but let

$$w_g(x) = \bar{w}_g + \beta px(1 - \tau)f(z_g),$$

with z_g fixed at the optimal level. For example, this wage equation could be the outcome of an implicit bargain between the firm and the worker, as is commonly analyzed in search equilibrium models.

The optimal z_g satisfies

$$\frac{xf'(z_g)}{r+\lambda}=1.$$

Similar reasoning for shadow jobs gives

$$\frac{xf'(z_b)}{r+\lambda+\rho}=1.$$

Shadow jobs break up for two reasons, because of the same separation process as in the legal sector and also when they are detected, at rate ρ. Under standard assumptions we get $z_g > z_b$. Interestingly the reason that there is more training in legal jobs is the same that drives the authors' results, namely that legal jobs are more stable than shadow jobs. But whereas the author's results depended on the cost of unemployment to the worker, with training the key result is driven by the fact that detection reduces on average the duration of a shadow job, and so gives less time to the firm to exploit the rewards from its investment.

It is straightforward to get the paper's single crossing property, namely the sorting according to skill. But the single crossing is now on the expected profit from the job, irrespective of the costs of unemployment. Under iso-elastic (Cobb-Douglas) $f(z)$, and if

$$\frac{p(1-\tau)-1}{(r+\lambda)^{1/1-\alpha}}>\frac{p-1}{(r+\lambda+\rho)^{1/1-\alpha}}$$

$$\bar{w}_g > \bar{w}_b,$$

the Js of legal and shadow employment cross only once, as shown in Figure 1. The sufficient conditions required are that taxes are not too high and detection is not too low—otherwise the whole economy is driven to the shadow sector—and that the outside opportunities of those in legal jobs are better than those in shadow jobs. The latter could be satisfied, for example, under the authors' assumption that workers in the legal sector receive unemployment compensation.

The model with training can reproduce the sorting results of this paper and in addition it formalizes the output costs of shadow employment, which is an important issue in the European policy debate. It can easily be incorporated into the model of this paper to yield more

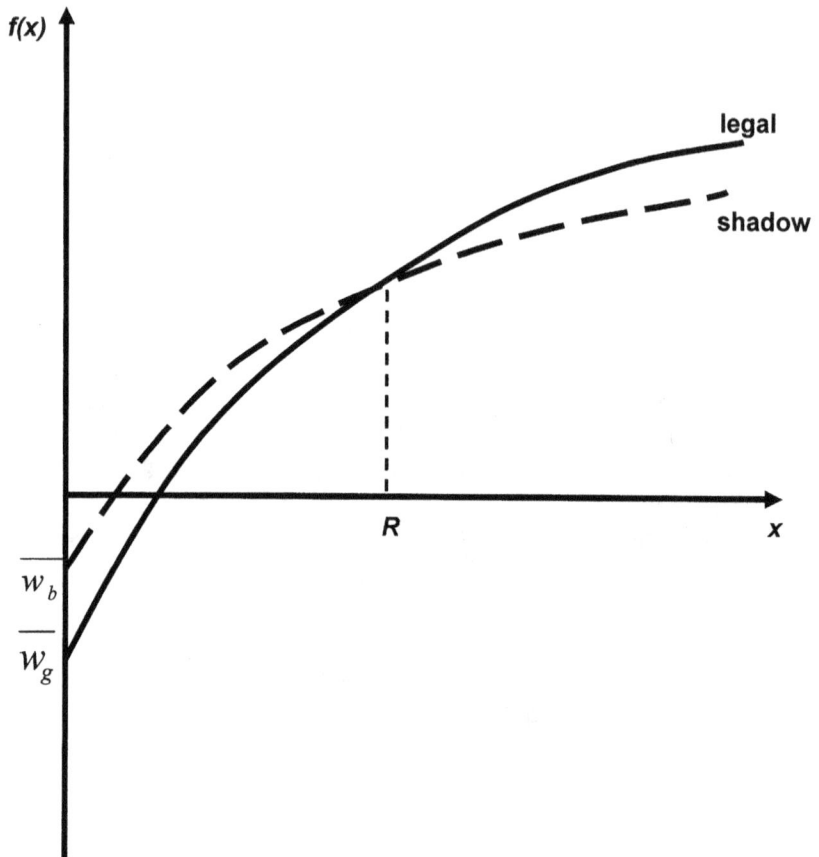

Figure 1
The value of legal and shadow jobs

general sorting results, which reflect both the training inefficiencies of
shadow employment and the unemployment costs. Full calibration of
this model may also avoid some implausible results in the reported
calibrations, like for example the very large wage differential between
the two sectors.

4

Globalization and Equilibrium Inflation-Output Tradeoffs

Assaf Razin, *Tel Aviv University, Cornell University, and NBER*
Prakash Loungani, *International Monetary Fund*

1. Introduction

In recent years there has been remarkably subdued inflation despite sharp rises in commodity prices, strong growth, and financial disturbances. Global inflation rates fell from 30 percent a year to about 4 percent a year in the 1990s. At the same time, a massive globalization process has swept emerging markets in Latin America, European transition economies, and the East Asian emerging economies. The establishment in 1992 of the Single Market in Europe, followed by the formation of the single currency area in 1999, are also notable landmarks of globalization over this period. Rogoff (2003, 2004) suggests that this association of globalization and disinflation is not accidental. While acknowledging that other favorable factors also helped drive down global inflation in the 1990s, he conjectures that "globalization—interacting with deregulation and privatization—has played a strong supporting role in the past decade's disinflation."[1] The impact of globalization on inflation will be temporary unless central banks change their inflation target. That is, unless globalization affects the objective function of the central bank.

Some empirical work supports Rogoff's conjecture. In early work, Romer (1993, 1998), and Lane (1997) showed that trade liberalization is associated with lower inflation in large (flexible exchange rate) OECD economies. More recently, Chen, Imbs, and Scott (2004) find, using disaggregated data for EU manufacturing over the period 1988–2000, that increased openness exerts a negative and significant impact on sectoral prices. They show further that this effect of openness on prices occurs both through lower markups and increases in productivity. Their results suggest that the increase in the trade volume can account for as much as a quarter of European disinflation over their sample period.

This paper explores the effects of globalization (namely, the opening of a country to trade in goods and the liberalization of its international capital markets) on the distortions associated with fluctuations in the output gap and the inflation rate, in a sticky price, New Keynesian model. The analysis shows how globalization alters the relative *weights* applied to the output gap and the inflation surprise in a utility-based loss function. The mechanism at play, not yet addressed by the existing literature, relies on the consumption-smoothing properties of capital market integration and the de-linking of the commodity composition of consumption spending from the commodity composition of domestic output, that characterize specialization in production under the goods market integration. These features of openness help reduce distortions associated with output gap fluctuations, while not affecting, to a first approximation, the inefficiency associated with fluctuations in inflation.

This theory provides a new way of interpreting the evidence on the effect of openness on the sacrifice ratio. It suggests that the forces of globalization could induce monetary authorities, guided in their policies by the welfare criterion of a representative household, into putting greater emphasis on reducing the inflation rate than on narrowing output gaps.

The organization of the paper is as follows. Section 2 describes the model. Section 3 provides a derivation of the closed-economy utility-based loss function from the viewpoint of the conventional expected utility maximization by the representative household. Sections 4 and 5 extend the derivation of the utility-based loss function to open economies. Section 6 provides evidence on the effect of openness on the equilibrium output-inflation tradeoffs. Section 7 concludes.

2. Analytical Framework

The analytical framework draws on the New Keynesian macroeconomics literature as in Woodford (2003). Main features of the model are as follows.

(1) There is a representative household whose utility is defined over consumption and leisure, as in standard micro-based welfare analysis.

(2) The domestic economy produces a continuum of varieties. The decisions of the representative household are governed by Dixit-Stiglitz preferences over varieties (generating fixed elasticities). Purchas-

ing power parity condition prevails and foreign firms' prices are taken as exogenous.

(3) A proportion of producers sets domestic currency denominated prices, one period in advance; the remaining proportion sets flexibly the domestic currency denominated prices, so that markets clear for these goods.

(4) The representative household's welfare depends on consumption and labor supply. From this standard construction we derive a quadratic loss function, which depends on the output gap and inflation surprise.

3.   The Model

Assume that the welfare criterion, from which a quadratic utility-based loss function is to be derived, is the standard expected utility of a representative household, given by:

$$E\left(\sum_{t=0}^{\infty}\beta^{i}u_{t}\right),$$

Where,

$$U_{t}=\left[u(C_{t};\xi_{t})-\int_{0}^{n}m(h_{t}(j);\xi_{t})dj\right].$$

Aggregate consumption, C_{t}, is an index of differentiated products:

$$C_{t}=\left[\int_{0}^{1}c_{t}(j)^{\frac{\theta-1}{\theta}}dj\right]^{\frac{\theta}{\theta-1}}.$$

Labor supply for a product variety j is denoted by $h_{t}(j)$. The production function of variety j is given by $A_{t}f(h_{t}(j))$. The vector (A_{t}, ξ_{t}) represents productivity and preference shocks. The $u(C_{t}; \xi_{t})$ function is concave in C, so that the consumer wants to smooth consumption fluctuations. The $m(h_{t}(j); \xi_{t})$ function is convex in h, so that the consumer prefers equality in the supply of labor across different varieties to cross-variety dispersion in the labor supply.

Aggregate domestic output is specified as

$$Y_{t}=\left[\int_{0}^{n}y_{t}(j)^{\frac{\theta-1}{\theta}}dj\right]^{\frac{\theta}{\theta-1}}.$$

If the economy is open to trade in goods, the number of domestically produced varieties is smaller than the number of domestically consumed varieties; i.e., trade-induced specialization in production. Thus, the commodity composition of the consumption basket is different from the commodity composition of the output basket. As a result, the correlation between fluctuations in output and consumption, which is perfect in the case of a closed economy, is less than perfect when the economy is opened to trade in goods. When the economy is financially open, output fluctuations are inter-temporally separated from consumption fluctuations, due to the consumption-smoothing property of international capital flows. Therefore these two types of openness result in a separation beetween output fluctuations and consumption fluctuations; the latter are the object of welfare evaluations, but not the former.

3.1 Price Setting

Firms behave *monopolistically* in the goods markets, and, at the same time, *monopsonistically* in the labor market (because producer j is the sole demander for labor of type-j and household supply of type-j labor is perfectively competitive).[2] A fraction γ of the monopolistically competitive firms sets their prices flexibly at p_{1t}, supplying y_{1t}; whereas the remaining fraction $1 - \gamma$ sets their prices one period in advance (in period $t - 1$) at p_{2t}, supplying y_{2t}. In the flexible price case, price is marked up above the marginal cost, s, by the factor:

$$\mu = \left(\frac{\theta}{\theta - 1} > 1 \right),$$

so that,

$$\frac{p_{1t}}{P_t} - \mu s \left(y_{1t}, C_t; \xi_t, A_t \right) = 0.$$

In the rigid price case, p_{2t} is set so as to maximize expected discounted profits subject to an implicit producer-consumer contract in which the producer supplies the entire demand that is realized at any state of nature. Thus, the price-setting rule for p_{2t} is obtained by maximizing

$$E_{t-1} \left[\frac{1}{1+i} (p_{2t} y_{2t} - w_t h_t) \right];$$

subject to:

$$y_{2t} = Y_t^W \left[\frac{P_{2t}}{P_t} \right]^{-\theta} \tag{1}$$

and

$$y_{2t} = A_t f(h_{2t}). \tag{2}$$

World output, Y^W, determines the overall demand for goods, as standard per open economies. Inverting the production function yields:

$$h_{2t} = f^{-1} \left(\frac{y_{2t}}{A_t} \right).$$

Substituting the demand function into the inverted function yields:

$$h_{2t} = f^{-1} \left(\frac{Y_t^W p_{2t}^{-\theta} P_t^{\theta}}{A_t} \right).$$

This means that the producer's maximization problem can be stated as:

$$\max_{p_{2t}} E_{t-1} \left[\frac{1}{1+i} \left(p_{2t}^{1-\theta} Y_t^W P_t^{\theta} - w_t f^{-1} \left(\frac{Y_t^W p_{2t}^{-\theta} P_t^{\theta}}{A_t} \right) \right) \right].$$

The first order condition is then given by:

$$E_{t-1} \left\{ \left(\frac{1}{1+i_{t-1}} \right) Y_t P_t^{\theta-1} \left[\frac{p_{2t}}{P_t} - \mu s \left(y_{2t}, C_t, \xi_t, A_t \right) \right] \right\} = 0.$$

The symbol i_{t-1} stands for the nominal rate of interest in period $t-1$.

How can one interpret the first-order condition? In the special case of perfect certainty, this is nothing but the standard equation describing price as a mark-up over marginal cost. With uncertainty, it becomes a weighted average of state-dependent mark-ups over marginal cost. Price is pre-determined by expectations of next period demand and costs, but the firm is committed to supplying quantities according to the actual realizations of demand and costs. That is, the realization of demand and supply shocks will affect actual output, with negative shocks leading to excess capacity and positive shocks to under-capacity. The model predicts that the mark-ups of the producers who preset their prices will be counter-cyclical. Negative demand shocks will induce the flex-price firms to adjust their prices downward, diverting demand away, and thus lowering the marginal costs of the flex-price firms and lowering mark-ups of the fixed-price firms.

Figure 1 describes equilibrium in one labor market. The downward-sloping marginal-productivity curve represents the demand for labor. The supply of labor, S_h, is implicitly determined by the utility-maximizing condition for h. The upward-sloping marginal factor cost curve is the marginal change from the producer monopsonistically point of view. It lies above the supply curve because, in order to elicit more hours of work, the producer has to offer a higher wage not only to that (marginal) hour but also to all the (infra-marginal) existing hours. Equilibrium employment occurs at a point where the marginal factor costs is equal to the marginal productivity of labor. Equilibrium wage is given by B, with the worker's real wage marked down below marginal product by the distance AB.

Full employment obtains because workers are offered a wage according to their supply schedule. This is why the aggregate supply curve will be stated in terms of excess capacity (which corresponds to the product market version of the Phillips curve) rather than unemployment (the labor market version of the Phillips curve).[3]

3.2 Transforming the Utility Function to a Loss Function

We now derive the quadratic loss function from a standard welfare criterion of a representative household, following Woodford (2003).[4] We first transform the labor disutility function to

$$v(y_{jt}) \equiv m(f^{-1}\left(y_{jt}\frac{1}{A_t}\right), j = 1, 2.$$

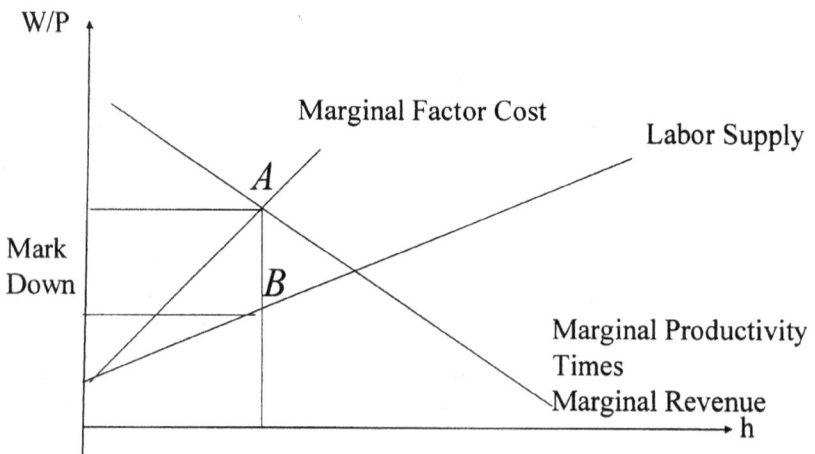

Figure 1
The labor market equilibrium

We employ the production function, $y_{jt} = A_t f(h_{jt})$, $j = 1, 2$, and transform period t utility function, as follows.

$$U_t = \left[u(C_t ; \xi_t)) - \int_0^1 v(y_t(j); \xi_t, A_t)dj \right].$$

Nominal marginal cost is:

$$\frac{\partial w_t h_{jt}}{\partial y_{jt}} = w_t f^{-1'} \left(\frac{y_{jt}}{A_t} \right) \frac{1}{A_t}.$$

Dividing through by P_t we get real marginal cost:

$$s_t(j) = w_t f^{-1'} \left(\frac{y_{jt}}{A_t} \right) \frac{1}{A_t P_t}, \quad j = 1, 2.$$

Labor supply is implicitly given by

$$\frac{v_h(h_{jt}, \xi_t)}{u_c(C_t, \xi_t)} = \frac{w_{jt}}{P_t}, j = 1, 2.$$

One can use the above conditions to get a reduced-form expression for the real marginal costs, as follows.

$$s_{jt} = \frac{v_h(h_{jt}, \xi_t)}{u_c(C_t, \xi_t)} f^{-1'} \left(\frac{y_{jt}}{A_t} \right) \frac{1}{A_t}, \quad j = 1, 2$$

where, v_y and u_c denote the marginal disutility of labor and the marginal utility of consumption, respectively.

The elasticity of $v_y (y(j); \xi, A)$ with respect to y is denoted by

$$\omega = \frac{\overline{C} v_{yy}(\overline{Y})}{v_y(\overline{Y})}.5$$

The inter-temporal elasticity of substitution is denoted by

$$\sigma^{-1} = -\frac{\overline{C} u_{cc}}{u_c} > 0.$$

To allow for stationarity in the stochastic process of consumption we assume that

$$\beta = \frac{1}{1 + \overline{r}}.$$

This implies a zero consumption growth rate in the deterministic steady state because in this case the familiar saving rule,

$$u_C(C_t) = \beta(1+i_t)E_t\left(u_C(C_{t+1})\frac{P_t}{P_{t+1}}\right),$$

reduces to $C_t = \bar{C}$. Upper bars denote the deterministic steady state.

3.3 Output Gap

We denote the output gap by x:

$$x_t = \hat{Y}_t - \hat{Y}_t^N .$$

A "hat" denotes a proportional deviation from steady state, and a superscript N indicates flexible price equilibrium. That is, $\hat{Y}_t$ is equal to deviations of actual output from its steady state level whereas $\hat{Y}_t^N$ is equal to deviations of potential output from its steady state level. Potential output is defined as the level of output the economy would produce if all prices and wages are fully flexible.

A different measure for an output gap in the steady state has to do with the monopolistic-competition distortion. In the shock-free steady state, the level of output, $\bar{Y}$, is implicitly given by:

$$s(\bar{C},\bar{Y};0,1) = v_y(\bar{Y};0,1) / u_c(\bar{C};0) = \frac{1}{\mu},$$

Recall that the mark up is defined in terms of the cross-variety elasticity of substitution, $\mu = \theta/\theta - 1$. The efficient (zero mark up) output in the shock-free steady state, Y^*, is implicitly given by:

$$s(C^*,Y^*;0,1) = 1.$$

The monopolistically based output gap measure is defined by the ratio of the flexible price monopolistic-competition output and the efficient output; namely

$$\bar{Y}/Y^*.$$

Log-approximation of the supply-side equations yields:

$$x^* = \log(\bar{Y}/Y^*) = -(\omega + \sigma^{-1})\frac{1}{\mu}.$$

Thus, the monopolistic output gap in logs, x^* is an increasing function of the markup.

4. Globalization and Efficiency

As is well known, when the economy opens up to trade in goods, it tends to specialize in production and to diversify in consumption. This means that the number of domestically produced varieties, equal to n, is less than the number of domestically consumed varieties. Consequently, the commodity composition of the consumption basket and the commodity composition of the output basket, that were identical in a closed economy, would diverge when the economy opens up. As a result, the correlation between fluctuations in output and consumption, which is equal to one in the case of a closed economy, falls short of one if the economy is opened to international trade in goods.

When the economy also becomes financially open, domestic consumption spending and domestic output typically diverge for a separate reason. The household can smooth aggregate consumption through international borrowing and lending. Hence, the aggregate output stochastic path diverges from the aggregate consumption path.

The upshot is that in both cases of openness, albeit for different reasons, the correlation between the fluctuations in the output gap and the fluctuations in aggregate consumption are significantly reduced. Because consumer welfare depends on consumption, not on output, the weight of the output gap in the loss function falls with both trade and capital openness. In what follows we formalize this intuition.

4.1 *International Mobility of Capital and Goods*

If capital is perfectly mobile, the domestic agent has a costless access to the international financial market. The saving rule, $u_c(C_t) = \beta(1 + r_t)E_t(u_c(C_{t+1}))$, where r_t equals the world risk free interest rate, implies that the representative consumer can smooth all the fluctuations in consumption that are caused by shocks to the domestic economy's output. In the neighborhood of the shock-free steady state, consumption smoothing is almost perfect and consumption growth has no trend because we assume $\beta = 1/1 + \bar{r}$. Thus, when the capital account is open and perfect consumption smoothing is achieved, the equilibrium proportional deviations of consumption from the steady state level are approximately the same in the fixed-price and flexible-price cases. That is,

$$\hat{C}_t = \hat{C}_t^N .$$

If goods are perfectly mobile, the number of product varieties is reduced from the closed-trade number of one to n. The approximate utility-based loss function for open-capital and open-trade regimes is:

$$L_t = (\pi_t - E_{t-1}\pi_t)^2 + \frac{1}{\theta} \frac{\gamma}{1-\gamma} \frac{n\varpi}{1+\varpi\theta} (x_t - x^*)^2 + residual$$

$$x^* = (\omega + \sigma^{-1})^{-1} \frac{1}{\mu}.$$

Distortions in the new Keynesian equilibrium can be grouped into two types:

(1) Consumption fluctuations are welfare-reducing, therefore output gap fluctuations, which are correlated with consumption fluctuations, are also welfare-reducing.

(2) An efficient allocation of the supply of labor across product varieties is to allocate labor equally across varieties because varieties have the same technologies and preferences concerning varieties are symmetric. Thus, any cross-variety output dispersion is welfare-reducing. An increase in unanticipated inflation rates, given that some prices are set in advance, would raise the labor supply dispersion. Hence, also, the unanticipated inflation is welfare-reducing.

The associated aggregate supply relationship (see Razin and Yuen (2002)) is:

$$\pi_t - E_{t-1}\pi_t = \frac{\gamma}{1-\gamma} \left[\frac{n\omega}{1+\omega\theta} (\hat{Y}_t^h - \hat{Y}_t^N) + \frac{(1-n)\omega}{1+\omega\theta} (\hat{Y}_t^f - \hat{Y}_t^N) \right]$$

$$+ \frac{1-n}{n} \left(\frac{1}{1-\gamma} \hat{e}_t - E_{t-1}\hat{e}_t \right).$$

The term $\hat{e}$ is the proportional deviation of the real exchange rate from its corresponding steady state level, $\hat{Y}_t^f$ is the proportional deviation of the rest-of-the-world output from its corresponding steady state level, and $1-n$ denotes the number of imported goods. Note that the relative weight that is placed upon the output gap term (normalizing the weight of the quadratic deviations of the inflation rate to one), is also equal to the (aggregate-supply based) sacrifice ratio times the inverse of the cross-variety elasticity of substitution, which is inversely proportional to the mark up of the flexible price firms.

The intuition for this is that the quadratic approximation to the utility function is derived from the original utility function by using the relation between nominal prices and real supply, which is based on the aggregate supply block of the macroeconomic model. This means that there is a direct link between the sacrifice ratio and the relative weight of the output gap term in the loss function, holding constant the flexible-price mark up,

$$\mu = \left(\frac{\theta}{\theta - 1} > 1 \right).$$

4.2 Closed Capital Account and Open Trade Account

If the domestic economy does not participate in the international financial market, then there is clearly no possibility of consumption smoothing. Thus domestic income must equal domestic spending: $PC = P_y Y$, where,

$$P_t = \left[\int_0^n p_t(j)^{1-\theta} dj + \int_n^1 (\varepsilon_t p_t^*(j))^{1-\theta} dj \right]^{\frac{1}{1-\theta}},$$

and

$$P_{Yt} = \left[\int_0^n p_t(j)^{1-\theta} dj \right]^{\frac{1}{1-\theta}}.$$

These conditions imply[6]:

$$\hat{C}_t - \hat{C}_t^N = \hat{Y}_t - \hat{Y}_t^N.$$

The approximate utility-based loss function becomes[7]:

$$L_t = (\pi_t - E_{t-1}\pi_t)^2 + \frac{1}{\theta} \frac{\gamma}{1-\gamma} \frac{n\omega + \sigma^{-1}}{1+\omega\theta} (x_t - x^*)^2 + residual.$$

4.3 Closed Economy

Under both trade and financial autarky (all the goods in the domestic consumption index are produced domestically), $n = 1$, because the commodity composition of the output and the consumption baskets are the same, and $\hat{c}_t = \hat{y}_t$; $\hat{c}_t^N = \hat{y}_t^N$. Consumption spending must equal output in the fixed price and the flexible price economies. The approximate utility-based loss function becomes:

$$L_t = (\pi_t - E_{t-1}\pi_t)^2 + \frac{1}{\theta}\frac{\gamma}{1-\gamma}\frac{\omega+\sigma^{-1}}{1+\omega\theta}(x_t - x^*)^2 + residual.\ ^{8}$$

5. Weights in the Loss Function

The relative weight attached to the output-gap term (recall: the unexpected-inflation weight is normalized to one) in each one of the openness scenarios is given by:

(1) $\psi_1 = \dfrac{1}{\theta}\dfrac{\gamma n\omega}{(1-\gamma)(1+\theta\omega)}$ (Open Capital and Trade Accounts)

(2) $\psi_2 = \dfrac{1}{\theta}\dfrac{\gamma(n\omega+\sigma^{-1})}{(1-\gamma)(1+\theta\omega)}$ (Closed Capital Account and Open Trade Account)

(3) $\psi_3 = \dfrac{1}{\theta}\dfrac{\gamma(\omega+\sigma^{-1})}{(1-\gamma)(1+\theta\omega)}$ (Closed Capital and Closed Trade Accounts

One can verify that $\psi_1 < \psi_2 < \psi_3.^{9}$

That is, the weight of the output-gap term in the utility-based loss function falls with openness. This result follows from the consumption-smoothing and trade-specialization intuitions presented in the previous subsection.

A simple one-period optimization problem of the central bank can serve to illustrate the finding that openness triggers more aggressive anti-inflation policy. Assume that the central bank minimizes the level of the utility-based quadratic loss function, subject to the aggregate supply constraint.[10] The resulting equilibrium trade-off is:

$$(\pi_t - E_{t-1}\pi_t) = -\frac{1}{\theta SR}(x_t - x^*)$$

where SR denotes the sacrifice ratio, and $1/\theta$ is proportional to the flexible-price mark up. The inverse of the sacrifice ratio is equal to

$$\frac{1}{\theta}\frac{\gamma n\omega}{(1-\gamma)(1+\theta\omega)},$$

$$\frac{1}{\theta}\frac{\gamma(n\omega+\sigma^{-1})}{(1-\gamma)(1+\theta\omega)},$$

or

$$\frac{1}{\theta}\frac{\gamma(\omega+\sigma^{-1})}{(1-\gamma)(1+\theta\omega)},$$

in the three cases of perfect international mobility of capital and goods, perfect mobility of goods but no mobility of capital, and no mobility of either goods or capital, respectively. That is, for any given level of the output gap, the equilibrium inflation surprise is lower as the economy becomes more open. In sum, the optimizing monetary rule implies that the central bank would become more aggressive with respect to inflation, as the economy opens up to trade in goods and flows of capital.

The de-facto output-inflation tradeoff characterizes the relative weight in the loss function which the policy maker puts on inflation. This consideration enables us to use the estimated general-equilibrium sacrifice ratio as an indicator for the de-facto weight of the output gap in the unobserved utility-based loss function. In the next section we review some empirical evidence on the association between the sacrifice ratio and openness.[11]

6. Globalization and the Sacrifice Ratio: Empirical Evidence

We present in this section some additional evidence on the impact of openness on equilibrium sacrifice ratios.[12] Our regressions focus on explaining the determinants of sacrifice ratios as measured by Ball. He starts out by identifying disinflations episodes, in which the trend inflation rate fell substantially. Ball identifies 65 such disinflation episodes in 19 OECD countries, over the period 1960 to 1987. For each one of these episodes he calculates the associated sacrifice ratio; the denominator of the sacrifice ratio being the change in trend inflation over an episode. The numerator of the Ball sacrifice ratio is the sum of output losses, the deviations between actual output and its trend ("full employment" level).

We also take from Ball data on determinants of the sacrifice ratios such as the initial level of inflation, the change in inflation over the course of the episode and the length of the disinflation episode.

Measuring the degree of openness of trade and capital accounts is always a heroic task. Since 1950, the IMF has issued an annual publication, which tries to describe the controls that its member countries have in place on various current account capital transactions. However, as Cooper (1999, p. 111) notes, these descriptions are very imperfect measures of the extent of capital-market restrictions, particularly for the case of the capital account:

"... Restrictions on international capital transactions ... come in infinite variety. Therefore an accurate portrayal requires knowledge not only of the laws and regulations in place, but also of how they are implemented—which often requires much official discretion—and of how easily they are circumvented, either legally or illegally. The IMF reports the presence of restrictions, but not their intensity or their impact."

Quinn (1997) takes the basic IMF qualitative descriptions on the presence of restrictions and translates them into a quantitative measure of restrictions using certain coding rules. This translation provides a measure of the intensity of restrictions on current account transactions on a (0, 8) scale and restrictions on capital account transactions on a (0, 4) scale; in both cases, a higher number indicates fewer restrictions. We use the Quinn measures, labeled CURRENT and CAPITAL, respectively, as our measures of restrictions. We also use the sum of the two measures, as an overall measure of the degree of restrictions on the openness of the economy; this measure is labeled OPEN. An econometrics advantage of using rule-based openness dummies over trade flows (e.g., the import to output ratios) and capital flows in the regression analysis has to do with the endogeneity problem associated with the latter measures).

For each one of the disinflation episodes identified by Ball, we use as an independent variable, the current account and capital account restrictions that were in place the year before the start of the episode. This at least makes the restrictions pre-determined with respect to the sacrifice ratios, though of course not necessarily fully exogenous.

6.1 Regressions

The first column of Table 1 reports a regression of the sacrifice ratio on initial inflation, the length of the episode (measured in quarters) and the change in inflation over the course of the episode. Not surprisingly, as all the data were taken from Ball's study, the results are qualitatively similar and quantitatively virtually identical to regressions reported in his paper. The key finding is that sacrifice ratios are smaller, the quicker

Table 1
Sacrifice ratios and restrictions on current account and capital account

Independent variables	(1)	(2)	(3)	(4)
Constant	−0.001	−0.059	−0.033	−0.058
	(0.012)	(0.025)	(0.022)	(0.026)
Initial inflation	0.002	0.003	0.003	0.003
	(0.002)	(0.002)	(0.002)	(0.002)
Length of disinflation episode	0.004	0.004	0.004	0.004
	(0.001)	(0.001)	(0.001)	(0.001)
Change in inflation during episode	−0.006	−0.007	−0.006	−0.007
	(0.003)	(0.003)	(0.003)	(0.003)
CURRENT	.	0.008	.	.
Index of current account restrictions		(0.003)		
CAPITAL	.	.	0.010	.
Index of capital account restrictions			(0.006)	
OPEN	.	.	.	0.006
Sum of CURRENT and CAPITAL				(0.002)
Adjusted R-square	0.16	0.23	.19	0.23
Number of observations	65	65	65	65

Note: Numbers in parentheses are standard errors.

is the speed with which the disinflation is undertaken. The change in inflation also enters with the predicted sign and is significant ($t = 1.8$, p-value = .076). Initial inflation is insignificant (but has the wrong sign from the perspective of the theory).

Now consider the impact of adding the measures of openness, which are shown in the next three regressions. Ball's findings continue to hold. The length of the episode and the decline in inflation become more significant, while initial inflation remain insignificant. The measures of openness enter with the positive sign predicted by the theory. The effect of openness on the sacrifice ratio is statistically significant, as reflected also in the perking up of the adjusted R square of the three regressions when compared to the first. The restrictions on the current account appear statistically more significant than the restrictions on the capital account. When we entered both CURRENT and CAPITAL in the regression, CURRENT remained significant but CAPITAL did not. The correlation between the two variables is almost 0.5; hence, our inability to tease out separate effects is not entirely surprising.

What the estimation method of the sacrifice ratio can deliver is an estimate of the *equilibrium* inflation-output trade off. It reflects both policymaker preference and aggregate supply conditions. Thus, the regressions in Table 1 provide some additional support to the notion that that relative weight, in equilibrium, of the inflation in the loss function increases with trade, capital, and overall openness.[13]

7.   Conclusion

This paper puts forward an efficiency argument for putting heavier weight on inflation, relative to output gap, in a utility-based loss function, as the economy opens up. With capital account liberalization the representative household is able to smooth fluctuations in consumption, and thus becomes relatively insensitive to fluctuations in the output gap. With trade liberalization the economy tends to specialize in production and diversify in consumption. The correlation between the fluctuations in the output gap and aggregate consumption is therefore weakened by trade openness; hence a smaller weight on the output gap in the utility-based loss function, compared to the closed economy situations.

The theory is based on a new mechanism of how globalization forces induce monetary authorities, guided in their policies by the welfare criterion of a representative household, to put greater emphasis on reducing the inflation rate than on narrowing the output gaps (see Gali and Monacelli (2005), Paoli (2004), and Benigno and Benigno (2003)). As noted by Kydland and Prescott (1977), Barro and Gordon (1983), and Rogoff (1985), central banks have an incentive to deviate from their pre-announced monetary rule, generating an inflation bias. Globalization lessens such temptation that leads to this bias because the central banker is less sensitive to output gap fluctuations. The theory provides a new way to interpret existing evidence of the empirical relationships between openness and the sacrifice ratio. Although the reduced-form evidence cannot sharply discriminate between alternative hypotheses, it is consistent with the theory's prediction that goods and capital markets' openness decreases the distortions associated with fluctuations in the output gap, while leaving unaffected, to a first approximation, the distortion associated with fluctuations in inflation.

Acknowledgements

We thank Robert King, Philip Lane, Chris Pissarides, Andrew Scott, and Ken West for useful comments.

Notes

1. See Appendix 1 for a description of trends in monetary policy and openness in the last two decades.

2. An alternative assumption is that producers behave competitively in a segmented labor market. This would not qualitatively change the results.

3. In fact, the model can also accommodate unemployment by introducing a labor union, which has monopoly power to bargain on behalf of the workers with the monopsonistic employer over the equilibrium wage. In this case, the equilibrium wage will lie somewhere between S_h and the marginal product schedule and unemployment can arise, so that the labor market version of the Phillips curve can be derived as well. To simplify the analysis, we assume in this paper that the workers are wage-takers. In the limiting case where the producers behave perfectly competitively in the labor market, the real wage becomes equal to the marginal productivity of labor and the marginal cost of labor curve is not sensitive to output changes. Thus, with a constant mark-up, $\theta/\theta - 1$, the aggregate supply curve becomes flat. That is, there exists no relation between inflation and excess capacity.

4. See a closed economy derivation in Appendix II.

5. All the elasticities are evaluated at the point:

$$C_t = \overline{C}, Y_t = \overline{Y}, \beta = \frac{1}{1+\overline{r}},$$

and $\overline{r}$ denotes the world rate of interest.

6. Log-linearizing the closed capital-account equality $PC = P_y Y$ yields:

$$\hat{C} = \hat{Y} - (\hat{P} - \hat{P}_Y)$$

$$(\hat{P} - \hat{P}_Y) = (1-n)((\varepsilon \hat{p}^*) - \hat{P}_Y) = (1-n)\hat{e}_Y$$

where,

$$P_{Yt} = \left[\int_0^n p_t(j)^{1-\theta} dj \right]^{\frac{1}{1-\theta}}$$

and

$$(\hat{P} - \hat{P}_Y) = (1-n)((\varepsilon \hat{p}^*) - \hat{P}_Y) = (1-n)\hat{e}_Y.$$

7. In this case, the aggregate-supply curve is given by:

$$\pi_t - E_{t-1}\pi_t = \frac{\gamma}{1-\gamma}\left[\frac{n\omega + \sigma^{-1}}{1+\omega\theta}(\hat{Y}_t^h - \hat{Y}_t^N) + \frac{(1-n)\omega}{1+\omega\theta}(\hat{Y}_t^f - \hat{Y}_t^N) \right] + \frac{1-n}{n}\left(\frac{1}{1-\gamma}\hat{e}_t - E_{t-1}\hat{e}_t \right).$$

8. The aggregate supply schedule is:

$$\pi_t - E_{t-1}\pi_t = \frac{\gamma}{1-\gamma}\left[\frac{\omega + \sigma^{-1}}{1+\omega\theta}(\hat{Y}_t^h - \hat{Y}_t^N) \right].$$

9. Note we implicitly assume that the price-setting fractions (γ, $1 - \gamma$) across the different openness scenarios are the same; empirically this (γ, $1 - \gamma$) can be relaxed. Also, the open economy steady state elasticities are assumed to be equal to the closed economy steady state elasticities. There is however no theory that can explain the fixed-flexible pricing structure for a closed economy; or one that can rationalize how the pricing structure changes in the presence of globalization. Thus we also do not know how

globalization affects the structure of price setting behavior by firms. The globalization proposition we just proved is therefore conditional on exogenous determination of the price-setting fractions (γ, $1 - \gamma$) across the different openness scenarios. The flexible price mark up term, $1/\theta$, is also assumed to be unaffected by the openness regime.

10. We focus here on the inflation-output tradeoff. In the quadratic loss function minimization problem the residual additive term in the loss function, residual, which is different across regimes, is essentially ignored. Therefore, the policy optimization problem yields the same equilibrium functional relationship between the equilibrium values of surprise inflation and the output gap, in each one of the three regimes.

11. Because the relative weight of the output gap term in the utility-based loss function is equal to $1/\theta$ times the sacrifice ratio, a working assumption that we make is that the parameter $1/\theta$ is uncorrelated, across the disinflation episodes, with the measures of openness.

12. Using Ball's (1994) sacrifice ratio estimates, Temple (2002) finds only a weak relationship between import-output ratios (as a measure of trade openness) and the sacrifice ratio in a cross-country analysis. However, his use of the (non-instrumented) import-output ratio as openness measures in the regressions raises acute issues of endogeneity. Indeed, when Daniels, Nourzad, and Vanhoose (2005) augment Temple's regressions with a measure of central bank independence, which allows them to condition on the interaction between central bank independence and the measure of trade openness, they find there is a positive and statistically significant relationship between trade openness and the sacrifice ratio.

13. Results are consistent with Loungani, Razin, and Yuen (2001) and Daniels, Nourzad, and Vanhoose (2005). See also Appendix 1 for indirect evidence on the linkage between globalization and tightness of monetary policy.

References

Ball, Laurence. 1993. "What Determines the Sacrifice Ratio?" NBER Working Paper no. 4306. Reprinted in Mankiw, N.G., ed., *Monetary Policy*. Chicago: University of Chicago Press, 1994.

Barro, Robert, and David Gordon. 1983. "A Positive Theory of Monetary Policy in a Natural Rate Model?" *The Journal of Political Economy* 91(4): 589–610.

Benati, L. 2004. "Evolving Post-World War II U.K. Economic Performance." *Journal of Money, Credit and Banking* 36(4): 691–717.

Benigno, Gianluca, and Pierpaolo Benigno. 2003. "Price Stability in Open Economies." *The Review of Economic Studies* 70: 743–764.

Blanchard, Olivier, and Francesco Giavazzi. 2002. "Current Account in The Euro Area: The End of The Horioka-Feldstein Puzzle?" MIT Department of Economics Working Paper no. 03–05.

Chen, Natalie, Jean Imbs, and Andrew Scott. 2004. "Competition, Globalization and the Decline of Inflation." CEPR Discussion Paper no. 6495.

Cooper, Richard. 1999. "Should Capital Controls be Banished?" *Brookings Papers on Economic Activity*: 89–125.

Daniels, Joseph P., Farrokh Nourzad, and David D. Vanhoose. 2005. "Openness, Central Bank Independence, and the Sacrifice Ratio." *Journal of Money, Credit and Banking* 37(2): 371–379.

Gali, Jordi, and Tommaso Monacelli. 2005. "Monetary Policy and Exchange Rate Volatility in a Small Open Economy." *The Review of Economic Studies* 72: 707–734.

Kydland, Finn, and Edward Prescott. 1977. "Rules Rather Than Discretion: The Inconsistency of Policy Plans." *Journal of Political Economy* 85(3): 473–491.

Lane, Philip. 1997. "Inflation in Open Economies." *Journal of International Economics* 42: 327–347.

Loungani, Prakash, Assaf Razin, and Chi-Wa Yuen. 2001. "Capital Mobility and the Output-Inflation Tradeoff." *Journal of Development Economics* 64: 255–274.

Paoli, Bianca. 2004. "Monetary Policy and Welfare in a Small Open Economy." CEP Discussion Paper Series no. 639. London School of Economics.

Quinn, Dennis. 1997. "The Correlates of Change in International Financial Regulation." *American Political Science Review* 91: 531–551.

Razin, Assaf, and Chi-Wa Yuen. 2002. "The "New Keynesian" Phillips Curve: Closed Economy vs. Open Economy." *Economics Letters* 75: 1–9.

Rogoff, Kenneth. 1985. "The Optimal Degree of Commitment to a Monetary Target." *Quarterly Journal of Economics* 100: 1169–1190.

Rogoff, Kenneth. 2003. "Disinflation: An Unsung Benefit of Globalization?" *Finance and Development* 40(4): 55–56.

Rogoff, Kenneth. 2004. "Globalization and Global Disinflation." In Federal Reserve Bank of Kansas City, *Monetary Policy and Uncertainty: Adapting to a Changing Economy*, proceedings of the 2003 Jackson Hole symposium sponsored by the Federal Reserve Bank of Kansas City.

Romer, David. 1993. "Openness and Inflation: Theory and Evidence." *Quarterly Journal of Economics* CVII(4): 869–904.

Romer, David. 1998. "A New Assessment of Openness and Inflation: Reply." *Quarterly Journal of Economics* CXII(2): 649–652.

Sgherri, Silvia. 2002. "A Stylized Model of Monetary Policy." *World Economic Outlook:* April 2002, ch. 2, p. 95–98.

Temple, Jonathan. 2002. "Openess, Inflation, and the Phillips Curve: A Puzzle." *Journal of Money, Credit and Banking* 34: 450–468.

Woodford, Michael. 2003. "Interest and Prices: Foundations of a Theory of Monetary Policy." Princeton, NJ: Princeton University Press.

Appendix I: Globalization and Disinflation—Recent Trends

Sgherri (2002) reports the parameter estimates for a monetary model for the U.S. economy, both for the high inflation period (1970Q1–1982Q1, hereafter the 1970s) and the subsequent move to the low inflation (1982Q2 onward) period. Similar results are obtained for other industrial countries with independent monetary policies included in the sample (Canada, Germany, and the United Kingdom). The parameter estimates indicate that—since 1982—policymakers have become significantly more aggressive on inflation, less responsive to the output gap, and more gradualist in adjusting their policy instruments. Benati (2004) investigates the changing nature of the Phillips relationship in the United Kingdom, with a flattening taking place in the 1980s and a particularly high degree of stability since the adoption of inflation targeting. International financial integration and the making of the single European market are other possible contributing factors.

Trade openness, as measured by a reduction in levels of assistance afforded to domestic industries through protectionist trade policies have raised: the protectionist policies have gradually fallen over the past 40 years. The average level of tariffs and the incidence of use of NTBs in most OECD countries for which data is available reached relatively low levels by the mid-1990s. Trends in the use of NTBs, as measured by incidence and frequency of use of NTBs, are shown in Table A1.

Controls on cross-border capital flows encompass a diversified set of measures. Typically, capital controls take two broad forms: (1) "administrative,"

Table A1
Pervasiveness of non-tariff barriers
(Percent)

	Frequency Ratio (a)			Import Coverage Ratio (b)		
	1988	1993	1996	1988	1993	1996
United States	25.5	22.9	16.8	16.7	17.0	7.7
European Union	26.6	23.7	19.1	13.2	11.1	6.7
Japan	13.1	12.2	10.7	8.6	8.1	7.4
Canada	11.1	11.0	10.4	5.7	4.5	4.0
Norway	26.6	23.7	4.3	13.8	11.1	3.0
Switzerland	12.9	13.5	7.6	13.2	13.2	9.8
Australia	3.4	0.7	0.7	8.9	0.4	0.6
New Zealand	14.1	0.4	0.8	11.5	0.2	0.2
Mexico	2.0	2.0	14.6	18.6	17.4	6.9

Source: OECD (1998), Trends in market openness.
OECD Economic Outlook, June, 1998.

involving outright prohibitions; and (2) "market based that attempt to discourage particular capital movements by making them more expensive, through taxation." Kaminsky and Schmukler (2001) study the progress of financial liberalization (reducing policy barriers to the purchase and sale of assets across national borders) over 1972–1999 periods in both the G–7 industrial economies and various regional sub-groups in the developing world. They prepared a composite index of liberalization of various segments of financial markets, including the capital accounts, domestic financial systems, and stock markets. They found that during the period under review removal of financially repressive measures was slow but continuous globally. They also concluded that the G–7 industrial economies were the first and the rapidest to liberalize their financial sectors. The rise in financial flows among industrial countries has enabled the United States to become both the world's largest creditor and its largest debtor, while financial flows to developing countries have remained steady at about 4 percent of the developing country GDP. Blanchard and Giavazzi (2002) observe that both Portugal and Greece have been running large current account deficits, with no effect on their financial ratings. Starting from this observation, they argue that Portugal and Greece are in fact representative of a broader evolution: Increasing goods and financial market integration is leading to an increasing decoupling of saving and investment within the European Union, and even more so within the Euro area. In particular, it is allowing poorer countries to invest more, save less, and run larger current-account deficits. The converse holds for the richer countries.

Appendix II: Closed Economy Quadratic Loss Function

The quadratic approximation of the utility function, around the steady state, in a closed economy, is given by:

$$U_t = -\frac{\overline{Y}u_c}{2}\left\{(\omega+\sigma^{-1})(x_t-x^*)^2 + (\omega+\theta^{-1})\operatorname{var}_j \hat{y}_{jt}\right\} \qquad (A1)$$

$$\hat{y}_{jt} \equiv \log\left(\frac{y_{jt}}{\overline{Y}}\right), j=1,2; x_t \equiv \hat{Y}_t - \hat{Y}_t^n; \hat{Y}_t = \log(Y_t/\overline{Y})$$

$$x^* = \log\left(\frac{Y^*}{\overline{Y}}\right)$$

$$\operatorname{var}_j \hat{y}_{jt} = \gamma[\hat{y}_{1t}-E_j\hat{y}_{jt}]^2 + (1-\gamma)[\hat{y}_{2t}-E_j\hat{y}_{jt}]^2$$

$$E_j\hat{y}_{jt} = \gamma\hat{y}_{1t}+(1-\gamma)\hat{y}_{2t}.$$

The terms $\operatorname{var}_j \hat{y}_t(j)$ and $E_j\hat{y}_t(j)$ denote cross-variety output variance and average output, respectively.

Note that the term $(\omega + \sigma^{-1})(x_t - x^*)^2$ originates from the sub-utility $[u(Y_t; \xi_t))]$.
    The term $(\omega + \theta^{-1})$ var$_j$ $\hat{y}_t(j)$ originates from the labor disutility

$$\int_0^1 v(y_t(j); \xi_t, A_t) dj .$$

The familiar Dixit-Stiglitz preferences over the differentiated goods (varieties)
imply

$$y_t(j) = Y_t \left(\frac{p_t(j)}{P_t} \right)^{-\theta} .$$

Taking logarithms yields:

$$\log y_t(j) = \log Y_t - \theta(\log p_t(j) - \log P_t).$$

The derived cross-variety variance is:

$$\text{var}_j \log y_t(j) = \theta^2 \, \text{var}_j \log p_t(j).$$

We can now substitute these derivations into equation (A1). The approximate
utility is expressed as a function of the output gap and price dispersion across
varieties:

$$U_t = -\frac{\overline{Y} u_c}{2} \{(\omega + \sigma^{-1})(x_t - x^*)^2 + \theta(1 + \omega\theta) \, \text{var}_j \log p_t(j)\} . \tag{A2}$$

We now exploit the rational-expectation property of mark up pricing and
express the price index in logarithms, as follows.

$$\log p_{2t} = E_{t-1} \log p_{1t}$$
$$\log P_t = \gamma \log p_{1t} + (1 - \gamma) \log p_{2t}.$$

These equations imply that:

$$\pi_t - E_{t-1}\pi_t = \gamma[\log p_{1t} - E_{t-1} \log p_{1t}]$$
$$= \gamma[\log p_{1t} - \log p_{2t}].$$

This step, in turn, yields:

$$\text{var}_j \log p_{jt} = \gamma(1 - \gamma)[\log p_{1t} - \log p_{2t}]^2 = \frac{1-\gamma}{\gamma}[\pi_t - E_{t-1}\pi_t]^2 .$$

Substituting this relationship into equation (A2) we get the closed economy
loss function:

$$L_t = (\pi_t - E_{t-1}\pi_t)^2 + \frac{1}{\theta} \frac{\gamma}{1-\gamma} \frac{\sigma^{-1} + \omega}{1 + \theta\omega}(x_t - x^*)^2 + \text{residual} \tag{A3}$$

where,

$$x^* = (\omega + \sigma^{-1})^{-1} \frac{1}{\mu} .$$

Comment

Robert G. King, Boston University and NBER

1. Introduction

Two outstanding facts about the last 20 years are that measures of world trade and financial openness have increased and that measures of world inflation have dramatically decreased. What is the connection between these facts?

This interesting and policy-relevant contribution by Prakash Loungani and Assaf Razin provides a formal model that links measures of openness to inflation, as well as developing some suggestive empirical evidence. That the contribution is timely as well is perhaps best illustrated by noting that the most recent *World Economic Outlook* (April 2006) produced by the International Monetary Fund is entitled "Globalization and Inflation."

2. A Quick Look at Some Facts

To fix some key ideas, it is useful to borrow some information from the third chapter of the WEO, which is entitled "How has Globalization affected inflation?" Figure 1 shows that the 1980s and 1990s witnessed a substantial decline in inflation in industrialized countries and in some—but not all—emerging market economies, although with the emerging market decline in inflation having occurred more recently. Figure 2 shows the pattern of increase in trade and financial openness in industrial economies and emerging markets. In the industrialized countries, there have been two rounds of major increases in international trade: the first took place while there was an acceleration of inflation in the 1970s, the second at the low inflation rates of the 1990s. Financial openness increased beginning in the mid-1980s and then accelerated dramatically in the 1990s. For emerging

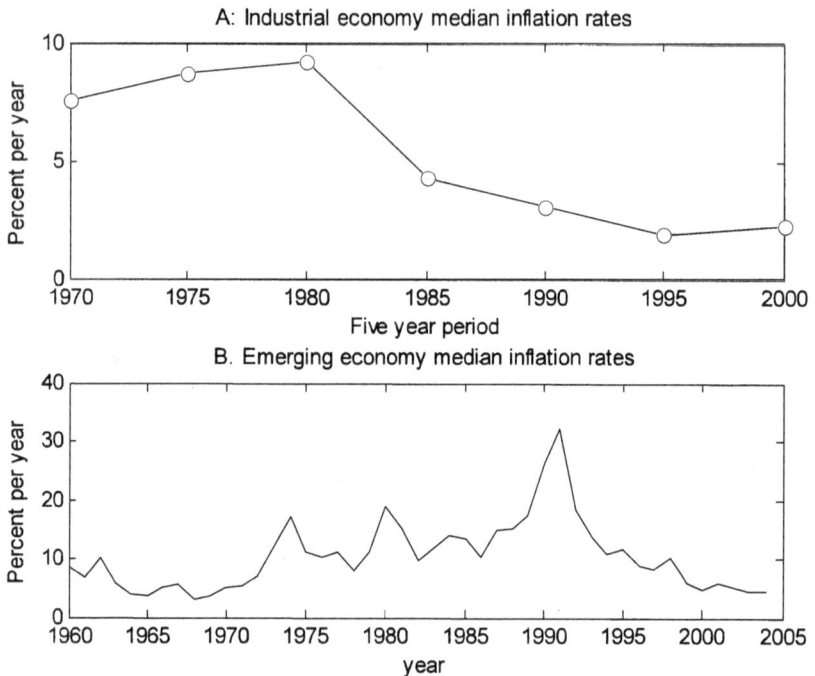

Figure 1
Source: *World Economic Outlook,* 2006, prepared by International Monetary Fund. Panel A is taken from Figure 3.1 in WEO and Panel B is taken from Box 3.1 in WEO.

markets, there has been a broadly similar pattern, although on a different base.

3. A Quick Overview of Some Theory

Many recent macroeconomic models are based on a mixture of Classical and Keynesian components. From the Classical side, they feature explicit microeconomic foundations and no long-run trade-off between inflation and real activity. From the Keynesian side, they feature inflation dynamics that are based on monopolistically competitive firms that set nominal prices in an optimal fashion, but also face some costs of adjusting prices in response to changes in economic conditions. In these models, there is a short-run trade-off between inflation and real activity, particularly if monetary policy is imperfectly credible.

In these monopolistic competition models, domestic adjusting firms—typically a subset of all domestic firms within any short period—set their price P^* as a markup (μ) over nominal marginal cost (Ψ).

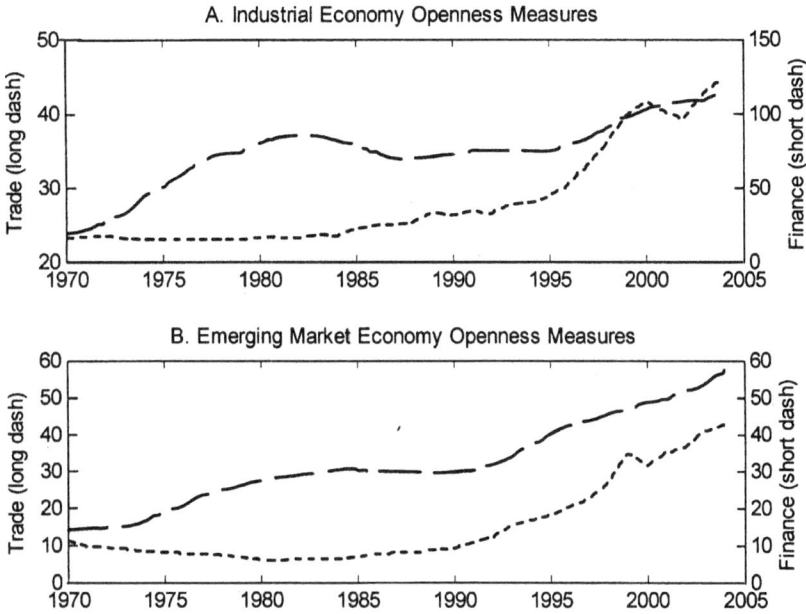

Figure 2
Source: *World Economic Outlook,* 2006, prepared by International Monetary Fund. Both panels are taken from Figure 3.4 WEO.

$$P_t^* = \mu_t * \Psi_t \tag{1}$$

and the price level is a weighted average of prices set now and in previous periods by domestic firms and the prices of some internationally traded goods.

$$\log(P_t) = \theta \left\{ \sum_{j=0}^{J-1} \omega_j \log(P_{t-j}^*) \right\} + (1-\theta)\log(\tilde{P}_t) \tag{2}$$

where $1 - \theta$ is the share of imported goods in the price level and $\log(\tilde{P}_t)$ is the average price of these imported goods. Finally, nominal marginal cost depend on real marginal cost and the price level via $\Psi_t = P_t \psi_t$. Taking all of these considerations together,

$$\pi_t = \Delta \log P_t = \log(P_t) - \log(P_{t-1}) \tag{3}$$

$$= \frac{\theta}{1-\theta\omega_0} \sum_{j=0}^{J-1} \omega_j (\Delta \log(\mu_{t-j}) + \Delta \log(\psi_{t-j}))$$

$$+ \frac{\theta}{1-\theta\omega_0} \sum_{j=1}^{J-1} \omega_j \pi_{t-j} + \frac{1-\theta}{1-\theta\omega_0} \tilde{\pi}_t.$$

So, in an accounting sense, inflation depends on changes in markups and real marginal cost, on past inflation, and on imported inflation.

Considering a major industrial country like the United States, globalization could therefore be important for inflation as (a) international competition affects markups or real marginal cost; (b) directly via imported inflation; or (c) via a changing share $1 - \theta$. For concreteness, let's think about the effect of trade with China, which is an important trading partner with the United States. Controversially, Chinese monetary policy seems to mainly involve keeping its currency low and stable vis-à-vis the U.S.

The key point built into the theory is that changes in the levels of real markups and real marginal cost affect the level of prices rather than the inflation rate. Hence, it is only *changes in the rate of growth* of these variables that affect inflation. For globalization to account for a decline in inflation, it must be increasing at an increasing rate. This does not seem to be the case for the United States. Therefore, we must look elsewhere for the sources of a decline in the inflation rate. Further, even with increased trade, the direct effect of imported inflation is not large for U.S. inflation. And, if we were to think carefully about this channel, we would also want to build in a theory of exchange rate determination.

4.   Money, Inflation, and Real Activity

It is thus natural that Loungani and Razin are led to consider the effect of financial and commodity market openness on the conduct of monetary policy. Modern macroeconomic models also contain effects of the monetary authority's actions on the evolution of prices. It is easiest to summarize these in terms of the familiar identity

$$M_t v = P_t y_t \tag{4}$$

where M_t is the money stock, v_t is its velocity (assumed constant), P_t is the price level as above, and y_t is output. According to this specification, then, inflation can be accounted for by changes in money, velocity, and real output growth.

$$\pi_t = \Delta \log(M_t) - \Delta \log(v_t) - \Delta \log(y_t). \tag{5}$$

Further, there are two sets of influences on the path of real output within modern macroeconomic models. First, it is influenced by real factors like changing productivity and changing competitive conditions that exert their impact via markups and marginal cost. Second, it is influenced by monetary policy, which also affects markups and marginal cost.

Globalization is certainly an important influence on the ongoing reorganization of United States economic activity, particularly for specific industries. Globalization may also be important for raising productivity growth in particular sectors, since greater returns can be realized from investments in new and better products.

However, from the aggregate perspective that is important for thinking about inflation, there are very modest effects on the growth rate of output. My sense is that little of the decline in inflation in industrialized countries can be explained by faster output growth, at most one out of the 8 percent median decline in Figure 1. So, as Milton Friedman suggested long ago, the explanation of the inflation decline in the United States and other industrialized countries must lie in the behavior of their monetary authorities.

4.1   Optimal Inflation with Commitment

Modern macroeconomic models suggest that the monetary authority has limited ability to affect the level of real economic activity via the average rate of inflation. This attribute is not much changed by openness. Thus, an optimizing monetary authority under commitment typically chooses a low rate of inflation (close to zero).

4.2   Equilibrium Inflation with Discretion

A discretionary monetary authority may choose a higher rate of inflation, for reasons familiar from Barro and Gordon's (1983) work on the inflation bias that arises when there is no commitment. Further, Romer (1993) uses an extension of the discretionary equilibrium to an open economy to develop the prediction that the extent of openness should be negatively related to the inflation rate (because the monetary authority's ability to influence real activity in the short-run is more modest) and finds that this holds in a cross-section of countries.

Loungani and Razin are therefore motivated to study the effect of commodity and financial market openness on the objectives and constraints of a monetary authority within a modern macroeconomic model. The idea—in line with some general observations and a simple model in Rogoff (2004)—is that increased openness has changed the objectives and constraints of monetary authorities in ways that account for reduced inflation. The Loungani-Razin analysis is carefully worked out and buttresses the arguments of Rogoff.

4.2.1 Inflation and Discretion from the Closed Economy Perspective

It is an open question whether a discretionary monetary policy model can explain the rise and fall of inflation in the United States, other industrialized economies, and emerging market economies. For economists working from a closed economy perspective, where time series analysis is key, there is embarrassing little applied research on this topic, despite the exhortations of Baxter (1988). Fortunately, the recent work of Ireland (1999), which suggests that U.S. inflation is driven by an evolving natural rate of unemployment as predicted by the Barro-Gordon model, is stimulating some further work on this important topic.

4.2.2 Inflation and Discretion from the Open Economy Perspective

Following the work of Romer (1993), there has been more applied work by open economy macroeconomists, which mainly focuses on a cross-section of countries. Using the import share as his measure of openness, Romer summarizes his core findings as follows:

"the estimated impact of openness on inflation is quantitatively large. The point estimates in column (I), for example, imply an average rate of inflation of 18 percent for a closed economy, 14 percent for an economy with an import share of 25 percent, 11 percent for an import share of 50 percent, and 8 percent for an import share of 75 percent. Finally, the fraction of the variation in inflation explained by the regression is non-trivial: openness alone accounts for over 10 percent of the cross-country variation in average inflation rates."

If import shares are one-half of the export+import shares used in Figure 2, then we can use these cross-sectional estimates to make a prediction about the time-series relationship: an increase in industrialized country trade openness in Figure 1 from about 36 in 1985 to about 43 in 2004 should correspond to an increase in the import share from about 18 to about 22. In terms of Romer's calculations, an increase from autarchy to 25 percent import share will change the inflation rate by only 4 percent. Thus, the prediction would be that a very small part—less than 1 percent—of the decline in industrialized country inflation from about 9 percent to about 2 percent was based on the interaction of openness with monetary policy outcomes. This is a fairly small effect and it seems completely consistent with my reading of the history of the major industrialized countries.

In terms of the emerging markets, export+import shares rose from about 29 percent in the early 1990s to about 57 percent in recent years. Cutting these in half (say, to 15 percent and 30 percent) and applying Romer's estimates, we would conclude that inflation should decline by at most a few percent. This is small potatoes in terms of the drop in median inflation from 30 percent to 5 percent shown in panel B of Figure 1.

Taking the results of these industrial and emerging market exercises together, my conclusion is that there is a substantial tension between the cross-section estimates of Romer and the attempt to attribute major parts of the decline in inflation in industrial and emerging market economies to increased globalization. At the same time, analysis along the lines of Loungani and Razin is useful because it potentially sharpens the predictions of the theory and allows for a more systematic empirical investigation.

References

Barro, Robert, and David Gordon. 1983. "A Positive Theory of Monetary Policy in a Natural Rate Model." *Journal of Political Economy* 91(4): 589–610.

Baxter, Marianne. 1993. "Toward an Empirical Assessment of Game-theoretic Models of Policymaking: A Comment." Carnegie-Rochester Conference Series on Public Policy, Volume 28: 141–151.

Goodfriend, Marvin, and Robert G. King. 1997. "The New Neoclassical Synthesis and the Role of Monetary Policy." *NBER Macroeconomic Annual*. Cambridge: MIT Press: 231–283.

Ireland, Peter. 1999. "Does the Time-consistency Problem Explain the Behavior of Inflation in the United States?" *Journal of Monetary Economics* 44(2): 279–291.

Rogoff, Kenneth. 2004. "Globalization and Global Disinflation." In Federal Reserve Bank of Kansas City, *Monetary Policy and Uncertainty: Adapting to a Changing Economy.* The Federal Reserve Bank of Kansas City.

Romer, David. 1993. "Openness and Inflation: Theory and Evidence." *Quarterly Journal of Economics* CVII(1): 869 904.

Comment

Kenneth D. West, University of Wisconsin and NBER

Razin and Loungani's paper links measures of openness to weights in a utility based loss function. Through policy that minimizes the loss function, openness is then tied to the tradeoff between output and inflation. The authors argue that disinflation data support the model's implication that more open economies have higher sacrifice ratios.

Their model builds on Razin and Yuen (2002), which in turn is an open economy extension of a closed economy formulation found in Woodford (2003). In Woodford (2003), there is a continuum of differentiated labor and differentiated products. Consumption is the familiar Dixit-Stigliz aggregate of the differentiated products, with substitution elasticity θ. Current period utility depends on current period consumption and leisure. Producers are a mix of flexible price firms and firms with one period price stickiness. Because prices are sticky for at most one period, the aggregate supply curve that results is of the new classical form familiar from work from the 1970s on monetary misperceptions models. Specifically, output deviates from steady state only insofar as there are inflation surprises (Woodford 2003: 397):

$$\pi_t = E_{t-1} \pi_t + \theta \psi x_t. \tag{1}$$

Here, x_t is the output gap, θ is the elasticity that figures into Dixit-Stiglitz aggregation, and ψ is a positive parameter that depends on θ and some other model parameters. These other model parameters are: the fraction of flex price firms (γ, in the notation of the present paper), the elasticity of consumption in consumer's utility function (σ), and the elasticity of leisure in consumer's utility function (ω). Woodford (2003: 398) shows that a quadratic approximation around the steady state yields a loss function:

$$\text{loss} = (\pi_t - E_{t-1}\,\pi_t)^2 + \psi(x_t - x^*)^2, \tag{2}$$

π_t = inflation, x_t = output gap, x^* = efficient output gap.

The ψ that appears in the aggregate supply curve (1) is the same as the ψ that appears in the loss function (2).

In Razin and Yuen's (2002) open economy extension, the home country produces good 1 to n, the foreign country goods n to 1, for given n. Aggregate supply is shown to depend on the foreign output gap and the deviation of the real exchange rate from steady state. The slope on domestic output gap ψ is shown to vary with openness as follows:

slope of aggregate supply when there is trade and capital mobility (3)

    < slope of aggregate supply when there is trade mobility
    but not capital mobility

    < slope of aggregate supply when there is neither trade
    nor capital mobility (i.e., closed economy).

As well, given trade mobility, the slope falls as the import share $1 - n$ increases, a result again consistent with the notion that increased openness lowers the slope of aggregate supply.

Recall the conventional wisdom that the sacrifice ratio is greater when aggregate supply is flatter: a shift downwards in aggregate demand will be associated with a relatively large fall in output and a relatively small fall in inflation when aggregate supply is relatively flat. The inequalities in (3) thus suggest that the sacrifice ratio is higher in more open (i.e., flatter slope [lower ψ]) economies. (A side comment: Some recent literature has focused on the upside of a flat [low ψ] aggregate supply curve—thanks to globalization, inflation is slow to take off, even when demand pressures are high. This paper focuses on the downside of a flat aggregate supply curve: disinflations are costly.)

The present paper shows that Razin and Yuen's (2002) results on the slope of aggregate supply translate to similar weights in a utility based loss function. As in section 5 of the present paper, let numerical subscripts 1, 2, and 3 denote the values of ψ that result across different assumptions about trade and capital mobility. Symbolically, then:

ψ_1 [loss function parameter when there is trade and capital mobility]   (4)

$< \psi_2$ [loss function parameter when there is trade mobility but notcapital mobility]

$< \psi_3$ [loss function parameter when there is neither trade nor capital mobility].

Razin and Loungani assume that policy will be set to minimize this loss function, and that tradeoffs between inflation and output that we see in the data will reflect the loss function weights. The empirical work considers whether greater openness (lighter restrictions on capital controls and trade) implies higher sacrifice ratios. It does so using disinflation episodes from Ball (1993). It adds ordinal measures of current and capital account openness to Ball's (1993) regressions of sacrifice ratios on inflationary variables. The result is that the sacrifice ratio increases with openness.

The basic idea of this paper—use modern monetary models to explain cross-sectional variation in the output-inflation tradeoff—is an excellent one. The paper, however, does not make nearly as much of this idea as it might. A list of questions and concerns might include:

1. The paper relies on an aggregate supply curve in which the output gap deviates from zero only when there are inflation surprises. This is a model of aggregate supply that in my view has little claim to empirical relevance. What happens if one allows for multiple periods of stickiness, using the Calvo or other model for price setting? What happens if one allows for an inertial component to inflation? What happens if one allows the fraction of flex price firms or the import share to change with secular changes in the rate of inflation?

2. Let us put aside such questions, and take the model as given. A needlessly small amount of data were used. According to the model and the argument of the authors, there is no particular reason to focus on disinflations. What happens if data from other time periods or other countries are used? Is the evidence from inflationary (as opposed to disinflationary) periods consistent with the model?

3. Let us also take as given the focus on disinflations. The paper does an incomplete job motivating and interpreting its regressions. Are the effects of openness economically large? Are they plausible, in terms of a rough calibration of parameters that determine the slope of the aggregate supply curve? In light of the model, shouldn't the regressions con-

trol for cross-country variation in other determinants of the slope (e.g., fraction of flexible price firms, share of imports)?

These are the sorts of questions that I hope the authors will answer in future research on this subject.

Acknowledgement

I thank the National Science Foundation for financial support.

References

Ball, Laurence. 1993. "What Determines the Sacrifice Ratio?" NBER Working Paper no. 4306, (March). Reprinted in Mankiw, N.G. (ed.), *Monetary Policy*, (University of Chicago Press, 1994).

Razin, Assat, and Chi-Wa Yuen. 2002. "The 'New Keynesian' Phillips Curve: Closed Economy vs. Open Economy." *Economics Letters* 75: 1–9.

Woodford, Michael. 2003. "Interest and Prices: Foundations of a Theory of Monetary Policy," (Princeton University Press).

Part II: Implications of an Expanding Monetary Union

5

Fiscal Externalities and Optimal Taxation in an Economic Community

Marianne Baxter, *Boston University and NBER*
Robert G. King, *Boston University and NBER*

1. Introduction

The Stability and Growth Pact is a continuing source of economic controversy within Europe. The pact is aimed at enforcing fiscal discipline on the member states of Europe, with the twin objectives of (1) maintaining the conditions for sustainable real growth in output and employment; and (2) providing the foundations for price stability. The pact recognizes that individual member states experience divergent business cycle conditions which may lead them to run deficits at certain points in time. However, the pact is designed to encourage member states to adopt fiscal policies which imply zero deficits on average and to limit their deficits to *3 percent of GDP* at any point in time.

The Stability and Growth Pact (SGP) involves two key ideas. First, it is based on the view that the fiscal policies of one member state are important to the other member states. Second, it is based on the view that the fiscal policy of the member states—particularly the national indebtedness—is important for the monetary policy of the European Central Bank and the behavior of the price level.

Our objective in this paper is to explore the first of these ideas in the context of a small and entirely real dynamic general equilibrium model of a multi-country economic union. We think that this is a logical starting point for two reasons. First, we believe that there are underlying real forces operating within economies that are highly important for the fiscal policies of member states. Therefore, it is important to understand the effects of these forces both on the individual member state and on the other members of the economic community. Second, modern models that give a central bank leverage over real economic activity frequently do so effectively by allowing the central bank to affect distortions arising from imperfect competition. These distortions have an alternative interpretation as tax rates, so that the consequences of alternative monetary policies and the design of optimal monetary policies are closely related to fiscal policy issues. Thus, monetary policy can frequently be given a fiscal policy interpretation. Further, desirable monetary policies depend heavily on the nature of fiscal policy.[1]

The model that we construct is parsimonious, designed to permit sharp focus on two key issues. First, we study the nature of fiscal externalities within an economic community such as the EU which lacks explicit rules for fiscal policy coordination. Second, to the extent that these externalities exist, we ask whether public sector deficits are a useful indicator of the extent of these fiscal externalities, as seems to have been believed by policymakers who framed the fiscal policy rules codified in the SGP. Our model abstracts from investment and capital formation and assumes that individual governments can commit to following dynamically optimal fiscal policies. Further, government expenditure is taken to be exogenous as is traditional in standard models of optimal taxation and optimal monetary policy.

There are two key observations about current fiscal policy in the EMU that we build into our model. First, all countries in the EMU employ national sales taxes (VAT) as well as income taxes, but there is considerable heterogeneity in terms of the relative use of these taxes. Second, in all countries, government expenditure contains four major components—purchases of goods and services; public employment; investment in government capital; and transfer payments. However, there is considerable heterogeneity across countries in the relative importance of these components.

The SGP is cast in terms of government deficits. However, our model highlights the international transmission of fiscal policy between countries not via the government deficit, but via the country's net exports, which we define as

$$x_{jt} \equiv y_{jt} - g_{jt}^c - c_{jt} \tag{1}$$

where y_{jt} is private output of country j at date t; c_{jt} is the amount of private consumption by country j at date t; and g_{jt}^c is the amount of government consumption in country j at date t. A higher level of net exports by an individual country in a given period has effects on other members of the economic community. If, for example, a country plans to run a surplus in net exports in a future period, that will have the effect of reducing the interest rate applicable to that period, with the strength of this effect depending on the relative size of the country running the surplus. The government surplus in our model is

$$s_{jt} = \tau_{jt}^n w_{jt} n_{jt} + \tau_{jt}^c c_{jt} - w_{jt} g_{jt}^n - g_{jt}^c \tag{2}$$

where w_{jt} is the wage rate; g_{jt}^n is government labor input, n_{jt} is total labor input; τ_{jt}^n is the tax on labor income; and τ_{jt}^c is the consumption tax. There are well-known economic mechanisms that make the trade deficit and the government deficit tend to move together. For example, holding other variables fixed, a rise in government consumption will increase both the fiscal deficit and the trade deficit. Through the trade channel, an individual country's fiscal policy can have effects on other countries which are transmitted via prices (here, the only price is the intertemporal price, i.e., the interest rate). However, the comovement of the fiscal and trade deficits clearly depends on the tax system, i.e., on the tax rates τ_{jt}^n and τ_{jt}^c. To learn about the character of "fiscal externalities" of national policies, we determine the behavior of optimal tax rates within several alternative settings. Our model also incorporates exogenous, time-varying levels of productivity, government purchases, and government labor input.

Our results can be briefly summarized as follows. For a small country within our basic model, which knows that its policies have no effect on community-wide interest rates, it is optimal to set tax rates constant over time. However, the model is silent on whether the necessary tax is applied to labor income, consumption, or both. Although the real equilibrium is invariant to the choice between τ^n and τ^c, the behavior of the public sector deficit obviously is not. Deficits can be highly variable if they involve mainly labor taxation, but relatively smooth if they involve mainly consumption taxation. Trade deficits, on the contrary, are invariant to the structure of taxation. Countries wishing to satisfy the SGP and avoid volatility in government deficits may wish to use the tax instrument that leads to smooth tax revenues. A closed economy will also choose to maintain a measure of tax rates constant over time, just as in the small open economy.

The character of the solution changes when we consider a community of several countries, each of which is "large" in the sense that it can affect community-wide prices via its fiscal policies. In this setting, which we propose as a model of the EMU, each country faces an intertemporal constraint on its net exports of the form:

$$\sum_{t=0}^{\infty} \beta^t \delta_t [y_{jt} - g_{jt}^c - c_{jt}] \geq 0 \tag{3}$$

where $\beta^t \delta_t$ is a discount factor applicable to date t. For a large open economy within an economic community, the effect of this constraint is quite different from the comparable effect for a single (closed) country or a small open economy, The government of a closed country knows that its fiscal policies affect the discount factors $\{\beta^t \delta_t\}_{t=0}^{\infty}$. However, in this closed economy, macroeconomic equilibrium requires that $[y_t - g_t^c - c_t] = 0$ so that the constraint is always satisfied in equilibrium and has no bearing on tax policy. By contrast, the government of a small country takes $\{\beta^t \delta_t\}_{t=0}^{\infty}$ as given and concentrates on the effects of its policies on net exports, $[y_{jt} - g_{jt}^c - c_{jt}]$, so as to assure that the constraint is satisfied. With an intermediate size country, tax policy takes into account effects on both intertemporal prices and net exports.

In community of "large" economies, a distinction emerges between coordinated and uncoordinated national policies. A coordinated community policy emphasizes the requirement that at each date

$$\sum_{j=1}^{J} \theta_j [y_{jt} - g_{jt}^c - c_{jt}] = 0 \qquad (4)$$

where θ_j is the relative size of country j. Essentially, equation (4) specifies that effects of tax policies on intertemporal prices do not create wealth at the community level. In Nash equilibrium, by contrast, governments have an incentive to choose tax rates that are high when the economy would otherwise run positive net exports, so as to make the "net wealth" on the left-hand side of (3), by reducing the world intertemporal price. That is, governments would tend to choose labor income tax policies that would stabilize their net exports relative to the constant-tax-rate-case. Lack of coordination in fiscal policy thus tends to stabilize net exports, relative to the coordinated fiscal policy regime.

2. Fiscal Policy in the European Monetary Union

This section presents information on the key fiscal policy variables in the European Monetary Union (EMU). For comparison, we will also include evidence for (1) countries that are part of the European Union (EU) but not in the EMU, and (2) countries that are not in the EU.

2.1 A Current Snapshot

This sub-section describes the current situation in the EMU. Table 1 presents information on government expenditure, receipts, and the

Table 1
EMU fiscal policy in 2004

	A. Government Expenditure: % of GDP			
Country	(i) Government non-wage consumption	(ii) Government wage consumption	(iii) Government investment	(iv) Government total current disbursements
Austria	8.9%	18.8%	1.0%	50.6%%
Belgium	10.3%	22.1%	1.5%	50.0%
Finland	8.3%	22.1%	2.7%	52.1%
France	10.5%	24.3%	2.9%	55.5%
Germany	11.3%	19.0%	1.5%	48.8%
Greece	3.2%	N/A	N/A	N/A
Ireland	6.8%	15.3%	4.9%	34.1%
Italy	7.8%	18.6%	2.5%	46.5%
Netherlands	13.9%	24.4%	3.3%	49.2%
Portugal	5.6%	20.5%	3.4%	46.3%
Spain	7.3%	17.8%	3.3%	39.5%
Median value	8.3%	19.7%	2.8%	49.0%

	B. Government Receipts: % of GDP			
Country	(i) Total direct taxes	(ii) Total indirect taxes	(iii) Total receipts	(iv) Government surplus
Austria	13.8%	14.6%	50.7%	1.5%
Belgium	17.4%	12.8%	49.7%	5.1%
Finland	18.9%	12.9%	52.8%	2.9%
France	11.8%	15.2%	50.9%	−0.1%
Germany	10.8%	12.2%	45.5%	−0.2%
Greece	N/A	14.2%	44.7%	4.3%
Ireland	11.1%	12.5%	33.3%	−1.1%
Italy	13.3%	14.5%	43.9%	1.5%
Netherlands	10.6%	12.8%	45.0%	0.3%
Portugal	9.5%	15.1%	42.7%	0.3%
Spain	10.5%	11.3%	39.6%	2.2%
Median value	11.4%	12.9%	45.0%	1.5%

Table 1 *(continued)*
EMU fiscal policy in 2004

	C. Employment: % of Working-age Population	
Country	(i) Government employment	(ii) Business sector employment
Austria	9.3%	63.5%
Belgium	11.1%	50.0%
Finland	16.7%	50.4%
France	14.8%	48.8%
Germany	7.5%	61.9%
Greece	7.3%	50.3%
Ireland	7.7%	58.8%
Italy	8.9%	54.2%
Netherlands	7.1%	52.5%
Portugal	12.7%	59.7%
Spain	9.2%	50.1%
Median value	9.2%	52.5%

sectoral structure of employment. Panel A contains details of some specific categories of government expenditures as a percentage of GDP. The median share of government total current disbursements (column (iv)) is 49 percent of GDP, ranging from a low of 34.1 percent (Ireland) to a high of 55.5 percent (France). Columns (i)–(iii) show government expenditures in three main categories: (1) non-wage consumption; (2) wage consumption; and (3) investment. (The remaining components of government disbursements are largely transfers, especially social security transfers.) Of the groups that we present, government wage consumption is substantially larger than either non-wage consumption or investment. Typically, wage consumption is about twice as large as non-wage consumption, and is an order of magnitude larger than government investment. In light of these facts, we develop a model with an important role for government wage consumption, i.e., government hiring of labor.

Panel B contains information on government receipts. Direct taxes and indirect taxes are about equally important in the EMU, each comprising about 12 percent of GDP. The difference between direct+indirect taxes and total receipts is again due largely to social security contributions by employers, employees, and the self-employed.

Column (iv) of Panel B shows the government primary surplus for 2005. According to these official OECD figures, only three EMU countries had deficits in 2004: France, Germany, and Ireland. The official figures show these deficits much smaller than those that would violate the SGP.

Panel C of Table 1 shows a breakdown of employment between the government sector and the business sector (this table does not include the self-employed), expressed as a fraction of the working-age population. Government employment is about one-sixth of the employment of the business sector, with some variation across countries.

Table 2 provides more detailed information on aspects of taxation in the EMU. For comparison, we also provide information for several non-EMU members of the EU. The first three columns of the table show the top marginal personal income tax rates for employees, with and without social security contributions. For comparison, column 3 lists the statutory income tax rate that would apply at the threshold for the highest tax bracket. When the effect of social security contributions is taken into effect, the median of the top marginal personal income tax rate is higher than the median of the statutory income tax rate. For some countries, the difference can be very large. For example, in Germany the statutory tax rate is 47.5 percent for an individual with the highest marginal tax rate (this corresponds to the actual tax rate, barring social security), but when social security is taken into account, the marginal tax rate is 13 percent higher than the statutory rate. Large discrepancies are also observed for Belgium, Greece, Ireland, Italy, Luxembourg, and Portugal. Only for France and Austria is the actual marginal tax rate (including social security) lower than the statutory rate. The non-EMU countries listed in the bottom panel of the table contain one very low-tax economy (the Slovak Republic), as well as two of the highest-tax-rate countries in Europe: Denmark and Sweden. The discrepancy between the statutory tax rate and the true marginal rate including social security is very large for Hungary in particular, where the statutory rate is 38 percent and the true rate is 69.5 percent. The corresponding rates for non-EU countries are listed at the bottom of the table. The median rates are in line with the EMU countries. The notable difference is that, among the non-EU countries, there is little difference between the true rates and the statutory rates.

In contrast to the high variation among countries in marginal personal income tax rates, there is little cross-country variation in the VAT. The median value is 19.3 percent. The highest VAT rate is in Finland (22 percent), while Luxembourg and Germany have relatively low VAT

Table 2
Taxation in the EMU and the EU (OECD members)

| Country | Top Marginal Personal Income Tax Rates for Employees (2004) | | Statutory income tax rate (2004) τ'' | VAT standard rate (2003) (%) τ^c | Corporate income tax (2005): Combined central plus sub-central rates | "Extent of taxation" $\dfrac{1-\tau''}{1+\tau^c}$ |
	Combined central plus sub-central rates	Including Social Security contributions				
Austria	42.9%	42.9%	50.0%	20.0	25.0	0.42
Belgium	45.1%	59.3%	53.5%	21.0	34.0	0.38
Finland	50.3%	56.7%	52.1%	22.0	26.0	0.39
France	37.0%	47.2%	55.7%	19.6	35.0	0.37
Germany	47.5%	60.5%	47.5%	16.0	38.9	0.45
Greece	33.6%	49.6%	40.0%	18.0	N/A	0.51
Ireland	42.0%	48.0%	42.0%	21.0	12.5	0.48
Italy	41.4%	51.6%	46.1%	20.0	33.0	0.45
Luxembourg	33.9%	47.8%	38.9%	15.0	30.4	0.53
Netherlands	52.0%	52.0%	52.0%	19.0	31.5	0.40
Portugal	35.6%	46.6%	40.0%	19.0	27.5	0.50
Spain	45.0%	45.0%	45.0%	16.0	35.0	0.47
Median	42.4%	48.8%	46.8%	19.3	31.5	0.45

EU, non-EMU

Czech Republic	28.0%	40.5%	32.0%	22.0	26.0	0.56
Denmark	54.9%	62.9%	59.7%	25.0	30.0	0.32
Hungary	56.0%	69.5%	38.0%	25.0	16.0	0.50
Poland	26.2%	51.6%	40.0%	22.0	n.a.	0.49
Slovak Republic	8.4%	21.8%	19.0%	20.0	19.0	0.68
Sweden	56.5%	56.5%	56.5%	25.0	28.0	0.35
United Kingdom	40.0%	41.0%	40.0%	17.5	30.0	0.51
Median	41.5%	54.1%	39.0%	23.5	26.0	0.49
Non-EU						
Australia	48.5%	48.5%	48.5%	10.0	30.0	0.47
Canada	46.4%	46.4%	46.4%	7.0	36.1	0.50
Iceland	42.0%	42.0%	43.6%	24.5	18.0	0.45
Japan	47.1%	47.8%	50.0%	5.0	n.a.	0.48
Korea	36.6%	39.2%	39.6%	10.0	27.5	0.55
Mexico	26.6%	28.9%	33.0%	15.0	30.0	0.58
United States	41.4%	42.9%	41.6%	n/a	39.3	n/a
Median	42.0%	42.9%	43.6%	10.0	30.0	0.51

rates at 15 percent and 16 percent, respectively. As a group, the non-EMU countries have higher VAT rates than the EMU countries. Notably, Denmark, Hungary, and Sweden have VAT rates of 25 percent—higher than any of the EMU countries. The non-EU countries rely much less heavily on the VAT, with the exception of Iceland.

The next-to-last column of Table 2 contains data on the corporate income tax rates. There is wide variation across countries in this tax rate, although the median in each group of countries is about 30 percent. Each group of countries has some members with low corporate taxes. In the EMU, Ireland has the lowest corporate tax rate, of only 12.5 percent. Hungary has the lowest rate (16 percent) of the non-EMU members of the EU, and Iceland (18 percent) has the lowest corporate tax rate in the non-EU group.

Finally, the last column of Table 2 contains a measure of what is commonly called the "wedge"

$$\frac{1-\tau_{jt}^{n}}{1+\tau_{jt}^{c}} \tag{5}$$

since it indicates the combined effect of labor and consumption taxation on the relative price of leisure and consumption. To compute this measure, we have used the statutory highest marginal personal income tax rate as our measure of τ^{n} and have used the VAT tax rate as our measure of τ^{c}. Given its prominence in public discussions of fiscal policy in Europe, we examine the behavior of the "wedge" under optimal fiscal policy in our analysis below.

2.2   A Longer View

This sub-section presents some evidence on the evolution of the key fiscal variables over the past 45 years. Figure 1 shows total government receipts and disbursements, expressed as shares of GDP. For most of the EMU countries, the government share of GDP has exhibited a rising trend since the early part of the sample. Ireland shows the opposite trend. Although government expenditure and receipts has been rising in Ireland, GDP has been rising faster still. Figure 2 shows the government "primary balance" as a share of GDP. Figure 3 graphs employment by the government and by the business sector as a fraction of the working age population. The self-employed are not included in the business-sector total. Employment in the government sector has been a gently rising fraction of the working-age population, and is smoother

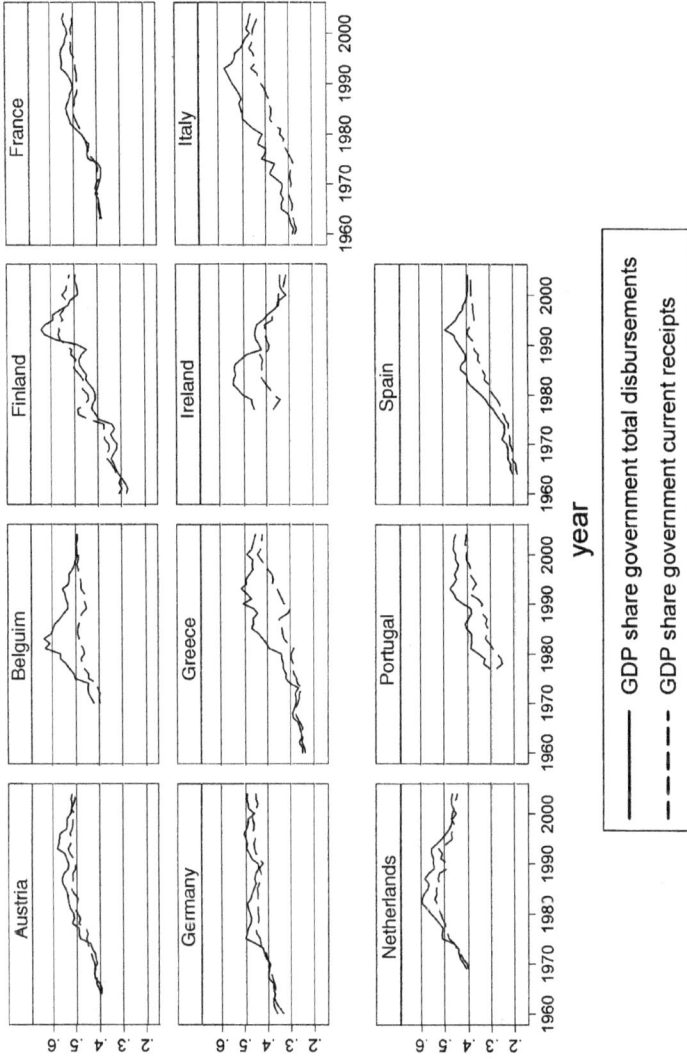

Graphs by country

Figure 1
Government receipts and disbursements

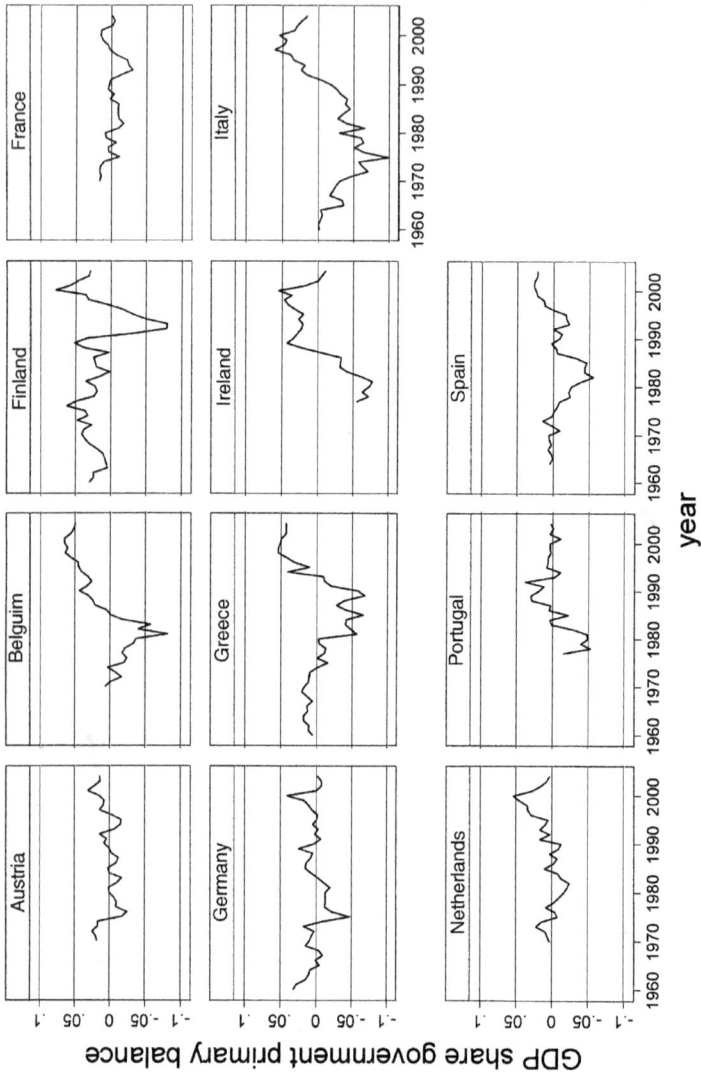

Graphs by country

Figure 2
Government surplus (primary balance)

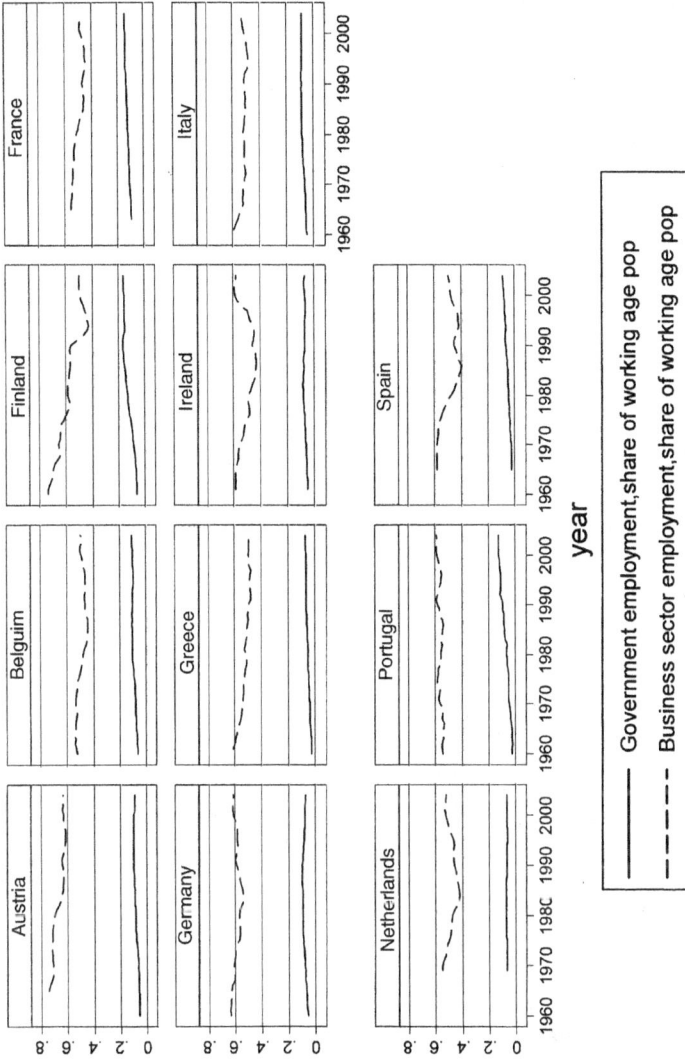

Graphs by country

Figure 3
Employment

than employment in the business sector. Figure 4 plots the government primary balance (the government surplus) against net exports. It may seem odd to graph these two variables together. However, our theoretical model highlights the relationship (actually, the potential lack thereof) between these two economic variables and we will refer back to this figure later on. Table 3 presents summary volatility and correlation statistics for the fiscal and trade deficits. The volatility measure is the standard deviation of annual growth rates. In most countries, the trade deficit is somewhat more volatile than the fiscal deficit. There is no clear pattern at all to the correlation between the fiscal deficit and the trade deficit: the correlations range from –0.32 (Spain) to 0.83 (Ireland). Our theory illustrates why, in an optimal tax setting, there need be no strong relationship between the trade and fiscal deficits.

Finally, Figure 5 plots three components of government expenditure, each measured as a fraction of GDP: (1) non-wage consumption (purchases of goods and services); (2) final wage consumption (purchases of labor), and (3) government fixed capital formation (investment). Government transfers are not included. Government wage expenditure is the largest of the three components of government expenditure, and shows a flat to slightly rising trend over the past 40 years. Government purchases of goods and services is one-half to two-thirds as large as government expenditure on labor, and exhibits a similar flat-to-slightly-rising trend over this period. Government investment represents the smallest GDP share of the three components, and has been falling as a fraction of GDP in several countries.

3.   A Model of an Economic Community

We will study a community with J countries which are indexed by $j = 1$, $2, \ldots J$. There will be several elements which distinguish a country. First, each country will have a unified labor market, with no labor mobility across countries. Second, countries will be subject to country-specific shocks to productivity and government purchases. Countries may differ in terms of size. We use θ_j to denote country j's fraction of community population, thus $\theta_j > 0$ and $\Sigma_{j=1}^{J} \theta_j = 1$.

3.1   Structure of Basic Model

In order to keep the analysis as simple as possible, all countries produce the same internationally traded final good, which can be used for public and private consumption.

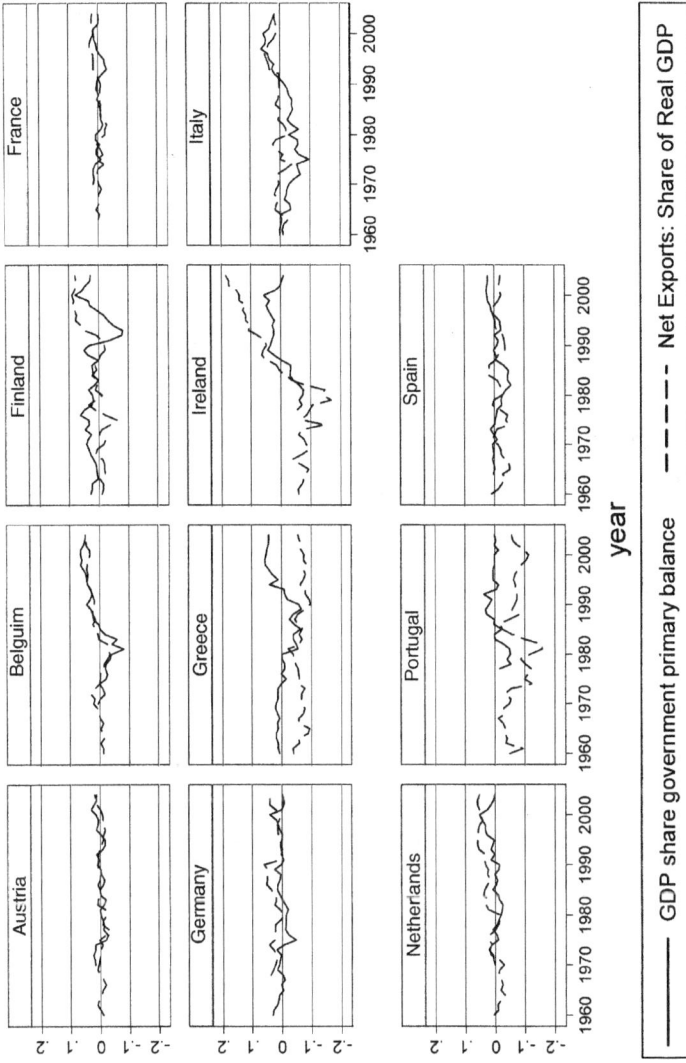

Figure 4
Government surplus and net exports

Table 3
Relationship between net exports and the fiscal deficit

| Country | Volatility of Growth Rate: % Per Year | | Correlation: net exports and fiscal deficit |
	Net exports	Fiscal deficit	
Austria	1.1%	1.4%	0.25
Belgium	2.3%	3.9%	0.87
Finland	4.0%	3.2%	−0.09
France	1.4%	1.2%	0.00
Germany	1.7%	1.5%	0.13
Greece	1.6%	3.4%	−0.14
Ireland	10.2%	4.2%	0.83
Italy	1.9%	3.9%	0.55
Netherlands	2.9%	1.8%	0.46
Portugal	3.5%	2.3%	0.50
Spain	1.8%	2.1%	−0.32
Median value	1.9%	2.3%	0.25

3.1.1 Production

We will assume that countries produce the single good according to constant-returns-to-scale production functions which depend only on labor input and have time-varying productivity levels. Private output is therefore of the form:

$$y_{jt} = a_{jt}(n_{jt} - g^n_{jt})$$

where a_{jt} is labor productivity. As above, y_{jt} is output in country j at time t, n_{jt} is total labor input, and g^n_{jt} is government use of labor input.

3.1.2 Labor Markets

We assume that there is a competitive labor market in each country. Competition ensures that the real wage—measured in units of the consumption good—in country j is given by

$$w_{jt} = a_{jt}$$

so we use these two symbols interchangeably below.

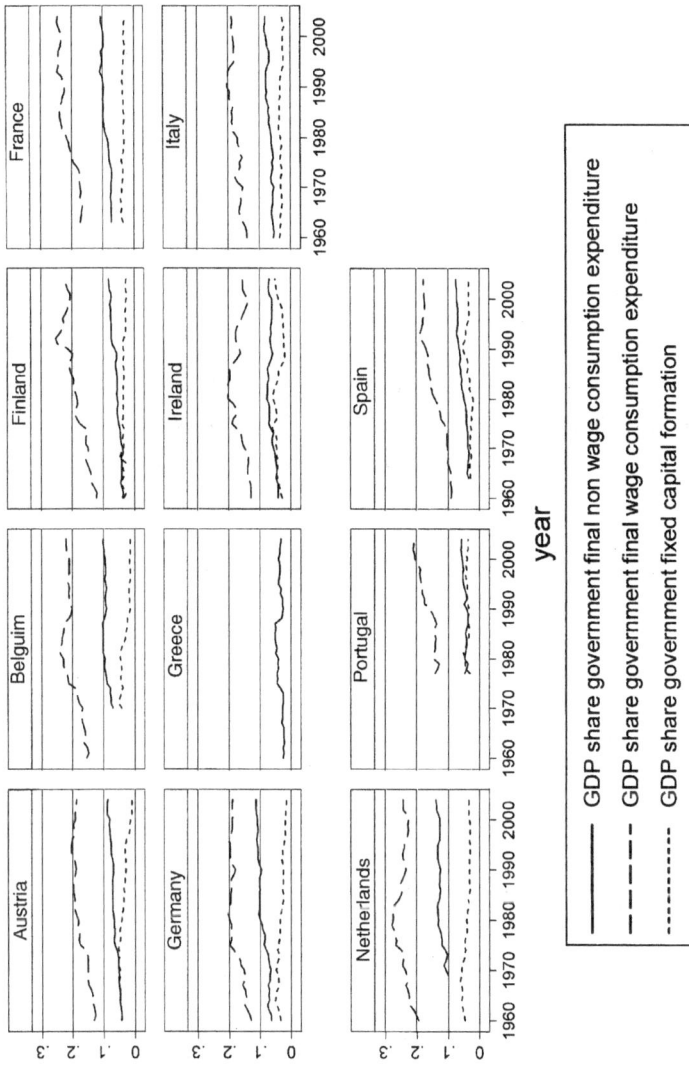

Graphs by country

Figure 5
Components of government expenditure

3.1.3   Government

We assume that each country's government faces an exogenous requirement for two types of purchases: (1) purchases of labor for its own use,
and (2) purchases of the consumption good. At date t, let g^c_{jt} be the
amount of purchases of goods and g^n_{jt} be country j purchases of labor.
Let τ^n_{jt} be the period t labor income tax rate in country j and let τ^c_{jt} be the
consumption tax rate.

3.2   Dynamic Elements

We assume that there is a single, community-wide market in which all
public and private financial instruments are traded. We assume that
this market establishes a discount factor, $\beta^t \delta_t$, which is the price of a
unit of the consumption good at t (β and δ_t will be discussed further
below).

3.2.1   Private and Public Intertemporal Budget Constraints

Private saving per capita in country j is

$$(1-\tau^n_{jt})w_{jt}n_{jt} - (1+\tau^c_{jt})c_{jt} \tag{6}$$

where c_{jt} is the amount of country j's private consumption demand for
the aggregate good. The representative household's budget constraint
is therefore

$$0 \le \sum_{t=0}^{\infty} \beta^t \delta_t[(1-\tau^n_{jt})w_{jt}n_{jt} - (1+\tau^c_{jt})c_{jt}]. \tag{7}$$

The country j government's primary surplus at date t is

$$s_{jt} = \tau^n_{jt}w_{jt}n_{jt} + \tau^c_{jt}c_{jt} - w_{jt}g^n_{jt} - g^c_{jt} \tag{8}$$

and the government's intertemporal budget constraint is

$$0 \le \sum_{t=0}^{\infty} \beta^t \delta_t s_{jt}. \tag{9}$$

These imply a country-wide constraint (3), as discussed in the introduction:

$$0 \le \sum_{t=0}^{\infty} \beta^t \delta_t[w_{jt}n_{jt} - g^c_{jt} - w_{jt}g^n_{jt} - c_{jt}] = \sum_{t=0}^{\infty} \beta^t \delta_t[y_{jt} - g^c_{jt} - c_{jt}]$$

which is the requirement that the discounted value of a country's net
exports is zero.

3.2.2 Intertemporal Consumption and Labor Supply Choices

Agents in country j maximize

$$U_j = \sum_{t=0}^{\infty} \beta^t u(c_{jt}, n_{jt})$$

subject to the household budget constraint. We assume that the momentary utility function takes the form

$$u(c, n) = \frac{1}{1-\sigma} c^{1-\sigma} - \frac{\chi}{1+\gamma} n^{1+\gamma}. \tag{10}$$

Intertemporally efficient consumption and labor supply plans require that

$$0 = u_c(c_{jt}, n_{jt}) - \Lambda_j \delta_t (1 + \tau_{jt}^c) \tag{11}$$

$$0 = u_n(c_{jt}, n_{jt}) + \Lambda_j \delta_t (1 - \tau_{jt}^n) w_{jt} \tag{12}$$

where Λ_j is a country-specific Lagrange multiplier which assures that the household's budget constraint is satisfied. Generally, these conditions define a set of Frischian behavioral equations for consumption and labor, which are each functions of $\Lambda_j \delta_t (1 + \tau_{jt}^c)$ and $\Lambda_j \delta_t (1 - \tau_{jt}^n) w_{jt}$. With the specified momentary utility function, we have a simpler, constant elasticity form of consumption demand,

$$c_{jt} = [\Lambda_j \delta_t (1 + \tau_{jt}^c)]^{-\frac{1}{\sigma}}.$$

Labor supply also takes on a constant elasticity form,

$$n_{jt} = [\Lambda_j * (1 - \tau_{jt}^n) w_{jt} \delta_t / \chi]^{\frac{1}{\gamma}}.$$

These rules imply that individuals substitute away from consumption and leisure when the intertemporal relative price, δ_t, is high. Individuals also substitute toward work in periods in which the after-tax wage rate is high.

The multiplier Λ_j has a number of properties of importance to us below. We illustrate the first of these by noting that, with the specified preferences, the multiplier which satisfies the household's budget constraint is

$$\Lambda_j = \left[\chi^{\frac{1}{\gamma}} \frac{\displaystyle\sum_{t=0}^{\infty} \beta^t [\delta_t (1 + \tau_{jt}^c)]^{1-\frac{1}{\sigma}}}{\displaystyle\sum_{t=0}^{\infty} \beta^t [\delta_t (1 - \tau_{jt}^n) w_{jt}]^{1+\frac{1}{\gamma}}} \right]^{\frac{\sigma\gamma}{\sigma+\gamma}}.$$

Hence, if all of the intertemporal prices are scaled up so that $\delta_t' = \phi\delta_t$, then the multiplier is scaled by $1/\phi$. This is just a consequence of the fact that real demands for goods and leisure are invariant to units in which prices are stated.

3.3 Community General Equilibrium

Our assumption is that the community is closed, which we think of as a workable approximation to the idea that the community is a large part of the world, as is Europe. We find it useful to think about the equilibrium in two steps. First, given aggregate demand and interest rates, the market for each country's goods and factors must clear. Second, aggregate demand and interest rates must be consistent with the overall equilibrium conditions of the community.

Community per-capita consumption demand is

$$C_t = \sum_{j=1}^{J} \theta_{jt} c_{jt}$$

and total government consumption is

$$G_t^c = \sum_{j=1}^{J} \theta_{jt} g_{jt}^c.$$

Aggregate world supply of the good, in per capita terms, is given by the weighted sum of all countries' outputs:

$$\sum_{j=1}^{J} \theta_{jt} y_{jt}.$$

Equating the aggregate supply and demand for goods implies an equilibrium sequence $\{\delta_t\}_{t=0}^{\infty}$.

Our interest is in studying settings in which each government must obey its budget constraint: there are no intergovernmental transfers. We explore two alternative assumptions about interactions across governments: (1) the community's governments cooperate to as to maximize the joint welfare of their citizens with the setting of their tax instruments; and (2) each government maximizes the welfare of its citizens, taking the policies of other governments as given. Before turning to this analysis, we discuss optimal taxation in simpler settings.

4. Background on Optimal Taxation

To establish some core ideas and benchmark results, this section studies three basic settings. First, following Ramsey, we consider a closed economy, as addressed in most analyses of fiscal policy. Second, we consider a small open economy, paralleling the Ramsey analysis of the closed economy. Third, we consider an alternative approach to the analysis of the small open economy, which is easier to extend to the analysis of interacting economies. In all of the settings that we study, an important element is the equilibrium form of the government budget constraint.

4.1 The Government Budget Constraint in Equilibrium

To study a formulation of the government's problem that does not involve taxes or market prices, we start by noting that the government budget constraint can be rewritten as

$$0 \leq \sum_{t=0}^{\infty} \beta^t \delta_t [-(1-\tau_{jt}^n)w_{jt}n_{jt} + (1+\tau_{jt}^c)c_{jt} - w_{jt}n_{jt} - g_{jt}^c - c_{jt} - w_{jt}g_{jt}^n] \tag{13}$$

$$= \sum_{t=0}^{\infty} \beta^t \delta_t [-(1-\tau_{jt}^n)w_{jt}n_{jt} + (1+\tau_{jt}^c)c_{jt} + y_{jt} - g_{jt}^c - c_{jt}]$$

$$= \sum_{t=0}^{\infty} \beta^t \delta_t [-(1-\tau_{jt}^n)w_{jt}n_{jt} + (1+\tau_{jt}^c)c_{jt}]$$

where the first line simply involves adding and subtracting consumption and labor income; the second makes use of the equilibrium wage rate and the production function; and the third imposes the requirement that $\sum_{t=0}^{\infty} \beta^t \delta_t [y_{jt} - g_{jt} - c_{jt}] = 0$.

Multiplying by Λ_j and imposing the private sector first-order conditions, we arrive at the requirement that

$$\sum_{t=0}^{\infty} \beta^t [u_c(c_{jt}, n_{jt})c_{jt} + u_n(c_{jt}, n_{jt})n_t] \geq 0. \tag{14}$$

That is: the government budget constraint in equilibrium is the requirement that the private sector must be able to afford to purchase the quantities that the government chooses for it, when the prices are stated in marginal utility units.

Since this expression will appear repeatedly below, it is convenient for us to have a short-hand version of it. Defining $q(c_t, n_t) = [u_c(c_t, n_t)c_t + u_n(c_t, n_t)n_t]$, we can thus write the equilibrium government budget constraint as

$$\sum_{t=0}^{\infty} \beta^t [q(c_{jt}, n_{jt})] \geq 0 \tag{15}$$

for country j.

4.2   Neutral Tax Changes

A standard result in public finance is that consumption taxes and labor income taxes are equivalent instruments when switches between these involve no change in government revenue. In intertemporal frameworks, such as those which we study in this paper, this equivalence arises when tax changes are considered which take the form

$$(1+\tau_t^c)' = \varsigma(1+\tau_t^c)$$

$$(1-\tau_t^n)' = \varsigma(1-\tau_t^n)$$

for all dates t. In view of the government budget constraint in equilibrium (15), it is clear that this policy is *revenue* neutral for any positive ς. Further, the government budget constraint in equilibrium implies the private sector budget constraint: both are essentially $\Sigma_{t=0}^{\infty}\beta^t\delta_t[-(1 - \tau_{jt}^n)w_{jt}n_{jt} + (1+\tau_{jt}^c)c_{jt}] = 0$. In view of the first order conditions, this policy is *behaviorally* neutral when the multiplier adjusts according to

$$\Lambda' = \frac{\Lambda}{\varsigma}$$

which in turn is consistent with the original budget constraint. So, such a switch in tax policy is neutral on all accounts.

Hence, for exploration of behavior—including the analysis of optimal policy—a country's fiscal policy is better summarized by an effective consumption wedge and an effective labor wedge,

$$\xi_{jt}^c = \Lambda_j(1+\tau_{jt}^c)$$

$$\xi_{jt}^n = \Lambda_j(1-\tau_{jt}^n)$$

than by the statutory tax rates themselves.

4.3   Single Country Benchmark

Our model is structured so that it would be optimal to have constant tax rates over time if there were a single country. To display this result and provide the background for some aspects of our analysis of an economic community, we start by supposing that there is a single country (the country subscript, j, will not appear). In this setting, the appropriate Ramsey tax problem is to maximize

$$U = \sum_{t=0}^{\infty} \beta^t u(c_t, n_t)$$

subject to the sequence of resource constraints

$$y_t = a_t(n_t - g_t^n) = c_t + g_t^c$$

the government budget constraint

$$0 \leq \sum_{t=0}^{\infty} \beta^t \delta_t [\tau_t^n w_t n_t + \tau_t^c c_t - g_t^c - w_t g_t^n]$$

and the private sector first order conditions ((11) and (12) above), which take the form

$$0 = u_c(c_t, n_t) - \Lambda(1 + \tau_t^c)\delta_t$$

$$0 = u_n(c_t, n_t) + \Lambda(1 - \tau_t^n)w_t\delta_t$$

for the closed economy.

There are a series of conceptual and technical issues about this closed economy problem that bear on our analysis below. First, a crucial component of the closed-economy Ramsey problem is that the government understands that it can have effects on prices—specifically the intertemporal prices δ_t—and takes this effect on its own budget constraint into account. Second, the closed-economy Ramsey problem is most often analyzed in its "primal" form, with optimal (second-best) quantities derived and their implications for taxes and market prices then deduced.

Accordingly, the constrained optimization problem has a Lagrangian of the form

$$L = \sum_{t=0}^{\infty} \beta^t u(c_t, n_t) + \Phi \left\{ \sum_{t=0}^{\infty} \beta^t [q(c_t, n_t)] \right\} + \sum_{t=0}^{\infty} \beta^t \lambda_t [u_t n_t - c_t - g_t^c - a_t g_t^n]$$

where the multiplier Φ has the interpretation as the cost of satisfying the equilibrium government budget constraint (15) and the multiplier λ_t has the conventional interpretation as the shadow value of goods at t. The Ramsey planner's first order conditions are

$$u_c(c_t, n_t) + \Phi q_c(c_t, n_t) - \lambda_t = 0 \tag{16}$$

$$u_n(c_t, n_t) + \Phi q_n(c_t, n_t) + \lambda_t a_t = 0$$

$$a_t n_t - c_t - g_t^c - a_t g_t^n = 0$$

at each date t. As Lucas and Stokey (1983) observe, these efficiency conditions look like those for a standard representative agent optimization problem, except that the preferences of the agent are modified from

$u(c_t, n_t)$ to $u(c_t, n_t) + \Phi q(c_t, n_t)$. In general, then, the second-best quantities can be determined by solving an optimization problem which includes the requirements that: consumption and work decisions satisfy the first-order conditions; the resource constraint and the equilibrium version of the government budget constraint.

We assume that the first order conditions are sufficient, as well as necessary, to determine optimal sequences of quantities, $\{c_t^*\}_{t=0}^{\infty}$ and $\{n_t^*\}_{t=0}^{\infty}$. The standard concavity assumptions on utility do not guarantee that this will be automatically satisfied in this "second best" setting, but we proceed under this assumption as in most other work in the optimal taxation literature.

4.3.1 Supporting Prices and Tax Rates

In order for optimal quantities to arise in competitive equilibrium, taxes and prices must satisfy

$$w_t = a_t \tag{17}$$

$$(1+\tau_t^c)\delta_t \propto u_c(c_t^*, n_t^*)$$

$$(1-\tau_t^n)a_t\delta_t \propto u_n(c_t^*, n_t^*).$$

These conditions highlight the following facts about supporting prices and tax rates. First, as in every real general equilibrium model, the prices δ_t are determined only up to a scale factor. Second, in terms of bringing about the optimal allocation, there are two alternative modes of taxation that are essentially perfect substitutes. Notice that the argument here is much stronger than the one discussed in section 4.2: the theory is silent on the composition of consumption and labor taxation at each date, simply specifying that a measure of the "wedge" is determined by

$$\frac{1-\tau_t^n}{1+\tau_t^c} = -\frac{1}{w_t}\frac{u_n(c_t^*, n_t^*)}{u_c(c_t^*, n_t^*)}.$$

Hence, the entire time path of consumption taxation may be viewed as arbitrary, with market discount prices responding to bring about a particular "full price" of consumption $(1+\tau_t^c)\delta_t$.

4.3.2 Implications for Tax Rates

With our specified preferences, even though we cannot solve explicitly for optimal quantities, it is direct to show that (a) there is one sense in which the burden of tax rates must be constant over time; and (b) there is a wide range of policies for τ^c and τ^n that are potentially optimal.

The planner sets

$$-\frac{u_n(c_t^*,n_t^*)+\Phi q_n(c_t^*,n_t^*)}{u_c(c_t^*,n_t^*)+\Phi q_c(c_t^*,n_t^*)}=a_t,$$

while private agents set

$$-\frac{u_n(c_t^*,n_t^*)}{u_c(c_t^*,n_t^*)}=\frac{1-\tau_t^n}{1+\tau_t^c}a_t.$$

The ratio of these conditions implies that

$$\frac{1-\tau_t^n}{1+\tau_t^c}=\frac{u_c(c_t^*,n_t^*)+\Phi q_c(c_t^*,n_t^*)}{u_n(c_t^*,n_t^*)+\Phi q_n(c_t^*,n_t^*)}\frac{u_n(c_t^*,n_t^*)}{u_c(c_t^*,n_t^*)}.$$

Since $q(c_t,n_t)=[u_c(c_t,n_t)c_t+u_n(c_t,n_t)n_t]=c_t^{1-\sigma}-\chi n_t^{\gamma+1}$, it follows that the right-hand side is invariant to the date-t values of consumption and work,

$$\frac{1-\tau_t^n}{1+\tau_t^c}=\frac{1+(1-\sigma)\Phi}{1+\Phi(\gamma+1)}. \tag{18}$$

Thus, the "wedge" depends on the preference parameters that control the elasticities of consumption demand and labor supply, as well as the multiplier that insures that the government budget constraint is satisfied. As this condition makes clear, optimal quantities are consistent with either labor income taxation, consumption taxation or a mixture of the two. But the "wedge," $(1-\tau_t^n)/(1+\tau_t^c)$, must be constant over time.

4.3.3 Dynamic Responses

Following a general strategy in modern macroeconomics, we can study the response of the economy to perturbations in the exogenous variables of the closed economy model via linear approximation methods around a stationary point. In particular, we consider a stationary point with a specific tax wedge, which is set so that the government balances its flow budget constraint (since every period is identical in the stationary economy, this also balances the economy's intertemporal budget constraint). The stationary point is then values of c, n, $(1-\tau^n)/(1+\tau^c)$ which satisfy

$$\left(\frac{1-\tau^n}{1+\tau^c}\right)a=-\frac{u_n(c,n)}{u_c(c,n)}$$

$$c + g^c = a(n - g^n)$$

$$\left(\frac{1-\tau^n}{1+\tau^c}\right)an=c\ .$$

The first two of these expressions are readily interpretable as involving (1) the equating of labor demand and labor supply; and (2) the equating of goods demand and goods supply. The third is a stationary version of the government budget constraint in equilibrium (13), which is also the stationary household budget constraint. Given these stationary values, the multiplier Φ is also determined, since it must satisfy (18).

We can then explore the implications of small perturbations in the sequences $\{a_t\}$; $\{g^c_t\}$; $\{g^n_t\}$; around the stationary values a, g^c, g^n. In the process, we hold fixed the multiplier Φ, so that the analysis corresponds to the effects of shocks in the presence of complete financial markets, as in Lucas and Stokey (1983).

In fact, in this setting, it is feasible to study the dynamic responses analytically by differentiating the Ramsey planner's first order conditions (16) and the equations governing supporting prices and tax rates (17). Essentially, the absence of production-side connections across periods means that the economy's outcomes correspond to those of a static model. Derivations along these lines produce a solution for optimal work effort, which takes the form

$$\log(n_t / n)=\frac{\sigma}{\sigma\phi+\gamma s_c}s_g \log(g^c_t / g^c)$$

$$+\frac{\sigma}{\sigma\phi+\gamma s_c}(\phi-1)\log(g^n_t / g^n)+\frac{s_c-\sigma}{\sigma\phi+\gamma s_c}\log(a_t / a)$$

where $s_c = c/(c + g^c)$, $s_g = g^c/(c + g^c)$ and $\phi = an/(c + g^c)$.[2] That is, increases in government consumption of goods and labor services lead to higher work effort, while productivity exerts an ambiguous effect (due, essentially, to offsetting income and substitution effects).

Consumption is correspondingly governed by

$$\log(c_t / c)=-\frac{\gamma}{\sigma\phi+\gamma s_c}s_g \log(g^c_t / g^c)$$

$$-\frac{\gamma}{\sigma\phi+\gamma s_c}(\phi-1)\log(g^n_t / g^n)+\left(\frac{\sigma+\gamma}{\sigma\phi+\gamma s_c}\right)\log(a_t / a)$$

so that it declines with both types of government purchases and rises with productivity.

4.4 Small Open Economy Benchmark

In the case where the economy is asymptotically small, actions by private agents or the government have no effect on the intertemporal prices that are determined at the community level. Accordingly, the government selects quantities subject to its budget constraint ((13), which continues to imply (15) in the small open economy) and the requirement that the country have net exports that obey the intertemporal constraint (3).

A Ramsey planner's constrained optimization problem for quantities thus has a Lagrangian of the form

$$L_j = \sum_{t=0}^{\infty} \beta^t u(c_{jt}, n_{jt}) + \Phi_j \left\{ \sum_{t=0}^{\infty} \beta[q(c_{jt}, n_{jt})] \right\}$$

$$+ \Upsilon_j \sum_{t=0}^{\infty} \beta^t \delta_t [a_{jt} n_{jt} - c_{jt} - g_{jt}^c - a_{jt} g_{jt}^n]$$

where the multiplier Φ_j may be interpreted as the cost of satisfying the government budget constraint and Υ_j is the shadow value of relaxing the constraint that the intertemporal market value of net exports is zero. The first-order conditions are

$$u_c(c_{jt}, n_{jt}) + \Phi_j q_c(c_{jt}, n_{jt}) = \Upsilon_j \delta_t$$

$$u_n(c_{jt}, n_{jt}) + \Phi_j q_n(c_{jt}, n_{jt}) = \Upsilon_j \delta_t a_{jt}$$

plus the two constraints.

4.4.1 Supporting Prices and Taxes
The small open economy faces exogenous intertemporal prices, $\{\delta_t\}$, so that the conditions for supporting prices and tax rates are

$$w_t = a_t \tag{19}$$

$$(1 + \tau_t^c) = \frac{1}{\Lambda \delta_t} u_c(c_t^*, n_t^*)$$

$$(1 - \tau_t^n) = \frac{1}{\Lambda a_t \delta_t} u_n(c_t^*, n_t^*).$$

4.4.2 Implications for Tax Rates

We can use these conditions to deduce three key results about optimal policy for the small open economy.

Result #1 Combining the foregoing with the private marginal rate of substitution implies that

$$\frac{1-\tau_{jt}^n}{1+\tau_{jt}^c}=\frac{1+(1-\sigma)\Phi_j}{1+\Phi_j(\gamma+1)}$$

should be constant over time, as we obtained in the prior closed economy case. Thus, the "wedge" is constant over time in the small open economy, just as it was in the closed economy.

Result #2 The ratio of the private to planner consumption first-order conditions for consumption requires that the consumption tax rate must be constant over time.

That is:

$$\frac{\Lambda_j(1+\tau_{jt}^c)\delta_t}{\Upsilon_j\delta_t}=\frac{u_c(c_{jt},n_{jt})}{u_c(c_{jt},n_{jt})+\Phi_jq_c(c_{jt},n_{jt})}=\frac{1}{[1+(1-\sigma)\Phi_j]}$$

implies that

$$(1+\tau_{jt}^c)=\frac{\Upsilon_j}{[1+(1-\sigma)\Phi_j]\Lambda_j}.$$

Since all three multipliers on the right-hand side of this expression are constant over time, the consumption tax rate is also constant over time. Hence, for the small open economy, optimal taxation implies no intertemporal distortions in consumption.

Result #3 The theory is silent on the determinants of the *levels* of the labor tax and the consumption tax. Either can be used to raise revenue efficiently—and yield precisely the same optimal quantities—when assumed constant over time. While the government of the small open economy cannot affect the intertemporal prices $\{\delta_t\}$, it can affect the relative price of consumption and work, which it can do either with a uniformly higher labor income tax or uniformly higher consumption tax.

This result for the small open economy is essentially the general neutral tax result discussed in section 4.2, operating at the level of a country rather than a representative individual. As discussed in the introduction, there are consequently a variety of efficient government deficit paths for the small open economy that are consistent with efficient taxation. For example, if the labor income tax rate is used alone, then the government surplus is

$$s_{jt} = \tau_j^n a_{jt} n_{jt} - g_{jt}^c - a_{jt} g_{jt}^n$$

where the constant tax rate is $\tau_j^n = \Sigma_{t=0}^\infty \beta^t \delta_t [g_{jt}^c + a_{jt} g_{jt}^n]/\Sigma_{t=0}^\infty \beta^t \delta_t [a_{jt} n_{jt}].^3$ By contrast, if the consumption tax rate is used alone, then the surplus is

$$s_{jt} = \tau_j^c c_{jt} - g_{jt}^c - a_{jt} g_{jt}^n$$

where constant tax rate is by $\tau_j^c = \Sigma_{t=0}^\infty \beta^t \delta_t [g_{jt}^c + a_{jt} g_{jt}^n]/\Sigma_{t=0}^\infty \beta^t \delta_t [c_{jt}]$. Since consumption likely would be much smoother than income for this small open economy, the government deficit would be much more volatile with labor income taxation.

4.4.3   Dynamic Responses

There are quite different dynamic responses for the small open economy relative to the closed economy. Variations in productivity stimulate strong intertemporal substitutions, in the sense that n_t^* moves together with a_t according to

$$\log(n_t^* / n) = \frac{1}{\gamma} \log(a_t / a) + \frac{1}{\gamma} \log(\delta_t / \delta)$$

while consumption is not affected by productivity,

$$\log(c_t^* / c) = -\frac{1}{\sigma} \log(\delta_t / \delta).$$

Variations in government consumption and government employment have no effect on either of the optimal quantities $\{c_t^*\}$ and $\{n_t^*\}$. These patterns of dynamic responses are characteristic of a small open economy under complete markets (see, for example, the discussion in Baxter 1995). Each derives from the effect that the wealth effects of shocks is insured away in these markets, leaving only substitution effects.

Intertemporal relative prices, $\{\delta_t\}$, also exert substitution effects, encouraging work and discouraging consumption in periods with high

δ. However, both the private sector and government of a small open economy view these prices as exogenous to their decisions.

4.5   The Direct Approach

In studying the small open economy above, we followed the Ramsey approach of computing optimal quantities, with the benefit that we could then deduce the implications for tax rates just discussed. An alternative look at the nature of the optimal taxation problem is afforded by the direct choice of optimal tax rates, given the conditions of government budget balance and macroeconomic equilibrium. We employ this direct approach within our analysis of community general equilibrium, but we start by considering its application in the context of the small open economy.

To implement the approach, it would be natural to write a representative agent indirect utility function that depends on tax rates as follows:

$$V(\{\tau^c_{jt}\}^\infty_{t=0}, \{\tau^n_{jt}\}^\infty_{t=0}, ...)$$

and then optimize with respect to tax rates, given a set of constraints. However, we have seen in section 4.2 that there are combinations of tax rates on labor income and consumption that are behaviorally equivalent if government revenue neutrality is imposed. This latitude is not desirable from the standpoint of the direct approach.

However, in section 4.2, we also saw that equivalent sequences of labor and consumption taxes could be readily related using a rescaling of the multiplier on the household's budget constraint. Hence, we use the effective wedges $\xi^c_{jt} = \Lambda_j(1 + \tau^c_{jt})$ and $\xi^n_{jt} = \Lambda_j(1 - \tau^n_{jt})$ as representing each class of equivalent tax rates. Then, we view small open economy as maximizing

$$V(\{\xi^c_{jt}\}^\infty_{t=0}, \{\xi^n_{jt}\}^\infty_{t=0}, \{a_{jt}\}^\infty_{t=0}, \{\delta_t\}^\infty_{t=0})$$

subject to decision rules for consumption and work,

$$c_{jt} = (\xi^c_{jt}\delta_t)^{-(1/\sigma)}$$

$$n_{jt} = (\xi^n_{jt}a_t\delta_t)^{(1/\gamma)}$$

the equilibrium version of the government budget constraint

$$\sum_{t=0}^{\infty} \beta^t \delta_t [-\xi^n_{jt}a_{jt}n_{jt} + \xi^c_{jt}c_{jt}] = \sum_{t=0}^{\infty} \beta^t [q(c_{jt}, n_{jt})] \geq 0$$

and the intertemporal constraint on net exports

$$\sum_{t=0}^{\infty} \beta^t \delta_t [a_{jt}(n_{jt} - g_{jt}^n) - g_{jt}^c - c_{jt}] \geq 0.$$

We think of the joint solution for optimal quantities and effective wedges as determining the fundamentals of fiscal policy. Once we have worked out this solution, we can construct any desired member of the class of equivalent fiscal policies, by calculating

$$(1+\tau_{jt}^c) = \frac{1}{\Lambda_j} \xi_{jt}^c$$

$$(1-\tau_{jt}^n) = \frac{1}{\Lambda_j} \xi_{jt}^n$$

for a specified value of Λ_j.

4.5.1   Efficiency Conditions for Taxation
The Lagrangian for the planner's problem is

$$L = \sum_{t=0}^{\infty} \beta^t u(c(\xi_t^c \delta_t), n(\xi_t^n a_t \delta_t)) + \Phi_j \sum_{t=0}^{\infty} \beta^t q(c(\xi_t^c \delta_t), n(\xi_t^n a_t \delta_t))$$

$$+ \Upsilon_j \sum_{t=0}^{\infty} \beta^t \delta_t [a_t n(\xi_t^n a_t \delta_t) - a_t g_t^n - g_t^c - c(\xi_t^c \delta_t)].$$

The efficiency condition for consumption is as follows:

$$0 = [u_{c_t} + \Phi_j q_{c_t} - \Upsilon_j \delta_t] \frac{\partial c_{jt}}{\partial \xi_t^n}.$$

The first three terms indicate that an efficient internal price of consumption ξ_{jt}^c takes into account: (1) the effect of the change in this price on utility; (2) the effect on the government budget constraint; and (3) the effect on the present discounted value of the country's net exports.

The efficiency condition for the internal price of labor ξ_{jt}^n takes a symmetric form

$$0 = [u_{n_t} + \Phi_j q_{n_t} + \Upsilon \delta_t a_t] * \frac{\partial n_t}{\partial \xi_t^n}.$$

Note that the bracketed terms are exactly the first-order conditions of the Ramsey method with respect to quantities. Hence, the Ramsey method and the direct method each require that the bracketed terms be set to zero at an optimum: the results of the Ramsey and the direct method for quantities and values of the effective wedges are therefore identical.

5. Optimal Policy without Coordination

If the governments of the countries cannot coordinate their actions, they nevertheless recognize that these actions will have implications for the prices and quantities that will prevail in community-wide markets. We are interested in a Nash equilibrium of the game between the J different countries governments. That is, in posing the optimal tax policy for an individual-country's government—for concreteness, country 1—we assume that the tax policies for the other governments are taken as given. In addition, country 1's government assumes that local and world markets clear.

Following the discussion in the previous section, we assume that each government chooses sequence of effective consumption and labor wedges, i.e., selects a fundamental fiscal policy. Then, when we consider a Nash game between the country governments, the strategy of the government of country j is given by $\{\xi_{jt}^c\}_{t=0}^{\infty}$ and $\{\xi_{jt}^n\}_{t=0}^{\infty}$.

5.1 Community Equilibrium with Exogenous Policies

In the intermediate case that we now study, a government's fiscal actions may have effect both on intertemporal prices and net exports. Community goods market equilibrium requires that

$$0 = \sum_{j=1}^{J} \theta_j [a_{jt} n_{jt} - c_{jt} - g_{jt}^c - a_{jt} g_{jt}^n]$$

$$= \sum_{j=1}^{J} \theta_j [a_{jt} n_{jt} - c_{jt}] - G_t$$

$$= Y_t - C_t - G_t$$

where $G_t^c = \Sigma_{j=1}^{J} \theta_j g_{jt}^c$, $G_t^n = \Sigma_{j=1}^{J} \theta_j a_{jt} g_{jt}^n$, $G_t = G_t^c + G_t^n$ and $C_t = \Sigma_{j=1}^{J} \theta_j c_{jt}$ as above. We also define a measure of community total output (the sum of private and public output),

$$Y_t \equiv \sum_{j=1}^{J} \theta_j [a_{jt} n_{jt}]. \tag{20}$$

The various supplies and demands are governed by

$$c_{jt} = (\xi_{jt}^c \delta_t)^{-(1/\sigma)}$$

$$n_{jt} = (\xi_{jt}^n a_{jt} \delta_t)^{(1/\gamma)}.$$

Accordingly, the market-clearing price is implicitly given by

$$0 = Y_t - C_t - G_t = \left[\delta_t^{\frac{1}{\gamma}} \sum_{j=1}^{J} \theta_j a_{jt}^{1+\frac{1}{\gamma}} (\xi_{jt}^n)^{\frac{1}{\gamma}} \right] - \left[\delta_t^{-\frac{1}{\sigma}} \sum_{j=1}^{J} \theta_j (\xi_{jt}^c)^{-\frac{1}{\sigma}} \right] - G_t \qquad (21)$$

so that the equilibrium price depends on productivity; consumption and labor tax rates; and the aggregate government expenditure shock. We write this price function as

$$\delta(\{a_{jt}\}_{j=1}^{J}, \{\xi_{jt}^c\}_{j=1}^{J}, \{\xi_{jt}^n\}_{j=1}^{J}, G_t).$$

The effects on intertemporal prices take a natural form. For example, since $Y_t = C_t + G_t$, we know that the effect of government demand on the intertemporal price is simply given by

$$\frac{\partial \delta_t}{\partial G_t} = \frac{1}{\frac{\partial Y_t}{\partial \delta_t} - \frac{\partial C_t}{\partial \delta_t}} = \delta_t * \frac{1}{\frac{1}{\gamma} Y_t + \frac{1}{\sigma} C_t} \qquad (22)$$

where the second line expresses the slope of the "excess supply of goods" using the relevant labor supply and consumption demand elasticities.

As an intermediate-size economy, the government in country 1 takes as given the fiscal policies in other countries, treating $\{\xi_{jt}^c\}_{t=0}^{\infty}, \{\xi_{jt}^n\}_{t=0}^{\infty}$ as parametric for all t and for $j = 2, \ldots, J$. It takes into account the effects of its own fiscal actions on intertemporal prices via the constraint above. The effect on the intertemporal prices due to country j fiscal policy decisions are:

$$\frac{\partial \delta_t}{\partial \xi_{jt}^n} = -\delta_t * \frac{\theta_j a_{jt}}{\frac{1}{\gamma} Y_t + \frac{1}{\sigma} C_t} * \frac{\partial n_{jt}}{\partial \xi_{jt}^n} \qquad (23)$$

$$\frac{\partial \delta_t}{\partial \xi_{jt}^c} = \delta_t * \frac{\theta_j}{\frac{1}{\gamma} Y_t + \frac{1}{\sigma} C_t} * \frac{\partial c_{jt}}{\partial \xi_{jt}^c}. \qquad (24)$$

Note that the effect of a country's fiscal actions on the intertemporal price involve the effect on its own labor supply or consumption and the effect of supply/demand shifts on the equilibrium price. More specifically, note that the magnitude of these intertemporal price effects of country j fiscal policy thus depends positively on the size of the country, θ_j.

5.2 Optimal Taxation for Country j

We now consider country j's optimal tax problem, using the "direct form" described above in the context of the small open economy:

$$L=\sum_{t=0}^{\infty}\beta^t u(c(\xi_{jt}^c\delta_t),n(\xi_{jt}^n a_{jt}\delta_t))+\Phi_j\sum_{t=0}^{\infty}\beta^t q(c(\xi_{jt}^c\delta_t),n(\xi_{jt}^n a_{jt}\delta_t))$$

$$+\Upsilon_j\sum_{t=0}^{\infty}\beta^t\delta_t[a_{jt}n(\xi_{jt}^n a_{jt}\delta_t)-a_{jt}g_{jt}^n-g_{jt}^c-c(\xi_{jt}^c\delta_t)].$$

To make the first-order conditions as simple as possible, we view the government of country j as choosing the relevant tax wedge, $\xi_{jt}^c\delta_t$ or $\xi_{jt}^n\delta_t$. This simplifies the algebra somewhat and corresponds to the idea that the country j government (1) understands the effects of its tax actions on intertemporal prices and (2) understands that its tax actions affect intertemporal prices through their effects on quantities supplied to or demanded from the international market.

5.2.1 Efficiency Conditions for Country j
The efficiency condition for $\xi_{jt}^c\delta_t$ takes the form

$$0=\{u_{c_{jt}}+\Phi_j q_{c_{jt}}-\Upsilon_j\delta_t\}\frac{\partial c_{jt}}{\partial(\xi_{jt}^c\delta_t)}+\Upsilon_j[a_{jt}n_{jt}-a_{jt}g_{jt}^n-g_{jt}^c-c_{jt})]\frac{\partial\delta_t}{\partial(\xi_{jt}^c\delta_t)}.$$

As in the case of the small open economy exported in section 4, the first three terms indicate that an efficient effective wedge—represented by $\xi_{jt}^c\delta_t$—takes into account: (1) the effect of the change in this price on utility; (2) the effect on the government budget constraint; and (3) the effect on the present discounted value of the country's net exports. However, in the current case of an intermediate size economy, there are two components to this last term: the direct expenditure effect $(\Upsilon_j\delta_t)$ also present in the small open economy case and a new indirect effect via the country's effect on the community discount factor $(\Upsilon_j x_{jt})$.

The efficiency condition for $\xi_{jt}^n\delta_t$ takes a symmetric form

$$0=\{u_{n_{jt}}+\Phi_j q_{n_{jt}}+\Upsilon_j\delta_t a_{jt}\}\frac{\partial n_{jt}}{\partial(\xi_{jt}^n\delta_t)}+\Upsilon_j[a_{jt}n_{jt}-a_{jt}g_{jt}^n-g_{jt}^c-c_{jt}]\frac{\partial\delta_t}{\partial(\xi_{jt}^n\delta_t)}.$$

As with the previous, there is an effect operating through the community discount factor,

$$\Upsilon_j x_{jt} \frac{\partial \delta_t}{\partial (\xi_{jt}^n \delta_t)}.$$

These expressions both contain effects of country j's fiscal actions on the world intertemporal price δ_t. These may be shown to be

$$\frac{\partial \delta_t}{\partial (\xi_{jt}^c \delta_t)} = \delta_t \frac{\theta_j}{\frac{1}{\gamma}(Y_t - \theta_j a_{jt} n_{jt}) + \frac{1}{\sigma}(C_t - \theta_j c_{jt})} \frac{\partial c_{jt}}{\partial \xi_{jt}^c}$$

$$\frac{\partial \delta_t}{\partial (\xi_{jt}^n \delta_t)} = -\delta_t \frac{\theta_j a_{jt}}{\frac{1}{\gamma}(Y_t - \theta_j a_{jt} n_{jt}) + \frac{1}{\sigma}(C_t - \theta_j c_{jt})} \frac{\partial n_{jt}}{\partial (\xi_{jt}^n \delta_t)}.$$

The preceding two first-order conditions imply basic restrictions that must be satisfied for a country that is following an optimal fiscal policy,

$$0 = u_{c_{jt}} + \Phi_j q_{c_{jt}} - \Upsilon_j \delta_t + \Upsilon_j \delta_t \theta_j \frac{x_{jt}}{z_{jt}} \tag{25}$$

$$0 = u_{n_{jt}} + \Phi_j q_{n_{jt}} + \Upsilon_j \delta_t a_{jt} - \Upsilon_j \delta_t a_{jt} \theta_j \frac{x_{jt}}{z_{jt}} \tag{26}$$

where z_{jt} is defined as

$$\left[\frac{1}{\gamma}(Y_t - \theta_j a_{jt} n_{jt}) + \frac{1}{\sigma}(C_t - \theta_j c_{jt}) \right].$$

Note that these country j fiscal policy conditions are those of the small open economy problem, modified by the presence of terms involving x_{jt}/z_{jt}. Accordingly, if $x_{jt} = 0$, then the intermediate size country chooses the same tax rates as the small country.

5.2.2 Implications for Optimal Taxation
More generally, we can use the equilibrium conditions (25) and (26) to determine aspects of the optimal tax structure.

First, we consider constancy of the "wedge." Taking the ratios of these two conditions, we see that

$$\left(\frac{-u_n}{u_c} \right) \frac{1 + \Phi_j(1+\gamma)}{1 + \Phi_j(1-\gamma)} = a_{jt} \frac{1 - \theta_j x_{jt}/z_{jt}}{1 - \theta_j x_{jt}/z_{jt}} = a_{jt}$$

so that the optimal policy involves

$$\frac{1-\tau_{jt}^n}{1+\tau_{jt}^c}=\frac{\xi_{jt}^n}{\xi_{jt}^c}=\frac{1+(1-\sigma)\Phi_j}{1+\Phi_j(\gamma+1)}$$

so that the "wedge" is constant over time as in all of the other models above. However, as we shall see below, it is no longer the case that the tax rates are constant over time, so that constancy of the "wedge" now implies that the labor income tax and the consumption tax must move inversely.

Second, we consider variation in components of the "wedge." The labor condition (25) implies that

$$\chi n_{jt}^\gamma[1+\Phi_j(1+\gamma)]=a_{jt}[1-\theta_j x_{jt}/z_{jt}]\Upsilon_j\delta_t$$

so that optimal labor is higher in situations where the country is a net importer ($x_{jt}<0$) and lower when it is a net exporter ($x_{jt}>0$).[4] In order to bring about this higher labor, it is necessary that there be a labor tax rate when the country is a net importer. Further, given that there is a lower labor tax, there must be a higher consumption tax, given the inverse relationship which we determined above. Both taxes thus work to cut net imports, thus lowering the price that the country faces for being a net importer.

5.3 Nash Equilibrium

In a Nash equilibrium, each country chooses its optimal tax policy taking as given the actions of the others. From above, we can see that there are two main mechanisms by which countries interact. First, the community discount factor δ_t affects the supply and demand for goods in all countries. Second, the fiscal policy within a given country is affected by

$$\frac{x_{jt}}{z_{jt}}=\frac{a_{jt}n_{jt}-a_{jt}g_{jt}^n-g_{jt}^c-c_{jt}}{\frac{1}{\gamma}(Y_t-\theta_j a_{jt}n_{jt})+\frac{1}{\sigma}(C_t-\theta_j c_{jt})}$$

so that other country's tax actions—which affect the aggregate quantities produced Y_t and consumed C_t—are relevant to country j's fiscal policy and production.

A Nash equilibrium, then, requires that each country j's choices of effective wedges are consistent with the conditions (equilibrium conditions (25) and (26)). In addition, a Nash equilibrium requires the conditions of community general equilibrium discussed in sections 3.3 and 4.1.

To study the dynamic responses of economies within such a Nash equilibrium, we then can adopt the same approach as used for the closed economy and the small open economy. First, we consider a stationary equilibrium in which all of the countries are the same in terms of a, g^c, and g^n, so that each has a position of zero net exports. In such a setting, the discussion above leads to the conclusion that each country will choose the same constant levels of ξ^c and ξ^n. Second, we log-linearize the relevant equilibrium conditions—including (25) and (26)—around this stationary position and then consider the response to small perturbations in productivity and government purchases.

Before doing so, we briefly consider how the Nash equilibrium outcomes would differ from those in a setting with policy coordination.

6. Optimal Policy with Coordination

If tax policy is coordinated across countries, then a natural objective is to maximize a weighted average of welfare for community members (these utility weights are ϑ_j). However, in considering this coordinated situation, we continue to require that each country satisfy its present value budget constraint and its government budget constraint: there are no transfers between governments or economies other than through the price system. The appropriate Lagrangian for this problem is then

$$L = \sum_{j=1}^{J} \vartheta_j \left\{ \sum_{t=0}^{\infty} \beta^t u(c(\xi^c_{jt}\delta_t), n(\xi^n_{jt} a_{jt}\delta_t)) \right\} + \sum_{j=1}^{J} \left\{ \Phi_j \theta_j \sum_{t=0}^{\infty} \beta^t q(c(\xi^c_{jt}\delta_t), n(\xi^n_{jt} a_{jt}\delta_t)) \right\}$$

$$+ \sum_{j=1}^{J} \left\{ \Upsilon_j \theta_j \sum_{t=0}^{\infty} \beta^t \delta_t [a_{jt} * n(\xi^n_{jt} a_{jt}\delta_t) - a_{jt} g^n_{jt} - g^c_{jt} - c(\xi^c_{jt}\delta_t)] \right\}$$

where the first line is the weighted-average objective; the second line represents the requirement that coordinated policy respect each of the government budget constraints; and the third line represents the requirement that coordinated policy represent each of the country budget constraints.

For the single decision maker, the first-order conditions with respect to country j's "prices" are as follows.

$$0 = \{\vartheta_j u_{c_{jt}} + \Phi_j \theta_j u_{c_{jt}} - \Upsilon_j \delta_t \theta_j\} \frac{\partial c_{jt}}{\partial(\xi_{jt}^c \delta_t)}$$

$$+ \left\{ \sum_{h=1}^{J} \Upsilon_h \theta_h [a_{ht} * n_{ht} - a_{ht} g_{ht}^n - g_{ht}^c - c_{ht})] \right\} \frac{\partial \delta_t}{\partial(\xi_{jt}^c \delta_t)}$$

$$0 = \{\vartheta_j u_{n_{jt}} + \Phi_j \theta_j u_{n_{jt}} - \Upsilon_j \delta_t \theta_j\} \frac{\partial n_{jt}}{\partial(\xi_{jt}^n \delta_t)}$$

$$+ \left\{ \sum_{h=1}^{J} \Upsilon_h \theta_h [a_{ht} * n_{ht} - a_{ht} g_{ht}^n - g_{ht}^c - c_{ht})] \right\} \frac{\partial \delta_t}{\partial(\xi_{jt}^n \delta_t)}$$

In each of these expressions, notice that the community decision-maker takes into account the effect on *all* countries' budget constraints of changing the community-wide discount factor. In this sense, the community decision-maker can choose tax rates that are quite different from those of the single country decision-maker.

An important reference case comes about when the decision-maker attaches the same weight to all country budget constraints ($\Upsilon_h = \Upsilon$). Then, the community general equilibrium condition,

$$\sum_{h=1}^{J} \theta_h [a_{ht} * n_{ht} - a_{ht} g_{ht}^n - g_{ht}^c - c_{ht})] = 0,$$

implies that the second line of both conditions above is zero. Accordingly, the community decision-maker will choose country tax rates on labor and consumption that are constant across time, resulting in the same deficit behavior in each country as if it were small.

7. Effects of Government Purchases

To study the nature of fiscal externalities within an economic community, we now consider a particular shock, an increase in government consumption in one country that is persistent but ultimately temporary. In particular, we suppose that

$$\log(g_{t+1}^c / g^c) = \rho \log(g_t^c / g^c) + e_t$$

where $0 < \rho < 1$ and e_t is a shock. Accordingly, the effect of a shock at date 0 is to cause a revision upward in the path of government purchases of goods, as shown in the first panel of Figure 6. We choose an $e_0 = .05$ as we assume that government purchases are 20 percent of total

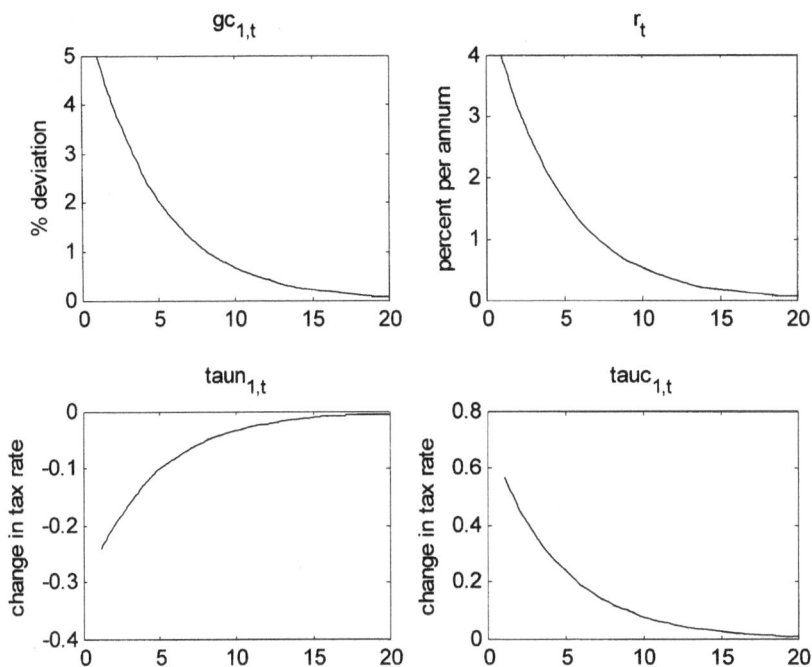

Figure 6
Effects of increase in country-1 government consumption

purchases $s_g = (g/(g + c)) = .2$ and we want to consider a shock that is equal to 1 percent of private output $(c + g)$.

7.1   Benchmarks

Our analysis in section 4 above provides two benchmarks.

Small open economy: If there is a surprise in government purchases in the small open economy, then the public and private sectors have previously assured against this adverse outcome—essentially a negative net income shock for the country—in the complete financial markets of the community. Tax rates are held constant in the face of this disturbance. There are no effects on either work or consumption. In fact, the only manifestations are in the country's net exports, which decline by Δg and in the government's primary deficit, which rises by Δg.

Closed economy: The private and public sectors of the closed economy would like to insure against this shock, but it is impossible for them to do so since there is no international trade in securities. Accordingly, as discussed in section 4.3, there must be a rise in work and a decline in consumption: each of these is stimulated by the prices δ_t for those periods which are affected by the increase in government expenditure. In particular, if we consider the implications for the real one period return implied by these prices,

$$r_t = r + \frac{1}{\sigma} E_t[\log(c_{t+1}) - \log(c_t)]$$

$$= r - \frac{1}{\sigma} \pi E_t[\log(g_{t+1}^c / g^c) - \log(g_t^c / g^c)]$$

$$= r - \frac{1}{\sigma} \pi(\rho-1)\log(g_t^c / g^c)$$

where $\pi = \gamma s_g / [\sigma\phi + \gamma s_c]$ with terms defined as shown in section 4.3.3. Hence, in the closed economy, the real rate of return rises if there is an increase in government consumption. The difference between these two responses lies in the fact that the small open economy can "export" the financing of higher government purchases to the world financial markets, while the closed economy cannot.

7.2 An Intermediate Size Country

We now consider the same disturbance in an intermediate size country, which is 40 percent of the economic community under two alternative assumptions.

7.2.1 Constant Tax Rates
If the country's fiscal decision-maker's ignored their influence on the prices $\{\delta_t\}_{t=0}^{\infty}$ in choosing their tax rates, then these would be constant over time. Further, under a coordinated fiscal policy, as discussed above, there are circumstances under which it is optimal for all countries to maintain constant tax rates. Accordingly, we begin by studying this case.

The economic community is assumed to be closed to the rest of the world. Therefore, the burden of higher government purchases must be borne by its citizens. Accordingly, all of the community's citizens work harder and consume less, with the market prices (interest rates) signaling that this is desirable. However, since the shock applies only to one of the community's economies, it has a smaller effect on prices and interest rates, scaled by the measure of θ_1 as in the discussions of general equilibrium above. In the simulations displayed in Figures 6 and 7, this fraction is .40, so that the interpretation is that the shock is equal to .40 percent of community private output $(C + G)$.

Accordingly, the constant tax responses shown in Figure 6—indicated by the solid lines—show that consumption declines and labor supply increases, following the path of the shock. Net exports from country decline by about .5 percent of its GDP on impact. That is, although the shock is initially 1 percent, part of it is offset by consumption declines and labor supply increases.

7.2.2 Nash Equilibrium Taxes

When fiscal planners of country 1 take into account their influence on the market prices $\{\delta_t\}$, they choose to cut the path of the labor income tax rate and raise the path of the consumption tax rate, as shown in the bottom panels of Figure 6 (the dashed lines indicate responses under Nash taxation throughout all panels). Consequently, there are responses of greater magnitude in country 1 labor and consumption than arise

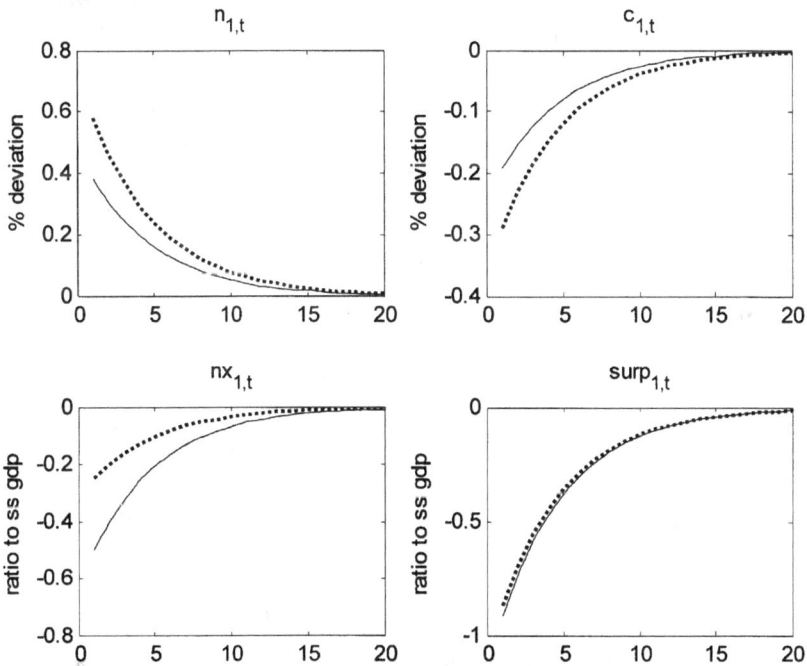

Figure 7
Effects on labor, consumption, net exports, and the fiscal surplus

under constant tax rates. Further, as discussed at the end of section 5, this policy has the effect of smoothing net exports: as shown in Figure 7, these become substantially less responsive to the government purchase shock in the home country. At the same time, declines in tax revenue mean that there is relatively little difference between the government's primary deficit under constant and optimal taxation. In each case, the deficit is dominated by the path of government purchases.

7.2.3   Fiscal Externalities

There are two types of externalities which we see as operating in this experiment and which bear further discussion.

First, treating the case of constant tax rates as proximately optimal under coordination, country 1 exerts a *pecuniary* externality on the economic community: the fact that it is using more goods leads to price variations that affect other members of the community. That is: there are gains to sharing the risk of variations in public purchases across members of the community. Markets handle these external effects efficiently.

Second, there are *policy externalities*—which can be interpreted as coordination failure or imperfect competition externalities—that arise because individual national fiscal policies take into account the effect of their policy actions on community prices. In the current setting of a government purchase (demand) shock, this lack of coordination means that the home country responds more and the community responds less to the shock, thus reducing the effectiveness of community risk-sharing.

8.   Summary and Conclusions

Motivated by the Stability and Growth Pact, we have laid the groundwork for studying the external effects of national fiscal policies within an economic community, working within an entirely real dynamic general equilibrium model. While the model is simplistic and abstract, there are some conclusions from the analysis that seem likely to apply to other more complicated and realistic models in the future.

First, the SGP is cast in terms of government deficits. However, our model highlights the international transmission of fiscal policy between countries not via the government deficit, but via the country's net exports.

Second, there are some economic mechanisms that make the trade deficit and the government deficit tend to move together. For example, holding other variables fixed, a rise in government consumption will increase both deficits. In this way, an individual country's fiscal policy can have effects on other countries, which are transmitted via interest rates.

Third, the comovement of these deficit measures clearly depends as well on the tax system, i.e., on how the tax rates and are determined.

Further, to learn about whether there can be important fiscal externalities of national policies when there are optimizing governments, we determined the behavior of optimal tax rates within some alternative settings. Again, there are important lessons that seem to be general.

For a small country within our basic model, which assumes that its policies have no effect on community-wide interest rates, it is optimal to make tax rates constant over time, but the model is silent on whether the necessary tax is applied to labor income or consumption. While the result on tax rate constancy is dependent on the specification of preferences, the model's stress that there are a variety of consumption and income tax policies that are consistent with a given real equilibrium is more general. Further, while the real equilibrium is invariant to the choice between consumption and income taxes, the behavior of the public sector deficit is not. Deficits can be highly variable if they involve mainly labor taxation, but relatively smooth if they involve mainly consumption taxation. That is: countries wishing to satisfy the SGP and avoid volatility in government deficits may wish to use the tax instrument that leads to smooth tax revenues. Hence, community agreements like the SGP may be subject to manipulation via changes in the structure of taxation. Our model highlights this by showing that a very wide range of behavior of government deficits is consistent with optimal taxation, yet these alternative deficits all involve the country having the same effect on the economic community because its net exports are invariant to the structure of taxation.

When we turn to countries that are "large" in the economic community, we stress that the government of a single large country knows that its fiscal policies affect the intertemporal prices determined in community asset markets. In such a setting, a distinction emerges between coordinated and uncoordinated national fiscal policies.

Fiscal policies which are coordinated at the community level will, as our model stresses, recognize that the effects of national tax policies intertemporal prices do not create wealth at the community level, but rather redistribute between its members.

By contrast, with uncoordinated fiscal policies—which we model using a Nash equilibrium—governments have an incentive to choose tax rates that increase the price of exports when the country is a net exporter and reduce the price when the country is a net importer. In our model, these effects operate on financial markets, with fiscal policy aimed at lowering the cost of financing national net export deficits and increasing the value of having national net export surpluses. In our model, we show that these national fiscal policies will therefore work to stabilize net exports relative to the constant tax rate solution, which is approximately optimal under coordinated policies.

Notes

1. Our analysis of optimal taxation follows the Ramsey approach of Lucas and Stokey (1983) and Chamley (1986); some aspects of our results on tax rates in Nash equilibrium are similar to the tariff equilibrium described in Kennan and Riezman (1990). Other recent analyses of international monetary and fiscal policy coordination include Feldstein (1988), Chari and Kehoe (1990) and Lambertini (2005).

2. Given that we have seen that the tax rate is constant over time, this equation for work and that below for consumption are most easily derived by approximating the conditions $(1 - \tau^i)/(1 + \tau^i)a_t = -u_n(c_t, n_t)/u_c(c_t, n_t)$ and $c_t + g_t^c = a_t(n_t - g_t^n)$ around the stationary point.

3. Notice that it is not appropriate to say that "world discount factors do not affect the optimal tax rate" since the labor income tax rate depends on two present values. However, world discount factors do not affect the desirability of smoothing the tax rate over time.

4. This discussion is somewhat heuristic, as the surplus is a function of labor and consumption, but it describes the direction of tax effects appropriately.

References

Baxter, Marianne. 1995. "International Trade and Business Cycles." *Handbook of International Economics*. Chapter 13, Amsterdam: North-Holland.

Chamley, Christophe.1986. "Optimal Taxation of Capital Income in General Equilibrium with Infinite Lives." *Econometrica* 54(3): 607–622.

Chari, V.V., and Patrick Kehoe. 1990. "International Coordination of Fiscal Policy in Limiting Public Good Economies." *Journal of Political Economy* 98(3): 617–636.

Feldstein, Martin. 1988. "Rethinking International Economic Coordination." *Oxford Economic Papers*, New Series 40(2): 205–219.

Kennan, John, and Raymond Riezman. 1990. "Optimal Tariff Equilibrium with Customs Unions." *Canadian Journal of Economics* 23(1): 70–83.

Lambertini, Luisa. 2005. "Fiscal Rules in a Monetary Union." Boston College Working Paper.

Lucas, Robert E., Jr., and Nancy Stokey. 1983. "Optimal Monetary and Fiscal Policy in an Economy without Capital." *Journal of Monetary Economics* 12(1): 55–94.

Comment

Pierpaolo Benigno, New York University and NBER

1. Introduction

Optimal taxation problems in open-economy models are not trivial extensions of similar analyses in closed-economy models. In this discussion, I emphasize two important caveats of open-economy optimal policy problems. First, the intertemporal budget constraint of the government is not a necessary restriction that a Ramsey government should consider in its maximization problem. This point revisits in the current framework a previous argument discussed in Woodford (1996). Second, the specification of the strategies followed by each government is critical for the outcome of the non-cooperative allocation. Finally, I argue that in the analysis of Baxter and King (2005), (BK), it would be interesting to know more about how the labor wedge is set across the different allocations and models analyzed.

2. Intertemporal Budget Constraint of the Government in Open Economy Models

In the so-called Ramsey's approach to optimal taxation, the government chooses taxes in order to maximize the utility of the households under the sequence of resource constraints of the economy and the constraints implied by the optimizing behavior of households. Government is then "benevolent." It would seem natural to assume that a relevant constraint for this optimal policy problem is the intertemporal budget constraint of the government. But, in the Ramsey's approach, this can be justified only if this constraint belongs either to the resource constraints of the economy or is an implication of the optimizing behavior of households.

In this section I show that the intertemporal budget constraint of the government is a relevant constraint for the optimization problem of a "Ramsey" government in a closed-economy model but not in an open-economy model.

Consider the closed-economy model presented in BK where households maximize

$$U = \sum_{t=0}^{\infty} \beta^t u(c_t, n_t) \tag{1}$$

in which β is the discount factor with $0 < \beta < 1$ and $u(\cdot)$ is the utility function of consumption, c, and labor, n, with standard properties. Households are subject to a flow budget constraint of the form

$$\frac{b_{t+1}^p}{1+r_t} = b_t^p + (1-\tau_t^n)w_t n_t - (1+\tau_t^c)c_t. \tag{2}$$

At time t, households' revenues are given by labor income, where w_t are wages taxed at the rate τ_t^n, and by the value of the financial assets carried over from the previous period, b_t^p; consumption is also taxed at the rate τ_t^c. Households can borrow or lend at time t using an asset, b_{t+1}^p, which is issued at discount and gives a return r_t. An initial condition on the assets at time 0 is given, $b_0 = 0$. The constraint (2) is not enough to impose a well-defined maximization problem, for consumption can be infinite. A natural borrowing limit conditions of the form

$$b_t^p \geq - \sum_{T=t}^{\infty} R_{t,T}(1-\tau_T^n)w_T n_T > -\infty \tag{3}$$

is added, stating that households' borrowing in a certain period cannot exceed the present discounted value, net of taxes, of wage revenues discounted by the appropriate factor defined as

$$R_{t,T} \equiv \prod_{s=t}^{T-1} \left(\frac{1}{1+r_s} \right)$$

for each $T > t$ while $R_{t,t} \equiv 1$. Household's optimization problem is to maximize (1) under the sequences of flow budget constraint (2) and the borrowing-limit constraints (3), given the initial condition b_0. This maximization problem has two other equivalent formulations. In the first, the utility is maximized under the sequences of flow budget constraints (2) and the intertemporal budget constraint of the households

$$\sum_{t=0}^{\infty} R_{0,t}(1+\tau_t^c)c_t \leq \sum_{t=0}^{\infty} R_{0,t}(1-\tau_t^n)w_t n_t.$$

In the second, the utility is maximized under the sequences of flow budget constraints (2) and the transversality condition

$$\lim_{T \to \infty} R_{0,T} b_T^p \geq 0.$$

In this economy, the government is subject to a flow budget constraint of the form

$$\frac{b_{t+1}^g}{1+r_t} = b_t^g + \tau_t^n w_t n_t + \tau_t^c c_t - g_t \tag{4}$$

in which b_t^g denotes government assets at time t carried over from the previous period; g_t represents exogenous government purchases of the only good produced in this economy. Government can borrow and lend freely from the private sector. Goods are produced in the economy with a technology of the form $y_t = a_t n_t$, where a_t is an exogenous productivity shock. Equilibrium in the goods and assets markets requires that

$$y_t = c_t + g_t, \tag{5}$$

$$b_t^p + b_t^g = 0, \tag{6}$$

respectively.

Firm's optimization problem implies that wages are equalized to productivity

$$w_t = a_t$$

Optimality conditions on the side of the consumers imply that: (1) the marginal rate of substitution between consumption and labor is equated to the labor wedge

$$\frac{u_n(c_t, n_t)}{u_c(c_t, n_t)} = \frac{(1-\tau_t^n)}{(1+\tau_t^c)} w_t; \tag{7}$$

(2) the marginal utilities of consumption between subsequent periods are related through the following Euler equation

$$\frac{u_c(c_t, n_t)}{(1+\tau_t^c)} = \beta(1+r_t) \frac{u_c(c_{t+1}, n_{t+1})}{(1+\tau_{t+1}^c)}; \tag{8}$$

(3) the intertemporal budget constraint of the consumer is satisfied with equality

$$\sum_{t=0}^{\infty} R_{0,t}(1+\tau_t^c) c_t = \sum_{t=0}^{\infty} R_{0,t}(1-\tau_t^n) w_t n_t \tag{9}$$

or alternatively the transversality condition is satisfied with equality

$$\lim_{T \to \infty} R_{0,T} b_T^p = 0. \tag{10}$$

As a consequence of this optimizing behavior, (9) together with the resource constraint of the economy

$$y_t = a_t n_t = w_t n_t = g_t + c_t \tag{11}$$

implies the intertemporal budget constraint of the government

$$\sum_{t=0}^{\infty} R_{0,t} [\tau_t^c c_t + \tau_t^n w_t n_t] = \sum_{t=0}^{\infty} R_{0,t} g_t \tag{12}$$

and vice versa (12) and (11) imply (9).

Although the government is only subject to a flow budget constraint of the form (4), the intertemporal budget constraint of the government is also an equilibrium condition as a consequence of the optimizing behavior of the consumers in this economy. The intertemporal budget constraint of the government mirrors through (11) that of the households.

In an alternative interpretation, the flow budget constraint (4) is not enough to imply that (12) holds. It would be the case were a transversality condition of the form

$$\lim_{T \to \infty} R_{0,T} b_T^g = 0 \tag{13}$$

holding. And indeed this is the case since the equilibrium in the asset markets (6) together with (10) implies (13).

In a multi-country open-economy model, this implication does not hold. Consider, for simplicity, a two-country (home and foreign) version of the above model. In this case, equilibrium in the goods and asset markets requires that

$$y_t + y_t^* = c_t + c_t^* + g_t + g_t^*, \tag{14}$$

$$b_t^p + b_t^{*p} + b_t^g + b_t^{*g} = 0, \tag{15}$$

where starred variables denote the respective variables for the foreign country. Conditions (7), (8), (9), and (10) hold for the home and foreign households. However, it is not the case that (12) holds for each country. Indeed the only implication of condition (10) together with the respective condition for the foreign households and the equilibrium condition (15) is that

$$\lim_{T \to \infty} R_{0,T} (b_T^g + b_t^{*g}) = 0$$

and then that an intertemporal budget constraint of the government holds at an aggregate level. i.e.,

$$\sum_{t=0}^{\infty} R_{0,t}[\tau_t^c c_t + \tau_t^{*c} c_t^* + \tau_t^n w_t n_t + \tau_t^{*n} w_t^* n_t^*] = \sum_{t=0}^{\infty} R_{0,t}[g_t + g_t^*].$$

As a consequence of the possible violation of the intertemporal budget constraint of the government at the country level, it is not necessarily the case that the intertemporal resource constraints

$$\sum_{t=0}^{\infty} R_{0,t}(y_t - g_t - c_t) = 0 \qquad \sum_{t=0}^{\infty} R_{0,t}(y_t^* - g_t^* - c_t^*) = 0 \qquad (16)$$

hold for each country, as it is instead assumed in BK. A benevolent Ramsey central planner that maximizes the aggregate utility of the households belonging to this union might not necessarily find it optimal to obey (16) in its optimal plan. Violation of (16) might even be possible in the non-cooperative allocation.

It would be interesting to investigate whether there are cases in which a central planner would prefer that (16) holds for both countries while in the non-cooperative allocation (16) would be instead violated. Perhaps it is even possible to argue for cases in which the equilibrium allocation for the endogenous variables that results from a strategic game can be non-stationary, even though exogenous disturbances are assumed stationary.

3.   Strategy Spaces in Open-economy Models

In the characterization of the optimal policy problem of a closed-economy model it does not really matter whether the instrument of policy is specified or not, unless this specification represents a constraint on the set of possible equilibrium allocations. Instead, in an open-economy problem, this can be an important issue and it is moreover critical when non-cooperative allocations are analyzed. Indeed, non-cooperative allocations depend on the concept of strategic equilibrium assumed and in particular on the strategies specified for each of the two governments. As an example, in a standard duopoly problem the equilibrium outcome is different whether prices or quantities are assumed as strategies. In this paper, it is assumed that the strategy of a generic government j is specified in terms of the variables ξ_{jt}^n, ξ_{jt}^c. In particular ξ_{jt}^n, ξ_{jt}^c are defined as

$$\xi_{jt}^n = \Lambda_j (1 - \tau_{jt}^n)$$

$$\xi_{jt}^c = \Lambda_j (1 + \tau_{jt}^c)$$

where

$$\Lambda_j = \Lambda_j(\{\tau_{jt}^n\}, \{\tau_{jt}^c\}, \{\delta_t\}, \{w_t\}).$$

Moreover δ_t depends also on the tax rates τ_{it}^n and τ_{it}^c for each $i \neq j$. A game in which each government chooses optimally $\xi_{jt'}^n \xi_{jt}^c$ under the constraints of the economy taking as given $\xi_{it'}^n \xi_{it}^c$ for each other government i, is likely not to correspond to a game in which the strategy space is specified in terms of τ_{jt}^n and τ_{jt}^c. Indeed in the latter case, government in country i can internalize the effect of its action on the variable Λ_j of country j, while this is precluded in the former case. Whether there is equivalence between the outcomes of these two games should be proved. The game in which the strategies are specified in terms of the tax rates τ_{jt}^n and τ_{jt}^c seems the one relevant for policy analysis. Indeed one might wonder how it is possible to assume that each government decides on the variables $\xi_{jt'}^n \xi_{jt}^c$ which are then non-linear functions of the tax rates, even of those of the other countries. It is important to note that this device is helpful to get an analytical solution, which otherwise I doubt it will be possible.

4. Other Comments

An interesting result, robust to the closed and open-economy versions of the model, is the fact that the labor wedge is required to be constant across time. The labor wedge, k, is given by the following expression

$$k = \frac{u_n(c_t, n_t)}{u_c(c_t, n_t)} \frac{1}{w_t} = \frac{1 - \tau_t^n}{1 + \tau_t^c}$$

and measures the distortions existing in this economy. The fact that this wedge is constant requires further investigation. In particular, it seems that an important aspect to know is the level at which this wedge is set across the different models and allocation. First, it would be interesting to know whether having a small-open economy model implies a different k with respect to the closed-economy case. Moreover, the size of the labor wedge would matter in the comparison between the cooperative and non-cooperative allocation for the evaluation of the magnitude of the externalities and gains from cooperation. Given the constant-labor-wedge result, the paper focuses on the fact that sometimes the single tax rates τ_t^n and τ_t^c can be time varying. However, I suspect that the time-varying properties of the tax rates is likely to be of second-order importance with respect to the wedge differences, if any. And indeed, fiscal policy is usually thought to have level (or structural) effect on the equilibrium allocation. The paper is silent on whether there is such a role of fiscal policy that comes out from this model and more research on this issue is needed.

References

Baxter, Marianne, and Robert G. King. 2005. "Fiscal Externalities and Optimal Taxation in an Economic Community." NBER International Seminar on Macroeconomics, forthcoming.

Woodford, Michael. 1997. "Control of the Public Debt: A Requirement for Price Stability?" In G. Calvo and M. King, eds., *The Debt Burden and Monetary Policy*. London: Macmillan.

Comment

Francesco Giavazzi, Bocconi University, MIT, and NBER

The accepted wisdom in Brussels is that coordination of fiscal policies among the countries that belong to the European economic and monetary union (Emu) is desirable. For instance, the "Sapir Report," a highly influential document commissioned by the President of the EU to a group of independent experts, recommends that *"There should be greater coordination among national budgeting processes."* The paper by Baxter and King is important in the European debate since it shows what might be the consequences of such coordination. Coordination of fiscal policies could reduce the political cost of an increase in government spending in one country by shifting part of this cost upon the residents of other countries.

To study the nature of the fiscal externalities within an economic community Baxter and King analyze the effects of an (unanticipated) shock to government consumption in one country: a temporary, but persistent increase in the amount of the consumption good used up by the government. Consider first the optimal response in a closed economy. Since insurance is impossible—because a closed economy does not trade with the rest of the world—the real interest rate rises inducing households to work more and consume less. Consumers must bear the full burden of the increase in government spending. On the contrary, in a small open economy, consumers are fully protected: there are no effects on either work or consumption since the country can borrow from the rest of the world at the given world interest rate.

Consider now an intermediate size country integrated in an economic community. The community is closed to the rest of the world, but country-specific shocks can be redistributed among the residents of all countries. The optimal response to a government spending shock consists in allowing the consumers in the country hit by the shock to insure borrowing from the rest of the community. Thus, following a government spending shock in one country, everybody in the community ends up working more and consuming less, but the effects in the country hit by the shock are dampened compared with the closed economy case. In a Nash equilibrium, on the contrary, the optimal response of the country hit by the shock would take into account its possibility to affect the community interest rate. This results in a lower degree of risk sharing: consumers in the country hit by the shock bear a greater burden, but consumers in the rest of the community are less affected by the spending shock in one country. This is a result of the Nash equilibrium. The large country has an incentive to shift upon its partners some of the burden of adjustment—this is why it tries to affect the community-wide interest rate. In equilibrium, however, it transmits less than it would in a coordinated solution and is thus worse off.

As Baxter and King point out, there are two types of externalities. The country where government spending increases exerts a pecuniary externality on the community: in order to consume more it must induce residents in other countries to consume less (and work more). This externality is largest under coordination. But there is also what Baxter and King define as a policy externality, which arises when countries fail to coordinate and thus to optimally insure. Lack of coordination means that the community does not take full advantage of the possibilities offered by region-wide risk sharing.

The point about the cost of coordinating fiscal policy could not be made in a sharper way. Coordination is undesirable because fiscal shocks exert a pecuniary externality. Under Nash the pecuniary externality is smaller than under coordination, which means that residents in the country where the increase in government spending occurs bear a larger burden. Baxter and King do not realize that there is a political economy corollary to their results. If the frequency and the size of shocks to government spending depend on the burden they impose upon a country's residents, coordination is the way to make such shocks larger and relatively frequent. In this context what matters is the pecuniary externality: correcting the policy externalities is a mistake. This is an important argument and one that is typically overlooked in Brussels.

6

Fiscal Divergence and Business Cycle Synchronization: Irresponsibility Is Idiosyncratic

Zsolt Darvas, *Corvinus University*
Andrew K. Rose, *University of California, Berkeley and NBER*
György Szapáry, *Magyar Nemzeti Bank*

1. Introduction

In 1998, European countries qualified for entry into European Monetary Union (EMU) on the basis of five "convergence criteria." The criteria were enshrined in the 1992 Maastricht Treaty and quantify targets concerning inflation, long-term bond yields, exchange rates, government debt, and the government budget. The Maastricht convergence criteria are of more than historical relevance, since they will also be applied to future EMU entrants. Further, the 1997 "Stability and Growth Pact" implies that the fiscal criteria are still, in principle, binding.[1]

Most economists—particularly non-Europeans—view the Maastricht convergence criteria with skepticism. The reason is simple: they have little to do with standard economic arguments concerning "optimal currency areas," monetary unions that are desirable and sustainable. The consensus in economics is that from a theoretical viewpoint, monetary unions make sense for countries with synchronized business cycles, integrated markets, flexibility, and mechanisms to share risk. The overlap between the Maastricht convergence criteria and the optimum currency area criteria is small.[2]

Clearly the direct correspondence between the (Maastricht) criteria actually applied for EMU entry and the appropriate (optimum currency area) criteria is poor. In this paper we ask if there is an *indirect* connection. We focus on the most controversial Maastricht criteria—the total government budget deficit/GDP ratio—and link it empirically to arguably the most important optimum currency area criterion, namely the synchronization of business cycles. Using a panel of data that includes 21 countries and 40 years of data, we show that countries with divergent fiscal policies (i.e., large average cross-country differences in the ratio of general government net lending/borrowing to GDP) tend to have less synchronized business cycles. We estimate that each percentage point of fiscal divergence between a pair of countries tends to lower the correlation coefficient of their business cycles by between .03 and .12. This effect is both statistically and economically significant. We also show that reduced *levels* of primary fiscal deficits (or increased primary surpluses) tend to increase the level of business cycle synchronization, though the evidence for this effect is somewhat weaker.

A concrete example may clarify things. When the Maastricht Treaty was signed in 1992, the total Italian budget deficit was 10.7 percent of GDP, and had been hovering at or above 11 percent of GDP for a decade. This was in sharp contrast to the typical German deficit, which was 2.6 percent of GDP in 1992.[3] The drive to enter EMU—that is, to satisfy the Maastricht criteria—encouraged this gap to shrink by around 8 percentage points; by the 1999 start, Italy's budget deficit had fallen to 1.7 percent, similar to the German deficit of 1.5 percent. In this paper, we ask: could such fiscal convergence have an effect on the synchronization of business cycles between Germany and Italy? Alternatively, the (cross-country) standard deviation of the government budget position/GDP ratio was 4.1 percent for the EURO-12 in 1991, and only 2.1 percent in 1999; did this convergence in fiscal positions affect business cycle synchronization at the start of EMU?[4] We find that the answer is generally positive; a larger panel of OECD data indicates that fiscal convergence (in either the total or primary budget balance) is systematically associated with more synchronized economic activity. *Whether or not it was intentional, the application of the Maastricht convergence criteria may have moved the EMU entrants closer to being an optimum currency area, since fiscal convergence tends to synchronize business cycles!*

We stress at this point that we know of no theoretical model formally linking fiscal convergence to business cycle synchronization. Still, we do not think it is difficult to understand our results. Fiscal convergence, by our definition, usually occurs because a country that has been fiscally irresponsible—that is, a country that has run persistently high budget deficits—reforms and closes the fiscal gap with other countries. Intuitively, countries that are fiscally irresponsible—i.e., countries that run persistently high budget deficits—are also countries that create idiosyncratic fiscal shocks. (This seems a natural association to us; irresponsible behavior is often idiosyncratic, for individuals as well as fiscal authorities.) In this case, reducing the budget deficit of a country simultaneously reduces its scope for idiosyncratic fiscal shocks, raising the coherence of its business cycle with the business cycle of others. That is, fiscal convergence raises business cycle synchronization since responsible fiscal behavior tends to be less idiosyncratic fiscal behavior.

We mention in passing that we know of no deliberate intent on the part of the creators of the Maastricht convergence criteria to affect the optimum currency criteria, either directly or indirectly. Our effect seems to have been an unintended side-benefit to the convergence process.

In section 2 we describe our methodology. Our results on the link between fiscal convergence and business cycle synchronization are presented in section 3; we link budget deficits to business cycle volatility more directly in the following section. The paper ends with a brief conclusion.

2. Methodology

What should the effect of persistent fiscal divergence be on business cycle synchronization? To our knowledge, there is no formal treatment of this topic in the extant literature.

Countries are subject to asymmetric shocks (e.g., exchange rate and/ or wage shocks). Further, similar shocks (e.g., oil price shocks) can have asymmetric effects across countries because of differing propagation mechanisms. If these asymmetries are persistent, and are partially offset with discretionary fiscal policy or automatic fiscal stabilizers, then fiscal divergence can, in principle, be associated with greater business cycle synchronization. For example, suppose that Austria and Belgium begin with identical budget positions and perfectly synchronized business cycles. Austria receives a persistent negative shock, and responds with expansionary fiscal policy that neutralizes any effect on its cycle. In this case, Austria's business cycle remains synchronized with the Belgian economy *ceteris paribus*, while the Austrian deficit diverges from the Belgian.

Of course, fiscal policy in some countries is pro-cyclic, as shown by Gavin and Perotti (1997) and Lane (2003); see also Kaminsky et al. (2004) and Aguiar et al. (2005). Fiscal policy can also be a source of shocks, for e.g., purely political reasons (e.g., Brender and Drazen 2005). Suppose that Austrian fiscal policy expands in the absence of shocks to either Austria or Belgium, and generates an Austrian expansion. In this case fiscal divergence will be associated with reduced business cycle synchronization.

From a theoretical viewpoint then, the matter is ambiguous. If fiscal policy divergence is a response to asymmetric shocks then it may be associated with enhanced business cycle coherence; if fiscal shocks themselves cause business cycles, then the opposite may be true. Without persistent shocks (or shocks with persistent effects), there may be no relationship at all between fiscal policy divergence and business cycle synchronization. The question is thus ultimately empirical. While the absence of a formal structural framework makes us uncomfortable, we see no alternative but to take the issue to the data.

The literature gives only a few hints about the matter. Several authors argue that a world business cycle exists (e.g., Gerlach 1988; Lumsdaine and Prasad 2003; Darvas and Szapáry 2007; Canova et al. 2004), consistent with the absence of important asymmetries. Fatás and Mihov (2003a) studied discretionary fiscal policy for 91 countries and conclude (p. 1419) "governments that use fiscal policy aggressively induce significant macroeconomic instability" i.e., output volatility. Similarly, Fatás and Mihov (2006) study the American states and conclude that budgetary restrictions lead to lower fiscal policy volatility and smoother business cycles; they conclude (p. 116) that "Fiscal policy is a source of business cycle volatility among US states and constraints on politicians lower policy volatility, which in turn leads to improved macroeconomic stability." Lane (2003) studies OECD countries and finds a link between output volatility and procyclic fiscal policy. Perhaps the work closest to ours is that of Kose et al. (2003) who study determinants of coherence of a country's business cycle with a global business cycle. One interpretation of their findings (p. 62) is that "fiscal policies exacerbate country-specific fluctuations."

Still, to our knowledge, no one has explored the link between differences of national fiscal policies and the synchronization of their business cycles. We now turn to that task.

2.1 Empirical Framework

We are interested in investigating the empirical linkages between persistent cross-country differences in the fiscal policy and business cycle synchronization. We are also interested in the effects of the average cross-country *level* of aggregate fiscal policy on business cycle synchronization.[5]

Our primary measure of fiscal divergence is the difference between countries in the general government budget surplus (+) or deficit (–), measured as a percentage of national GDP. In 1999, the Austrian deficit was 2.3 percent of GDP, while the Belgian deficit was .4 percent. Thus our measure of Austrian-Belgian fiscal divergence in 1999 is 1.9 percent. Taking the average of this over a decade of annual data yields our measure of fiscal divergence (.98 for average Austrian-Belgian fiscal divergence during 1994–2003). That is, we measure fiscal divergence as:

$$\text{FiscalDiverge}_{ij\tau} \equiv .1^* \Sigma_\tau \left(\mid \text{Budg}_{it} - \text{Budg}_{jt} \mid \right)$$

where Budg_{it} is the general government budget surplus (+) or deficit (–) at time t expressed as a percentage of nominal GDP for country i, and the averaging is done over a decade of annual data. A larger value of FiscalDiverge corresponds to higher average divergence between the fiscal positions of the two countries over a long period of time.[6]

The total government budget position as a percentage of GDP is of great relevance; the Maastricht convergence criteria focus on this measure. However, we also examine the analogue using the cyclically adjusted primary budget position (also measured as a percentage of GDP). Since the primary balance excludes interest payments (and thus the impact of the government debt level), it better captures discretionary fiscal policy (as well as acting as a robustness check).

We note that our measure of international fiscal divergence indicates little about the pro- or counter-cyclic nature of national fiscal policy. A standard argument used against the Stability and Growth Pact is that countries that are constrained to have the same monetary policy should have good access to counter-cyclic fiscal policy. But the average *level* of the budget deficit is unrelated to its counter- or pro-cyclic stance, especially when the data is smoothed over a decade. Countries that use fiscal policy counter-cyclically sometimes have persistent deficits, but so do countries with pro-cyclic fiscal policy.[7] In any case, our focus is on the average *difference* between fiscal positions.

Fiscal policy was highly divergent at the signing of the Maastricht Treaty. In 1992, four European countries had total government budget deficits in excess of 6 percent of GDP (Belgium 8 percent; Greece 12.2 percent; Italy 10.7 percent; and UK 6.5 percent), while another four had deficits of less than 3 percent of GDP (Austria 1.9 percent; Denmark 2.2 percent; Germany 2.6 percent; and Luxembourg .3 percent).[8] The Maastricht treaty encouraged fiscal convergence since it pointed potential EMU entrants towards lower deficits. For this reason, we find it interesting to determine the consequences, if any, of fiscal convergence. But clearly the treaty encouraged members to converge to *lower* deficits (of no more than 3 percent of GDP), not to similar deficits irrespective of their level. Accordingly, we also examine the effect of the average cross-country *level* of the total government budget deficit, measured as a percentage of GDP. We measure this by:

$$\text{AvgFiscal}_{ij\tau} \equiv .1^*\Sigma_{\tau}\,(\text{Budg}_{it} + \text{Budg}_{jt})/2$$

Again, we also examine the analogy for the primary budget position.

Our other important variable is business cycle synchronization. We focus on this because it is arguably the most important criteria of the traditional Mundell optimum currency area criteria. Regions with more synchronized business cycles have less need of individual monetary policies, and are thus better candidates for currency union. While it is by no means the only criteria, it seems a natural place to search for an overlap between Maastricht and Mundell.

We are interested in the bilateral correlation between real activity in country i and country j over decade τ. There is no obvious single measure for this; accordingly, we construct a number of proxies. We begin by using two standard measures of real economic activity: (the natural logarithm of) real GDP and the unemployment rate. We then de-trend the variables so as to focus on business cycle fluctuations (i.e., the combination of shocks and propagation mechanisms), in two different ways: (1) we take simple first-differences of annual variables; (2) we use the well-known Hodrick-Prescott ("HP") filter (with the standard annual smoothing parameter of 100). After de-trending our variables over the entire available sample, we are able to compute bilateral correlations for real activity. These correlation coefficients are estimated (for a given concept of real economic activity and de-trending technique), *between* two countries *over* a given span of time. Thus, for instance, we estimate the correlation between (HP-de-trended real) Austrian and Belgian GDP, between 1964 and 1973. We also investigate a number of other measures of business cycle synchronization below to ensure that our results are insensitive to the underlying measure of economic activity, the de-trending technique, etc. Thus we also use industrial production, we de-trend with the Baxter-King "BK" (1999) band-pass filter, and so forth.

2.2   The Data Set

Our default sample includes 21 OECD countries; these are listed in the Appendix, Table A1. We stick to the OECD *Economic Outlook* data set because it is both high quality and the most relevant for e.g., questions concerning EMU. Our underlying data set consists of annual observations (though with some gaps); we also use quarterly data (which has more holes) as a robustness check. The data set spans 1964 through 2003, which we then split into four decades (1964–1973, 1974–1983, 1984–1993, and 1994–2003). We are thus left with a panel of data; the maximum possible sample size is 840 observations; 210 bilateral country-pair "dyads" [=(21 × 20)/2], with four decadal observations per country-pair.[9] Descriptive statistics for key variables are provided in the Appendix, Table A2.

Figure 1 provides a set of four simple scatterplots of our four default measures of business cycle synchronization (GDP/Unemployment, differenced/HP-filtered) graphed against budget divergence. Non-parametric data smoothers are also provided in the graphs; these demonstrate a loose negative relationship between the two variables. Figures 2 and 3 are analogues that portray observations from the most recent (1994–2003) decade and EMU members respectively. Figure 4 is the analogue that portrays divergence in the *primary* (instead of the total) fiscal balance. Finally, Figures 5 and 6 are scatterplots of business cycle synchronization against the average cross-country levels of the total and primary budget positions respectively. There is reasonably consistent ocular evidence of a negative relationship between fiscal divergence and business cycle synchronization. However, there is no sign of a strong link between the latter and the average total fiscal *level*, though the correlations are higher for the average *primary* budget position.

2.3   Estimation

Our general empirical strategy follows that of Frankel and Rose (1998) who focused on the endogeneity of business cycle synchronization with respect to trade.

The benchmark regressions we estimate are non-structural and take the simple form:

$$\text{Corr}(v,s)_{i,j,\tau} = \alpha + \beta \text{FiscalDiverge}_{i,j,\tau} + \varepsilon_{i,j,\tau}.$$

$\text{Corr}(v,s)_{i,j,\tau}$ denotes the correlation coefficient between country i and country j over decade τ for activity concept v (corresponding to log real GDP or the unemployment rate), de-trended with method s (corresponding to differencing or HP-filtering). $\text{FiscalDiverge}_{i,j,\tau}$ denotes the average (over decade τ) absolute difference in the government budget position (measured as a percentage of national GDP) between countries i and j. Finally, $\varepsilon_{i,j,\tau}$ represents the myriad influences on bilateral activ-

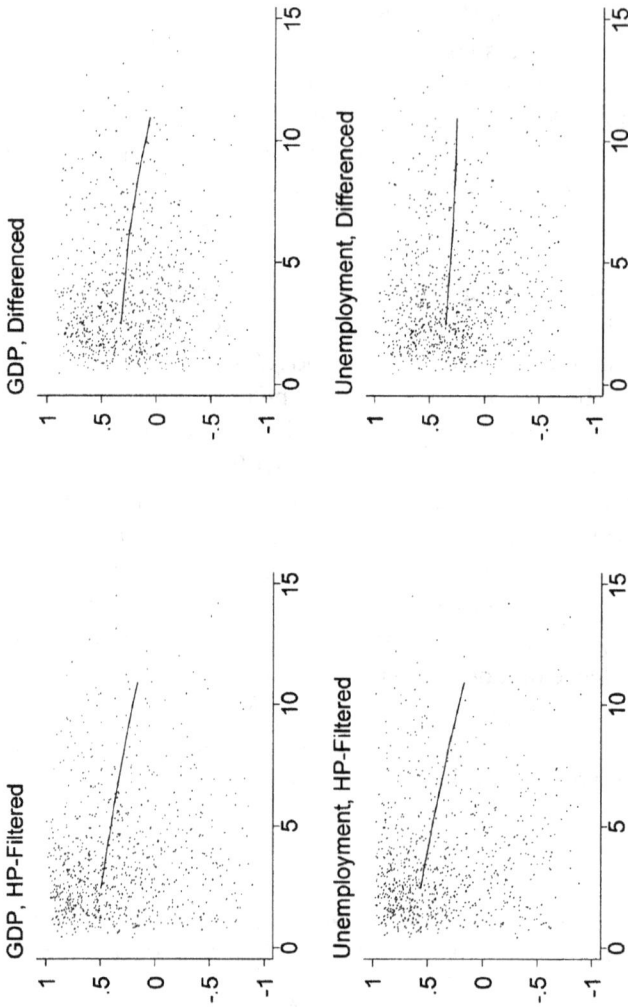

Figure 1
Simple scatterplots of key variables, 1964–2003

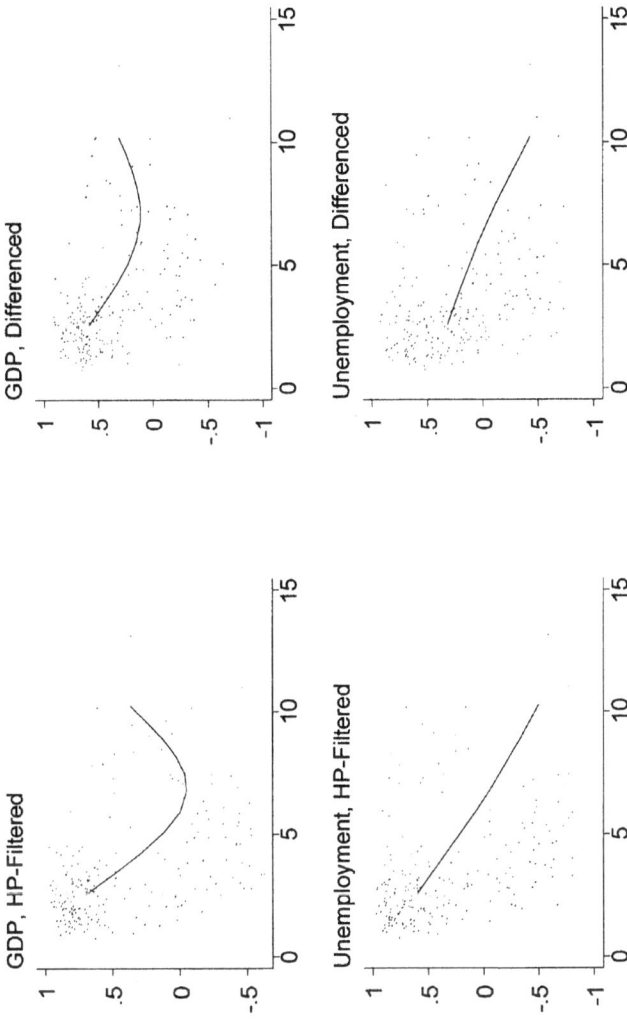

Corr Coefficients (y); Avg Abs-Val Budget/GDP Differentials (x)
Business Cycle and Budgets, 1994-2003

Figure 2
Scatterplots for most recent decade

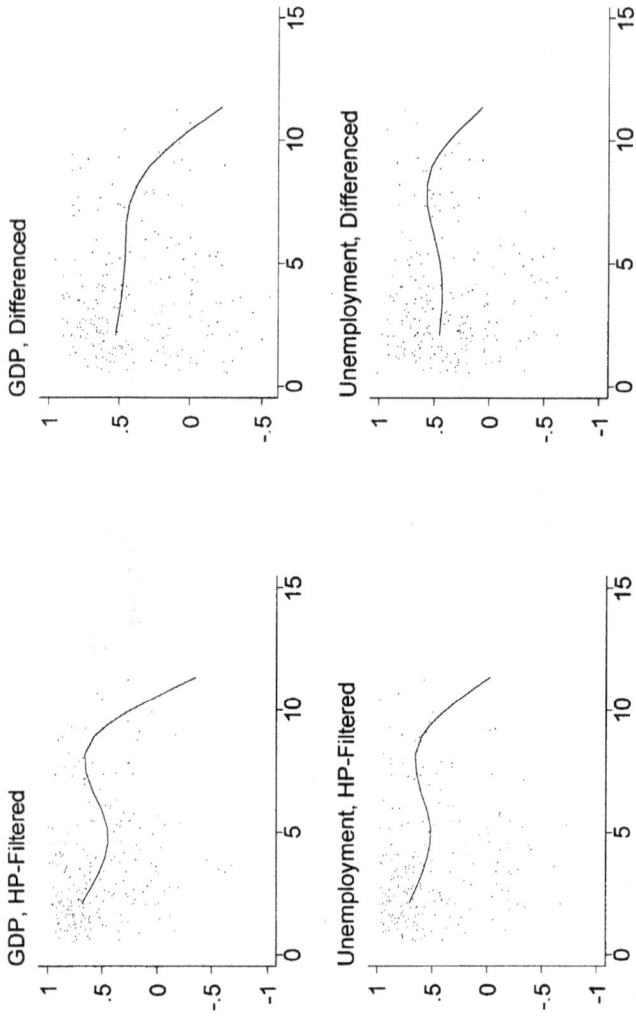

Figure 3
Scatterplots for the Ins, 1964–2003

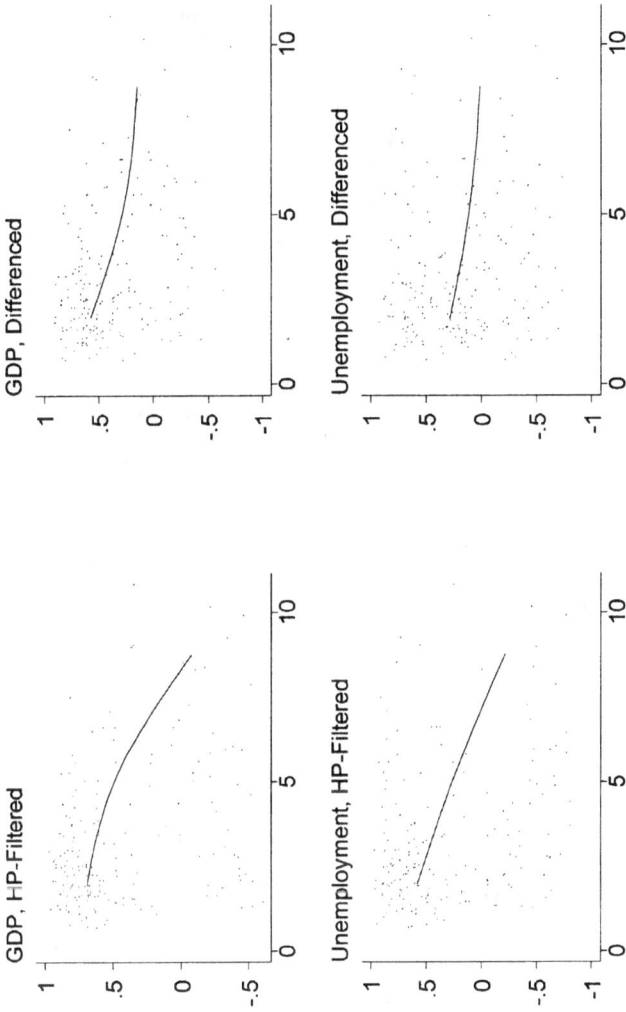

Corr Coefficients (y); Avg Abs-Val Primary Budget/GDP Diffl (x)
Business Cycles and Budgets, 1964-2003

Figure 4
Primary fiscal divergence

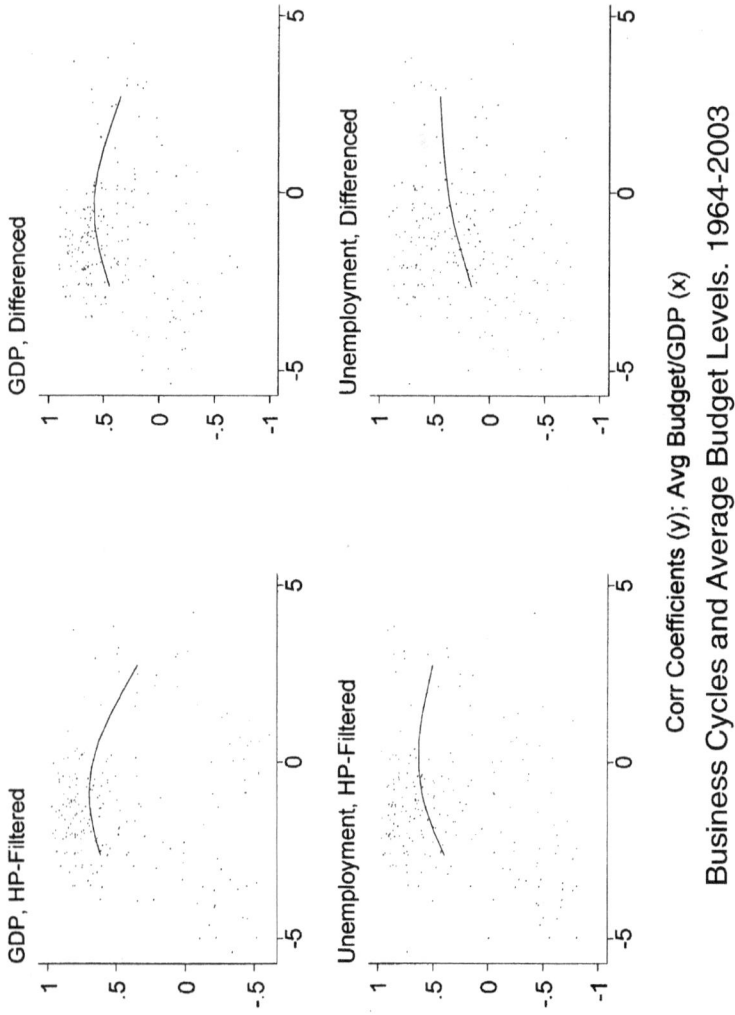

Figure 5
Average total government budget level

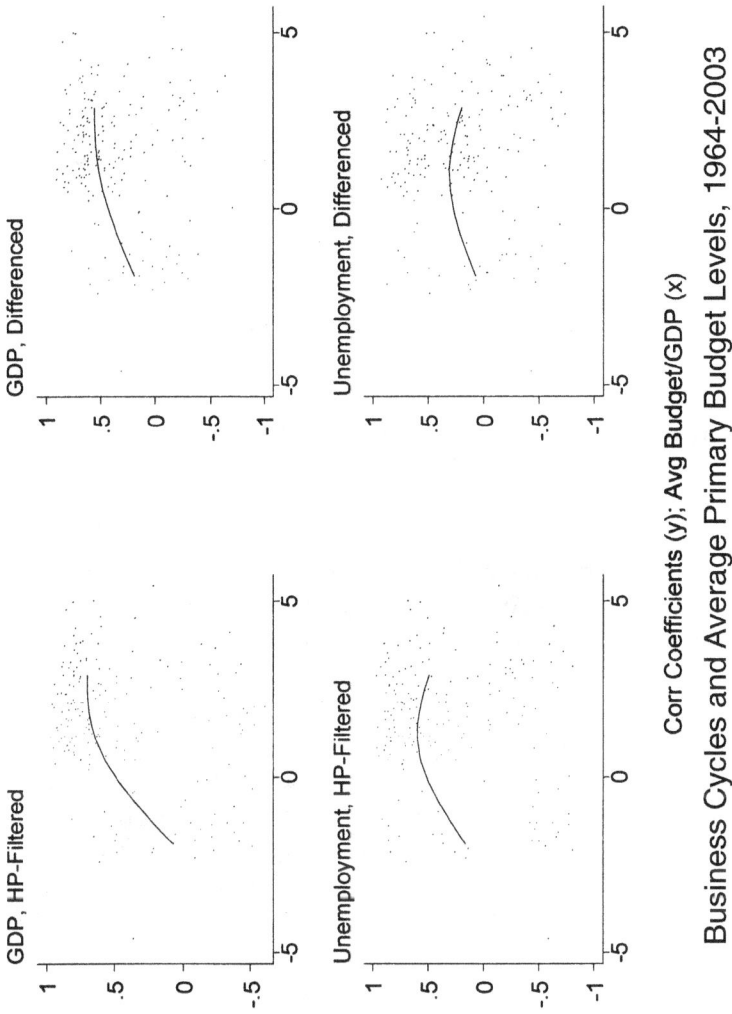

GDP, Differenced

GDP, HP-Filtered

Unemployment, Differenced

Unemployment, HP-Filtered

Corr Coefficients (y); Avg Budget/GDP (x)

Business Cycles and Average Primary Budget Levels, 1964-2003

Figure 6
Average primary government budget level

ity correlations above and beyond the influences of fiscal divergence (hopefully unrelated to our regressor), and α and β are the regression coefficients to be estimated.

The object of interest to us is the slope coefficient β. A negative estimate of β indicates that an increase in fiscal divergence is associated with reduced business cycle coherence. That is, fiscal policy convergence is linked to more synchronized business cycles.

A simple OLS regression of bilateral activity income correlations on fiscal divergence might be inappropriate for a couple of reasons. First, there may be non-trivial measurement error in fiscal divergence (especially since measuring the general government budget position itself seems difficult). A potentially more important worry is simultaneity. Suppose that for some exogenous reason a high-deficit country decides to engage in long-term fiscal consolidation. If this leads to a recession, *ceteris paribus*, we might expect fiscal convergence to coincide with lower business cycle synchronization, at least over a short period of time.[10] Alternatively, suppose that a high-deficit country decides to engage in fiscal consolidation and convergence simultaneously (e.g., during the drive to EMU); in this case, the effect goes the opposite way.

Accordingly, our default estimation is conducted with both OLS and instrumental variables. Our instrumental variables are associated with (cross-country differences in) the size and composition of public sector activity, since the public finance/political economy literature has shown these to be of relevance (e.g., Alesina and Perotti 1997 and Lane 2003). Thus we use expenditure variables (such as government investment and non-wage consumption), as well as revenue variables (e.g., direct business and household taxes), all expressed as percentages of GDP. We check that our OLS and IV results are consistent and also show that our results are insensitive to the exact choice of instrumental variables.

3.   Empirics

3.1   Benchmark Results on Fiscal Convergence and Business Cycle Synchronization

Our main results are presented in Tables 1 and 2. These display estimates of β, the estimated effect of fiscal divergence on business cycle synchronization. Robust standard errors (clustered by country-pair dyads) for the slope coefficients are presented beneath the coefficients in parentheses. One (two) asterisk(s) mark a coefficient that is signifi-

Table 1
Effect of fiscal divergence on business cycle synchronization, OLS

	GDP, HP-filtered	GDP, differenced	Unemployment, HP filtered	Unemployment, differenced
Benchmark	−.036**	−.024**	−.048**	−.028**
	(.006)	(.005)	(.006)	(.005)
Pair-specific fixed effects	−.022**	−.010	−.034**	−.005
	(.008)	(.007)	(.009)	(.008)
Without decade effects	−.027*	−.013**	−.032**	−.016**
	(.006)	(.005)	(.006)	(.006)
Without EMU pairs	−.039**	−.026**	−.050**	−.029**
	(.007)	(.006)	(.007)	(.006)
Add EMU-pairs intercept	−.036**	−.024**	−.048**	−.028**
	(.006)	(.005)	(.006)	(.005)
Last half of sample	−.055**	−.040**	−.073**	−.045**
	(.009)	(.007)	(.010)	(.009)
Without 2σ outliers	−.040**	−.024**	−.046**	−.028**
	(.006)	(.004)	(.006)	(.005)
Without six small	−.016	.000	−.075**	−.052**
	(.011)	(.009)	(.011)	(.010)
G7 only	−.012	−.010	−.064*	−.061*
	(.019)	(.017)	(.025)	(.023)
Add trade/GDP ratio	−.030**	−.018**	−.042**	−.022**
	(.006)	(.005)	(.006)	(.005)
With gravity regressors	−.036**	−.023**	−.050**	−.028**
	(.006)	(.005)	(.006)	(.005)
Regressor variant	−.031**	−.023**	−.044**	−.027**
	(.006)	(.005)	(.005)	(.005)
Primary deficit measure	−.054**	−.044**	−.051**	−.027**
	(.009)	(.007)	(.010)	(.009)
Primary deficit without six small	−.047**	−.029**	−.075**	−.035*
	(.015)	(.012)	(.017)	(.014)
Primary deficit measure, G7 only	−.042	−.035	−.073*	−.055*
	(.028)	(.020)	(.031)	(.025)
Maastricht deviation	−.013	−.012	−.041**	−.023**
	(.009)	(.007)	(.008)	(.007)
Std dev (not mean) of budget	−.084**	−.049**	−.077**	−.034*
	(.014)	(.011)	(.015)	(.014)
With average fiscal position	−.044**	−.026**	−.050**	−.027**
	(.006)	(.005)	(.006)	(.006)
With avg primary fiscal position	−.040**	−.026**	−.057**	−.032**
	(.008)	(.007)	(.008)	(.008)

Regressand is correlation coefficient (computed over decades) between country i and j detrended series.
Coefficients recorded are effect of (average of absolute-value of differential of) government budget surplus/deficit, as percentage of GDP. Robust standard errors (clustered by country-pair dyads) recorded in parentheses. Decade effects and constant included but not recorded.
Coefficients significantly different from zero at .05 (.01) level marked with one (two) asterisk(s). OLS estimation unless noted.
Data set has maximum of 21*20/2=210 country pairs for four decades (1964–1973, 1974–1983, 1984–1993, 1994–2003).
Six small countries: Denmark, Finland, Greece, Ireland, Norway, and New Zealand.
Regressor variant is absolute value of average of differential (not average of absolute-value of differential). Std Dev is standard deviation over time of absolute value of differential of government budget surplus/deficit, % GDP.

Table 2
Effect of fiscal divergence on business cycle synchronization, IV

	GDP, HP-filtered	GDP, differenced	Unemployment, HP filtered	Unemployment, differenced
Benchmark	−.16**	−.11**	−.15**	−.11**
	(.04)	(.03)	(.04)	(.03)
Pair-specific fixed effects	−.23**	−.16**	−.25**	−.14*
	(.08)	(.06)	(.08)	(.06)
Without decade effects	−.17**	−.13**	−.16**	−.11**
	(.04)	(.04)	(.04)	(.03)
Without EMU pairs	−.12**	−.07**	−.11**	−.07**
	(.03)	(.02)	(.03)	(.02)
Add EMU-pairs intercept	−.12**	−.08**	−.11**	−.07**
	(.03)	(.02)	(.03)	(.02)
Last half of sample	−.19**	−.11**	−.16**	−.11**
	(.04)	(.03)	(.04)	(.03)
Without 2σ outliers	−.19**	−.13**	−.19**	−.14**
	(.03)	(.02)	(.04)	(.03)
Without six small	−.15*	−.13**	−.20**	−.11*
	(.06)	(.05)	(.06)	(.04)
G7 only	−.14	−.16	−.23*	−.12*
	(.09)	(.09)	(.10)	(.06)
Add trade/GDP ratio (Gravity IV)	−.09**	−.05**	−.06**	−.04*
	(.02)	(.01)	(.02)	(.02)
With gravity regressors	−.08**	−.05**	−.06**	−.03
	(.02)	(.02)	(.02)	(.02)
Regressor variant	−.14**	−.10**	−.14**	−.09**
	(.03)	(.03)	(.03)	(.02)
Primary deficit measure	−.15**	−.13**	−.19**	−.10**
	(.04)	(.03)	(.05)	(.03)
Primary without six small	−.12**	−.09**	−.16**	−.06*
	(.04)	(.03)	(.04)	(.03)
Primary deficit measure, G7 only	−.16*	−.14*	−.18	−.07
	(.08)	(.06)	(.09)	(.05)
Deviation from Maastricht	−.03	−.05	−.09*	−.06*
	(.04)	(.03)	(.04)	(.03)
With average fiscal position	−.15**	−.12**	−.16**	−.11**
	(.04)	(.03)	(.04)	(.03)
With avg primary fiscal position	−.14**	−.09**	−.12**	−.10**
	(.05)	(.03)	(.04)	(.03)

Table 2 *(continued)*
Effect of fiscal divergence on business cycle synchronization, IV

	GDP, HP-filtered	GDP, differenced	Unemployment, HP filtered	Unemployment, differenced
IV Variant 1	–.16** (.05)	–.12** (.04)	–.29** (.06)	–.25** (.06)
IV Variant 2	–.14** (.04)	–.08* (.03)	–.08** (.03)	–.03 (.03)
IV Variant 3	–.18** (.06)	–.10* (.04)	–.12** (.05)	–.07* (.03)
IV Variant 4	–.19** (.06)	–.15** (.05)	–.20** (.05)	–.15** (.04)

Regressand is correlation coefficient (computed over decades) between country i and j de-trended series.

Coefficients recorded are effect of (average of absolute-value of differential of) government budget surplus/deficit, as percentage of GDP. Robust standard errors (clustered by country-pair dyads) recorded in parentheses. Decade effects and constant included but not recorded.

Coefficients significantly different from zero at .05 (.01) level marked with one (two) asterisk(s).

Instrumental Variable estimation unless noted. IVs include: (1) government non-wage consumption/GDP; (2) government investment/GDP; (3) direct business taxes/GDP; and (4) direct household taxes/GDP. IVs are average of absolute value of cross-country differentials.

Data set has maximum of 21*20/2=210 country pairs for four decades (1964–1973, 1974–1983, 1984–1993, 1994–2003). Six small countries: Denmark, Finland, Greece, Ireland, Norway, and New Zealand.

Regressor variant is absolute value of average of differential (not average of absolute-value of differential). Std Dev is standard deviation over time of absolute value of differential of government budget surplus/deficit, % GDP.

IV Variant 1: (1) government non-wage consumption/GDP; (2) government investment/GDP; (3) effective labor taxes as percentage of labor costs; and (4) indirect taxes/GDP. Variant 2: (1) government social benefits/GDP: (2) government wages/GDP; and (3) direct business taxes/GDP. Variant 3: (1) direct household taxes/GDP; (2) indirect taxes/GDP; and (3) direct business taxes/GDP. Variant 4: (1) government non-wage consumption/GDP; (2) government wages/GDP; and (3) government investment/GDP.

Gravity regressors are: (1) log distance; (2) log product land area; (3) common land border dummy; (4) common language dummy.

cantly different from zero at the .05 (.01) confidence level. Table 1 presents OLS results, while our IV estimates are tabulated in Table 2.

The first row of each table present four benchmark estimates, one for each of our four default ways of measuring business cycle synchronization (arranged in columns). All four coefficients are negative and distinguishable from zero with a high level of statistical confidence, for both OLS and IV. Moreover, the effects are economically important. A simple average of the four coefficients is −.034 for OLS. This implies that a reduction in fiscal divergence of (say) 2.5 percentage points—equal to one standard deviation in fiscal divergence—around its mean tends to raise the correlation of business cycles between a pair of countries, *ceteris paribus*, by around .085. Since the *average* correlation coefficient in the sample is around .3, this effect is neither trivial nor implausible. The IV results are approximately four times larger, and remain highly statistically significant. We try to be conservative in estimating the magnitude of our effect (especially when the model is so simple), but are reassured by the fact that OLS and IV deliver the same sign.

Succinctly, our initial results show that fiscal convergence tends to raise business cycle synchronization.

3.2 Sensitivity Analysis

Our benchmark estimates are derived from a simple setup; before taking them seriously, it is critical to establish their robustness. The remainder of Tables 1 and 2 is devoted to sensitivity analysis. In particular, we explore the robustness of our finding to: (1) differences in the estimation technique; (2) differences in the sample; (3) the inclusion of other controls; and (4) different measures of fiscal policy. None of these alters our basic finding that fiscal convergence is associated with increased business cycle synchronization.

Our analysis examines pairs of countries over different periods of time. It is thus natural to add country pair-specific (dyadic) fixed effects. When we do so, β remains negative; its statistical significance falls somewhat, while its economic importance grows substantially with IV, and shrinks with OLS. Further, the fixed effects themselves are jointly insignificant at standard levels (except for two of the OLS equations). It seems that dyadic fixed effects are not the reason for our finding of a negative β. Similarly, removing the decade (time-specific) fixed effects does not change our conclusion.

Our results seem insensitive to the exact handling of EMU observations. Dropping country-pairs that eventually joined EMU does not destroy our result; neither does adding a separate intercept for EMU dyads. Our significantly negative β estimate also survives dropping observations from the first two decades of our sample, and dropping all observations with residuals lying more than two standard deviations from zero.[11]

When we drop the six smallest countries from our sample (thereby halving the number of bilateral observations available to us), our results remain negative and significant when we use unemployment to measure the business cycle; the same is true when we use only G7 data.

Frankel and Rose (1998) demonstrated that trade integration had the effect of raising business cycle synchronization. Baxter-Kouparitsas (2005) showed that among the various candidates (not including our fiscal variables) suggested in the literature to determine business cycle synchronization, only trade integration has a robust effect. Might including trade in the regression reduce the effect of fiscal divergence? No. We add bilateral trade between countries i and j, normalized by the ratio of their GDPs, using four geographic determinants of the gravity model of bilateral trade as instrumental variables.[12] As expected, trade has a positive and usually significant effect on business cycle synchronization, but its presence makes little difference to the effect of fiscal divergence on business cycles.[13] Our results are also not substantially affected when we include the four gravity variables directly in our equation.[14]

Our next sensitivity analyses use different variants of the fiscal divergence regressor. First, we use the absolute value of the average (over time) gap between the two countries' budget positions, instead of using the average of the absolute value. Since budget balances are persistent, this variant delivers almost identical results to our benchmark. Second, we use (averages of absolute values of) primary budget deficits instead of total budget deficits; this delivers economically large results that remain statistically significant.[15] Interestingly, these significantly negative estimates persist when we restrict our attention to either the G7 countries or the largest 15 countries in our sample (for both GDP and unemployment). It seems that our results do not stem from any particular set of countries.

We also use the gap between the two countries' actual government budget deficits and the Maastricht targets of a maximal 3 percent deficit/GDP ratio.[16] Here we find weaker results; there is a statistically significant result only when we use unemployment. That is, cross-country deviations from the Maastricht convergence criteria (and thus the Stability Pact's ceiling of 3 percent deficits) do not seem to have a substantial consistent effect on cycle synchronization.[17]

Towards the bottom of Table 1, we also use the standard deviation (computed over the ten years inside each decadal observation) of the gap between the two countries' budget/GDP ratios, in place of our default measure of fiscal divergence. OLS estimates indicate that variation in the budget deficit positions between the countries tends to lower their business cycle synchronization, which support our benchmark results.

It is comforting to us that OLS and IV estimates both sign β negatively. Nevertheless, we do not have vast confidence in our instrumental variables themselves.[18] (Our first stage is tabulated in the Appendix, Table A3; while three of the instrumental variables are significant, the R^2 of the first stage is only .18.) Accordingly, we use four different sets of instrumental variables, combining measures of government revenue and expenditure series in different ways. We tabulate these results towards the bottom of Table 2. Both the economic and statistical significance of β varies depending on the estimator and measure of business cycle coherence. Still, all the estimates are negative, and the vast majority are significantly so.[19]

We also check whether our finding (that fiscal divergence lowers business cycle synchronization) is immune to the addition of the average *level* of the government budget position. That is, we add AvgFiscal to our default equation and re-estimate. As can be seen from the bottoms of Tables 1 and 2, the effect of fiscal divergence on business cycle synchronization is unaffected when we control for the level of the average (cross-country) fiscal deficit; β remains economically and statistically significant.

3.3 Further Robustness Checks

Table 3 provides more sensitivity checks, using a number of different measures of business cycle synchronization. Rather than rely on a single measure of business cycle coherence in the benchmark results, we used four measures in Tables 1 and 2. Still, there is no reason not to try others. The rows of Table 3 correspond to the estimated effect of fiscal divergence on 15 further measures of business cycle synchronization. In different columns we provide OLS and IV estimates of β.

Table 3
Fiscal divergence and different measures of business cycle synchronization

	OLS	IV
Industrial production, HP-filtered	−.027**	−.08**
	(.005)	(.02)
Industrial production, differenced	−.014**	−.06**
	(.005)	(.02)
GDP, Alesina-Barro-Tenreyro	.0005**	.0019**
	(.0001)	(.0005)
GDP p/c, Alesina-Barro-Tenreyro	.0004**	.0018**
	(.0001)	(.0005)
Unemployment, Alesina-Barro-Tenreyro	.026**	.027
	(.009)	(.026)
Industrial production, Alesina-Barro-Tenreyro	.0009**	.0046**
	(.0002)	(.0010)
GDP, Baxter-King	−.029**	−.15**
	(.005)	(.03)
Unemployment, Baxter-King	−.030**	−.11**
	(.005)	(.03)
Industrial production, Baxter-King	−.023**	−.07**
	(.005)	(.02)
Quarterly GDP, HP-filtered	−.012*	−.09**
	(.005)	(.02)
Quarterly GDP, differenced	−.023**	−.12**
	(.006)	(.03)
Quarterly GDP, Baxter-King	−.027**	−.18**
	(.004)	(.04)
Quarterly industrial production, HP-filtered	−.021**	−.06**
	(.004)	(.02)
Quarterly industrial production, differenced	−.016**	−.05**
	(.004)	(.02)
Quarterly industrial production, Baxter-King	−.025**	−.07**
	(.004)	(.02)
Quarterly GDP, Alesina-Barro-Tenreyro	.0003**	.0022**
	(.0001)	(.0005)
Quarterly industrial production, Alesina-Barro-Tenreyro	.0008**	.0013*
	(.0001)	(.0006)

IVs include: (1) government non-wage consumption/GDP; (2) government investment/GDP; (3) direct business taxes/GDP; and (4) direct household taxes/GDP. IVs are average of absolute value of cross-country differentials.

Coefficients recorded are effect of (average of absolute-value of differential of) government budget surplus/deficit, as percentage of GDP.

Coefficients significantly different from zero at .05 (.01) level marked with one (two) asterisk(s).

Data set has maximum of 21*20/2=210 country pairs for four decades (1964–1973, 1974–1983, 1984–1993, 1994–2003).

Decade effects and constant included but not recorded.

Alesina-Barro-Tenreyro measure is root mean squared error of residual from AR(2) of log ratios (lower => greater comovement).

Robust standard errors (clustered by country-pair dyads) recorded in parentheses.

The first rows of Table 3 use industrial production (rather than GDP or unemployment) as the underlying measure of economic activity. Next, we follow Alesina, Barro, and Tenreyro (2002) in measuring business cycle divergence. Alesina-Barro-Tenreyro first construct the ratio of the two countries' log real GDP; they then regress that ratio on two of its lags and an intercept. The root mean squared error of the residual is their measure of business cycle divergence. Since a smaller number implies greater synchronization, we expect the sign of β to be reversed (compared with that of the correlation coefficient of de-trended business cycles). We construct Alesina-Barro-Tenreyro measures for log real GDP, log real GDP per capita, the unemployment rate, and the log of industrial production.

A third set of checks uses the Baxter-King (1999) band-pass filter to de-trend the underlying data (we use 2–8 years, corresponding to their 6–32 quarters). Finally, we switch to using underlying quarterly data rather than annual data. The finer frequency comes at a cost of a smaller data span.

None of the results in Table 3 alter our conclusions. The checks work well in the sense that β remains significantly negative for almost all the perturbations.[20]

As an additional robustness check, we broadened the country coverage to include developing countries as well. This extended database covers 115 countries (hence it has a maximum of 6555 [=115*114/2] bilateral country-pairs) for four decades. Since the unemployment rate and our instrumental variables are missing for many observations, we are constrained to use only GDP and OLS. The results are tabulated in the Appendix, Table A6. As in Tables 1 and 2, we find a negative and mostly significant relationship between fiscal divergence and business cycle synchronization (though when pair-specific effects are included, the coefficients lose significance).

3.4 Does the Average Budget Position have an Effect on Business Cycle Synchronization?

Thus far we have found strong evidence that persistent cross-country *differences* in government budget positions have a (negative) effect on the synchronization of their business cycles. An interesting but different question is whether the average (cross-country) *levels* of government budget positions also affect business cycle synchronization. We now investigate that issue.[21]

Table 4 contains estimates of the effect of the average (across pair of countries) government budget position on business cycle synchronization. Since we analyze two underlying concepts of economic activity (GDP and unemployment), three de-trending techniques (HP-filtering, differencing, and BK-filtered), two estimators (OLS and IV), and two budget concepts (total and primary), we provide 24 (=2*3*2*2) different point estimates and their standard errors.

We find little evidence that the total budget deficit has a consistent effect on business cycle synchronization. Seven of the 12 estimates are negative (two of those are statistically significant), while five are positive (non significant). All are small. However, all 12 of the coefficients for the primary budget effects are positive, three-quarters of them significantly so. We interpret the evidence as indicating that lower primary fiscal deficits (or higher primary surpluses) enhance business cycle synchronization. Further, when we use our extended sample of 115 countries, the average total budget balance has a positive and significant effect on synchronization, as can be seen from the last column of Table A6 in the Appendix.

Table 4
Average budget positions and business cycle synchronization

	GDP, HP	GDP, diff.	GDP, BK	Unem, HP	Unem, diff	Unem, BK
Total budget (% GDP) IV	−.04 (.02)	−.00 (.02)	−.04 (.02)	.00 (.02)	.00 (.02)	−.01 (.02)
Total budget (% GDP) OLS	.02* (.01)	−.00 (.01)	−.02** (.01)	.01 (.01)	.01 (.01)	.01 (.01)
Primary budget (% GDP) IV	.11** (.03)	.09** (.03)	.12** (.03)	.10** (.04)	.03 (.03)	.07** (.03)
Primary budget (% GDP) OLS	.03** (.01)	.02* (.01)	.05** (.01)	.02 (.01)	.01 (.01)	.03** (.01)

IVs include: (1) government non-wage consumption/GDP; (2) government investment/GDP; (3) direct business taxes/GDP; and (4) direct household taxes/GDP. IVs are average of absolute value of cross-country differentials.
Coefficients recorded are effect of cross-country average level of total/primary government budget surplus/deficit, as percentage of GDP.
Coefficients significantly different from zero at .05 (.01) level marked with one (two) asterisk(s).
Data set has maximum of 21*20/2=210 country pairs for four decades (1964–1973, 1974–1983, 1984–1993, 1994–2003).
Decade effects and constant included but not recorded.
Robust standard errors (clustered by country-pair dyads) recorded in parentheses.

Still, we do not wish to over-interpret our findings. The average primary budget position is negatively correlated with our default measure of fiscal divergence (as can be seen in the Appendix, Table A2). When we include both fiscal divergence and the average primary budget position in our regressions, the former remains significantly negative (as can be seen from Tables 1 and 2), while the latter effect loses the horse-race (its effect becomes economically and statistically small, and varies across specifications). We have searched without success for a non-linear or interactive effect, and consider this to be a good topic for future research. That is, there is evidence that primary fiscal consolidation enhances business cycle synchronization, but it is weak. By way of comparison, there is strong evidence that fiscal divergence (of both total and primary balances) reduces the coherence of business cycles.[22]

4.   Interpretation: Fiscal Irresponsibility tends to be Idiosyncratic

In section 3, we established that fiscal convergence seems to induce greater business cycle synchronization. If one takes the finding as given, the question remains: Why? We think the answer is that fiscal divergence tends to occur when one country runs a substantially and persistently higher budget deficit than other countries, and simultaneously creates fiscal shocks. That is, irresponsible fiscal policy (a persistently high deficit) coincides with idiosyncratic (fiscal) instability. When the budget deficit is closed (fiscal convergence), the fiscal shocks diminish; business cycles tend to become more synchronized. Succinctly, fiscal policy that is irresponsible is also fiscal policy that creates idiosyncratic shocks and thus macroeconomic volatility. This idea is both intuitive and consistent with the literature (e.g., Fatás and Mihov 2003a, 2006).

4.1   Direct Evidence on Budgets and Macroeconomic Volatility via a Unilateral Panel

We now test our intuition in a straightforward way. We are interested in testing for a (negative) link between a country's average budget position and its business cycle volatility. Our evidence thus far has relied on bilateral data, comparing fiscal policy of pairs of countries to the synchronization of their business cycles. It is also possible to check this idea more directly using a unilateral (though still non-structural) approach. Accordingly, we gather a panel of annual data for 115 countries (see the Appendix, Table A1, Part B) between 1960 and 2003 (with gaps), consisting of data on real GDP and the total government budget position (as a percentage of GDP; surpluses are positive, deficits negative).[23] We then de-trend the output data by differencing and using both the HP and BK filters to create measures of business cycle fluctuations. We compare both the average absolute value of these business cycle deviations, and their volatility—proxied by the standard deviation (estimated for a country over time)—to the average level of the government's fiscal position. A negative relationship between the two indicates that smaller deficits or larger surpluses are associated with reduced business cycle volatility, consistent with our hypothesis.

We exploit our (country x year) panel of data in three different ways. First, we estimate panel regressions of the effect of the government budget position on business cycle deviations from trend at the annual frequency. Second, we split our 44-year data set into four 11-year periods, so that each country contributes a maximum of four observations. Finally, we average over all 44 years, creating a single cross-section where each country contributes a single observation. For the first two cases, we estimate our models with differing sets of country- and time-specific fixed effects.

Our results are contained in Table 5. The top panel portrays annual results; the middle presents results estimated at the 11-year frequency; and the bottom shows cross-sectional results that average out the entire 44-year sample.

The point estimates from our annual results are all negative; a higher fiscal surplus (or lower deficit) is associated with smaller (in absolute value) business cycle deviations from trend. The results are statistically significant at conventional levels for 12 perturbations. When we shift to a lower frequency, we can examine both the average (over 11 years) of the mean absolute value of business cycle deviations, and the volatility of business cycles (the standard deviation of de-trended log real GDP). Twenty of the 24 point estimates are negative, eight significantly so; none of the positive coefficients is economically or statistically large. Finally, when we examine a single cross-section of our countries, we again find that larger fiscal surpluses/smaller deficits are associated with lower business cycle volatility. At this very low frequency, all six point estimates are negative and half of them are significantly different from zero at standard confidence levels.

We do not consider this evidence to be overwhelming. Since we have essentially no structure in our empirical model, our results are suggestive rather than definitive. Still, we have not found evidence inconsis-

Table 5
Government budgets and business cycle volatility

	Annual Panel Results		
	Hodrick-Prescott	Baxter-King	Differenced
Common intercept	−.057**	−.050**	−.080**
	(.014)	(.011)	(.016)
Year effects	−.038**	−.040**	−.072**
	(.014)	(.011)	(.017)
Country effects	−.058**	−.042**	−.066**
	(.015)	(.012)	(.019)
Year and country effects	−.038**	−.032**	−.060**
	(.015)	(.012)	(.019)
Observations	3371	2944	3308

Regressands are the absolute value of detrended log real GDP, either (1) Hodrick-Prescott filtered, (2) Baxter-King band-pass filtered or (3) differenced (country specific mean growth removed from differences before taking absolute values). Regressor is government budget, % GDP.

	Long-run Panel Results (for Data Averaged over 11-year Periods)					
	Standard Deviation			Mean Absolute Value		
	Hodrick-Prescott	Baxter-King	Differenced	Hodrick-Prescott	Baxter-King	Differenced
Common intercept	−.062*	−.067**	−.083	−.070**	−.051*	−.115**
	(.035)	(.033)	(.057)	(.033)	(.027)	(.040)
Period effects	−.039	−.052	−.068	−.046	−.040	−.111**
	(.036)	(.033)	(.059)	(.036)	(.027)	(.044)
Country effects	−.033	−.029	.010	−.076**	−.032	−.073*
	(.048)	(.046)	(.072)	(.038)	(.035)	(.043)
Period, country effects	.012	.000	.039	−.032	−.010	−.072
	(.047)	(.046)	(.071)	(.040)	(.035)	(.047)
Observations	365	349	364	368	354	365

Regressands are either (1) standard deviation or (2) mean absolute value of log real GDP, either (1) Hodrick-Prescott filtered, (2) Baxter-King band-pass filtered or 3) differenced (country specific mean growth removed from differences before taking absolute values) over four 11-year long periods. Regressor is mean of government budget, % GDP.

Table 5 *(continued)*
Government budgets and business cycle volatility

	Cross-sectional Results (for Data Averaged over Entire Sample)					
	Standard Deviation			Mean Absolute Value		
	Hodrick-Prescott	Baxter-King	Differenced	Hodrick-Prescott	Baxter-King	Differenced
Intercept	−.064	−.117**	−.139*	−.025	−.058*	−.077
	(.070)	(.047)	(.073)	(.050)	(.030)	(.049)
Observations	115	115	115	115	115	115

Regressands are either (1) standard deviation or (2) mean absolute value of log real GDP, either (1) Hodrick-Prescott filtered, (2) Baxter-King band-pass filtered or (3) differenced (country specific mean growth removed from differences before taking absolute values) over entire period, 1960–2003. Regressor is the mean of government budget, % GDP.

Notes for all blocks.
Coefficients from OLS regressions, multiplied by 100. Robust standard errors (clustered by country) in parentheses (also multiplied by 100).
Coefficient significantly different from zero at .01 (.05) marked by two (one) asterisks.
Based on annual data for 115 countries, 1960–2003 (with gaps).

tent with our hypothesis either in the literature or in our own empirical work. The hypothesis that larger fiscal deficits tend to be associated with greater business cycle volatility seems reasonable and awaits further scrutiny.

5. Conclusion

The motivation for this paper is simple. The criteria that make a currency area optimal were established long ago by Mundell and have essentially no intersection with the "Maastricht convergence" criteria used to govern the actual entry of countries into European Monetary Union. In this paper, we ask: does Maastricht indirectly overlap with Mundell?

The answer is positive. We find that fiscal convergence—similarity in the aggregate budget positions across countries—is systematically associated with enhanced business cycle synchronization. Fiscal convergence raises business cycle synchronization by eliminating idiosyncratic fiscal shocks. We find evidence that reduced primary fiscal deficits (or higher surpluses) also increase the coherence of business cycles across countries. The Maastricht convergence process encouraged both fiscal convergence and reduced deficits for the Euro-12 during the run-up to EMU. Our results indicate that this fiscal convergence would have raised their business cycle coherence, making them better candidates for currency union. Even if not by design, Maastricht mimics Mundell!

There is a different (though consistent) interpretation of our results. Conventional wisdom tells us that national fiscal policy is the sole macroeconomic tool to smooth the business cycle when a country is hit by asymmetric shocks in a currency union. Yet the Maastricht criteria impose convergence of budget deficits at low levels. Consequently, Maastricht *could* reduce business cycle synchronization and increase volatility. In fact though, fiscal convergence seems to *increase* cycle synchronization by reducing volatile fiscal shocks.

If our finding is corroborated, it is of more than academic interest. The Maastricht criteria continue to govern future entry into the euro zone. Further, the Stability and Growth Pact continues, in principle, to constrain fiscal policy for the EU. If either or both of these institutions induce fiscal convergence, they indirectly enhance the desirability and sustainability of EMU. Two cheers!

Acknowledgements

Darvas is Assistant Professor, Department of Mathematical Economics and Economic Analysis, Corvinus University. Rose is B.T. Rocca Jr. Professor of International Trade and Economic Analysis and Policy in the Haas School of Business at the University of California, Berkeley, NBER research associate and CEPR Research Fellow. Szapáry is deputy governor of the Magyar Nemzeti Bank. The idea of this paper stemmed from a conversation with Miriam Green. Rose thanks the Banco de España for hospitality during the course of this research. For comments we thank: Dave Backus, Fabrizio Balassone, Marianne Baxter, Péter Benczúr, Helge Berger, Paul de Grauwe, Antonio Fatás, Jon Faust, Jeff Frankel, Joe Gagnon, Francesco Giavazzi, Linda Goldberg, Jim Harrigan, Dale Henderson, Zoltán Jakab, Olivier Jeanne, Sebnem Kalemli-Ozcan, Pat Kehoe, Phil Lane, Jacques Melitz, Roberto Perotti, Paolo Pesenti, Lucrezia Reichlin, Roberto Rigobon, John Rogers, Eric van Wincoop, Charles Wyplosz, and seminar participants at ISOM 2005, the Bundesbank, the Federal Reserve Bank of New York, the Federal Reserve Board, the International Monetary Fund, the Magyar Nemzeti Bank, and the National Bank of Poland. The views expressed do not necessarily represent those of the Magyar Nemzeti Bank or its staff. A current version of this paper, key output, and the data set used in the paper are available at http://faculty.haas.berkeley.edu/arose and at http://www.uni-corvinus.hu/darvas.

Notes

1. In EU terminology, EMU technically refers to Economic and Monetary Union, which is different from the euro area. All EU countries are members of the Economic and Monetary Union, but only 12 members are currently members of the euro area. In the academic literature, EMU generally refers to the European monetary union. In this paper we follow conventional practice and use EMU to refer to the euro area.

2. We ignore the design of monetary institutions and policies for the time being. These are relevant to both the Maastricht Treaty and Optimum Currency Area considerations, but are not intrinsically either national or international. In any case, there is considerable overlap between the two sets of criteria in this respect.

3. Table 7A of "Cyclical Adjustment of Budget Balances" produced by ECFIN, EC, Spring 2005, available at http://europa.eu.int/comm/economy_finance/indicators/general_government_data/2005/cabb_spring2005en.pdf.

4. Again, we use Table 7A of "Cyclical Adjustment of Budget Balances." For further analysis, see Fatás and Mihov (2003b).

5. We also briefly examine effects of other Maastricht criteria, such as those for inflation, exchange rates, etc.

6. We rely on the fact that a decade is substantially longer than the span of a typical business cycle, so that business cycle effects are likely to wash out.

7. See, e.g., Gavin and Perotti (1997).

8. Ditto, Table 7A of "Cyclical Adjustment of Budget Balances." Buti and Gudice (2002) provide a recent review of the Maastricht criteria and references.

9. In practice there are often gaps in our data set.

10. Further, short-run fiscal spillovers results in the same problem. We try to minimize such issues by estimating our business cycle synchronizations using decades, but the issue remains.

11. Controlling for exchange rate volatility does not change our key result; neither does restricting the sample to countries with only limited exchange rate volatility.

12. The four instrumental variables are: (1) the natural logarithm of the great circle bilateral distance between the two countries; (2) the log of the product of the countries' land areas; (3) a common land border dummy; and (4) a common language dummy.

13. This is unsurprising since trade is almost always uncorrelated with fiscal divergence.

14. Our results also do not change when we control for the inflation differential (an imperfect measure of monetary policy).

15. We use the OECD's measure "Primary Government Balance, Cyclically Adjusted, % Potential GDP."

16. We formalize this as follows. If both countries meet the 3 percent target, the gap between them is zero. If one meets the criterion and one has a deficit of say 4 percent of GDP, the gap is 1 percent (of GDP). If neither meets the criteria, one country's deficit is 5 percent and the other's is 6 percent, the difference between them is also 1 percent (of GDP).

17. This may be unsurprising, since there is little reason to think that convergence to 3 percent should have a different effect on business cycle synchronization than convergence to another deficit level.

18. For instance, we cannot exclude the possibility of simultaneity from any available fiscal aggregate.

19. We have experimented extensively with our instrumental variables, focusing especially on their cyclical sensitivity, and find that our results are robust.

20. We have also used 20- and 40-year periods instead of decades, and our key results remain.

21. We have already shown in Tables 1 and 2 that controlling for the average level of the government budget position (i.e., including AvgFiscal in our regressions) has little effect on the economic or statistical significance of .

22. We have also briefly investigated the effects of other Maastricht criteria on business cycle synchronization; estimates appear in Table A5. There is some evidence that exchange rate volatility, and divergence in inflation, long interest rates, and government debt levels all tend to lower business cycle synchronization. However, none of the effects is particularly strong or consistent. We view this as an area worthy of future research.

23. We do not know of a source that systematically provides primary fiscal positions for countries outside the OECD.

References

Aguiar, Mark, Manuel Amador, and Gita Gopinath. 2005. "Efficient Fiscal Policy and Amplification." NBER Working Paper no. 11490 (Cambridge, MA).

Alesina, Alberto F., Robert J. Barro, and Silvana Tenreyro. 2002. "Optimal Currency Areas." In M. Gertler and K. Rogoff, eds., NBER Macroeconomics Annual. Cambridge: MIT Press.

Alesina, Alberto F., and Roberto Perotti. 1997. "Fiscal Adjustments in OECD Countries: Composition and Macroeconomic Effects." IMF Staff Papers 44(2): 210–248.

Baxter, Marianne, and Robert G. King. 1999. "Measuring Business Cycles: Approximate Band-Pass Filters for Economic Time Series." The Review of Economics and Statistics 81(4): 575–593.

Baxter, Marianne, and Michael A. Kouparitsas. 2005. "Determinants of Business Cycle Comovement: A Robust Analysis." Journal of Monetary Economics 52: 113–157.

Brender, Adi, and Allan Drazen. 2005. "Political Budget Cycles in New versus Established Democracies." Journal of Monetary Economics 52(7): 1271–1295.

Buti, Marco, and Gabriele Gudice. 2002. "Maastricht's Fiscal Rules at Ten: An Assessment." *Journal of Common Market Studies* 5: 823–848.

Canova, Fabio, Matteo Ciccarelli, and Eva Ortega. 2004. "Similarities and Convergence in G-7 Cycles." CEPR DP no. 4534.

Darvas, Zsolt, and György Szapáry. 2007. "Business Cycle Synchronization in the Enlarged EU." Open Economies Review (forthcoming).

Fatás, Antonio, and Ilian Mihov. 2003a. "The Case for Restricting Fiscal Policy Discretion." *Quarterly Journal of Economics* 118(4): 1419–1447.

Fatás, Antonio, and Ilian Mihov. 2003b. "Fiscal Policy and EMU: Challenges of the Early Years." In Buti and Sapir, eds., *EMU and Economic Policy in Europe*. Cheltenham, England: Edward Elgar.

Fatás, Antonio, and Ilian Mihov. 2006. "The Macroeconomic Effects of Fiscal Rules in the US States." *Journal of Public Economics* 90(1/2): 101–117.

Frankel, Jeffrey A., and Andrew K. Rose. 1998. "The Endogeneity of the Optimum Currency Area Criteria." *Economic Journal* 108(449): 1009–1025.

Gavin, Michael, and Roberto Perotti. 1997. "Fiscal Policy in Latin America." *NBER Macroeconomics Annual* 12: 11–61.

Gerlach, H.M.S. 1988. "World Business Cycles under Fixed and Flexible Exchange Rates." *Money Market and Banking* 20(4): 621–632.

Kaminsky, Graciela, Carmen Reinhart, and Carlos Vegh. 2004. "When it Rains, it Pours." *NBER Macroeconomics Annual* 19: 11–53.

Kose, A.A., E.S. Prasad, and M. Terrones. 2003. "How Does Globalization Affect the Synchronization of Business Cycles?" *American Economic Review* 93(2): 57–62.

Lane, Philip R. 2003. "The Cyclical Behaviour of Fiscal Policy: Evidence from the OECD." *Journal of Public Economics* 87: 2661–2675.

Lumsdaine, Robin L., and Eswar S. Prasad. 2003. "Identifying the Common Component of International Economic Fluctuations: A New Approach." *Economic Journal* 113(484): 101–127.

Mundell, Robert. 1961. "A Theory of Optimum Currency Areas." *American Economic Review* LI: 657–665.

Reinhart, Carmen M., and Kenneth S. Rogoff. 2004. "The Modern History of Exchange Rate Arrangements: A Reinterpretation." *Quarterly Journal of Economics* CXIX(1): 1–48.

Appendix

Table A1—Part A
Countries in default OECD sample

Australia	Austria	Belgium	Canada	Denmark	Finland
France	Germany	Greece	Ireland	Italy	Japan
Netherlands	Norway	New Zealand	Portugal	Spain	Sweden
Switzerland	UK	USA			

Table A1—Part B
Additional countries in wide sample

Argentina	Bahrain	Bangladesh	Barbados	Belarus	Belize
Bhutan	Bolivia	Botswana	Brazil	Bulgaria	Burk. Faso
Burundi	Cameroon	Chile	China	Colombia	Congo
Costa Rica	Croatia	Cyprus	Czech Rep.	Dominican R.	Egypt
El Salvador	Estonia	Fiji	Ghana	Guatemala	Guyana
Haiti	Honduras	Hungary	Iceland	India	Indonesia
Iran	Israel	Jamaica	Jordan	Kazakhstan	Kenya
Korea	Kyrgyz Re.	Latvia	Lesotho	Lithuania	Madagascar
Malawi	Malaysia	Malta	Mauritius	Mexico	Mongolia
Morocco	Myanmar	Nepal	Nicaragua	Nigeria	Oman
Pakistan	Panama	Pap. N. Guinea	Paraguay	Peru	Philippines
Poland	Romania	Russia	Rwanda	Saudi Arabia	Senegal
Seychelles	Sierra Leone	Singapore	Slovak Republic	Slovenia	South Africa
Sri Lanka	St. Lucia	St.Vin. & Gren.	Swaziland	Syria	Thailand
Tunisia	Turkey	Uganda	Ukraine	Uruguay	Venezuela
Vietnam	Yemen	Zambia	Zimbabwe		

Table A2
Descriptive statistics

	Obs.	Avg.	Std. dev.	Min.	Max.	Corr.
Correlation coefficient, GDP, HP-filtered	840	.36	.44	−.88	.99	−.22
Correlation coefficient, GDP, differenced	840	.27	.37	−.83	.96	−.13
Correlation coefficient, unemployment, HP-filtered	840	.39	.45	−.89	.98	−.29
Correlation coefficient, unemployment, differenced	840	.29	.39	−.74	.99	−.22
Government budget/GDP divergence	840	3.65	2.52	.41	14.5	n/a
Average government budget/ GDP level	840	−2.77	2.47	−11.9	4.2	−.14
Primary government budget/ GDP divergence	617	3.12	1.90	.14	10.8	.47
Average primary government budget/GDP level	617	−.03	2.04	−6.63	5.43	−.41
Gov't budget/GDP divergence, Maastricht deviation	840	1.91	2.23	0	9.82	.70
Government non-wage consumption/GDP divergence	800	2.46	1.76	.15	9.89	−.16
Government investment/GDP divergence	722	1.00	.66	.06	4.01	.08
Direct business taxes/GDP divergence	638	1.27	.86	.10	5.05	.25
Direct household taxes/GDP divergence	602	5.25	4.36	.17	21.95	−.00
Trade/GDP ratio	840	.49	.77	.01	7.21	−.07
Inflation divergence	840	3.48	3.18	.36	18.2	.11
Long interest rate divergence	742	2.55	2.44	.08	16.3	.22
Government debt/GDP divergence	592	28.0	20.2	.58	106.8	.38
Standard deviation of exchange rate	840	.12	.09	.003	.58	.03
Maximum change of exchange rate	840	.28	.13	.02	.67	.15

Corr. is simple correlation coefficient between variable and government budget/GDP.

Table A3
First stage

Government non-wage consumption/GDP	−.23** (.06)
Government investment/GDP	.44** (.14)
Direct business taxes/GDP	.44** (.11)
Direct household taxes/GDP	−.02 (.02)

Regressand is (average of absolute-value of differential of) government budget surplus/ deficit, as percentage of GDP. Coefficients estimated via OLS. Standard errors recorded in parentheses.

All regressors are average of absolute value of cross-country differentials.

Data set has maximum of 21*20/2=210 country pairs for four decades (1964–1973, 1974–1983, 1984–1993, 1994–2003).

Decade effects and constant included but not recorded.

Coefficients significantly different from zero at .05 (.01) level marked with one (two) asterisk(s).

Table A4
Business cycle synchronization in different fiscal regimes

	Surplus/deficit < 1%	Deficit in (1,6)%	Deficit > 6%
A: GDP HP-filtered, Total Deficit			
Surplus/deficit < 1%	.30 (85)		
Deficit in (1,6)%	.35 (278)	.42 (293)	
Deficit > 6%	.07 (32)	.35 (136)	.46 (16)
B: GDP Differenced Total Deficit			
Surplus/deficit < 1%	.30 (85)		
Deficit in (1,6)%	.26 (278)	.29 (293)	
Deficit > 6%	.13 (32)	.27 (136)	.38 (16)
C: Unemployment HP-filtered Total Deficit			
Surplus/deficit < 1%	.39 (85)		
Deficit in (1,6)%	.35 (278)	.47 (293)	
Deficit > 6%	−.11 (32)	.38 (136)	.49 (16)
D: Unemployment Differenced Total Deficit			
Surplus/deficit < 1%	.38 (85)		
Deficit in (1,6)%	.25 (278)	.32 (293)	
Deficit > 6%	.02 (32)	.30 (136)	.38 (16)

	Primary surplus > 1.5%	Balance in (−1.5,1.5)%	Primary deficit > 1.5%
E: GDP HP-filtered, Primary Surplus/Deficit			
Primary surplus > 1.5%	0.45 (62)		
Balance in (−1.5,1.5)%	0.45 (145)	0.44 (132)	
Primary deficit > 1.5%	0.18 (56)	0.39 (165)	0.35 (57)
F: GDP Differenced, Primary Surplus/Deficit			
Primary surplus > 1.5%	0.34 (62)		
Balance in (−1.5,1.5)%	0.39 (145)	0.34 (132)	
Primary deficit > 1.5%	0.19 (56)	0.28 (165)	0.25 (57)
G: Unemployment HP-filtered, Primary Surplus/Deficit			
Primary surplus > 1.5%	0.27 (62)		
Balance in (−1.5,1.5)%	0.39 (145)	0.53 (132)	
Primary deficit > 1.5%	0.15 (56)	0.41 (165)	0.36 (57)
H: Unemployment Differenced, Primary Surplus/Deficit			
Primary surplus > 1.5%	0.15 (62)		
Balance in (−1.5,1.5)%	0.32 (145)	0.40 (132)	
Primary deficit > 1.5%	0.17 (56)	0.30 (165)	0.26 (57)

Deficits expressed as percentages of national GDP. Number of observations recorded in parentheses. Data tabulated are average correlations of business cycles. Thus for the (85) cases where both countries are in total surplus or have deficits < 1 percent GDP, the average correlation of de-trended GDP is .30.

Table A5
Different criteria and business cycle synchronization

	GDP, HP-filtered	GDP, differenced	Unemployment, HP filtered	Unemployment, differenced
		OLS		
Inflation	−.01	−.01	−.02**	−.02**
	(.01)	(.01)	(.01)	(.01)
Long interest rate	−.02*	−.01	−.03**	−.02**
	(.01)	(.01)	(.01)	(.01)
Government debt/GDP	−.001	−.001	−.004**	−.003**
	(.001)	(.001)	(.001)	(.001)
Standard deviation of exchange rate	−.43	−.36	−.92**	−.77**
	(.23)	(.21)	(.23)	(.21)
Maximum change of exchange rate	−.42*	−.40**	−.61**	−.53**
	(.18)	(.14)	(.16)	(.14)
		IV		
Inflation	−.04	−.09*	−.13	−.05
	(.06)	(.04)	(.07)	(.04)
Long interest rate	−.13**	−.13**	−.18**	−.09*
	(.04)	(.04)	(.05)	(.04)
Government debt/GDP	−.006	−.007*	−.008	−.005
	(.004)	(.004)	(.005)	(.004)
Standard deviation of exchange rate	−4.99**	−4.83**	−6.51**	−3.42*
	(1.56)	(1.26)	(1.95)	(1.32)
Maximum change of exchange rate	−1.93**	−1.79**	−2.49**	−1.53**
	(.57)	(.43)	(.67)	(.52)

Regressand is correlation coefficient (computed for individual decades of annual data) between country i and j de-trended series.

Coefficients recorded are effect of (average of absolute-value of differential of) variable tabulated in left column. Coefficients significantly different from zero at .05 (.01) level marked with one (two) asterisk(s).

IVs include: (1) government non-wage consumption/GDP; (2) government investment/GDP; (3) direct business taxes/GDP; and (4) direct household taxes/GDP. IVs are average of absolute value of cross-country differentials.

Data set has maximum of 21*20/2=210 country pairs for four decades (1964–1973, 1974–1983, 1984–1993, 1994–2003).

Decade effects and constant included but not recorded.

Robust standard errors (clustered by country-pair dyads) recorded in parentheses.

Table A6
Fiscal divergence and business cycle synchronization; OLS on a wide panel

	Benchmark effect of fiscal divergence	Pair-specific fixed effects	With average fiscal position	Only average fiscal position
HP-filtered	−0.005**	−.001	−0.004**	.007**
	(.001)	(.003)	(.001)	(.002)
First-differenced	−0.002**	.001	−0.001	.005**
	(.001)	(.002)	(.001)	(.001)

Regressand is correlation coefficient (computed over decades) between country i and j de-trended series.
Coefficients recorded are effect of (average of absolute-value of differential of) government budget surplus/deficit, as percentage of GDP.
OLS estimation. Robust standard errors (clustered by country-pair dyads) in parentheses.
Decade effects and constant included but not recorded. 14,961 observations.
Coefficients significantly different from zero at .05 (.01) level marked with one (two) asterisk(s).

Data Sources

OECD Economic Outlook (Annual series): Consumer Price Index; Direct Taxes, Households; Direct Taxes, Business; Fixed Investment, Government, Value; Government Consumption, Excluding Wages; Government Consumption, Wages; Gross Domestic Product (Market prices), Value; Gross Domestic Product (Market prices), Volume; Gross Government Debt, % GDP; Indirect Taxes; Interest Rate, Long-Term; Interest Rate, Short-Term; Primary Government Balance, Cyclically Adjusted, % Potential GDP; Social Benefits Paid by Government; Unemployment Rate.

OECD Quarterly National Accounts: Gross Domestic Product, Volume.

OECD Tax Database (Annuals series): Income tax plus employee and employer contribution less cash benefits (as % of labor costs), one-earner family with two children.

IMF International Financial Statistics (Annual series): General Government Deficit (−) or Surplus; Gross Domestic Product, Volume and Value (for developing countries included in the wide sample); Industrial Production (Volume). (Quarterly series): Industrial Production. (Volume). (Monthly series): Exchange rate (National Currency per US Dollar, line RF)

IMF Direction of Trade Statistics (Annual series for 1980-2003): Exports, f.o.b.; Imports, c.i.f.

Frankel-Rose (1998) (Annual series for 1960-1979): Exports, f.o.b.; Imports, c.i.f.

EC AMECO database (Annual series): Net lending (+) or net borrowing (–): general government, Percentage of GDP at market prices.

Reinhart-Rogoff (2004) (Monthly series): Parallel or Black Market Exchange Rate

Comment

Roberto Rigobon, MIT and NBER

Since Gavin and Perotti (2004) highlighted the strong pro-cyclicality of fiscal policy in emerging markets, the international literature has devoted an enormous amount of research to two main aspects: first, continue documenting how pro-cyclical fiscal policy is, and second, understanding why it is pro-cyclical.

It is fair to say that the consensus is that fiscal policy is pro-cyclical in emerging and developing nations, but is far less in developed countries.[1] However, even a casual reader will find that the reasons behind the pro-cyclicality of fiscal policy are not clear at all. The main problem is the endogeneity of fiscal policy. The simplest framework to understand this dilemma is the following:

$$y = \alpha g + \varepsilon$$
$$g = \beta y + \eta$$

where y stands for output, and g stands for fiscal policy—either expenditures or fiscal deficit. For expositional simplicity, this comment will assume g are government expenditures.[2]

The first equation is the typical fiscal multiplier. The idea is that an increase in expenditure increases aggregate demand, and output. Hence, in general, we expect the coefficient of that equation to be positive—as in the traditional Keynesian multiplier. The second equation is the fiscal policy response. The classical theory predicts that if taxation or expenditures are distortionary, then government consumption should smooth out output fluctuations. In that regard, booms should be accompanied with government cuts, and conversely during recessions. That means that the standard theory predicts a counter cyclical policy. More precisely, the coefficient in the second equation should be negative if fiscal policy is used to smooth output fluctuations.

In reality, both equations are at work; the first one implying a positive correlation, the second one implying a negative correlation. Therefore, what is the correlation measured in sample? The reduced form is

$$y = \frac{1}{1-\alpha\beta}(\alpha\eta + \varepsilon)$$

$$g = \frac{1}{1-\alpha\beta}(\eta + \beta\varepsilon).$$

Which means that if the residuals are uncorrelated, that the correlation between output and expenditures is?

$$\rho = \frac{\alpha\sigma_\eta^2 + \beta\sigma_\varepsilon^2}{\sqrt{\left(\alpha^2\sigma_\eta^2 + \sigma_\varepsilon^2\right)\left(\sigma_\eta^2 + \beta^2\sigma_\varepsilon^2\right)}} = \frac{\alpha + \beta\theta}{\sqrt{\left(\alpha^2 + \theta\right)\left(1 + \beta^2\theta\right)}}$$

where θ is the relative variance of the two shocks.

$$\theta = \frac{\sigma_\varepsilon^2}{\sigma_\eta^2}.$$

When we compare two countries there are three reasons why their correlations can be different. First, a different correlation can be the outcome of how fiscal policy responds to output shocks. It is possible that because of credit constraints, or other inefficiencies, governments in emerging markets cannot smooth government expenditures as much as desired; and therefore, the coefficient β is too small, or even positive, in comparison to the benchmark. This is one of the preferred explanations in the literature, and the first one advanced by Gavin and Perotti. By far, most of the discussion in the literature is about this coefficient—although, I have rarely seen it estimated (with the exception of one paper). I come back to this point below.

Second, similarly, it is possible that fiscal policy is just extremely effective in smaller/emerging countries, and less effective in developed nations. This will point out to the pro-cyclicality being the outcome of a very strong Keynesian multiplier—i.e., the coefficient α is relatively big in emerging markets.

Lastly, a country can have a higher correlation because it is hit by a different combination of shocks. Under the assumption that α is positive and β is negative, a decrease in θ increases the correlation unambiguously. In other words, a country that is subject to a higher proportion of supply shocks has a small—and possibly negative—correlation.

My reading of the literature is that very few papers have disentangled these possibilities properly. The best attempt is Gali and Perotti (2004) where they use GDP of the trading partners as an instrument of domestic output to estimate β. Surprisingly, they find that it is negative—meaning that if there is a positive relationship between output and expenditures it is because there is a positive feedback that drives it.

The paper by Darvas, Rose, and Szapary (2005) offer a different approach to the resolution of this dilemma, one that I find particularly interesting, and convincing. The general idea of the paper is very simple, because countries embarked in a process of fiscal reform after signing the Maastricht Treaty, whose aim was to reduce the level and the volatility of fiscal deficits in Europe; we can evaluate what occurs to the correlation of GDP's across countries. Let's see how this question is related to the previous discussion.

Assume that there are two countries described as follows:

$$y_1 = \alpha_1 g_1 + \varepsilon_1$$

$$g_1 = \beta_1 y_1 + \eta_1$$

$$y_2 = \alpha_2 g_2 + \varepsilon_2$$

$$g_2 = \beta_2 y_2 + \eta_2$$

where we assume that the innovations to output are correlated, but the fiscal policy shocks are not. This is one of the crucial assumptions that the authors make, but one that I find reasonable. Outputs across European countries has very good reasons to be correlated—through trade, productivity, migration, etc.—while fiscal policy decisions (the shocks not the automatic response) are less likely to be correlated.

In this setup, output of each country is given by

$$y_1 = \frac{1}{1 - \alpha_1 \beta_1} (\alpha_1 \eta_1 + \varepsilon_1)$$

$$y_2 = \frac{1}{1 - \alpha_2 \beta_2} (\alpha_2 \eta_2 + \varepsilon_2)$$

which implies that the correlation between outputs is given by:

$$\rho_{y_1 y_2} = \frac{\alpha_1 \alpha_2 \operatorname{cov}(\varepsilon_1 \varepsilon_2)}{\sqrt{(\alpha_1^2 \sigma_{\varepsilon,1}^2 + \sigma_{\eta,1}^2)(\alpha_2^2 \sigma_{\varepsilon,2}^2 + \sigma_{\eta,2}^2)}}.$$

Notice that the assumption that countries are involved in a process of fiscal restructuring implies that both $\sigma^2_{\eta,1}$ and $\sigma^2_{\eta,2}$ are coming down. If that is the case, then the correlation between outputs increases. In the limit, when the variance of the fiscal shocks becomes zero, outputs are going to be correlated in the same way output innovations are.

This is exactly the hypothesis that this paper tests. They assume that the Maastricht criteria includes a heavy dose of fiscal reform—which is a sound assumption—and evaluate what are the implications of such policy on the comovement of output. They do not test their model using correlations. They use the average absolute deviation, but the implications are very similar. It is important to mention, that their results survive this minor change in the definition. I believe that concentrating on the correlation makes the intuition much simpler (as I did in my discussion), but the authors have decided to highlight the absolute deviation, instead.

One interesting aspect is to draw the yearly average correlation between all country pairs. This is done in Figure 1. As can be easily seen, the correlation of output growth among all developed nations increases substantially: from an average of 35 percent to an average of 45 percent. This is exactly what the authors would have expected if fiscal shocks are idiosyncratic and the fiscal reform makes them smaller.

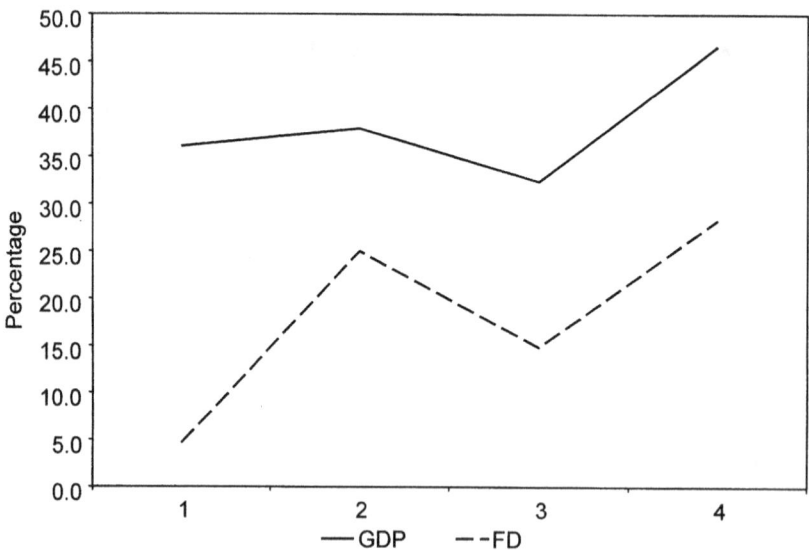

Figure 1

In addition to the GDP correlation, we can check this hypothesis by observing the behavior of the fiscal accounts. Using the exact same model it is easy to check that the correlation between any two expenditures is

$$\rho_{g_1 g_2} = \frac{\text{cov}(\varepsilon_1 \varepsilon_2)}{\sqrt{\left(\sigma_{\varepsilon,1}^2 + \beta_1^2 \sigma_{\eta,1}^2\right)\left(\sigma_{\varepsilon,2}^2 + \beta_2^2 \sigma_{\eta,2}^2\right)}}.$$

Again, if the variances of the fiscal shocks become smaller, then the correlation between fiscal expenditures has to increase. In the limit, if the variance of the fiscal shocks is zero, then the correlation between the fiscal accounts is exactly the correlation of the output shocks. In Figure 1, I also depicted the average correlation between fiscal deficits in the region (the exact same pattern arises if we look at expenditures). Notice the extremely large increase in the fiscal deficit co-movement—from 5 percent to almost 30 percent!

This very simple exercise shows—also confirms—the hypothesis raised by the authors. In their paper, they make two important claims: (1) that fiscal shocks are idiosyncratic; and (2) that the Maastricht criteria reduced fiscal shocks. Because of these two assumptions, the movement toward fiscal responsibility has made the countries better candidates for a currency union.

In summary, this paper studies the implications of the movement toward fiscal responsibility that took place in Europe after the Maastricht Treaty, and its implications on output comovement across the member nations. The claim is that if the fiscal shocks are idiosyncratic, and if the fiscal effort implies a reduction in the variance of those shocks, then the Maastricht criteria implies an increase in the comovement of output across European countries, making them better candidates for a currency union. They find evidence that supports this view, and here I have presented further evidence.

All their results depend on the two assumptions. The second one is easily checked in the data. Fiscal deficits indeed came down, and their volatility was reduced significantly. The second claim is much harder to prove. In fact, it is the only critique I could see to the paper: fiscal shocks are not necessarily idiosyncratic. However, if you have ever worked in public office, as I did briefly, you will know this is not an assumption, it is a description of reality.

Notes

1. Kaminsky et al. (2005) also show that this pattern is also true for monetary policy.

2. If you would like to think about it as fiscal deficit, you are welcome to do the search and replace.

References

Darvas, Zsolt, Andrew K. Rose, and György Szapáry. 2007. "Fiscal Divergence and Business Cycle Synchronization: Irresponsibility is Idiosyncratic." In *NBER International Seminar on Macroeconomics 2005*. Jeffrey A. Frankel and Christopher A. Pissarides, eds., (Cambridge, MA: The MIT Press), p. 261–298.

Gali, Jordi, and Roberto Perotti. 2004. "Fiscal Policy and Monetary Integration in Europe." Economic Policy, forthcoming.

Kaminsky, Graciela, Carmen Reinhart, and Carlos Végh. 2005. "When It Rains It Pours: Procyclical Macropolicies and Capital Flows." In *NBER Macroeconomics Annual 2004*. Mark Gutler and Kenneth S. Rogoff, eds., (Cambridge, MA: The MIT Press), p. 11–53.

Rigobon, Roberto. 2004. "Comments on: "When it Rains, it Pours" by Graciela Kaminsky, Carmen Reinhart, and Carlos Vegh. NBER Macro Annual.

Comment

Lucrezia Reichlin, European Central Bank and CEPR

1. The Main Result of the Paper

The idea of the paper is simple and appealing: the Maastricht Treaty, to the extent that it has enforced fiscal convergence, may have also induced business cycle synchronization. In other words, assuming that in the last 15 years we have observed an increase in business cycle synchronization, this is likely to have been endogenous.

The paper analyzes 21 OECD countries on the basis of a simple panel regression where correlations between the GDP growth of countries' pairs is regressed against indicators of fiscal divergence between the same pairs. The correlation coefficient is found to be negative, large, and significant. The interpretation is that persistent high deficits generate idiosyncratic shocks (idiosyncratic fiscal instability) and therefore idiosyncratic business cycle dynamics. When budget deficits decrease, business cycle synchronization increases and idiosyncratic dynamics explain a smaller part of output.

This is an interesting observation and a warning for discussions on optimal currency areas. Observed comovements of economic activity are endogenous to policy and regulatory regimes. As Frankel and Rose (1998) had observed for trade, it might be the case that fiscal rules also affect output synchronization.

Can this result be true? A first observation is that, while it is uncontroversial that for Euro area countries there has been fiscal convergence, business cycle relations among G7 and Euro area countries seem to have been stable at least since the seventies, with no clear change in the degree of synchronization. Of course, facts about business cycle are difficult to establish since they depend on definitions and data transformation.

The next section will present some facts based on GDP growth rates.

2. Some Stylized Facts

Let us look at some numbers and some charts.

First of all, Table 1 shows that the correlation of GDP growth between different G7 countries has been pretty stable over time.

The same fact emerges from Figure 1 which shows the correlation of per-capita GDP growth rates with respect to the Euro area for different sub-periods, and a larger selection of countries, grouped according to different criteria. Correlations, with the exception of few countries, have remained stable over time.

The fact that cross-country business cycle synchronization has remained stable over time, at least for the largest countries, is well

Table 1

Average correlation GDP growth G7 countries with respect OECD average

1964–1973	0.42
1974–1983	0.69
1984–1993	0.69
1994–2003	0.68

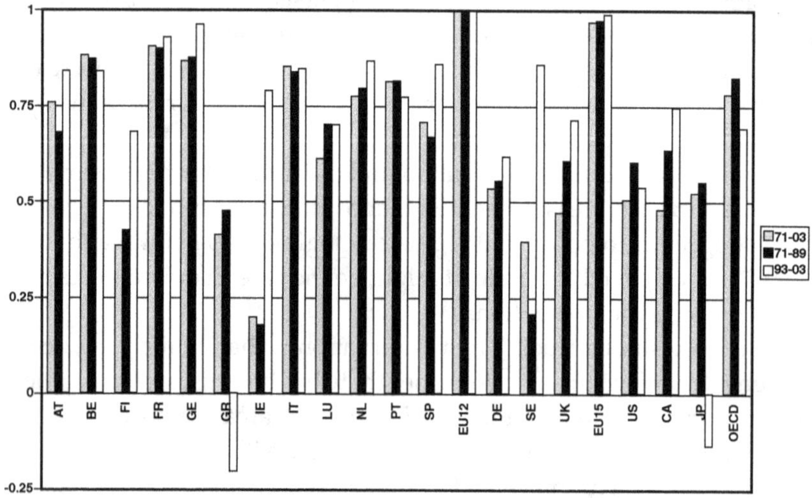

Figure 1
Correlation with respect to the Euro area average GDP per-capita growth

documented and based on different measurement criteria. See, for example, Canova, Ciccarelli, and Ortega (2004), Giannone and Reichlin (2005), Harding and Pagan (2004), and Stock and Watson (2005).

This suggests that the result in the paper may be driven by a specific group of countries or that the regression result is picking up something else.

Output volatility, for example, has decreased over time in most countries (Figure 2 shows the variance of per-capita GDP growth rates for different sub-periods and for Euro area countries). This might be the effect of fiscal policy, as suggested by Fatas and Mihov (2003), but it is not what the paper is focusing on.

Finally, Figure 3 shows the percentage of forecast error of GDP per capita explained by country-specific shocks for Euro area countries. These numbers are estimated by Giannone and Reichlin (2005) (methods and data described in that paper).

As Giannone and Reichlin (2005) document, idiosyncratic shocks (country specific) are small and they have been so even before Maastricht and the recent period of fiscal convergence. This should imply that fiscal/national shocks or national fiscal responses to idiosyncratic shocks have little to do with business cycle correlations.

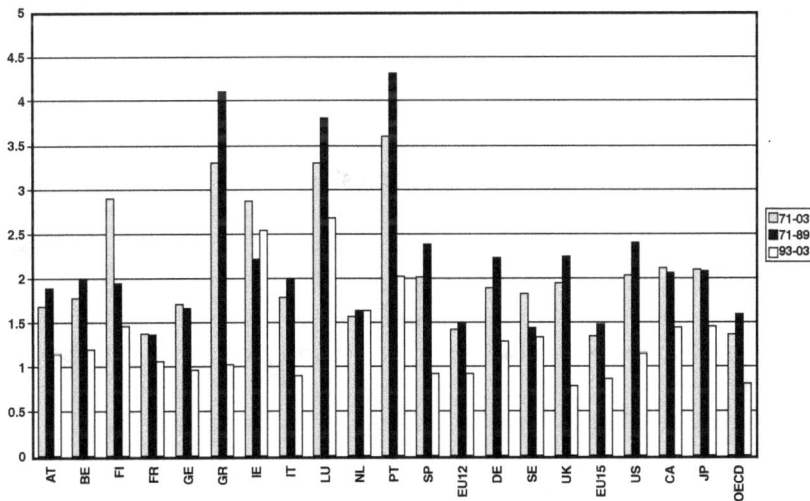

Figure 2
Variance—GDP per-capita growth

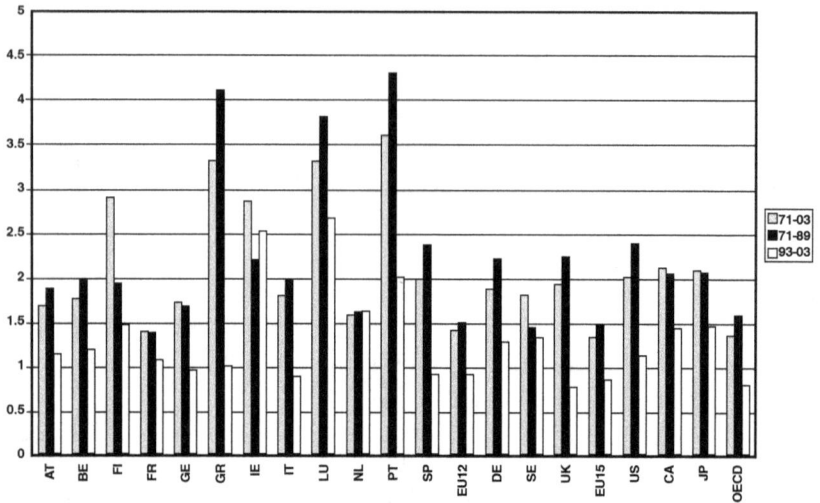

Source: Giannone and Reichlin (2005)

Figure 3
Percentage of GDP per capita forecast errors explained by country-specific shocks

3.   What Is Going On?

If business cycle synchronization among OECD countries has remained stable and so have correlations amongst European countries despite Maastricht and if idiosyncratic shocks on output are small, what can possibly drive the results of the paper?

To answer this question, I will run the same panel regressions of business cycle dispersion on fiscal dispersion performed by the authors, but allow for some heterogeneity in countries' responses.

Heterogeneity across countries is taken into consideration by estimating the regressions on different country groups. I will group countries by their economic size, defined as share of GDP in the OECD total.

Table 2 reports the size in terms of GDP of the 21 OECD countries analyzed in the paper and will help interpreting regression results presented below.

As in the benchmark regression in the paper, I estimate:

$$\text{Corr}_{i,j,t} = \alpha + \gamma_t + \beta \text{FD}_{i,j,t} + \text{var}\varepsilon_{i,j,t}$$

where the dependent variable is the correlation coefficient between GDP growth rate of countries i and j in decade t. The independent variable is given by a measure of fiscal divergence between the same country

Table 2
GDP (constant PPP 2000) in year 2000. Percentage in OECD Total GDP and in total GDP of 21 countries in the paper
Unit: billions of dollars

Country	GDP	Marginal/OECD	Cumulative	Marginal/21	Cumulative
USA	9765	36%	36%	40%	40%
Japan	3309	12%	48%	14%	54%
Germany	2069	8%	56%	9%	63%
France	1552	6%	62%	6%	69%
UK	1503	6%	68%	6%	75%
Italy	1444	5%	73%	6%	81%
Canada	860	3%	76%	4%	85%
Spain	822	3%	79%	3%	88%
Australia	509	2%	81%	2%	90%
Netherlands	435	2%	82%	2%	92%
Belgium	269	1%	83%	1%	93%
Sweden	239	1%	84%	1%	94%
Austria	230	1%	85%	1%	95%
Switzerland	219	1%	86%	1%	96%
Portugal	178	1%	86%	1%	97%
Greece	178	1%	87%	1%	97%
Norway	163	1%	88%	1%	98%
Denmark	152	1%	88%	1%	99%
Finland	133	0%	89%	1%	99%
Ireland	108	0%	89%	0%	100%
New Zealand	79	0%	89%	0%	100%

pairs. The coefficient γ_t measures decade effects (1964–1973, 1974–1983, 1984–1993, 1994–2003) in the benchmark regression of the paper and captures global changes in correlations between country pairs across time. The results from this benchmark regression are reported in the column headed D.E. in Tables 3A and 3B. Results considering only a common intercept, excluding decade effects (C.I. column) and adding fixed effects (F.E.+D.E.) to account for heterogeneity in the country pairs are also reported, as in the paper.

Results for different country groups are reported in different rows in Table 3A and 3B. The second row reports results for the seven largest OECD countries (G7). Spain, Australia, Belgium, and the Netherlands, the four richest non G7 countries, are added to the G7 in the third row. In the fourth row, this group is augmented by Austria, Sweden, and Switzerland (Table 3A) or the latter subgroup plus Portugal (Table 3B). Finally, the last row reports the results of the paper, derived by running the regression on the whole set of the 21 OECD countries considered in the paper.

Results indicate that a significant and negative coefficient of fiscal dispersion on business cycle dispersion is only present when all countries are included, but the result does not hold for other groupings. As it is showed in column two of the tables, the negative relation does not hold for groups accounting for up to 86 percent of the total OECD income per capita.

A further confirmation of the lack of robustness of the authors' findings emerges from simple visual analysis.

Let me define a convenient synthetic measure of divergence for both fiscal and output variables.

Fiscal dispersion in decade j for country i will be defined as:

$$\text{FD}_{i,j,t} = \frac{1}{10} \sum_{t=1}^{10} | g_{it}^j - G_t^j |$$

where g_{it}^j is the deficit-GDP ratio of country i (N countries) at time t in decade j.

The global fiscal deficit will then be the cross-country average:

$$G_t^j = \frac{1}{N} \sum_{i=1}^{N} g_{it}^j.$$

This measure should be understood as a sort of standard deviation of fiscal policy of country i around the cross section (OECD wide) average.

Table 3A
Regression results

Panel	% OECD	C. I.	C.I. + D.E.	F.E. + D.E.
G7	73 [81]	0.008 [0.016]	−0.01 [0.016]	−0.012 0.025
G7 plus 4	82 [92]	0.013 [0.012]	−0.002 [0.012]	−0.02 0.017
G7 plus 7	86 [96]	0.008 [0.009]	−0.008 [0.009]	−0.012 0.013
All	89 [100]	−0.0013** [0.005]	−0.024** [0.005]	−0.010 [0.007]

Table 3B
Regression results

Panel	% OECD	C. I.	C.I. + D.E.	F.E. + D.E.
G7	73 [81]	0.008 [0.016]	−0.01 [0.016]	−0.012 0.025
G7 plus 4	82 [92]	0.013 [0.012]	−0.002 [0.012]	−0.02 0.017
G7 plus 8	86 [97]	0.013 [0.008]	−0.006 [0.008]	−0.005 0.012
All	89 [100]	−0.0013** [0.005]	−0.024** [0.005]	−0.010 [0.007]

- One (two) asterisk indicates 5 (1) % significance.
- Full cross section is the 21 OECD countries.
- G7 plus 4 is G7 Countries plus Spain, Australia, Belgium, and Netherlands.
- G7 plus 7 is G7 plus 4 plus Austria, Sweden, and Switzerland.
- G7 plus 8 is G7 plus 4 plus Austria, Sweden, Switzerland, and Portugal.
- C.I. column: Common Intercept.
- C.I. + D.E. column: Common Intercept plus Decade Effects (time dummies).
- F.E. + D.E. column: Fixed (country pairs) effects (F.E.) and Decade Effects (D.E.).
- In the second column, we indicate the % of GDP of the group of countries over the sample of all OECD countries while the number in parenthesis is the same % over the smaller set of the 21 OECD countries considered by the authors.

I will define business cycle dispersion in decade j for country i as:

$$BCD_{i,j,t} = \frac{1}{10} \sum_{t=1}^{10} |y_{it}^j - Y_t^j|$$

where y_{it}^j = is the GDP growth rate of country i at time t in decade j and

$$Y_t^j = \frac{1}{N} \sum_{i=1}^{N} Y_{it}^j$$

is a sort of (decade) standard deviation of the growth rate of country i around the cross section (OECD wide) average, say the world business cycle.

Figure 4 shows the scatterplot of fiscal dispersion and business cycle dispersion for the different decades.[1] The six smallest countries in the figures are indicated by the "rounds," while the biggest 11 with the "stars." Clearly, if the "rounds" are not taken into accounts, no clear relation between business cycle synchronization and fiscal divergence seems to emerge!

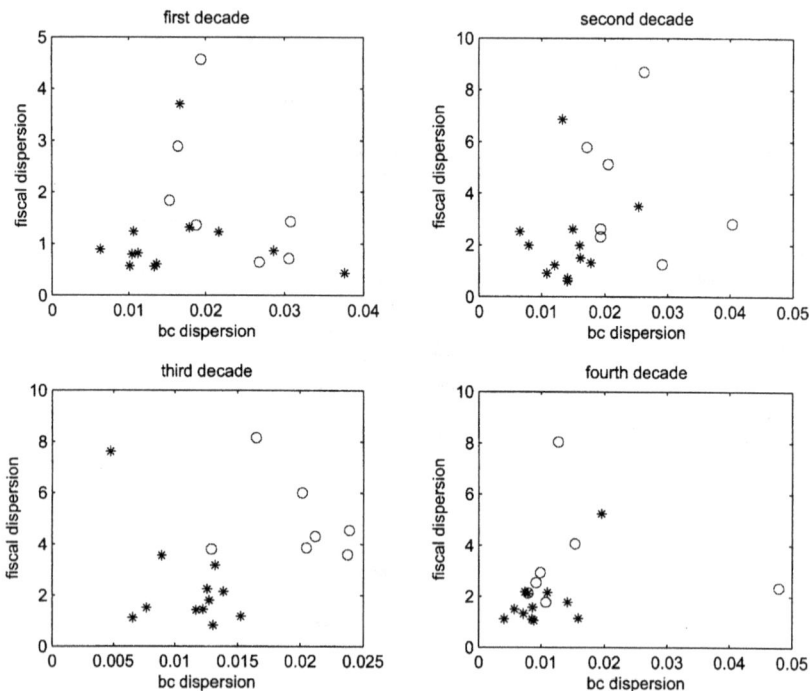

Figure 4
Scatterplot: fiscal dispersion - business cycle dispersion

Note

1. Australia, Belgium, Portugal, and New Zealand are excluded from the figures because of missing observations in the fiscal series

References

Canova, F., M. Ciccarelli, and E. Ortega. 2004. "Similarities and Convergence in G-7 Cycles." EABCN/CEPRD Discussion Paper 5.

Fatás, A., and I. Mihov. 2003. "The Case for Restricting Fiscal Policy Discretion." *Quarterly Journal of Economics* 118(4): 1419–1447.

Frankel, J., and A. K. Rose. 1998. "The Endogeneity of the Optimum Currency Area Criteria." *Economic Journal* 108: 1009–1025.

Giannone, D., and L. Reichlin. 2005. "Euro Area and US Recessions, 1970–2003." In L. Reichlin, ed., *Euro Area Business Cycle: Stylized Facts and Measurement Issues.* CEPR: 83–93.

Harding, D., and A. Pagan. 2004. "Synchronization Of Cycles." Cama Working Papers, Australian National University, Centre for Applied Macroeconomic Analysis.

Stock, J. H., and M. W. Watson. 2005. "Understanding Changes in International Business Cycle Dynamics." *Journal of the European Economic Association* 3(5): 969–1006.

7

Dual Inflation and the Real Exchange Rate in New Open Economy Macroeconomics

Balázs Világi, *Magyar Nemzeti Bank (Central Bank of Hungary)*

1. Introduction

The traditional approach in international macroeconomics has attempted to explain real exchange rate behavior by the movements of domestic relative prices, that is, by the *internal real exchange rate.* This was a consequence of the assumptions it employed: strong homogeneity in international goods markets, where *purchasing power parity* (PPP) is dominant and the only source of heterogeneity is the distinction between *tradables* and *non-tradables.* In recent years, however, the literature has switched sides. According to the recent approach consumer markets are segmented, PPP has little explanatory power, and the main determinant of real exchange rate movements is the *external real exchange rate,* which is the relative price of domestic and foreign tradables. This new focus of research was initiated on the basis of empirical findings, see, e.g., the papers of Engel (1999) and Rogoff (1996). It appeared that, as Obstfeld (2001) put it "apparently, consumer markets for tradables are just about as segmented internationally as consumer markets for non-tradables."

After the collapse of the Bretton Woods system, floating exchange rate regimes became widespread. This enabled scrutiny of the relationship between nominal and real exchange rate behavior: It turned out, as was first forcefully documented by Mussa (1986), that nominal and real exchange rates were strongly correlated, and moving from fixed to floating exchange rate regimes resulted in a dramatic rise in the variability of the real exchange rate. The need for a comprehensive explanation for the aforementioned empirical findings stimulated the birth of *new open economy macroeconomics* (NOEM), initiated by the seminal paper of Obstfeld and Rogoff (1995), which combines the heterogeneity of goods with *nominal rigidities* in models with micro-foundations.

Although the empirical literature related to NOEM revealed the importance of the external real exchange rate, in fast-growing and emerging market countries there are considerable movements of the internal real exchange rate. Permanent *dual inflation,* namely a significant divergence of inflation rates for tradable and non-tradable goods, is a frequent phenomenon of such markets: the inflation rate of non-tradables is permanently higher than that of tradables, which results in long-run real appreciation of the CPI-based real exchange rate. This phenomenon was documented by Ito, Isard, and Symansky (1997) for the case of Japan and some Southeast Asian countries, as well as by Coricelli and Jazbec (2001), Halpern and Wyplosz (2001), Égert (2002), Égert, Drine, Lommatzsch, and Rault (2002) and Kovács (2002) for European post-communist countries. Of course, this does not mean that in these countries the empirical phenomena emphasized in the NOEM literature are not present. For example, the required disinflation efforts, related to future EMU accession, have revealed that the connection between the consumer price index and the nominal exchange rate is weak, which, of course, violates the PPP and implies a strong comovement of nominal and real exchange rates.

The objective of this paper is to build a NOEM model which is able to replicate both sets of empirical facts observable in emerging markets: the strong correlation of the nominal and real exchange rate, and dual inflation accompanied by appreciation of the CPI-based real exchange rate.

The problem is the following. The majority of empirical studies explain the coexistence of dual inflation and the appreciation of the CPI-based real exchange rate in emerging markets by the Balassa-Samuelson (BS) effect, i.e., the relatively rapid productivity growth in the tradable sector. However, dual inflation accompanies appreciation of the CPI-based real exchange rate only if growth in tradable productivity does not result in a significant depreciation of the external real exchange rate. But the external real exchange rate does not depreciate considerably if the common currency prices of domestically produced and foreign tradables cannot deviate strongly from each other, i.e., if domestically produced and foreign tradables are *close* substitutes. On the other hand, the strong comovement of the nominal and real exchange rates stressed by the NOEM literature requires considerable deviations in the short run between domestic and foreign tradable prices (denominated in the same currency). Yet this requirement can be fulfilled only if the products of the aforementioned sectors are *distant* substitutes and/or *pricing to market* (PTM) is possible.

The paper demonstrates that no intermediate degree of international substitution exists that simultaneously guarantees the operation of the BS effect and strong comovement of the nominal and real exchange rate. One possible remedy is an assumption of PTM. In this case, it is possible that domestically produced export goods are close substitutes of foreign tradables, which ensures the existence of the BS effect. On the other hand, with PTM the common currency price of the exported and locally sold domestically produced goods can be substantially different over the short-run. Hence, nominal-exchange-rate movements can influence the behavior of the real exchange rate.

The paper also shows that the presence of decreasing returns to scale, which can be rationalized by a certain combination of real and nominal rigidities, has significant impact on the magnitude of the difference between sectoral inflation rates. As a consequence, the size of the effect of asymmetric sectoral productivity growth, in line with empirical observations, becomes smaller than predicted by the models of the traditional approach.

The paper is structured as follows. Section 2 surveys the empirical literature which initiated the research of this study. Section 3 presents the model and the solution technique employed. In section 4 the Balassa-Samuelson hypothesis is examined; under study is how the model can reproduce the co-existence of dual inflation and appreciation of the CPI-based real exchange rate, and the relationship between asymmetric productivity growth and the magnitude of sectoral inflation differentials is examined. Section 5 presents the conclusions.

2. Previous Empirical Results

This section briefly reviews the empirical literature which initiated the research of this paper. First, findings related to the internal real exchange rate are surveyed. On this issue the evidence is ambiguous. In developed economies, internal-real-exchange-rate movements are negligible, while in several emerging economies dual inflation is an important phenomenon. Second, findings on the strong relationship between the nominal and real exchange rates are considered, which are relevant in both developed and emerging economies.

2.1 Dual Inflation and Real Appreciation

As mentioned in the introduction, NOEM literature focuses on the behavior of the external real exchange rate, instead of the internal one, which was mainly studied by the previous traditional literature. This switch of interest was partly initiated by the findings of Engel (1999), who, using U.S. data, showed that the volatility of the real exchange rate can be explained nearly perfectly by the movements of the external real exchange rate.

However, the validity of this finding is not general. Even in developed countries one can observe significant movements of the internal real exchange rate, as De Gregorio and Wolf (1994), or more recently, López-Salido, Restoy, and Vallés (2005) have documented, but the real importance of this phenomenon is manifested in high growth and emerging market countries. Several empirical studies demonstrate that the BS effect plays a significant role in these countries.

Balassa (1964) and Samuelson (1964) formulated the hypothesis that the difference in productivity growth rates in tradable and non-tradable sectors results in dual inflation, and, as a consequence, appreciation of the CPI-based real exchange rate.[1] Ito, Isard, and Symansky (1997) showed that mainly in Japan, Korea, and Taiwan, but to some extent in other Southeast Asian countries as well, the BS effect was determinant at particular stages of their development process. It also plays an important role in the transition of European post-communist countries, as the empirical studies of Coricelli and Jazbec (2001), Halpern and Wyplosz (2001), Égert (2002), Égert, Drine, Lommatzsch, and Rault (2002), and Kovács (2002) have documented.

Coricelli and Jazbec (2001) examined the determinants of the real exchange rate in 19 transition economies between 1991 and 1998.[2] Halpern and Wyplosz (2001) studied the relevance of the BS effect in nine European post-communist countries by estimating a panel regression for the period 1991–1998.[3] Égert (2002) used time series and panel cointegration techniques to study the BS effect in five east European accession countries between 1991 and 2001.[4] Égert, Drine, Lommatzsch, and Rault (2002) examined the BS effect in nine European accession countries by panel cointegration techniques on a data set covering the period from 1995 to 2000.[5] The paper edited by Kovács (2002) summarizes the results of research on the BS effect conducted by the central banks of central European accession countries.[6]

The above studies demonstrate that in most European post-communist countries the coexistence of dual inflation and appreciation of the CPI-based real exchange rate can be observed in their transition period. In addition, dual inflation is related to sectoral productivity growth differentials, and appreciation of the CPI-based real exchange rate is due to the appreciation of both the external and internal real exchange rates.

Coricelli and Jazbec (2001), Halpern and Wyplosz (2001), Égert (2002), and Égert, Drine, Lommatzsch, and Rault (2002) estimated the relationship between the relative price of non-traded to traded goods and the sectoral productivity differential.[7] Their findings are summarized in Table 1.

According to Coricelli and Jazbec (2001, equation 19), if the productivity differential rises by 1 percent, the relative price rises by 0.87 percent. Égert (2002, Table 1-7) found a significant cointegration relationship between the relative price and productivity differential. The cointegration coefficient measuring the long-run relationship between the relative prices and productivity factors varies from 0.49 to 0.95 in individual country estimates, and 0.72 is the common estimate for the coefficient provided by the panel cointegration analysis. In Égert, Drine, Lommatzsch, and Rault (2002, Table 5) the same cointegration coefficient ranges from 0.73 to 1, depending on the applied definition of tradable and non-tradable sectors. Unlike the previous studies, Halpern and Wyplosz (2001, Table 7) estimated the effects of tradable and non-tradable productivity developments separately. They found significant coefficients with correct signs, although the estimated coefficients

Table 1
Empirical long-run relationship between sectoral prices and productivity measures

	Type of regression	Estimated coefficient
Coricelli–Jazbec (2001)	price differential on productivity differential	0.87
Égert (2002)	panel, price differential on productivity differential	0.72
Égert (2002)	individual, price differential on productivity differential	0.49–0.95
Égert et al. (2002)	price differential on productivity differential	0.73–1
Halpern–Wyplosz (2001)	tradable price on tradable productivity	0.43
Halpern–Wyplosz (2001)	non-tradable price on non-tradable productivity	0.32

are quite small. If tradable productivity rises by 1 percent, the sectoral relative price rises by 0.24 percent in the short-run and by 0.43 percent in the long-run. A 1 percent rise of non-tradable productivity results in a 0.18 percent decrease of the relative price in the short-run and a 0.32 percent decrease in the long-run.

In summary, all papers found a significant relationship between sectoral prices and productivity measures. Magnitudes of estimated coefficients locate in quite a wide range. However, according to all but one estimate, productivity differentials are greater than the accompanying price differentials.

According to the original BS hypothesis, productivity induced real appreciation of the internal real exchange rate results in CPI-based real appreciation, since the external real exchange rate is fixed due to the assumed validity of PPP.

Kovács (2002, Table 1-1) documented that between 1993 and 2002 the annual average CPI-based real appreciation of the examined countries varied from 2.2 to 5.8 per cent. However, the BS effect does not fully explain the observed CPI-based real appreciations. Only 33–72 percent of it can be attributed to productivity growth induced internal real exchange rate movements; the rest can be assigned to the external real exchange rate. Égert (2002, Table 9) also reveals that productivity induced appreciation of the internal real exchange rate cannot completely explain CPI-based real appreciation. According to his panel analysis, it is responsible for 38–60 percent of CPI-based appreciation. He also stresses the importance of a trend appreciation of the external real exchange rate to explain the observed phenomena. Égert et al (2002) presented similar findings and reinforced the conclusions of the above papers.

Although in this paper I study only productivity induced dual inflation, I should mention that studies analyzing the BS effect have often detected other non-productivity factors in the determination of the sectoral relative price. Moreover, Arratibel, Rodríguez-Palenzuela, and Thiman (2002) do not simply provide alternative explanations for dual inflation, they deny the role of productivity factors in the determination of the examined countries. However, the authors admit that one should interpret this result with caution because of the poor quality of productivity data.[8]

2.2   The Comovement of the Nominal and Real Exchange Rates

As mentioned in the introduction, the NOEM literature was partly initiated by the empirical findings of Mussa (1986), who first documented the strong connection between the nominal and real exchange rates. Using Monacelli (2004), I summarize some important findings. The post-1971 data from 12 developed countries reveal that the unconditional correlation of real and nominal depreciation rates is 0.98. In flexible exchange rate regimes the unconditional variance of the real depreciation rate is nearly equal to the unconditional variance of the nominal depreciation rate.

Violation of PPP is a necessary condition for the above findings. Moreover, the violation of PPP is not a transitory phenomenon, as several empirical studies have shown. Chari, Kehoe, and McGrattan (2002) studied the persistence of the real-exchange-rate shocks using HP-filtered quarterly data for the USA and 11 developed European countries for the period 1973:1–2000:1. Their estimated quarterly autocorrelation is 0.84.[9] Though the above empirical results are all related to developed countries, the violation of PPP can also be detected in European post-communist countries, which are the primary focus of this study,[10] although the supporting evidence is mainly only stylized facts.

3. The Model

This paper studies how to construct a model which can simultaneously guarantee the empirical regularities characterized in section 2, i.e., the comovement of the nominal and real exchange rates and generate the BS effect, i.e., the coexistence of productivity based dual inflation and appreciation of the CPI-based real exchange rate.

To guarantee the empirically observable correlation between the nominal and real exchange rates the model needs sticky prices and heterogeneous international tradable markets. Obviously, to consider the BS effect it is necessary to have two sectors with different total factor productivities (TFP).

International market heterogeneity can be captured in different ways. I therefore examine whether model versions with different descriptions of market heterogeneity can generate the BS effect. I consider a version (version A) without pricing to market (PTM) and with the assumption that domestic and foreign tradables are imperfect substitutes. In version B PTM combined with local currency pricing (LCP) is added to the model.[11]

The paper also considers the relationship between the magnitude of sectoral relative price and productivity differential. In frictionless, sectorally symmetric models the two quantities are equal. Yet this is not in line with empirical results, which reveal that the relative price of non-tradables to tradables is smaller than the sectoral productivity differential. Nominal rigidities help to explain this phenomenon: if prices are sticky the adjustment of the sectoral relative price is not immediate. In addition, *decreasing returns* amplify the impact of sticky prices, making the adjustment process even slower and incomplete, which provides a better fit in terms of empirical results.

Decreasing returns are guaranteed in the model by the assumption of *fixed capital stock*. This approach makes the model simple and tractable. Besides, it can be considered as the limiting case of the *firm-specific-investments* model of Altig, Christiano, Eichenbaum, and Linde (2005) and Woodford (2005). As they show, even if technology exhibits constant returns to scale, the lack of an economy-wide rental market for physical capital and frictions in investments formation combined with sticky asynchronized price setting results in suboptimal input allocation, and decreasing returns to scale.

3.1 Households

The domestic economy is populated by a continuum of infinitely-lived identical households. To simplify the notation, household indices are dropped, since this does not cause confusion. The utility accrued to a given household at date t is

$$U(c_t, l_t) = \frac{c^{1-\sigma}}{1-\sigma} - \frac{l^{1+\varphi}}{1+\varphi},$$

where c_t is the consumption, l_t is the labor supply of the representative household at date t, and $\sigma, \varphi > 0$.

The consumption good c_t is composed of *tradable* and *non-tradable* consumption goods:

$$c_t = \left[a_T^{\frac{1}{\eta}} (c_t^T)^{\frac{\eta-1}{\eta}} + a_N^{\frac{1}{\eta}} (c_t^N)^{\frac{\eta-1}{\eta}} \right]^{\frac{\eta}{\eta-1}}, \tag{1}$$

where c_t^T is the tradable, c_t^N is the non-tradable consumption good, η and $a_T = 1 - a_N$ are non-negative parameters.

The intertemporal budget constraint of a given household is the following:

$$P_t^T c_t^T + P_t^N c_t^N + P_t^B B_t = \zeta_t B_{t-1} + W_t l_t + T_t,$$

where P_t^T and P_t^N are the price indices of tradables and non-tradables, B_t is the household's nominal portfolio at the beginning of date t, P_t^B is its price, and ζ_t is its stochastic payoff. W_t is the nominal wage, while T_t is a lump-sum tax/transfer variable.

It is well known that the linear homogeneity of function (1) implies that the households' problem can be solved in two steps. First, they maximize the intertemporal objective function

$$\sum_{t=0}^{\infty} \beta^t E_0[U(c_t, l_t)],$$

with respect to c_t and l_t subject to the following modified budget constraint:

$$P_t c_t + P_t^B B_t = \zeta_t B_{t-1} + W_t l_t + T_t, \tag{2}$$

non-negativity constraints, and no-Ponzi schemes, where $0 < \beta < 1$ is the discount factor of households. In the budget constraint (2) the consumer price index P_t is defined by the following expression:

$$P_t = [a_T (P_t^T)^{1-\eta} + a_N (P_t^N)^{1-\eta}]^{\frac{1}{1-\eta}}. \tag{3}$$

Second, knowing c_t it is possible to determine c_t^T and c_t^N by the demand functions

$$c_t^T = a_t \left(\frac{P_t}{P_t^T}\right)^{\eta} c_t, \quad c_t^N = a_N \left(\frac{P_t}{P_t^N}\right)^{\eta} c_t. \tag{4}$$

The assumption of complete asset markets implies that the optimal intertemporal allocation of consumption is determined by the following condition in all states of the world:

$$\beta \frac{\Lambda_{t+1} P_t}{\Lambda_t P_{t+1}} = D_{t,t+1}, \tag{5}$$

where Λ_t is the marginal utility of consumption,

$$\Lambda_t = c_t^{-\sigma},$$

and $D_{t,t+1}$ is the stochastic discount factor, which satisfies the condition

$$P_t^B = E_t[D_{t,t+1} \zeta_{t+1}].$$

Since in this economy the asset markets are also complete internationally, the foreign equivalent of equation (5) is also held:

$$\beta \frac{\Lambda_{t+1}^* e_t P_t^{F*}}{\Lambda_t^* e_{t+1} P_{t+1}^{F*}} = D_{t,t+1}, \tag{6}$$

where Λ^*_t is the marginal utility of foreign households, P^{F*}_t is the foreign consumer price index in foreign currency terms, and e_t is the nominal exchange rate. For simplicity P^{F*}_t is assumed to be constant. Combining equations (5) and (6) and applying recursive substitutions yields formula

$$\frac{\Lambda_t e_t P^{F*}_t}{\Lambda^*_t P_t} = \iota, \tag{7}$$

where ι is a constant, which depends on initial conditions.

The solution of the households' problem implies that the real wage w_t is equal to the marginal rate of substitution between consumption and labor, i.e.,

$$w_t = c^\sigma_t l^\varphi_t ,$$

which determines the labor supply decision.

3.2   Production

There are two stages of production in the model: in the first step import goods and labor are transformed into differentiated intermediate goods in both the tradable and non-tradable sectors,[12] while in the second step homogenous final goods are produced and distributed using intermediate products.

Final goods are produced in competitive markets by constant-returns-to-scale technologies from a continuum of differentiated inputs, $y^s_t(i)$, $i \in [0, 1]$, where $s = T, N$, with T referring to tradable sector and N to non-tradable.

In version A there are two types of final goods, a tradable one, used for domestic consumption and exports, and a non-tradable one, used only for domestic consumption. The technology of final goods production is represented by the following CES production function:

$$y^s_t = \left(\int_0^1 y^s_t(i)^{\frac{\theta-1}{\theta}} di \right)^{\frac{\theta}{\theta-1}} ,$$

where $\theta > 1$. As a consequence, the output price P^s_t is given by

$$P^s_t = \left(\int_0^1 P^s_t(i)^{1-\theta} di \right)^{\frac{1}{1-\theta}} ,$$

where $P^s_t(i)$ denotes the price of differentiated good i in sector s. The demand for differentiated goods is determined by

$$y_t^T(i) = \left(\frac{P_t^T}{P_t^T(i)}\right)^\theta (c_t^T + x_t), \quad y_t^N(i) = \left(\frac{P_t^N}{P_t^N(i)}\right)^\theta c_t^N, \tag{8}$$

where x_t denotes exports.

In version B intermediate goods are also manufactured in sector T and N, and the non-tradable final good is produced and distributed in the same way as in version A. However, the market for tradable final goods is segmented, domestic consumption and export goods are sold in different markets. This market structure is represented by the assumption that two diverse final good producers/distributors operate in these markets. As a consequence, domestic and foreign prices of tradables denominated in the same currency can diverge. Final goods distributors apply the previously described CES technologies, and export prices are set in local currency. Hence, the demand for tradable intermediate goods are given by the following functions:

$$c_t^T(i) = \left(\frac{P_t^T}{P_t^T(i)}\right)^\theta c_t^T, \quad x_t(i) = \left(\frac{P_t^{x*}}{P_t^{x*}(i)}\right)^\theta x_t, \tag{9}$$

where $P_t^{x*}(i)$ is the foreign currency price of exported tradables, $y_t^T(i) = c_t^T(i) + x_t^T(i)$, and

$$P_t^{x*} = \left(\int_0^1 P_t^{x*}(i)^{1-\theta} di\right)^{\frac{1}{1-\theta}}.$$

The continuum of goods $y_t^s(i)$ are produced in a monopolistically competitive market in each sector ($s = T, N$). Each $y_t^s(i)$ is made by an individual firm using the following uniform technology:

$$y_t^s(i) = A_t^s(\bar{k}^s)^\alpha z_t^s(i)^{1-\alpha}, \tag{10}$$

where $0 < \alpha < 1$, A_t^s is total factor productivity of sector s, $\bar{k}^s$ is the stock of fixed physical capital in sector s, and $z_t^s(i)$ denotes an individual firm's utilization of the composite input z_t^s defined in the following way:

$$z_t^s(i) = N_s l_t^s(i)^{n_s} m_t^s(i)^{1-n_s}, \tag{11}$$

where $l_t^s(i)$ is an individual firms' utilization of labor l_t, and $m_t^s(i)$ is the utilization of imported good m_t, n_s is a given non-negative parameter, and $N_s = n_s^{-n_s}(1 - n_s)^{n_s - 1}$. The price of z_t^s is given by

$$W_t^{z,s} = W_t^{n_s}(e_t P_t^{m*})^{1-n_s}, \tag{12}$$

where P_t^{m*} is the foreign currency price of the imported good.

Intermediate goods producers solve the standard static cost minimization problem. The solution of the cost minimization problem determines the labor and import demand of a particular firm by

$$l_t^s(i)=n_s\frac{W_t^{z,s}}{W_t}z_t^s(i), \quad m_t^s(i)=(1-n_s)\frac{W_t^{z,s}}{e_t P_t^{m*}}z_t^s(i). \tag{13}$$

Intermediate goods producers follow a sticky price setting practice.
As in the model of Calvo (1983), each individual firm in a given time
period changes its price in a rational, optimizing, forward looking manner with probability $1-\gamma_s$. Those firms which do not optimize at a given
date follow a rule of thumb, as in Christiano, Eichenbaum, and Evans
(2001) and Smets and Wouters (2003), and update their prices according
to the past sectoral inflation rate.

In version A all firms in sector $s = T, N$ which follow the simple index-
ation rule at date t update their prices according to formula

$$P_t^s(i)=P_{t'}^s(i)\left(\frac{P_{t-1}^s}{P_{t'-1}^s}\right)^{\vartheta_s}. \tag{14}$$

Those which set their prices rationally at date t' take into account that
$P_t^{s'}(i)$ will exist with probability $\gamma_s^{t-t'}$ at date t. Thus, they maximize the
expected profit function

$$\sum_{t=t'}^{\infty}E_{t'}\left[\gamma_s^{t-t'}D_{t',t}\left\{(1-\tau)P_{t'}^s(i)y_t^s(i)-W_t^{z,s}\left(\frac{y_t^s(i)}{A_t^s}\right)^{\frac{1}{1-\alpha}}(\bar{k}^s)^{\frac{\alpha}{1-\alpha}}\right\}\right], \tag{15}$$

with respect to $P_t^{s'}(i)$ and $y_t^s(i)$ subject to the constraints (8) and (14),
where τ is a tax/transfer variable which modifies firms' markup.[13] I used
equation (10) to derive the marginal-cost term in the above formula.

In version B export prices of non-optimizing firms are given by

$$P_t^{x*}(i)=P_{t'}^{x*}(i)\left(\frac{P_{t-1}^{x*}}{P_{t'-1}^{x*}}\right)^{\vartheta_T}. \tag{16}$$

In sector N optimizing firms set their prices the same way as in version A. In sector T instead of equation (15), they maximize the expected
profit function

$$\sum_{t=t'}^{\infty}E_{t'}[\gamma_s^{t-t'}D_{t',t}(1-\tau)\{P_t^T c_t^T(i)+e_t P_{t'}^{x*}(i)x_t(i)\}] \tag{17}$$

$$-\sum_{t=t'}^{\infty}E_{t'}\left[\gamma_s^{t-t'}D_{t',t}W_t^{z,T}\left(\frac{c_t^T(i)+x_t(i)}{A_t^T}\right)^{\frac{1}{1-\alpha}}(\bar{k}^T)^{\frac{\alpha}{1-\alpha}}\right],$$

with respect to $P_t^T(i)$, $P_t^{x*}(i)$, $c_t^T(i)$ and $x_t(i)$, subject to the constraints (9), (14), and (16).

3.3   Exports Demand

Foreign behavior is not modeled explicitly. It is assumed that the following *ad hoc* equation determines demand for exports:

$$x_t = \left(\frac{P_t^{FT*}}{P_t^{x*}} \right)^{\eta^*} x^*, \tag{18}$$

where P_t^{x*} is the foreign currency price of the export goods, P^{FT*} is the foreign currency price of the rival goods (which is constant by assumption), x^* is an exogenous parameter representing the volume of demand, and $\eta^* > 0$ is an exogenous parameter.

In version A of the model, exported goods are produced by the tradable sector, and $P_t^{x*} = P^T/e_t$. While in version B local tradables and export goods are different, hence their prices denominated in the same currency can be different, i.e., it is possible that $P_t^{x*} \neq P^T/e_t$.

3.4   Real Exchange Rate Indices

In this study the following real exchange indices will be considered:

$$q_t = \frac{e_t P_t^{F*}}{P_t}, \quad q_t^T = \frac{e_t P_t^{FT*}}{P_t^T}, \quad P_t^R = \frac{P_t^N}{P_t^T}, \tag{19}$$

where q_t is the CPI-based real exchange rate and q_t^T is the external real exchange rate. The movements of P_t^R, the domestic relative price of non-tradables to tradables, unambiguously determine the fluctuation of the internal real exchange rate, since it is assumed that P^{FT*} and P^{FN*} are constant.

3.5   The Log-linearized Model

To solve the model its log-linear approximation around the steady state is taken. In this section, instead of the description of the complete log-linearized model, the most important equations of the system are reviewed. Variables without time indices refer to their steady-state values, and the tilde denotes the log-deviation of a variable from its steady-state value.

3.5.1 Domestic Price Setting

Following Woodford (2005, chapter 3) and using equations (12) and (19), one can show that the solution of the maximization of the expected profit functions (15) and (17) yields formula

$$\pi_t^s - \vartheta_s \pi_{t-1}^s = \beta E_t [\pi_{t+1}^s - \vartheta_s \pi_t^s] \tag{20}$$

$$+ \xi_s \left[\frac{\alpha}{1-\alpha} \frac{c^s \tilde{c}_t^s + \overline{x}^s \tilde{x}_t}{c^s + \overline{x}^s} - \frac{1}{1-\alpha} \tilde{A}_t^s + n_s \tilde{w}_t + (1-n_s)\tilde{q}_t + \chi_s \tilde{P}_t^R \right]$$

for determining domestic prices, where $s = T, N$, $\pi_t^s = \tilde{P}_t^s - \tilde{P}_{t-1}^s$ is the sectoral inflation rate and

$$\xi_s = \frac{(1-\gamma_s)(1-\beta\gamma_s)}{\gamma_s \left(1 + \theta \dfrac{\alpha}{1-\alpha} \right)}. \tag{21}$$

Furthermore, $\overline{x}^T = x$, $\overline{x}^N = 0$, $\chi_T = a_N$ and $\chi_N = -a_T$.

3.5.2 Export Market

In version A of the model $\tilde{q}_t^T = \tilde{P}_t^{x*}$, hence the log-linearized version of the exports demand equation (18) becomes

$$\tilde{x}_t = \eta^* \tilde{q}_t^T. \tag{22}$$

In version B the log-linearized exports demand is

$$\tilde{x}_t = -\eta^* \tilde{P}_t^{x*}. \tag{23}$$

Since in version A the law of one price is valid in tradable goods market, the foreign currency price of exported goods is determined by the nominal exchange rate and the domestic price of tradables. However, in version B the assumption of pricing to market implies that one needs an additional equation to determine export prices. The maximization of (17) yields the following log-linear formula for export prices:

$$\pi_t^{x*} - \vartheta_T \pi_{t-1}^{x*} = \beta E_t [\pi_{t+1}^{x*} - \vartheta_T \pi_{t-1}^{x*}] \tag{24}$$

$$+ \xi_T \left[\frac{\alpha}{1-\alpha} \frac{c^T \tilde{c}_t^T + xx_t}{c+x} - \frac{1}{1-\alpha} \tilde{A}_t^T + n_T(\tilde{w}_t - \tilde{q}_t) - \tilde{P}_t^{x*} \right],$$

where $\pi_t^{x*} = \tilde{P}_t^{x*} - \tilde{P}_{t-1}^{x*}$.

3.5.3 Policy Rule

In this model monetary policy is represented by the following simple log-linear nominal exchange rate rule:

$$d\tilde{e}_t = -\omega(a_T \pi_{t-1}^T + a_N \pi_{t-1}^N) + S_t^{de}, \tag{25}$$

where $d\tilde{e}_t = \tilde{e}_t - \tilde{e}_{t-1}$ is the nominal depreciation rate, and S_t^{de} is an exogenous nominal depreciation shock.

3.6 Model Solution and Parameterization

To solve the model, Uhlig's (1999) implementation of the *undetermined coefficients* method is used and the numerical results are generated by the aforementioned author's MATLAB algorithm.

Benchmark values of the basic parameters are found in Table 2.

The value of β is taken from King and Rebello (1999). The value α is chosen in such a way that capital's share in GDP is 0.4.[14] The values of σ, φ, a_T, and η are widely accepted in the literature. The value of θ was chosen in such a way as to obtain the same degree of strategic complementarity of price setting as in Woodford (2003, 2005). I take the values of γ_s and ϑ_s from the study of Galí, Gertler, and López-Salido (2001), which also contains Euro area estimates.[15] The value of parameter $\eta*$ is not fixed: in the simulation exercises of section 4 several different val-

Table 2
Parameter values of the benchmark economy

	Parameter	
	Name	Value
	β	0.984
	σ	1.000
	φ	3.000
	a_T	0.500
	η	1.000
	α	0.250
	θ	10.80
	γ_s	0.817
	ϑ_s	0.365
	ω	1.000

Note: $s = T, N$.

ues are considered. Finally, ω was chosen in such a way that the model fits the empirical findings of section 2.

4. Examination of the Balassa-Samuelson Effect

As discussed in section 2, there is a strong relationship between the nominal and real exchange rates, and asymmetric sectoral productivity growth results in dual inflation and appreciation of the CPI-based real exchange rate in developing countries. Under study in this section is how it is possible to reproduce both sets of evidence in a NOEM model.

First, it will be demonstrated that, unlike in the models of the traditional approach, in NOEM models productivity induced dual inflation is not necessarily accompanied by CPI-based real appreciation, which contradicts the empirical findings discussed previously. It will be shown that the international substitution parameter η^* in equations (22) and (23) has a key role in generating appreciation of the CPI-based real exchange rate. On the other hand, η^* also influences the degree of comovement of the nominal and real exchange rates. According to my numerical simulations, the assumption of pricing to market (PTM) is necessary to find such a value of η^* which ensures both the strong comovement of the nominal and real exchange rates and the CPI-based real appreciation related to asymmetric productivity growth.

Second, it will be shown that it is difficult to reproduce the observed slow adjustment of the sectoral relative price to the sectoral productivity differential by frictionless models. However, decreasing returns to scale, which can be rationalized by the coexistence of heterogeneity in capital accumulation and sticky prices, help to explain this phenomenon.

4.1 Productivity Induced Dual Inflation and Real Appreciation

As discussed in section 2.1, in European post-communist countries in the 1990s the fast productivity growth of the tradable sector resulted in dual inflation, i.e., appreciation of the internal real exchange rate, which accompanied the appreciation of the external and the CPI-based real exchange rate.

Usually productivity induced coexistence of dual inflation and CPI-based real appreciation, i.e., the BS effect, is analyzed with models of the traditional approach. These models can successfully explain the coexistence of dual inflation and appreciation of the CPI-based real exchange rate, since in these models PPP is assumed, which prevents external real exchange rate movements. On the other hand, due to PPP they cannot reproduce the observable appreciation of the external real exchange rate.

It seems that with NOEM models it is even more problematic to explain the discussed empirical phenomena. It is typical in NOEM models that although a positive productivity shock in the tradable sector results in appreciation of the internal real exchange rate, at the same time, due to increasing productivity, domestic tradables become cheaper, i.e., the external real exchange rate depreciates. As Benigno and Thoenissen (2002) demonstrated, the latter effect suppresses internal appreciation, hence the CPI-based real exchange rate also depreciates.

This possibility is especially important in version A. Consider the exports demand equation (22). If the international substitution parameter $\eta^* = +\infty$ then $\tilde{q}_t^T = 0$, i.e., the external real exchange rate becomes constant, and there will not be any relationship between the nominal and the real exchange rate, which contradicts empirical results. On the other hand, if η^* is low, and $\tilde{P}_t^T$ is sticky, i.e., it responds to shocks slowly, then $\tilde{q}_t^T = \tilde{e}_t - \tilde{P}_t^T$ will move together with the nominal exchange rate. However, in this case high tradable-productivity growth may cause strong external-real-exchange depreciation. The question is whether there is an intermediate value of η^* which can replicate both sets of empirical findings in version A of the model.

In version B even a high value of η^* can guarantee a strong comovement of the nominal and real exchange rates. On the other hand, in this case the foreign currency price of domestically produced export goods $\tilde{P}_t^{x*}$ does not deviate much from the prices of their foreign rivals. As a consequence, $\tilde{P}_t^T - \tilde{e}_t$ remains stable, since the marginal costs of domestic tradable and export productions are the same. Thus, the conjecture is that in version B it is possible to find appropriate values for the substitution parameter, which guarantee that asymmetric sectoral productivity growth results in appreciation of the CPI-based real exchange rate.

First, it is studied which value of the substitution parameter η^* is consistent with the strong comovement of the nominal and real exchange rates discussed in section 2. In the simulation exercises the depreciation shock S_t^{de} is the only source of nominal-exchange-rate movements. This approach is supported by several empirical studies. In a closed economy context Smets and Wouters (2003) and Ireland (2004) demonstrated by their estimated models that nominal shocks have a primary role while technological shocks have only an auxiliary role in explaining business cycles. Clarida and Galí (1994) showed that in open economies 35–41 percent of real exchange rate movements can be attributed to nominal shocks. The prominent importance of the nominal-exchange-rate shocks in emerging markets is documented by Calvo and Reinhart (2002).

Instead of calculating simple contemporaneous correlations, I use statistics, which describe movements of the considered variables in a more complex way. Simple correlation coefficients can capture only a certain qualitative property of comovement. Namely, if the nominal and real exchange rates usually move to the same direction, then the value of the coefficient will be high, even if the size and time pattern of the movements are different. I therefore follow Chari, Kehoe, and McGrattan (2002), and study the autocorrelation structure of the CPI-based real exchange rate in response to nominal-exchange-rate shocks.[16] I also considered the relative variance of depreciation of the nominal and the CPI-based real exchange rates, which measure the relative magnitude of their movements and can capture varying magnitudes of real-exchange-rate reactions to nominal-exchange-rate shocks.

In the following simulations all parameters, except for η^*, are set to their benchmark values (see Table 2). Table 3 displays the results. Empirical values of the statistics in the table are taken from section 2.2.

Let us consider the autocorrelation function. If $\eta^* = 1$ both versions of the model reproduce the 1-quarter value of empirical autocorrelation quite well. However, they undershoot the observed 1-year of and 2-year autocorrelation coefficients.[17]

In version A all autocorrelation coefficients significantly diminish as η^* increases. In particular, the 1-year and 2-year coefficients become very small compared to the empirical values. On the other hand, in version B the auto-correlation coefficients are much less sensitive to the substitution parameter, moreover as η^* increases the fit of the model slightly improves.

Another measure indicating the strength of the comovement of nominal and real exchange rates is the relative variance of nominal and real depreciations. In version A this statistic decreases as η^* increases, and becomes definitively smaller than the empirical value. On the other hand, in version B the relative variance does not react to changes of the substitution parameter.

In summary, while model version B is quite insensitive to changes of η^*, version A is sensitive to the variation of the substitution parameter. It can approximate the empirical results only if η^* has low values,

Table 3
The relationship between the nominal and the CPI-based real exchange rate in the model
economy

Statistics	Data	Parameter values of η^*			
		1	5	15	20
Version A					
Autocorrelation of the real exchange rate					
1 quarter	0.84	0.78	0.74	0.67	0.64
1 year	0.50	0.34	0.26	0.16	0.13
2 years	0.25	0.10	0.06	0.03	0.03
The relative variance of the real and nominal depreciations	1	0.93	0.91	0.87	0.86
Version B					
Autocorrelation of the real exchange rate					
1 quarter	0.84	0.80	0.81	0.82	0.82
1 year	0.50	0.37	0.40	0.42	0.43
2 years	0.25	0.13	0.16	0.18	0.19
The relative variance of the real and nominal depreciations	1	0.93	0.93	0.93	0.93

i.e., domestically produced export goods and their foreign rivals are far
substitutes.

The next issue is whether dual inflation induced by asymmetric sectoral productivity growth is accompanied by CPI-based real appreciation. The role of the international substitution parameter η^* in equations
(22) and (23) will be studied by numerical simulations.

In the simulation exercises I imitate some characteristics of productivity developments of transition countries. The model's steady state
represents the state of the economy at the beginning of its transition
process. Foreign productivity growth is normalized to zero, hence the
productivity variables $\tilde{A}_t^T$ and $\tilde{A}_t^N$ represent relative productivity of
the examined small open economy. In the model transition is driven
by increasing productivity. The start of the process is captured by an
unexpected productivity shock. It is assumed that during transition the
growth rate of productivity is constant. After the transition process the
growth rate of productivity in the small open economy will be equal to
zero as well. The steady state belonging to the new level of productivity
represents the after-transition state of the economy. However, this new

state of the economy is beyond my focus. I assume that the transition process is mainly driven by tradable productivity, hence I assume that in the examined transition period the growth rate of non-tradable productivity is equal to zero. In the simulation exercises I set the annual growth rate of the tradable TFP to 1 percent.

In the following simulation exercises differences between the responses of the two model versions are negligible, since nominal-exchange-rate rate movements are small. Hence, it is sufficient to report the outcomes belonging to version B. Figure 1 displays the simulation results for the benchmark economy with $\eta^* = 1$. The first panel of the figure plots the difference between the growth rates of sectoral productivity factors $d\hat{A}_t^T - d\hat{A}_t^N$, and the inflation differential $\pi_t^R = \pi_t^N - \pi_t^T$. The latter determines the movements of the internal real exchange rate. If π_t^R is positive, then the internal real exchange rate appreciates. The second panel plots the depreciation of the CPI-based real exchange rate $d\tilde{q}_t$, and the external real exchange rate $d\tilde{q}_t^T$. Positive values of $d\tilde{q}_t$ and $d\tilde{q}_t^T$ mean deprecation. Formulas (3) and (19) imply that the connection between the real exchange rate indices is

$$d\tilde{q}_t = d\tilde{q}_t^T - a_N \pi_t^R.$$

The third panel displays $\bar{y}_t^T = (c^T \tilde{c}_t^T + x\bar{x}_t)(c^T + x)^{-1}$ and $\bar{y}_t^N = \tilde{c}_t^N$. As equation (20) reveals, beyond productivity factors these quantities also influence sectoral inflation rates. Finally, the fourth panel plots the growth rates of the real wage and exports. All growth rates are expressed in annualized terms.

Simulation results reveal that although the internal real exchange rate appreciates, the real exchange rate depreciates since the effect of the depreciating external rate is stronger then that of the internal rate. The reason is that productivity growth of the tradable sector is higher than those of the non-tradable sector and foreign tradable sectors. As a consequence, the relative price of domestically produced tradables to foreign tradables decreases. That is, the external real exchange rate depreciates. If domestically produced and foreign tradables were perfect substitutes, then the reduced relative price would induce a large instant increase of demand for domestic tradables. Hence, domestic real wages and tradable prices would increase and the prices of domestic and foreign tradables denominated in the same currency would equalize immediately. But in the studied case domestic and foreign tradables are far substitutes, hence increasing demand does not result in equalized prices.

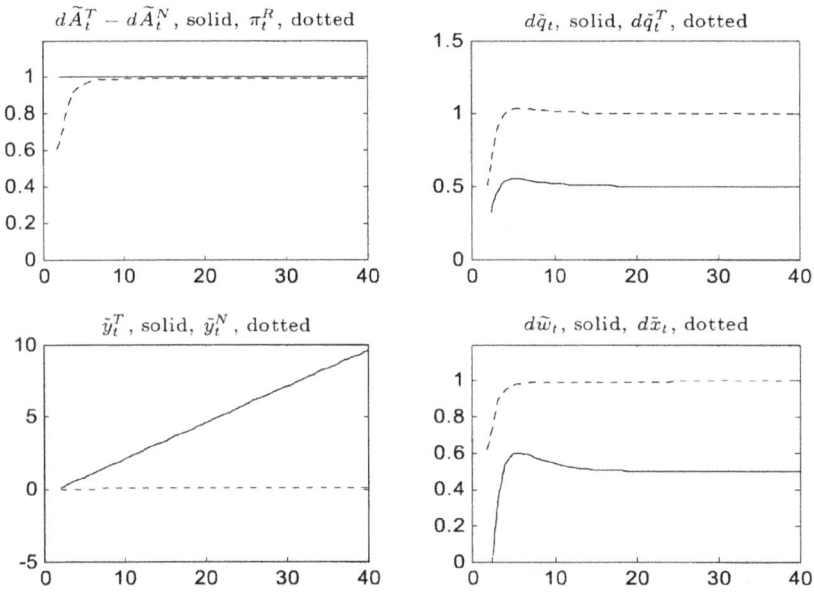

$d\widetilde{A}_t^T - d\widetilde{A}_t^N$, solid, π_t^R, dotted

$d\tilde{q}_t$, solid, $d\tilde{q}_t^T$, dotted

$\tilde{y}_t^T$, solid, $\tilde{y}_t^N$, dotted

$d\tilde{w}_t$, solid, $d\tilde{x}_t$, dotted

Units on a horizontal axis represent quarters, on a vertical axis percentage points.
Growth rates are displayed in annualized terms.

Figure 1
Balassa-Samuelson effect
PTM – version B
$\eta^* = 1$

Figure 2 plots simulation results belonging to a higher value of the substitution parameter ($\eta^* = 15$). The figure reveals that if domestic and foreign tradables are closer substitutes than in the previous case, then the depreciation of the external real exchange rate becomes more moderate. However, even this moderate level of depreciation prevents appreciation of the CPI-based real exchange rate. As a consequence, even this value of the international substitution parameter η^* is insufficient to reproduce empirical findings.

Figure 3 displays the results belonging to $\eta^* = 20$. Since in this case export goods are relatively close substitutes of their foreign rivals their prices cannot deviate much, hence the depreciation of the internal real exchange rate is moderate. As a consequence, the CPI-based real exchange rate appreciates in the long run.

In summary, it was demonstrated that the international substitution parameter η^* had a key role in reproducing empirical facts related to the BS effect. If η^* is low, i.e., domestic and foreign tradables are far substitutes, then the external real exchange rate depreciates too much, and

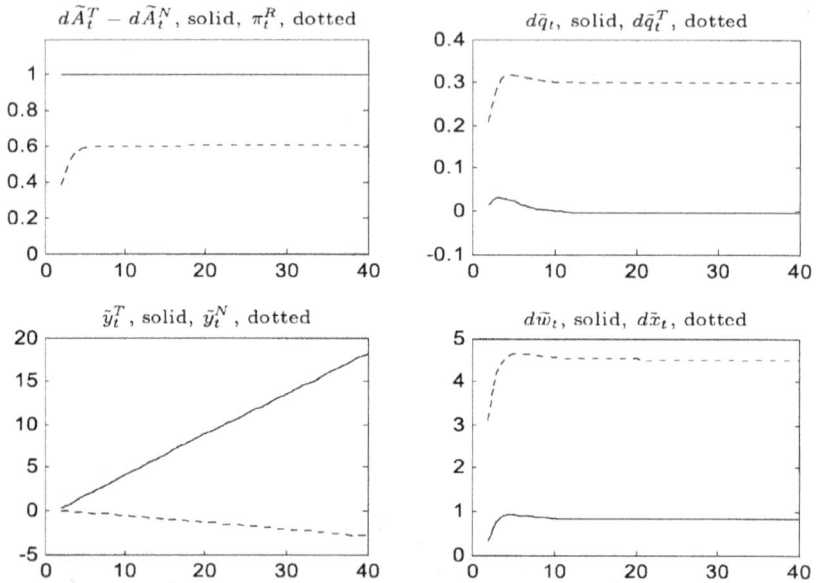

$d\tilde{A}_t^T - d\tilde{A}_t^N$, solid, π_t^R, dotted

$d\bar{q}_t$, solid, $d\bar{q}_t^T$, dotted

$\tilde{y}_t^T$, solid, $\tilde{y}_t^N$, dotted

$d\tilde{w}_t$, solid, $d\tilde{x}_t$, dotted

Units on a horizontal axis represent quarters, on a vertical axis percentage points.
Growth rates are displayed in annualized terms.

Figure 2
Balassa-Samuelson effect
PTM – version B
$\eta^* = 15$

prevents the appreciation of the CPI-based real exchange rate. Hence, relatively high values of parameter η^* are the only possible candidates to generate results consistent with empirical findings. However, in version A, when PTM is not allowed, sufficiently high values of η^* result in an insufficient and weak relationship between the nominal and real exchange rates. In version A to generate CPI-based real appreciation η^* > 15 is necessary, but these parameter values induce small autocorrelation coefficients and relative variance of the real exchange rate (recall Table 3). Hence, PTM seems necessary to appropriately describe the BS effect in NOEM models.

One may criticize the applied high values of the substitution parameter η^*, since estimates using macro data are usually much lower, around 1.5 to 2. However, micro data yields estimates in the range of 5 to 20; see the references in Obstfeld and Rogoff (2000b). Moreover, recent estimation of an open economy macro model by Adolfson, Laseén, Lindé, and Villani (2005) also supports high values of the elasticity of substitution. I provide some further informal arguments why it is reasonable to assume high values of η^* in the case of European post-communist econ-

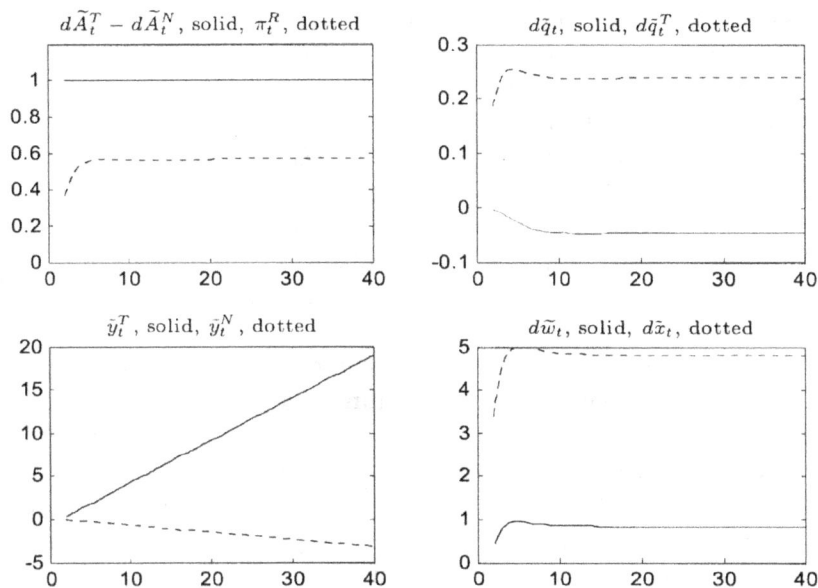

Units on a horizontal axis represent quarters, on a vertical axis percentage points.
Growth rates are displayed in annualized terms.

Figure 3
Balassa-Samuelson effect
PTM – version B
$\eta^* = 20$

omies. First, traditionally they exported little differentiated goods, e.g., agriculture products. Second, during the transition as a result of adoption of developed foreign technologies they started exporting highly differentiated products. However, those are manufactured by plants of foreign multinational firms, which usually produce the same product varieties in these countries as in any other countries. Hence, the majority of export products of European post-communist countries are still very similar to foreign products, and the main source of their imperfect substitutability is not variety but transportation and distribution costs.

One more remark related to market segmentation. To simplify the exposition I did not discuss the possibility of PTM with producer currency pricing (PCP), but it is possible to show that in the present framework it provides practically the same results as version B. As a consequence, I would rather not take sides in the LCP vs. PCP debate since both approaches can be consistent with the BS effect.[18] PCP can be applied without the assumption of price discrimination. Moreover, in most cases PCP is applied without PTM, which is equivalent to applying version A. The reason for this is that the arguments of the supporters of PCP remain valid without PTM. However, my results point out that if one wants to capture the particularities of emerging markets, then the PCP approach cannot be applied without the assumption of international price discrimination.

As was discussed in section 2.1, in European post-communist countries the observed long-run appreciation of the CPI-based real exchange rate is only partly caused by dual inflation; the long-run appreciation of the external real exchange rate also lies behind this phenomenon. The presented model is not able to reproduce the long-run appreciation of the external real exchange rate.[19]

To explain this phenomenon it seems necessary to relax the assumption of constant quality, or fixed structure of goods in the model. García Solanes, Flores, and Portero (2005) provide indirect evidence that increasing demand for tradables due to their improving quality results in appreciation of the external real exchange rate in new member states of the European Union. Broda and Weinstein (2004) demonstrate that in the U.S. increasing variety of goods is not properly captured by the statistical system, hence the rise of tradable price index is overestimated by 1.2 percent per year. This finding suggests that the appreciation of the external real exchange rate in European post-communist countries can partly be explained by measurement errors as well.

4.2   The Adjustment of the Relative Price of Non-tradables to Tradables

As discussed in section 2.1 and displayed in Table 1, according to most of the estimations of Coricelli and Jazbec (2001), Halpern and Wyplosz (2001), Égert (2002), and Égert, Drine, Lommatzsch, and Rault (2002), in the long-run the magnitude of the relative price of non-tradables to tradables $(\tilde{P}_t^R)$ is significantly smaller than that of the sectoral productivity differential $\tilde{A}_t^T - \tilde{A}_t^N$. In addition, Halpern and Wyplosz found that the short-run adjustment of the relative price was very slow.

It is difficult to explain these facts by models of the traditional approach. Applying classical assumptions to the present model,[20] it is easy to show that the relative price is determined by

$$\tilde{P}_t^R = \frac{n_N}{n_T} \tilde{A}_t^T - \tilde{A}_t^N , \tag{26}$$

where n_T and n_N are the labor utilization parameters in the technological equation (11). If the tradable productivity process $\tilde{A}_t^T$ is dominant, then the only way to reproduce the aforementioned empirical long-run relationship is to assume that the tradable sector is more labor intensive than the non-tradable one. But this is counterfactual. In addition, the above formula implies instant adjustment of the relative price to the productivity differential.

In this section I show how the presence of decreasing returns, which can be rationalized as the limiting case of the firm-specific-investments model of Altig, Christiano, Eichenbaum, and Linde (2005) and Woodford (2005), helps to explain the above empirical findings, even if $n_N \geq n_T$. For expositional simplicity, I assume that $n_N = n_T$. Combine sectoral sticky price equations represented by formula (20), and for expositional simplicity assume that $\xi_T = \xi_N = \xi$ and $\vartheta_T = \vartheta_N = \vartheta$. Then the inflation differential $\pi_t^R = \pi_t^T - \pi_T^N$ is determined by

$$\pi_t^R - \vartheta\pi_{t-1}^R = \beta E_t[\pi_{t+1}^R - \vartheta\pi_t^R] + \frac{\xi}{1-\alpha}(\tilde{A}_t^T - \tilde{A}_t^N) \tag{27}$$

$$+\frac{\xi\alpha}{1-\alpha}\left(\tilde{c}_t^N - \frac{c^T\tilde{c}_t^T + x\tilde{x}_t}{c^T + x}\right) - \xi\tilde{P}_t^R.$$

Terms $\tilde{c}_t^N$, $\tilde{c}_t^T$, and $\tilde{x}_t$ appear in the above equation, due to decreasing returns to scale. In the constant-returns-to-scale version of the present model, i.e., when $\alpha = 0$, only the productivity factors $\tilde{A}_t^T$, $\tilde{A}_t^N$ and the relative price $\tilde{P}_t^R$ would influence the evolution of the inflation differential.

Relative price adjustment in the presence of sticky prices is definitely slower than in flexible price models of the traditional approach represented by formula (26). Obviously, speed of adjustment of $\tilde{P}_t^R$ depends on the magnitude of parameter ξ. The smaller ξ is, the slower is the adjustment process. However, nominal rigidities without decreasing returns are not sufficient to reproduce the empirical estimates, as the simulation exercise belonging to Figure 4 demonstrates. The figure plots the adjustment process of the relative price to the sectoral productivity differential: it displays the fraction of the relative price to the productivity differential, i.e., $\tilde{P}_t^R/(\tilde{A}_t^T - \tilde{A}_t^N)$. In the simulation exercise I apply the same productivity process as previously, and use version B with $\eta^* = 20$, but I assume that $\alpha = 0$, i.e., technology exhibits constant returns to scale. Hence, terms $\tilde{c}_t^N$, $\tilde{c}_t^T$ and $\tilde{x}_t$ are missing from formula (27). To compare simulation results with empirical estimates I calculated the OLS regression

$$\tilde{P}_t^R = \rho(\tilde{A}_t^T - \tilde{A}_t^N) + u_t$$

using the simulated ten-year-long time series. The obtained OLS coefficient ρ represents the empirical "long-run" estimates of the studied relationship. The magnitude of the OLS coefficient ρ is also displayed

$$\tilde{P}_t^R / (\tilde{A}_t^T - \tilde{A}_t^N), \text{ dotted, } \rho, \text{ solid}$$

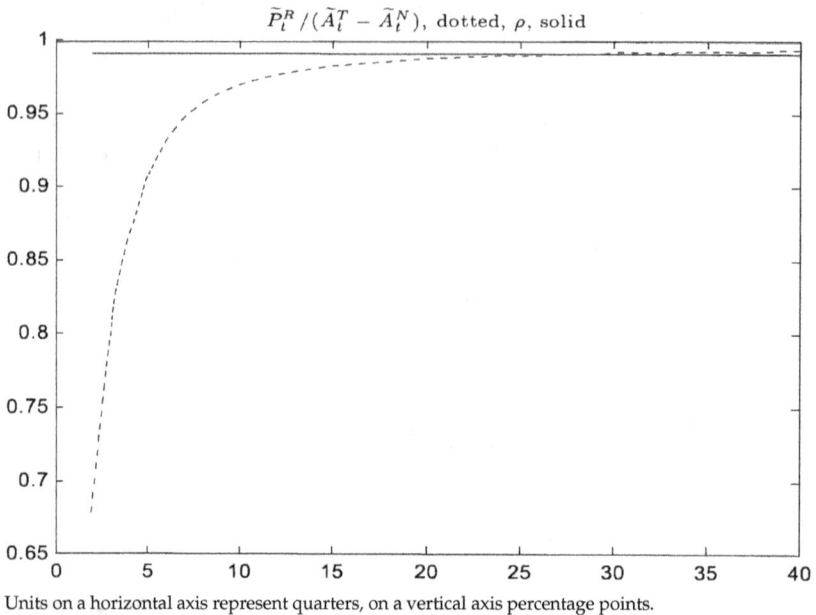

Units on a horizontal axis represent quarters, on a vertical axis percentage points.

Figure 4
Adjustment of the relative price of non-tradables to tradables
PTM – version B, constant returns to scale, $\eta^* = 20$

in the figure. Figure 4 reveals that although the adjustment of $\tilde{P}_t^R$ is not instant, ρ is nearly equal to 1. However, with one exception the empirical estimates are significantly smaller than this.

In the presence of decreasing returns to scale the adjustment process becomes slower and incomplete. First, as formula (21) reveals, if $\alpha > 0$, then ξ becomes smaller than in the constant-returns-to-scale case, which slows down the adjustment process. Second, terms $\tilde{c}_t^N$, $\tilde{c}_t^T$, and $\tilde{x}_t$ in the real marginal cost function triggers a feedback effect. As $\tilde{A}_t^T$ increases π_t^R and $\tilde{P}_t^R$ start increasing as well. As a consequence, the demand for $\tilde{c}_t^T$ and $\tilde{x}_t$ will rise and for $\tilde{c}_t^N$ will decrease. But according to formula (27) this change of demand will decrease the rise of π_t^R and $\tilde{P}_t^R$, hence the adjustment process will be slower. Third, the sectoral consumption and export terms make the adjustment incomplete, since the long-run rise of productivity in the tradable sector results in a long-run rise of tradable consumption and exports, see Figures 1–3. Hence, formula (27) implies that sectoral price differential will not converge to productivity differential.

Figure 5 illustrates this. In this simulation exercise I used the original decreasing-returns-to-scale ($\alpha > 0$) form of version B with $\eta^* = 20$. The

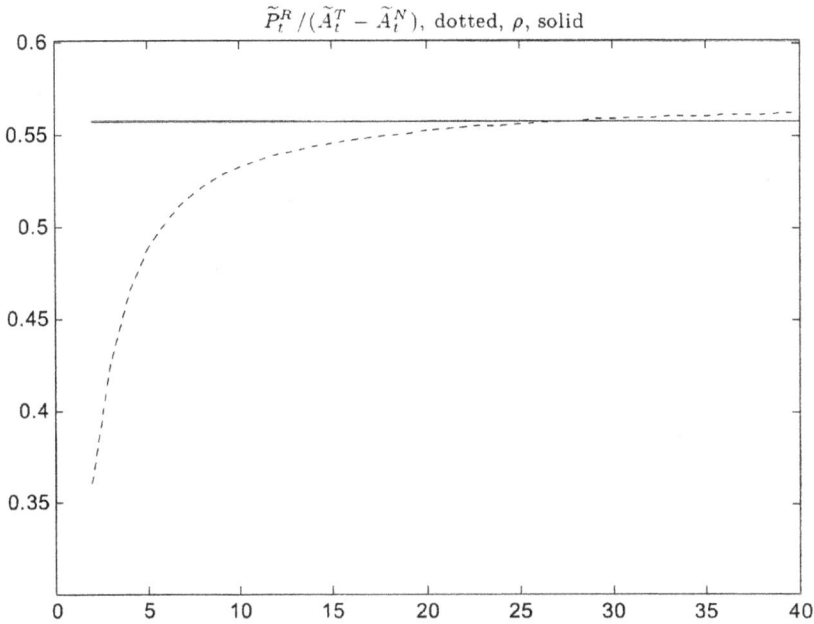

Figure 5
Adjustment of the relative price of non-tradables to tradables
PTM – version B, benchmark economy, $\eta^* = 20$

figure reveals that now the adjustment is slower and $\rho = 0.56$, which is in line with empirical estimates.

In summary, although both flexible price models and sticky price models with constant returns to scale can roughly capture the relationship between sectoral price and productivity differentials, they fail to reproduce the exact empirical magnitudes. The presence of decreasing returns to scale, which can be rationalized by the coexistence of frictions in capital accumulation and nominal rigidities, helps to explain the observed phenomena.

5. Conclusions

This paper has reviewed how models of the new open economy macroeconomics (NOEM) can explain the permanent dual inflation and the accompanying appreciation of the CPI-based real exchange rate often observed in emerging markets.

The coexistence of dual inflation and CPI-based real appreciation is usually explained by the BS effect, i.e., by the faster productivity growth in the tradable sector. Traditionally, the BS effect is derived from models with flexible prices and internationally homogenous tradable goods markets. On the other hand, NOEM models assume sticky prices and/or wages and heterogeneous goods markets. The traditional approach focuses on the determinants of the internal real exchange rate, while NOEM emphasizes the importance of the external real exchange rate.

It was shown that a NOEM model can simultaneously guarantee the strong comovement of the nominal and real exchange rates and can generate the BS effect only if there is pricing to market in the model.

The study also investigates how the presence of decreasing returns to scale, which can be rationalized by the coexistence of nominal rigidities and frictions in capital accumulation, modifies the effects of asymmetric productivity growth on dual inflation and the external real exchange rate. The paper demonstrated that decreasing-returns-to-scale features help to explain the slow and incomplete adjustment of the relative price of non-tradables to tradables observable in post-communist European countries.

Although it was not studied in this paper, it is worth mentioning here that decreasing returns to scale can also explain the role of demand factors in generating dual inflation as documented in Arratibel, Rodríguez-Palenzuela, and Thiman (2002) and López-Salido, Restoy, and Vallés (2005).

Acknowledgements

This paper was presented at the *NBER International Seminar on Macroeconomics* held 17–18 June, 2005 at Magyar Nemzeti Bank (Central Bank of Hungary). I would like to thank my discussants, Richard Clarida and Refet S. Gürkaynak. I am also grateful to Péter Benczúr, Giancarlo Corsetti, Chris Pissarides, Philip Lane, David López-Salido, Hugo Rodríguez Mendizábal, and János Vincze. All errors are, of course, my own.

Notes

1. On the Balassa-Samuelson effect see Obstfeld and Rogoff (1996, chapter 4).

2. The examined countries were Armenia, Azerbaijan, Belarus, Bulgaria, Croatia, Czech Republic, Estonia, Hungary, Kazakhstan, Kyrgyzstan, Latvia, Lithuania, Poland, Romania, Russia, Slovakia, Slovenia, Ukraine, and Uzbekistan.

3. The countries in the sample were the Czech Republic, Estonia, Hungary, Latvia, Lithuania, Poland, Russia, Romania, and Slovenia.

4. The examined countries are the Czech Republic, Hungary, Poland, Slovakia, and Slovenia.

5. The studied countries are Croatia, the Czech Republic, Estonia, Hungary, Latvia, Lithuania, Poland, Slovakia, and Slovenia.

6. The examined countries and the length of the data set: the Czech Republic (1994–2001), Hungary (1992–2001), Poland (1990–2001), Slovakia (1995–2000), and Slovenia (1992–2001).

7. Since reliable estimates of total factor productivity were not available, due to the lack of capital stock data, they used labor productivity measures.

8. In their paper they studied the inflation processes in ten European post-communist countries. Their results support the existence of dual inflation in these countries. However, according to their estimations a positive productivity shock negatively influences the inflation rate in the non-tradable sector.

9. Diebold, Husted, and Rush (1991) and Lothian and Taylor (1996) using long annual time series of different currencies found much more persistent real-exchange-rate shocks than Chari, Kehoe, and McGrattan (2002). It is difficult to explain their findings purely by nominal rigidities. Rogoff (1996) refers to this phenomenon as the "*PPP puzzle*." Engel and Morley (2001) built an empirical model, which may help to resolve this puzzle.

10. Hornok, Jakab, Reppa, and Villányi (2002) tried to perform econometric estimations on very short time series and the half-time they found is approximately 2.8 years. On the other hand, Darvas (2001) using the data of the Czech Republic, Hungary, Poland, and Slovenia found very short, less than one year, half-lives. But in the studied time periods narrow-band crawling peg regimes were typical in these countries, which may explain his results.

11. Although it is rarely studied in the literature, there is a third logical possibility, namely PTM with producer currency pricing. For the sake of clear presentation, I omit discussion of this case.

12. Thus, I apply the approach of McCallum and Nelson (2001), Smets and Wouters (2002), and Laxton and Pesenti (2003), who consider imports as a production input.

13. Since the government's budget is balanced, the tax/transfer represented by τ is compensated by T_t lump-sum tax/transfer variable in equation (2). In the present model the only role of τ is to simplify steady-state calculations, see the Appendix.

14. In this model α is not equal to capital's share in GDP since one has to subtract the value of imports from the value of total output to obtain GDP.

15. In their study they interpret inflation persistence differently from the approach I use. They use the model of Galí and Gertler (2000) and assume that each firm updates its price in a given period by probability $1 - \gamma$. Hence, according to the law of large numbers in a given period $1 - \gamma$ fraction of the firms change their prices. But only $1 - \vartheta$ fraction of the price setters choose their prices in an optimal forward-looking manner, the rest update their prices according to the past inflation rate. If $\beta = 1$, then the approach I use and the one used by Galí and Gertler coincides, if $\vartheta_s = \vartheta/\gamma$ and $(1 - \gamma_s)^2 \, \gamma_s^{-1} = (1 - \vartheta)(1 - \gamma)^2 \gamma^{-1}$, $s = T$, N. Although in our case $\beta \neq 1$, as an approximation I used the above mentioned formula to determine the values of γ_s and ϑ_s.

16. The speed of the pass-through of the nominal exchange rate to domestic CPI, a key issue both in academics and policy applications, is also related to the autocorrelation of the CPI-based real exchange rate.

17. This contradicts the simulation results of Chari, Kehoe, and McGrattan (2002), who found weaker simulated autocorrelations. However, Benigno (2004) demonstrated that if monetary policy is described by a rule with inertia, and the foreign and home country are asymmetric in such a way that monetary shocks result in terms of trade changes, then the required persistence can be attained by the model. These conditions are fulfilled in my model.

18. LCP vs. PCP is one of the most important undecided debates in the NOEM literature, since the choice of the optimal exchange rate is not independent of this problem. One can read pro LCP arguments in Engel (2002a, 2002b). Obstfeld (2001, 2002) and Obstfeld and Rogoff (2000a) present arguments supporting the PCP approach. Two recent studies on this topic are Bergin (2004), which provides evidence supporting LCP, and Koren, Szeidl, and Vincze (2004) with findings reinforcing PCP.

19. As it is shown in an extended version of the present study, see Világi (2005), applying Woodford's (2005) firms-specific-investments model can explain initial appreciation of the external real exchange rate due to initial bias of investments demand for tradables. However, it cannot account for its long run appreciation.

20. Flexible price setting, internationally homogeneous goods and capital markets.

References

Adolfson, M., S. Laseén, J. Lindé, and M. Villani. 2005. "Bayesian Estimation of an Open Economy DSGE Model with Incomplete Pass-Through." Sveriges Riksbank Working Paper no. 179.

Altig D., L.J. Christiano, M. Eichenbaum, and J. Linde. 2005. "Firm-Specific Capital, Nominal Rigidities and the Business Cycle." NBER Working Paper no. 11034. Cambridge, MA: National Bureau of Economic Research.

Arratibel, O., D. Rodríguez–Palenzuela, and C. Thiman. 2002. "Inflation Dynamics and Dual Inflation in Accession Countries: A "New Keynesian Perspective." European Central Bank Working Paper no. 132.

Balassa, B. 1964. "The Purchasing Power Doctrine: a Reappraisal" *Journal of Political Economy* 72: 584–596.

Benigno, G. 2004. "Real Exchange Rate Persistence and Monetary Policy Rules." *Journal of Monetary Economics* 51: 473–502.

Benigno, G., and C. Thoenissen. 2002. "Equilibrium Exchange Rates and Supply-Side Performance." Bank of England Working Paper no. 156.

Bergin, P.R. 2004. "How Well Can the New Open Economy Macroeconomics Explain the Exchange Rate and Current Account?" NBER Working Paper no. 10356. Cambridge, MA: National Bureau of Economic Research.

Betts, C., and M. Devereux. 1998. "Exchange Rate Dynamics in a Model of Pricing to Market." *Journal of International Economics* 47: 569–598.

Broda, C., and D.E. Weinstein. 2004. "Globalization and the Gains from Variety." NBER Working Paper no. 10314. Cambridge, MA: National Bureau of Economic Research.

Calvo, G. 1983. "Staggered Price Setting in a Utility Maximizing Framework." *Journal of Monetary Economics* 12: 383–398.

Calvo, G., and C. Reinhart. 2002. "Fear of Floating." *Quarterly Journal of Economics* 117(2): 379–408.

Chari, V.V., P.J. Kehoe, and E.R. McGrattan. 2002. "Can Sticky Price Models Generate Volatile and Persistent Real Exchange Rates?" Federal Reserve Bank of Minneapolis Research Department Staff Report 277.

Christiano, L.J., M. Eichenbaum, and C.L. Evans. 2001. "Nominal Rigidities and the Effects of a Shock to Monetary Policy." NBER Working Paper no. 8403. Cambridge, MA: National Bureau of Economic Research.

Clarida, R., and J. Galí. 1994. "Sources of Real Exchange rate Fluctuations: How Important are Nominal Shocks?" *Carnegie Rochester Conference Series on Public Policy* 41: 1–56.

Coricelli, F., and B. Jazbec. 2001. "Real Exchange Rate Dynamics in Transition Economies." CEPR Discussion Paper no. 2869.

Darvas, Z. 2001. "Exchange Rate Pass Through and Real Exchange Rate in the EU Candidate Countries." Discussion Paper of the Economic Research Centre of the Deutsche Bundesbank 10/01.

De Gregorio, J., and H.C. Wolf. 1994. "Terms of Trade, Productivity and the Real Exchange Rate." NBER Working Paper no. 4807. Cambridge, MA: National Bureau of Economic Research.

Diebold, F.X., S. Husted, and M. Rush. 1991. "Real Exchange Rate under the Gold Standard." *Journal of Political Economy* 99: 1252–1271.

Égert, B. 2002. "Investigating the Balassa-Samuelson Hypothesis in Transition: Do We Understand What We See?" Bank of Finland Discussion Papers 2002/6.

Égert, B., I. Drine, K. Lommatzsch, and C. Rault. 2002. "The Balassa-Samuelson Effect in Central and Eastern-Europe: Myth or Reality?" William Davidson Working Paper no. 483.

Engel, C. 1999. "Accounting for U.S. Real Exchange Rate Changes." *Journal of Political Economy* 107: 507–538.

Engel, C. 2002a. "The Responsiveness of Consumer Prices to Exchange Rates and Implications for Exchange-Rate Policy: A Survey of a Few Recent New Open-Economy Macro Models." NBER Working Paper no. 8725. Cambridge, MA: National Bureau of Economic Research.

Engel, C. 2002b. "Expenditure Switching and Exchange Rate Policy." NBER Working Paper no. 9016. Cambridge, MA: National Bureau of Economic Research.

Engel, C., and J.C. Morley. 2001. "The Adjustment of Prices and the Adjustment of the Exchange Rate." NBER Working Paper no. 8550. Cambridge, MA: National Bureau of Economic Research.

Galí, J., and M. Gertler. 2000. "Inflation Dynamics: A Structural Econometric Analysis." NBER Working Paper no. 7551. Cambridge, MA: National Bureau of Economic Research.

Galí, J., M. Gertler, and J.D. López-Salido. 2001. "European Inflation Dynamics." NBER Working Paper no. 8218. Cambridge, MA: National Bureau of Economic Research.

García Solanes, J., F. Torrejón Flores, and I. Sancho Portero. 2005. "Más allá de la Hipótesis de Balassa–Samuelson en los Países de la Ampliación Europea: El Sesgo de Calidad y la Segmentación de Mercados." Mimeo, Universidad de Murcia.

Halpern, L., and C. Wyplosz. 2001. "Economic Transformation and Real Exchange Rates in the 2000s: The Balassa-Samuelson Connection." In *Economic Survey of Europe 2001*, No. 1, Chapter 6. Geneva: United Nations Economic Commission for Europe.

Hornok, C., M.Z. Jakab, Z. Reppa, and K. Villányi. 2002. "Inflation Forecasting at the Magyar Memzeti Bank." Mimeo, Magyar Nemzeti Bank (Central Bank of Hungary).

Ito, T., P. Isard, and S. Symansky. 1997. "Economic Growth and Real Exchange Rate: An Overview of the Balassa-Samuelson Hypothesis in Asia." NBER Working Paper no. 5979. Cambridge, MA: National Bureau of Economic Research.

Ireland, P. 2004. "Technology Shocks in the New Keynesian Model." NBER Working Paper no. 10309. Cambridge, MA: National Bureau of Economic Research.

King, R.G., and S.T. Rebello. 1999. "Resuscitating Real Business Cycles." In J.B. Taylor and M. Woodford, eds., *Handbook of Macroeconomics* Vol. 1. Amsterdam: Elsevier Science B.V.

Koren, M., Á. Szeidl, and Vincze J. 2004. "Export Pricing in New Open Economy Macroeconomics: An Empirical Investigation." Mimeo, Harvard University and Corvinus University of Budapest.

Kovács M.A., ed. 2002. "On the Estimated Size of the Balassa-Samuelson Effect in Five Central and Eastern European Countries." MNB (Central Bank of Hungary) Working Paper no. 2002/5.

Laxton, D., and P. Pesenti. 2003. "Monetary Rules for Small, Open, Emerging Economies." NBER Working Paper no. 9568. Cambridge, MA: National Bureau of Economic Research.

López-Salido, D., F. Restoy, and J. Vallés. 2005. "Inflation Differentials in EMU: the Spanish Case." Banco de España, paper presented at the European Central Bank Workshop on *Monetary Policy Implications of Heterogeneity in a Currency Area*, 13 and 14 December, 2004, Frankfurt am Main.

Lothian, J.R., and M.P. Taylor. 1996. "Real Exchange Rate Behavior: The Recent Float from the Perspective of the Past Two Centuries." *Journal of Political Economy* 107: 507–538.

McCallum, B.T., and E. Nelson. 2001. "Monetary Policy for an Open Economy: An Alternative Framework with Optimizing Agents and Sticky Prices." NBER Working Paper no. 8175. Cambridge, MA: National Bureau of Economic Research.

Monacelli, T. 2004. "Into the Mussa Puzzle: Monetary Policy Regimes and the Real Exchange Rate in a Small Open Economy." *Journal of International Economics* 62: 191–217.

Mussa, M. 1986. "Nominal Exchange Regimes and the Behavior of Real Exchange Rates: Evidence and Implications." *Carnegie-Rochester Conference Series on Public Policy* 25:117–214.

Obstfeld, M. 2001. "International Macroeconomics: Beyond the Mundell-Fleming Model." NBER Working Paper no. 8369. Cambridge, MA: National Bureau of Economic Research.

Obstfeld, M. 2002. "Exchange Rate and Adjustment: Perspectives from the New Open Economy Macroeconomics." NBER Working Paper no. 9118. Cambridge, MA: National Bureau of Economic Research.

Obstfeld, M., and K. Rogoff. 1995. "Exchange Rate Dynamics Redux." *Journal of Political Economy* 103: 624–660.

Obstfeld, M., and K. Rogoff. 1996. *Foundations of International Macroeconomics.* Cambridge, MA: MIT Press.

Obstfeld, M., and K. Rogoff. 2000a. "New Directions for Stochastic Open Economy Models." *Journal of International Economics* 50(1): 117–153.

Obstfeld, M., and K. Rogoff. 2000b. "The Six Major Puzzles in International Macroeconomics: is There a Common Cause?" In B. Bernanke and K. Rogoff, eds., *NBER Macroeconomics Annual.* Cambridge, MA: MIT Press.

Rogoff, K. 1996. "The Purchasing Power Parity Puzzle." *Journal of Economic Literature* 34(2): 647–668.

Samuelson, P.A. 1964. "Theoretical Notes on Trade Problems." *Review of Economics and Statistics* 46: 145–54.

Smets, F., and R. Wouters. 2002. "Openness, Imperfect Exchange Rate Pass-Through and Monetary Policy." *Journal of Monetary Economics* 49: 947–981.

Smets, F., and R. Wouters. 2003. "An Estimated Stochastic Dynamic General Equilibrium Model of the Euro Area." *Journal of the European Economic Association* 1: 1123–1175.

Uhlig, H. 1999. "A Toolkit for Analyzing Dynamic Stochastic Models Easily." In R. Marimon and A. Scott, eds., *Computational Methods for the Study of Dynamic Economies.* Oxford: Oxford University Press.

Világi, B. 2005. "Dual Inflation and the Real Exchange Rate in New Open Economy Macroeconomics. Available at <http://www.ecb.int/events/conferences/html/mpimphet.en.html>.

Woodford, M. 2003. *Interest and Prices: Foundations of a Theory of Monetary Policy.* Princeton, NJ: Princeton University Press.

Woodford, M. 2005. "Firm-Specific Capital and the New Keynesian Phillips Curve." NBER Working Paper no. 11149. Cambridge, MA: National Bureau of Economic Research.

Appendix

The Steady State

In this section the non-stochastic steady state of the benchmark model is described. Variables without time indices refer to their steady-state values.

In the steady state there is no difference between the two model versions, and there is no intra-household and intra-sector heterogeneity. Therefore the index *i* of firms are omitted to simplify the notations. The level of fixed capital stock used in the model is set to be equal to the steady state capital stock of the variable capital version of the model with zero depreciation rate and steady state level of investments.

It is assumed that $P = P^T = P^N = 1$. Then the demand equations of formula (4) imply that

$$c^T = a_T c, \quad c^N = a_N c. \tag{28}$$

Furthermore, it is assumed that $P^T x = e P^{m^*} m$. Hence,

$$GDP = a^T c^T + a^N c^N = c.$$

The real interest rate r is determined by

$$r = \frac{1}{\beta} - 1.$$

The values of τ is set in such a way that the markup is equal to 1,

$$1 - \tau = \frac{\theta}{\theta - 1}.$$

Then it is true for all sectors that the marginal product of capital is equal to r. Thus, equation (10) implies that

$$\kappa = \left(\frac{r}{\alpha}\right)^{\frac{1}{1-\alpha}},$$

where $\kappa = z^T/k^T = z^N/k^N$. Furthermore, equation (10) implies that

$$c^T + x = k^T \kappa^{1-\alpha}, \quad c^N = k^N \kappa^{1-\alpha}. \tag{29}$$

It is assumed that $w = W = eP^{m^*}$, then equation (12) implies that $w^z = w$. Since in each sector w^z is equal to the marginal product of z^s

$$w = (1 - \alpha)\kappa^{-\alpha}.$$

In the benchmark economy $w = 1.865$. Let us denote the exogenous exports/GDP ratio by s_x, and I set $s_x = 0.6$. Since $x = eP^{m^*} m$,

$$s_x = \frac{x}{c} = \frac{eP^{m^*} m}{c}. \tag{30}$$

It is assumed that in the benchmark economy $n_N = n_T = n$. Then the imports demand equation in formula (13) implies that

$$m = (1 - n)(z^T + z^N).$$

Then one can show that

$$m = (1 - n)\,\kappa(k^T + k^N) = (1 - n)\kappa k. \tag{31}$$

Using the previous expression for m and equation (30) yields

$$c = Kk, \tag{32}$$

where

$$K = eP^{m^*}(1 - n)\kappa s_x^{-1}.$$

By equation (29) one can similarly show that

$$k\kappa^{1-\alpha} = c + \delta k + x = eP^{m^*}(1 - n)\kappa s_x^{-1}k + eP^{m^*}(1 - n)\kappa k.$$

This implies that

$$n = 1 - \frac{\kappa^{1-\alpha}}{eP^{m^*}\kappa(1+s_x^{-1})}.$$

In the benchmark economy $n = 0.5$.

In the steady state the labor supply function of households takes the form

$$w = c^\sigma l^\varphi. \tag{33}$$

As for imports, one can derive a similar expression for labor:

$$l = n\kappa k. \tag{34}$$

Substituting equations (32) and (34) into equation (33) yields an expression for the capital stock:

$$k = [wK^{-\sigma}(n\kappa)^{-\varphi}]^{\frac{1}{\sigma+\varphi}}.$$

Using this expression one can calculate the steady-state value of the capital stock and investments. In the benchmark economy $k = 67.296$. Then using formula (32) yields the value of consumption, $c = 2.736$, and equation (34) provides the value of labor, $l = 0.88$.

Comment

Richard H. Clarida, Columbia University and NBER

We observe trend appreciations of CPI real exchange rates in rapidly growing economies. This is usually explained by more rapid productivity growth in the tradables sector, which pushes up the relative price of non-tradables, sometimes called "dual inflation." We also observe high frequency correlations between nominal exchange rates, CPI real exchange rates, and relative price of tradables. This is usually explained by imperfect substitutability among traded goods combined with sticky prices.

In a textbook Balassa-Samuelson model, the terms of trade are exogenous and thus not a function of tradables productivity. This can explain trend real appreciation. In a textbook Dornbusch model, prices are sticky and terms of trade endogenous but all goods are traded. This can explain high correlation between nominal, CPI real, and relative traded goods prices. However, if we add endogenous terms of trade to the Balassa-Samuelson framework, the same trend productivity that can explain "dual inflation" will also cause the terms of trade to worsen and thus offset or even reverse the appreciation of the CPI real exchange that we sought to explain in the first place. And of course, even if the CPI real exchange appreciates, it will move in the opposite direction of the relative price of tradables, the "external real exchange rate."

The objective of this paper is to see if a two sector small open economy optimizing model with sticky prices can simultaneously generate (1) trend real CPI appreciation in response to "real" shocks; and (2) high, positive correlation among nominal, CPI real, external real exchange rates in response to "nominal shocks." To do this, one needs at least two sectors, sticky prices, and at least two shocks, a supply shock and a nominal shock. There is a reason why the literature has tended to specialize in either sticky price models with only traded goods or flexible price models with non-traded goods but exogenous terms of trade—it is very hard to do both and solve in closed form. Thus, the paper must resort to simulation which is appropriate. That being said, I am not convinced that the basic story requires capital accumulation or pricing to market. I found the capital accumulation part of the model hard to understand. I also think the pricing to market version of the model is overly complex.

The model is a bit of hybrid—there is optimization at home for agents, but the monetary authority follows a crawling peg exchange rate target. Could one consider other monetary policy rules with inflation targeting? The author chooses the NOEM set up with imports as an intermediate input. In this framework a terms of trade deterioration is an adverse supply shock, which is realistic. But imported goods are also consumed directly, and thus a terms of trade decline lowers real income and thus demand. This effect would go the other way and is worth modeling since the model is being solved numerically anyway.

The model can generate a lot of persistent real exchange rates and a high correlation between real and nominal exchange rates. The model is better at matching these moments for low price elasticities of foreign demand η^* than for high elasticities. In response to faster productivity growth in tradables, the model can always generate dual inflation. However, for low values of η^*, it cannot generate appreciation of the real CPI exchange rate. The terms of trade effect swamps the dual inflation effect. For $\eta^* = 5$, it can generate real CPI appreciations, but not trend as real exchange rate ultimately depreciates. For very high $\eta^* = 15$, it can generate trend real CPI appreciations. However, even in this case, the model is not able to reproduce the trend appreciation of the external real exchange rate in response to a shift in the supply of tradables.

This is an important area for research, especially for central banks in small open economies with flexible exchange rates. It has implications for inflation targeting in open economies, and the results in this paper add to our knowledge in this area.

Comment

Refet S. Gürkaynak, Bilkent University and CEPR

1. Introduction

International finance is not a sui generis field just because there is an exchange rate floating around (forgive the pun). International finance is open economy macroeconomics and should be studied with the tools of macroeconomics. That open economy macroeconomics *is* macroeconomics was a motivating argument of the new open economy macroeconomics (NOEM) literature and this paper takes that point seriously.

The paper displays an impressive technical mastery and makes a nice contribution to the new open economy macroeconomics literature. It is also a quite complicated paper, using a lot of heavy machinery. In my discussion I will try to provide an intuitive overview of the paper while pointing out that the machinery sometimes obscures some labeling issues.

2. Definitions

We can distinguish between three conceptually different definitions of real exchange rates. First, there is the internal real exchange rate, the price of non-tradables relative to tradables. Defining this exchange rate does not require an open economy; it is a simple relative price. In the paper's notation this is given as

$$P_t^R = \frac{P_t^N}{P_t^T},$$

where P_t^R is the internal real exchange rate, P_t^N is the price of non-tradables and P_t^T is the price of tradables.

A second real exchange rate is the one newspapers usually refer to—relative prices of the consumption basket in the foreign country and the home country. This external real exchange rate is CPI based and uses the consumption basket which involves the prices of non-tradables as well the prices of tradables. This definition of the external real exchange rate is

$$q_t = \frac{e_t P_t^{F*}}{P_t},$$

where q_t is the CPI-based real exchange rate, P_t is the domestic price level, P_t^{F*} is the foreign price level and e_t is the nominal exchange rate.

Lastly, to abstract from the price differences of non-tradables in different countries, an alternative external real exchange rate can be defined as the relative price of the tradable good in the home and foreign countries

$$q_t^T = \frac{e_t P_t^{FT*}}{P_{t_t}^T},$$

where q_t^T is the external real exchange rate and P_t^{F*} is the price of the tradable good in the foreign country.

3. The Question

All three measures of the real exchange rate show significant time variation. The main question of the paper is, can we make sense of this using microfounded models?

The internal real exchange rate appreciates considerably in developing economies, i.e., non-tradables become relatively more expensive. (Note that this *dual inflation* need not be an open economy issue.) However, in open economies q_t and q_t^T also move around a lot, importantly with q_t^T being very highly correlated with e_t. That is, fluctuations in nominal exchange rates translate into fluctuations in the real external exchange rates. Is there a unifying framework that explains both of these?

4. The Answer

Two different strands of the literature provide answers to different parts of this question. First, the time variance in P_t^R and q_t are related to each other via the Balassa-Samuelson effect. To the extent that productivity in the tradables sector grows faster than that of non-tradables in developing economies, which seems to be the case, there will be dual inflation. Assuming that purchasing power parity (PPP) holds, the price (or the growth rate of the price) of the tradables in the two countries must be the same, thus relative deflation in the tradables sector in the home country will cause an appreciation of the nominal exchange rate which will cause an appreciation of the CPI-based real exchange rate (as non-tradables productivity is not improving at the rate of tradables').

On the other hand, the new open economy macroeconomics literature tackles the question of the correlation of the nominal exchange rate, e_t, and the real exchange rate, q_t^T. In a frictionless, flexible price world q_t^T should be unity. To allow it to deviate from this value and show time variation we need to introduce some frictions. The standard NOEM literature assumes price stickiness (following the New Keynesian macroeconomic models) to introduce this friction. In the limiting case of fixed prices P_t^T and $P_t^{FT^*}$ are constant and thus all movements of e_t are directly reflected in movements of q_t^T.

The problem with the above explanation is that these two answers are not mutually consistent. If PPP does not hold and productivity growth in tradables leads to dual inflation (relative deflation in tradables), the CPI based exchange rate will depreciate, not appreciate. Thus, to motivate the appreciation of the CPI based real exchange rate with dual inflation via the Balassa-Samuelson mechanism PPP is needed while PPP has to fail by definition to explain the variance of the external real exchange rate.

Purchasing power parity, of course, can fail at various degrees. In particular, the less substitutable the home and foreign tradables, the more scope there is for deviations from PPP and the more substitutable the two tradables, the more scope for the Balassa-Samuelson effect. It is important to note that imperfect substitutability of home and foreign tradables can simultaneously generate the Balassa-Samuelson effect and the positive covariance of nominal and real external exchange rates. Although this is qualitatively possible, Vilagi argues that the magnitudes observed in data cannot be matched by any degree of substitutability.

Vilagi's preferred solution is to introduce pricing to market (PTM) into the model. When PTM is possible, producers are able to price the same tradable good differently in different counties. To allow for this, the model is expanded into three sectors, non-tradables, domestic tradables, and export tradables. PPP holds for export tradables while PTM takes place in the domestic tradable goods market. This device helps explain both types of stylized facts as the nominal exchange rate still appreciates when productivity in the tradables sector improves (as PPP holds for some tradables), helping generate the Balassa-Samuelson effect and the nominal and real (external) exchange rates, q_t^T, are correlated as PPP fails for the domestic tradables.

While introducing PTM helps simultaneously replicate the two stylized facts, it seems that some of this is due to labeling changes. Introducing PTM comes with the introduction of a domestic tradable good, which, unlike the export tradable, is not internationally traded—hence PTM is possible. It is not all that clear to me how non-traded tradables differ from non-tradables.

In particular, the reason we care about the external real exchange rate (and not only the CPI based real exchange rate) is that we do not expect PPP to hold for non-tradables. In this model, the domestic tradables that are subject to PTM are included in the tradable definition and therefore enter the calculation of the external real exchange rate. It is the inclusion of these that generates the failure of PPP for the tradables, broadly defined.

An alternative argument would be to assert that we only expect PPP to hold for goods that are actually traded and to define the external real exchange rate only for the export goods. In this model, the traded goods still satisfy PPP (depending on substitutability) and the real exchange rate defined over these goods would not be correlated with the nominal exchange rate to the extent such correlation is present in the data. It therefore seems that part of the success of the model comes from labeling some non-traded (but not non-tradable) goods as tradable.

This paper over all is a fine contribution to the NOEM literature in that it makes an important observation about the internal and external real exchange rates and their relationship with nominal exchange rates and then provides an explanation of the stylized facts using a microfounded model. The paper provides a valuable service by coherently presenting the stylized facts and pointing out an important question, which will likely lead to more interest in the topic.

Trade Invoicing in the Accession Countries: Are They Suited to the Euro?

Linda S. Goldberg, *Federal Reserve Bank of New York and NBER*

1. Introduction

The accession countries to the euro area are increasingly binding their economic activity, external and internal, to the euro area countries. One aspect of this phenomenon concerns the currency invoicing of international trade transactions. There has been a substantial shift away from the use of the U.S. dollar by accession countries in international trade transactions. In this paper, I explore the theoretical drivers of optimal invoicing choices for exporters, highlighting the importance of the composition of goods in exports and imports, and the partner composition of these forms of trade. I explore whether accession country exporters, by invoicing in euros and thus closely aligning their trade with that of the rest of the euro area, are pursuing economically appropriate strategies. Perhaps some of the accession country export transactions are not as well suited to euro invoicing, leading producers with overly high euro shares in pricing to expose themselves to excessive risk in international markets.

The analysis draws on lessons from the theoretical model of Goldberg and Tille (2005), which presents the determinants of the relative importance of hedging motives and herding motives in currency invoicing (and exchange rate pass through) choices by exporters. This model motivates an empirical application to the accession countries. The model shows the role of macroeconomic volatility and industry composition in exporter pricing strategies, demonstrating that optimal currency invoicing strategies consist of a mix of hedging considerations and herding. Macroeconomic volatility considerations have been emphasized in a range of papers, from Giovannini (1988) through recent contributions by Devereux, Engel, and Storegaard (2004), Oi, Otani, and Shirota (2004), and Engel (2005). By introducing an explicit role for elasticities of substitution in demand and decreasing returns to scale in pricing, Bacchetta and van Wincoop (2005) and Goldberg and Tille (2005) [GT] show that macroeconomic volatility may mainly play a role in pricing and currency invoicing decisions for producers of differentiated products.[1] Instead, they stress that industry structure, emphasized early on by McKinnon (1979), is the key determinant of how much herding occurs in pricing and currency invoicing decisions. Producers in highly competitive industries, and producers facing a high degree of decreasing returns to scale in production, may optimally mimic the pricing strategies of their competitors in markets in which their goods are sold. This leads to herding in invoice currency selection, while not explicitly seeking to identify which currencies will be used in such herding. Various strategies have been offered elsewhere to pin down the equilibrium choice of herding currency. One example is through introducing "network externalities" in foreign exchange markets interacting with transaction costs in securities markets, as in Portes and Rey (1998). Using reasonable ranges of parameters, GT show that this herding activity could be much more important in decision making than the influence of hedging and macroeconomic volatility.

These considerations are applied to the trade transactions of 11 countries aspiring to join the euro area: Bulgaria, Cyprus, the Czech Republic, Estonia, Hungary, Latvia, Lithuania, Malta, Poland, Slovakia, and Slovenia. A simple picture drawn from GT motivates the focus of the paper, which explores the extent to which accession country exporters use dollars, euros, or other currencies in invoicing their international trade transactions. Using mostly data for 2002, GT compared the actual share of dollar use in invoicing country exports to what might be "expected" purely on the basis of trade with the United States and the composition of country trade. The pattern of this relationship for a broad sample of countries is shown in Figure 1.

Figure 1 works with the assumption that all exports to the United States and all exports of "referenced priced" and "organized-exchange" traded goods ("RW goods") to other countries are invoiced in dollars, the standard currency for pricing most of these transactions. If this assumption were true, a country would have its observations lie along the 45 degree line in this figure. Observe that many of the accession countries have invoicing patterns above the 45 degree line, suggesting that they have fewer exports invoiced in dollars compared with what would be predicted by this simple metric. Estonia, Slovenia, Slovakia, Hungary, and the Czech Republic all fit this description. The exception

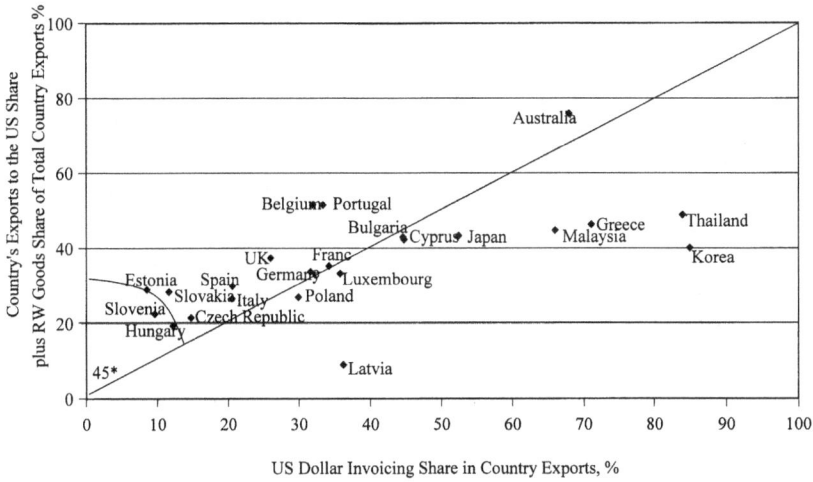

Source: DOTS and various national sources.
Euro-area country data, with the exception of Italy data, refer to extra-euro area trade and invoicing.
Reproduced from Figure 5, Goldberg and Tille (2005). 2002 data used.

Figure 1
Vehicle currency use of the dollar and "commodity" type exports

is Latvia which, like Greece, had considerably more use of dollars in invoicing exports than expected purely on the basis of Latvia's trade with the United States and exports of highly substitutable goods.

What are the consequences of exporters making invoice currency choices that are inappropriate, given observed industry features and the volatility of macroeconomic conditions? These choices would lead to lower expected profits and more volatile profits than are optimal. As a hypothetical, consider the case of an accession country exporter invoicing in euros while competitors in euro area countries or in the United States are invoicing in dollars. Suppose as well that there is a high degree of product substitutability between the exporter's goods and its competitors' goods. With fluctuations in exchange rates, the exporter's relative price will vary ex post, even if ex ante the common currency expected prices of the goods were identical.

An unanticipated dollar appreciation against the euro would lead the exporter to experience a sharp increase in demand for its goods. Given decreasing returns to scale, the exporter would also have an increase in his marginal costs. The net effect on expected profitability will depend on the elasticities of substitution, the returns to scale in his production function, and a mix of covariances between the revenue and cost conditions he faces. In the reverse case of an unexpected dollar depreciation against the euro, the exporter's goods are ex post excessively expensive, leading to substitution away from his products.

This example shows that, even in cases where accession country exporters are overwhelmingly trading with euro area countries, dollars may still be more appropriate for invoicing trade with the euro area for those goods on which dollars are vehicle currencies for pricing. Indeed, exporters in euro area countries use dollars for invoicing similar products even on trade transactions within the euro area, as recently discussed by the European Central Bank (ECB 2005).

Below, to explore these questions for the accession countries I start with the model of Goldberg and Tille (2005). After briefly presenting the theoretical motivation (section 2), I present empirical detail on the direction of trade of accession countries with respect to euro area countries, the rest of the European Union, the United States markets, and other "dollar bloc" countries, followed by detail on the product composition of accession country exports and imports. For this work the Rauch (1999) indices, constructed to highlight the role of types of networks used in goods market transactions, are applied to detailed accession country export and import data. This application produces shares of goods in trade that are best described as differentiated, referenced priced, or priced in and traded on organized exchanges. Organized exchange trade goods, such as commodities, are assumed to be highly substitutable and the theory predicts that producers of such goods should herd in their invoicing choices. In practice, the dollar typically has been the currency used in such herding, at least in post war transactions. Conceptually, as long as this remains the case, the share of these types of goods in exports is treated as a lower bound on dollar invoicing.

The paper's focus next turns to the second consideration: the role of hedging in optimal invoicing decisions by exporters. The theory predicts that optimal hedges should cover expected shocks to producer marginal costs. In other words, for stable expected profits, a producer should invoice in a currency that yields positive revenue shocks at the same time that the producer faces high marginal costs, either because wages fluctuate or because aggregate demand fluctuates in an environment of non-constant returns to scale. An invoice currency should be selected for hedging purposes if it provides the highest covariance between an exchange rate (on the producer export revenue) and marginal costs, so that it helps limit demand for a product at precisely the time when marginal costs of production are high. Thus, revenue will be high just at the times that marginal costs are high. For each country, we explore whether the dollar or the euro better suits this objective in export transactions to the United States, to the euro area, or to the rest of the European Union.

A number of interesting observations are generated based on this analysis. First, there is considerable cross-country heterogeneity in the portion of exports invoiced in dollars versus in euros. On average, in 2000 to 2002 more than half of the exports of accession countries were invoiced in euros, while the average share of exports invoiced in dollars was closer to 25 percent. Euro use has been increasing, with some of this euro gain matched by declines in dollar use in export invoicing. Indeed, dollar use as an invoicing currency has declined even for some countries that initially had surprisingly low use of dollars. On accession country exports to countries other than the United States and the euro area, euro invoicing is roughly 37 percent, a lower share than observed for euro area countries.[2]

The United States is not a major export destination for the goods of most accession countries, typically receiving less than 5 percent of these exports. Most of the accession country exports go to the euro area and the rest of Europe. Between 60 and 85 percent of the total exports of accession countries are characterized as differentiated products. While the remaining exports are often in reference priced goods, for example paper, some countries also export substantial amounts of organized exchange traded goods like copper and aluminum. Much of the latter types of exports have dollar pricing worldwide. Controlling both for the structure of partners in trade and the composition of traded goods products, some accession countries use euros more heavily and use dollars less frequently in invoicing than do euro area countries.

Examination of the optimal currencies in invoicing for hedging purposes also yields interesting conclusions for accession country exports to the United States, the euro area, the rest of the European Union, and Asia. The covariance analysis for this work compares the desirability of invoicing in euros versus dollars in exports to each destination market. In most cases, neither the dollar nor the euro are appropriate choices for hedging the demand and marginal cost risks to profits from exporter perspectives. Lithuania significantly favored the dollar as a hedging currency prior to 2000, but this relationship then disappeared. Since 2000, neither the dollar nor euro was theoretically a strong hedge, except in the limited case of Hungarian exports to Asia, which would have favored the euro. Based on hedging motives, exporters in accession countries should be indifferent to the euro or dollar as an invoice currency choice on their exports to Europe, the United States, and Asia.

Overall, if the dollar is the key vehicle currency for many countries on reference priced and exchange traded goods, our results suggest that some accession countries may have moved further toward the euro in trade invoicing than is potentially optimal. This argument relies on an assumption that the dollar has retained a central role as a vehicle currency in the goods that are reference priced and traded on organized exchanges. The validity of this assumption, and its relation to exchange rate regimes, is discussed in the concluding remarks of section 4.

2.   A Three-Country / Three Currency Model of Invoice Currencies

The theoretical exposition closely follows the model of Goldberg and Tille (2005) [GT] on currency choice for trade invoicing. As exposited above, GT develop the interaction between industry features and macroeconomic variability in a new open-economy macro model with three countries and price rigidities, building on both Devereux, Engel, and Storegaard [DES] (2004) and Bacchetta and van Wincoop (2005). While GT do not derive a general equilibrium version of the DES model, they extend the existing theory of invoice currency selection in several critical dimensions. First, GT move from the DES two-country / two-currency world to a three-country / three-currency one, allowing for invoicing in a vehicle currency that belongs neither to the exporter nor the importer home market. Second, GT develop the contrasting roles in optimal invoice currency selection of *industry characteristics*, such as the substitutability between competitors' goods, and *macro-economic factors*, such as business cycle and exchange rate volatility. The firm's incentive to limit the fluctuations of its relative price by choosing a trade invoicing strategy close to that of its competitors leads to a type of "herding" behavior in invoice currency choices for the exporters of relatively homogeneous products. This feature is also emphasized in Bacchetta and van Wincoop (2005). Third, GT introduce decreasing returns to scale in production, so that increases in output increase marginal costs even when wages are not responsive.

Overall, GT conclude that macroeconomic variability is an important consideration in optimal invoicing only for trade in differentiated products. The degree of macroeconomic volatility needed to disturb an invoicing status quo for trade in more homogeneous products would need to be exceptionally large. The theoretical prediction is that—even within a country where all economic agents face the same degree of macroeconomic volatility—different producers will make different invoice currency choices. Moreover, an exporter with two distinct trading partners is more likely to use distinct currencies on invoicing his exports to these distinct partners when his production is in differentiated goods and when he faces lower levels of decreasing returns to scale in production.

2.1 The Model Set-up

Before turning to the empirical implementation for accession countries, this section presents an abridged version of GT. An exporting firm is assumed to have to post a price for its goods before knowing the realization of various shocks affecting the economy. The exporter is located in country e, produces a brand z, and sells her goods to the destination country d. Goods are produced using a technology with decreasing returns to scale:

$$Y_{ed}(z) = (\alpha)^{-1}[H_{ed}(z)]^\alpha, \qquad 0 < \alpha \leq 1 \tag{1}$$

where $Y_{ed}(z)$ is the output of z, $H_{ed}(z)$ is the labor input, and α is the returns to scale parameter. The firm faces the following demand in destination country d:

$$Y_d(z) - [P_{ed}(z)/P_d]^{-\lambda}C_d \tag{2}$$

where C_d is the total demand for brands of the relevant sector in country d, $P_{ed}(z)$ is the price, in country d currency, of the brand z produced in country e, and P_d is the price index, in country d currency, across all brands of the relevant sector sold in country d. $\lambda > 1$ is the elasticity of substitution between the various brands. According to (2), the demand for a specific brand depends on its price, relative to the prices of other brands in the sector, and on the strength of overall demand in the destination market.

The exporter producing brand z sets its price in currency k, $P^k_{ed}(z)$, before the realization of the shocks affecting the economy. The currency of invoicing can be the currency of the country in which the exporter is located ($k = e$), the currency of the country of destination ($k = d$), a third vehicle currency ($k = v$), or a combination of these three currencies. The exporter's price is set in currency k to maximize expected profits represented by (3):

$$\Pi_{ed}^k(z)= ED_e\left\{ S_{ek}P_{ed}^k(z)\left[\frac{S_{ek}P_{ed}^k(z)}{S_{ed}P_d}\right]^{-\lambda} C_d - W_e(\alpha)^{\frac{1}{\alpha}}\left[\left[\frac{S_{ek}P_{ed}^k(z)}{S_{ed}P_d}\right]^{-\lambda} C_d\right]^{\frac{1}{\alpha}}\right\} \quad (3)$$

where S_{ek} is the exchange rate between currency e and currency k, in terms of units of currency e per unit of currency k so that an increase corresponds to a depreciation of currency e. D_e is the state-specific discount factor at which profits are evaluated, and W_e is the nominal wage. With its price set in currency k, the unit revenue for the exporter in currency e is $S_{ek}P_{ed}^k(z)$. Similarly, the price in currency d paid by consumers in the destination country is $[S_{ed}]^{-1}S_{ek}P_{ed}^k(z)$.

2.2 Optimal Invoice Currency Selection

Maximized profits are obtained through the exporter choice of the currency k in which her goods are invoiced. In making this selection, the exporter regards all the other variables in (3), such as the destination market demand, exporter wages, aggregate prices in the destination market and the bilateral exchange rate as exogenous to her invoicing decision, with lower case variables denoting log deviations from the steady state ($x = \ln X - \ln X_{ss}$). Without constraining the exporter to invoice entirely in any currency e, d, or v, the invoicing decision is a choice of weights of the three available currencies in the invoicing currency basket k. Specifically, the weights of currencies d and v in the invoicing of exports to country d are β_d^d and β_d^v respectively, with the weight of currency e being $1 - \beta_d^d - \beta_d^v$, and with the sum of the weights bounded between 0 and 1. The case of pricing in one currency only is given by setting the weights to 0 or 1. Specifically, producer currency pricing (PCP), which corresponds to the producer keeping unit revenues fixed in his own currency, corresponds to $\beta_d^d = \beta_d^v = 0$. Local currency pricing (LCP), in which the producer has unit revenue stabilized in the buyer's currency, corresponds to $\beta_d^d = 1$, $\beta_d^v = 0$. Vehicle currency pricing (VCP) is given by $\beta_d^d = 0$, $\beta_d^v = 1$.

The sensitivity of p_d, the relative price between brand z and the competing brands, to exchange rate movements plays a central role in the invoice currency choice. Some brands are invoiced in currency d, so the price paid by the consumers for these brands is unaffected by exchange rate movements. Other brands are invoiced in currency e, and the consumer price in currency d moves with the exchange rate between the two currencies, s_{ed}, with consumer paying a higher price when currency e appreciates (i.e., $s_{ed} < 0$). A final set of brands are invoiced in currency v, so the price paid by consumers is higher when currency v appreciates (i.e., $s_{ed} - s_{ev} < 0$). We denote the total share of competing brands invoiced in currency d by η^d_d, and the shares invoiced in currency e and v by η^e_d and η^v_d respectively. In this case, the exporter's relative price of the good sold in the destination market becomes:

$$q^k_{ed} = (\beta^d_d - \eta^d_d)s_{ed} + (\beta^v_d - \eta^v_d)s_{ev}. \tag{4}$$

Expression (4) shows that, while stabilization of *unit revenues* requires $\beta^d_d = 1$, full stabilization of his *relative price* instead requires an exporter to choose weights on the different currencies that exactly correspond to their shares in the industry wide price index: $\beta^d_d = \eta^d_d, \beta^v_d = \eta^v_d$. However, stabilization of the relative price is not the only consideration driving the exporter's decision.

Optimal invoicing weights β^d_d and β^v_d maximize expected profits under the constraint that $\beta^d_d, \beta^v_d,$ and $\beta^d_d + \beta^v_d$ do not fall outside the [0,1] interval and given the structure of demand and costs shocks to which the exporter is subjected. GT show that the optimal invoicing basket solution for the case where an exporter is selling only to one destination market is:[3]

$$\beta^d_d = \Omega \eta^d_d + (1-\Omega)\rho(m_{ed}, s_{ed}) \tag{5}$$

$$\beta^v_d = \Omega \eta^v_d + (1-\Omega)\rho(m_{ed}, s_{ev}) \tag{6}$$

$$\beta^e_d = 1 - \beta^d_d - \beta^v_d = (1-\Omega) + \Omega \eta^e_d - (1-\Omega)[\rho(m_{ed}, s_{ed}) + \rho(m_{ed}, s_{ev})] \tag{7}$$

where:

$$\Omega = \frac{\lambda(1-\alpha)}{\alpha + \lambda(1-\alpha)}, \quad m_{ed} = w_e + \frac{1-\alpha}{\alpha}c_d.$$

The term m_{ed} entering into equations (5)–(7) is a covariance reflecting the influence of exogenous factors, for example exporter wages, productive inputs, and destination market aggregate demand, on the firm's marginal cost. Because of decreasing returns to scale, a 1 percent increase in demand requires a $1/\alpha$ percent increase in the labor input, hence a $1/\alpha$ percent increase in cost, holding the wage constant. The increase in demand also leads to a 1 percent increase in revenue, holding the price constant. The net increase in the marginal cost is then $1 - 1/\alpha = (1 - \alpha)/1$ percent. The terms $\rho(m_{ed}, s_{ed})$ and $\rho(m_{ed}, s_{ev})$ in (5)–(7) are regression coefficients that capture the covariances between marginal cost, m_{ed}, and the exchange rates s_{ed} and s_{ev}.

2.3   Components of Optimal Invoicing

While invoicing in the exporter's currency has the advantage of fully stabilizing the exporter's marginal revenue, this full stabilization ($\beta^e_d = 1$) is not necessarily an optimal choice for two reasons shown in equations (5)–(7). The first reason reflects a "herding" motive, captured by the terms $\Omega \eta^d_d$ and $\Omega \eta^v_d$. The exporter optimally limits the movements of her relative price by choosing an invoicing strategy close to that of her competitors: the exporter places a higher weight on invoicing in the destination currency, β^d_d, when her competitors have a higher share η^d_d of their own sales invoiced in that currency.

The second motive for a producer to move away from PCP is due to "hedging," as captured by the terms $(1 - \Omega)\rho(m_{ed}, s_{ed})$ and $(1 - \Omega)\rho(m_{ed}, s_{ev})$. These terms measure the potential for an exporter to have an invoicing strategy that helps profits by limiting the impact of fluctuations in marginal costs on her profits. If she invoices in the destination currency, d, a depreciation of her currency vis-à-vis the destination currency ($s_{ed} > 0$) increases unit revenue, in her own currency. If depreciations of this exchange rate tend to be correlated periods of increases in marginal costs, i.e., $\rho(m_{ed}, s_{ed}) > 0$, invoicing in the destination currency induces a positive correlation between marginal revenue and marginal costs, reducing some of the volatility in profits. A similar logic applies to the vehicle currency. Indeed, if we were to consider alternative vehicle currencies for use in an export transaction, the model implies that the hedging portion of the invoicing decision should favor the currency (i.e., the bilateral exchange rate) that is significantly and most positively correlated with the shocks to exporter costs, regardless of whether these arise through prices of imported inputs, local currency wages, or fluctuations in aggregate destination market demand.

The balance of influence on the herding dimension versus the hedging dimension in (5)–(7) is given by the term Ω, which solely reflects the structural parameters of the model, namely the elasticity of substitution between goods, λ, and the degree of returns to scale, α. The herding dimension is more pronounced (Ω is large) in industries where goods are more substitutable (λ is large), since movements in relative prices then leads to large fluctuations in quantities sold. The effect is also stronger when the technology exhibits larger decreasing returns to scale (α is small), because fluctuations in output generate large movements in marginal cost.[4]

Clearly, this theoretical exposition argues that optimal invoicing has both country-specific and industry-specific considerations. The country-specific macroeconomic correlations mainly apply to the exporters of highly differentiated products. By contrast, exporters in industries producing a more homogenous good (i.e., goods that are more substitutable with those of their competition) would optimize by following industry practices and invoicing in a basket of currencies close to that of their competitors.[5]

3. Invoicing Trade for Accession Countries

A recent ECB report[6] provides data on euro invoicing of imports and exports for eight euro zone countries (Belgium, France, Germany, Greece, Italy, Luxembourg, Portugal, and Spain), all ten newly accepted countries to the European Union (Cyprus, the Czech Republic, Estonia, Hungary, Latvia, Lithuania, Malta, Poland, Slovakia, and Slovenia), and Bulgaria, a European Union candidate country. In the analysis below, Bulgaria is included with the "euro area accession countries," misusing the terminology for brevity purposes.

The ECB data run from 2000 to 2003, with less complete coverage across countries in the early years. The data from the ECB report are supplemented with data on euro, dollar, and local country invoicing gathered from individual country sources, as detailed in the appendix tables of Goldberg and Tille (2005). The accession country data are presented in Table 1, with the top panel providing broad details for 2000, and the lower panel providing details for 2002, the last year for which dollar invoicing data are widely available.

Accession countries invoice their imports and exports largely in euros, with an average euro share well over 50 percent in 2002. However, the cross-country variation in the role of the euro in export invoicing is large, ranging from below 25 percent for Cyprus and Lithuania to over 60 percent for the Czech Republic, Estonia, Hungary, Poland, Slovakia, and Slovenia. With the exception of Cyprus, the data indicate a significantly smaller share of exports and imports invoiced in U.S. dollars. Most accession countries do not report local currency invoicing shares. The two countries that do, the Czech Republic and Latvia,

Table 1
Dollar and euro shares of trade invoicing in accession countries

	Exports		Imports	
	Euro share	Dollar share	Euro share	Dollar share
Invoicing Patterns in 2000				
Average	**46.0**	**39.3**	**48.5**	**37.8**
Bulgaria	37.0	60.1	47.0	50.2
Czech Republic*	65.4	14.1	63.1	19.7
Latvia**	35.5	43.6	35.5	43.6
Invoicing Patterns in 2002				
Average	**58.6**	**23.1**	**58. 5**	**27.6**
Bulgaria	52.0	44.5	60.0	37.1
Cyprus	21.8	44.7	45.5	34.9
Czech Republic	68.8	14.7	65.0	19.5
Estonia†	70.0	8.5	61.0	22.0
Hungary	83.0	12.2	73.0	18.5
Latvia **	47.7	32.1	47.7	32.1
Lithuania†	22.0		53.0	
Malta			34.7	48.8
Poland	60.0	29.9	60.0	28.6
Slovakia	73.9	11.6	60.1	21.2
Slovenia	87.0	9.6	83.0	13.3

* data from 2001 instead of 2000.
† data from 2003 instead of 2002.
** Latvian data are for overall invoicing of imports and exports combined.
All shares are for invoicing of goods and services combined except for the Czech Republic (goods only).
Source: ECB (2001, 2003, 2005) and individual country sources (details in Appendix Table 2).

report home currency shares for imports and exports at or below 10 percent. Since the sum of euro and dollar are closer to 80 percent than 100 percent for some countries (e.g., Cyprus, Czech Republic, Estonia, Latvia), it is evident that currencies other than the dollar and euro still play a role in invoicing trade.

Among these countries, only a few have invoicing data published both for 2000 and 2002, thereby providing only a limited perspective on how invoicing patterns are changing over time. The available data are consistent with the euro growing in its role as the currency used in invoicing both export and import transactions. This pattern is shown in Figure 2, where the left most bars indicate the increase in average annual euro use in invoicing the exports of the accession countries for which we have 2000 and 2002 data. To provide perspective on these developments, in the right-most bars I introduce comparable information for the euro area countries.[7] Among the three accession countries reported, the biggest increase in euro share over 2000 through 2002 is for Bulgaria, at almost 8 percent annually, followed by Latvia at 6 percent, and the Czech Republic at under 4 percent. The increase in euro use on export invoicing by euro area countries has been within a similar range over this time frame, again with variation across countries. Referring back to Figure 1, only Greece and Latvia had an increase in euro use in invoicing that might be expected based on the prior "unexplained" large vehicle role of the dollar in its exports.[8]

Figure 3 shows the extent to which increasing uses of euros in export invoicing came through reduction in the use of U.S. dollars for these purposes. For those countries for which relevant information is available, there has been both an (average annual) increase in the euro and an (average annual) decline in the dollar in export invoicing. Among the three accession countries for which there is appropriate data, euro gains

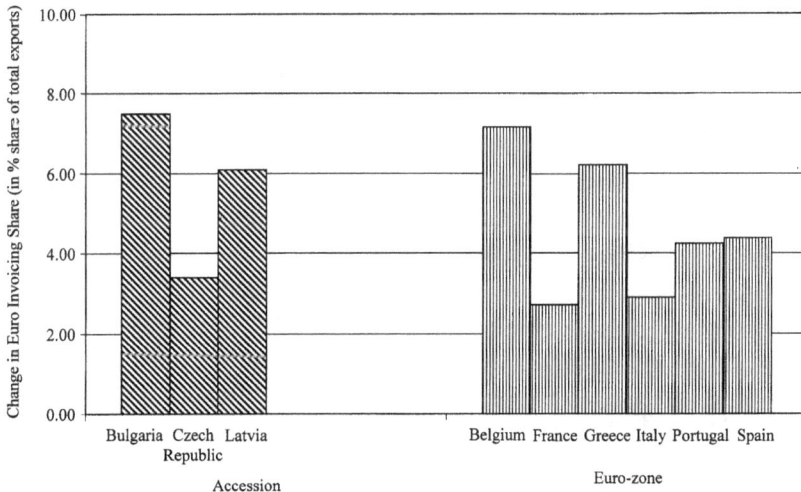

* or longest available period. Details of time periods in Table 1.

The data cover all exports for accession countries and Italy; otherwise, extra euro area exports.

Source: Author's calculations using data from the ECB report and local country sources (details in appendix).

Figure 2
Average annual rise in euro invoicing of exports, 2000–2002.*

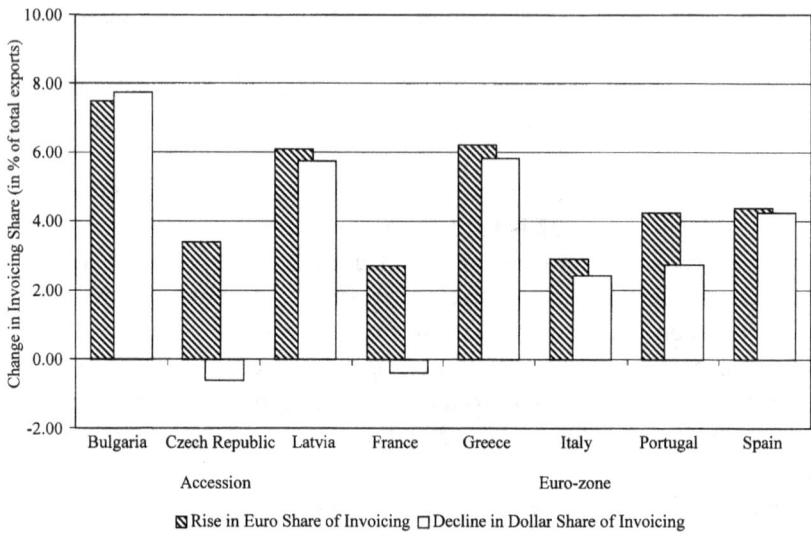

Source: Author's calculations using data from the ECB report and local country sources (details in appendix).

Figure 3
Average annual rise in euro invoicing and fall in dollar invoicing of exports, 2000–2002

have roughly matched dollar declines for Bulgaria and Latvia. For the Czech Republic, where dollar share in invoicing started low, increased euro use came through reduced use of other currencies. The experience among the euro area countries has also been mixed. For Greece, Spain and Italy, most of the increase in euro use came in parallel to reduced use of dollars. This was not the case for France, and was only partially the case for Portugal.

These changes in invoicing patterns may be consistent with a number of complementary hypotheses. First, there may be an increased prominence of the euro area and rest of Europe, or a decline in the United States or dollar bloc countries, as a destination for exports. Second, the increase in euro use and related decline in dollar use may be because accession countries have reduced the share of commodity type goods in their exports. Third, these changes may be driven by producer optimization under changing covariance structures in macroeconomic fluctuations. Alternatively, there may have been a switch in market invoicing behavior from use of dollars to use of euros on the same products, with the same partners.[9] This change in behavior might occur because of a change over time in macroeconomic correlations, highlighted in equations (5)–(7), with such changes possibly induced by shifts in exchange rate regimes. The analysis below addresses these hypotheses and provides perspective on whether accession countries are invoicing as predicted by the theory and implied exporter optimization, or are potentially exposing themselves to profits that are excessively volatile and lower than expected.

3.1 Destinations for Accession Country Exports

Did euro use increase in accession country trade because of increasingly close trade relationships with countries tied to the euro? Figure 4 provides data on euro share in invoicing exports versus euro area share in total accession country exports for the years 2000 (indicated with lighter points) and 2003 (darker points). If all euro area trade was invoiced in euros, and only euro area trade was invoiced in euros, the data points of this chart would lie along the 45 degree line.

The proximity of the three country-data points for 2000 to the 45 degree line indicate that initial use of euros in invoicing roughly matched shares of the euro zone countries in exports for accession countries in that year. Yet by 2003 use of the euro in invoicing accession country exports far exceeded the expanded share of the euro area in country

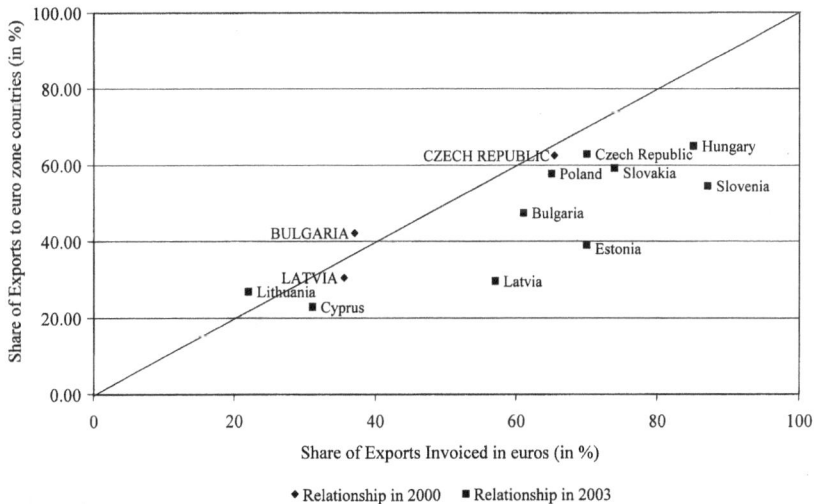

Figure 4
Export invoicing in euros versus exports to the euro zone, 2000 and 2003

exports. All accession countries, with the single exception of Lithuania, had euros play a larger role in export invoicing than would be expected purely due to trade with countries within the euro area (ignoring, at this point, the issue of the composition of trade, which should reduce euro use even within the area to the extent that other currencies are used in invoicing homogeneous commodities and goods). As reflected in distance from the 45 percent line, chart 4 shows that measured increases in euro invoicing between 2000 and 2003 well exceeded the mild increases observed in accession country exports to the euro area.

Another potential explanation is that accession country exporters are increasingly using euros to invoice exports to countries outside of the euro zone, for example to the rest of the European Union or to countries tied to the euro through exchange rate arrangements. Some of this change may be attributable to changes in the exchange rate or currency orientation of trade-partner countries. Such changes might induce changes in the structure of covariances entering the invoice currency selection criteria, or might even induce shifts in the herding currency equilibria for a particular type of good. Within these partner countries, a key related question is whether the competitors to accession country exporters are largely invoicing in euros or, for example, dollars.[10]

Tables 2A and 2B provide details on the concentration of accession country trade with European markets, the United States, and other countries heavily using the euro or the dollar. Table 2A shows that in 2003, the euro area accounts for between one-quarter and 60 percent of accession exports. Other "euro bloc" countries are not big export destinations. Much more influential are exports to the rest of the countries in the European Union but outside the euro area. Malta is a consistent outlier, but otherwise these countries collectively account for close to three-quarters of accession exports.[11]

Table 2B shows that accession countries export much less to the United States and other countries with exchange regimes tied to the dollar, both in East Asia[12] and other regions.[13] The United States purchases less than 5 percent of euro area exports of goods, except for Malta and Latvia. Accession countries also have low direct export links with other dollar bloc countries.

Available data does not differentiate invoicing patterns as accession country exports to the euro area versus exports to other Europe and euro-bloc countries. Speculatively, given the dominance of trade with the rest of Europe in accession exports, these might also be the markets where accession countries are invoicing in euros. Consider the

Table 2A
Accession country exports to the euro bloc and the rest of the European Union, 2003

Country	Euro area	Other euro bloc	Non-euro area European Union	Total euro bloc and EU
Bulgaria	50.7	3.1	7.1	60.9
Cyprus	31.5	0.1	34.6	66.2
Czech Republic	61.7	0.2	22.6	84.5
Estonia	39.7	0.0	36.9	76.6
Hungary	62.9	1.3	15.7	79.9
Latvia	27.4	0.0	47.0	74.4
Lithuania	33.1	0.0	36.0	69.2
Malta	25.8	0.2	12.5	38.5
Poland	57.7	0.3	22.4	80.4
Slovakia	58.8	0.6	26.7	86.0
Slovenia	57.6	7.3	11.5	76.4

Table 2B
Accession country exports to the United States and the dollar bloc, 2003

Country	United States	East Asia	Other dollar bloc	Total dollar bloc
Bulgaria	6.1	1.4	1.6	9.0
Cyprus	1.6	1.4	0.6	3.7
Czech Republic	3.0	1.3	0.9	5.2
Estonia	3.3	1.6	1.3	6.2
Hungary	6.3	1.7	1.1	9.0
Latvia	10.4	0.7	0.7	11.8
Lithuania	5.5	1.0	0.9	7.4
Malta	12.1	15.2	1.6	29.0
Poland	2.7	1.1	1.3	5.2
Slovakia	4.9	0.7	0.5	6.1
Slovenia	3.6	0.6	0.9	5.1

Source: International Monetary Fund, *Direction of Trade Statistics*.

following hypothetical invoicing. Suppose that 100 percent of accession country trade with the euro area is invoiced in euros (an overstatement given the composition of this trade across differentiated versus homogeneous and commodity-type goods) and 100 percent of accession country trade with the United States is invoiced in dollars. The implied use of euros on accession country exports to other countries are shown in Figure 5, with these residual exports primarily directed at the rest of Europe.[14] These computations imply that euro invoicing occurs on an average of 37 percent of accession exports to countries outside of the euro area and the United States. The variation across countries is large. Lithuania has zero implied euro invoicing on transactions outside the euro area, while Hungary and Slovenia have euro invoicing have shares exceeding 70 percent on export transactions directed outside the United States and euro area.

Such statistics can be compared with invoicing patterns of countries already within the euro area, where the euro serves as the producer currency as well as a potential vehicle currency elsewhere. Starting

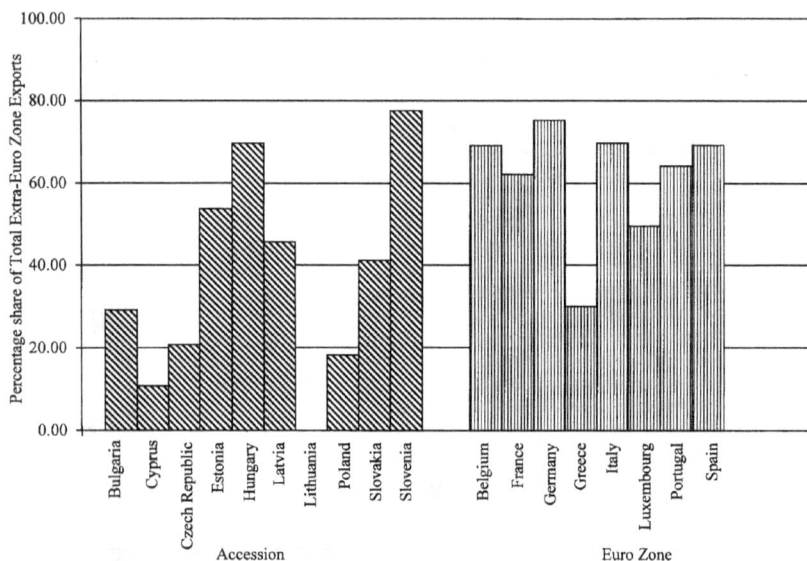

* With Accession country shares estimated assuming that 100% of exports to the euro zone are invoiced in euros and 100% of exports to the U.S. are invoiced in dollars. Slovakia data for 2002. Lithuania adjusted to zero from an estimated share of -7.4%.

Figure 5
Euro invoicing share in exports to countries other than the euro zone and United States, 2003*

with data on extra-euro area trade, euros are used in invoicing approximately 50 percent of extra euro-area exports. Under the assumption that trade with the United States is exclusively in dollars, the computation implies that euros are used in invoicing nearly 60 percent of the remaining exports. The range is from a low of 30 percent for Greece to about 75 percent for Germany.

3.2   The Composition of Accession Country Exports

The previous section focused exclusively on destination markets, without taking into account the composition of trade. Recall that the theoretical model predicts a dominant role of herding in invoice currency choice for producers whose goods face high elasticities of substitution in export markets. To highlight this point, this section categorizes accession country exports according to whether they are differentiated "N" (as are many manufactured goods), have uniform prices referenced in industry periodicals "R" (used for uniform goods not widely traded enough to have a world market, such as paper), or are considered Walrasian "W," which are homogeneous goods, mainly commodities such as ore with world market prices, typically quoted in a single currency and traded on organized exchanges. Box 1 presents examples of Walrasian and reference priced goods, with specific reference to exports of accession countries. For this construction of export composition shares, I use Rauch (1999) indices, which classify industries into N, R, or W groups, and apply these indices to sort country-specific 4-digit SITC data on exports for each accession country. Table 3 presents the resulting shares of differentiated (N), reference priced (R), and organized exchange traded (W) goods in each country's exports.

Differentiated products account for 62 to 83 percent of accession country exports. Organized exchange traded goods, often priced in dollars, are typically a small proportion of the remaining exports and are generally less than 8 percent of exports.[15] Reference priced goods are between 15 percent and 30 percent of accession country exports, with shares for Cyprus, Estonia, Latvia, and Lithuania all above 25 percent. All of the accession countries had reduced shares of the more homogeneous goods (the R+W share) between 2000 and 2003. Declines were large for Cyprus and Lithuania.

Taken together the shares of reference-priced and organized exchange traded goods represent between 17 and 35 percent of accession country exports. While reductions in these shares since 2000 may have

Table 3
The composition of accession country exports in 2003, shares by pricing method

Country	Differentiated "N"	Reference-priced "R"	Organized exchange "W"	Total R+W	
				2000	2003
Bulgaria	64.9	20.5	14.7	42.5	35.1
Cyprus	61.7	30.6	7.7	61.9	38.3
Czech Republic	83.0	14.5	2.5	19.5	17.0
Estonia	70.2	26.0	3.8	35.0	29.8
Hungary	81.8	13.7	4.5	19.8	18.2
Latvia	64.8	30.1	5.1	36.1	35.2
Lithuania	68.2	25.6	6.2	52.2	31.8
Malta*	80.3	6.3	13.4	19.7	—
Poland	75.5	18.7	5.8	28.5	24.5
Slovakia	82.0	14.6	3.4	22.0	18.0
Slovenia	80.8	16.7	2.5	21.9	19.2

*Source: Trade data from UN Comtrade, and author's calculations. Malta data from 2000.

accounted for some of the decline in dollar use in invoicing exports of accession countries, R+W goods still represent a large portion of accession country exports. For the most part, the observed declines are too small to explain shifts away from dollars in accession country export invoicing. Recall that the evidence on invoicing changes between 2000 and 2003 was only available for Bulgaria, Czech Republic, and Latvia. Accounting for the changing share of trade with the euro area, Latvia and Bulgaria had larger increases in invoicing in euros, while the Czech Republic had relatively small changes. This pattern is not matched by R+W share declines across these three countries, where the Czech Republic had the largest change, Latvia some change, and Bulgaria very little change in composition of exports.

If these R+W goods are invoiced in dollars in European markets, the model would suggest that many accession countries under-utilized dollars in invoicing exports in 2003. In some cases, the share of dollars used in invoicing total country exports is below the share of R+W goods in the export basket (Czech Republic, Estonia, Hungary, Latvia, Slovakia, Slovenia). Even though accession country exporters conduct much of their trade with other European countries, they still compete with producers from around the world, many of whom are likely invoicing these types of goods in dollars. The examples of pricing of copper, aluminum and paper pulp, shown in Box 1, illustrate the pervasiveness of dollar pricing on some products in these categories. If the accession country exporters are in fact invoicing less of their R+W type goods in dollars and instead invoicing these goods in euros, they may be exposing themselves to excess profit risk under circumstances of movements of the euro-dollar exchange rate.

3.3   Macroeconomic Covariances and Hedging in Export Invoicing

The theory exposition of section 2 emphasizes that specific macroeconomic covariances could impact producer pricing and invoicing, with these effects potentially economically important for producers of goods with lower elasticities of substitution. In our empirical exercise, these goods are classified and interpreted as the "N" goods, i.e., the ones that are differentiated products mostly found within manufacturing. From equations (5) to (7), the key hedging terms are the covariances between the alternative exchange rates for the exporter currency and

$$m_{ed} = w_e + \frac{1-\alpha}{\alpha} c_d .$$

Recall that w_e is the quarter-to-quarter percent change in an index of production costs, α is a parameter indicating the degree of diminishing returns to scale in production, and c_d captures the business cycle conditions of the destination market. The herding role in invoicing exports is given by the term $(1 - \Omega)\rho(m_{ed}, s_{ed})$ for the destination market currency, and by $(1 - \Omega)\rho(m_{ed}, s_{ev})$ for a vehicle currency on transactions with the destination market d.

We derive values for w_e, c_d, m_{ed} using data spanning the period 1980Q1–2005:Q3 and primarily drawn from Eurostat and the International Financial Statistics (IMF).[16] We confine our analysis to a discussion of the dollar and the euro as currency alternatives, and to the United States, the euro area, the rest of Europe, and Asia as destination markets. For each accession country exporter, wages w_e are quarter-to-quarter percent changes in nominal data.[17] Exchange rates are nominal and bilateral between each accession country currency and either the euro or the U.S. dollar. Exporter wages are the proxy for marginal costs, thereby excluding by construction consideration of correlations that might arise through the costs of imported inputs into production. To the extent that these imported inputs are commodities, the analysis will

Box 1
Sample industry profiles for reference priced and world market priced goods

Unwrought Copper: a world market priced good.
Rauch classifies commodity 6821, "Copper and copper alloys, refined or not, unwrought" (SITC rev. 2 4-digit classification), as a world priced good. Accession countries export large quantities of unwrought copper, $942 million in 2003 (UN Comtrade), representing 0.5 percent of total Accession country exports.

The main world market for unwrought copper is the London Metal Exchange (LME), with industry profiles and reports referencing the LME prices. The official prices quoted by the LME are in U.S. dollars per ton. The LME also trades unwrought aluminum, which also is a major export for the accession countries ($740 million in 2003), suggesting potential similarities in pricing and invoicing across both commodity categories.

The largest accession copper exporters are Bulgaria and Poland (unwrought copper comprises 6.0 percent of Bulgaria's total exports by value in 2003). Almost all of Bulgaria's copper is smelted at Pirdop, which is owned by Umicore, a Belgian company. The smelt copper is then exported to Umicore's headquarters in Belgium to be refined. So, Bulgaria's "export" prices are transfer prices not market prices, subject to qualification because they represent transfers within a corporation.

Poland's main copper producer is KGHM Polska Miedz, which supplies 6 percent of the world's copper according to AME Mineral Economics. KGHM posts a lot of information about its pricing structure on its website. They base their price on the LME and add a "producers premium" which is based on the annual price announcements of Codelco (the biggest world copper producer), which are also made in dollars. KGHM reports that the vast majority of copper sales are based on annual contracts where buyers agree to buy a certain tonnage a month whatever the market conditions, then pay each month based on the average market price over that month. A small share of sales is made with "spot contracts" to deal with unexpected shifts in supply or demand.

Paper: a reference priced good.
Paper is another major export for a number of the accession countries, including Estonia (2.5 percent of total exports in 2003), Poland (2.1 percent), Slovakia (2.0 percent), and Slovenia (1.8 percent). Pricing information is a little vaguer for this industry because, by definition, there is not an open world market with frequently published price quotes. Industry publications, such as Paperloop and Pulp & Paper Week, list monthly or quarterly market prices for various grades of paper, with these prices usually only made available to subscribers.

These periodicals publish prices for specific markets. Newsprint and pulp, both "W"-type goods, only have world markets listed, but the industry publications list printing and writing paper prices separately for North American, European, and sometimes Asian markets. When specific prices are mentioned, Asian markets and North American markets were quoted in U.S. dollars and Europe markets were quoted in euros. One publication listed a full table of prices from FOEX (Finnish Options Exchange) which were all in euros.

London Metal Exchange: http://www.lme.co.uk/
AME Mineral Economics: http://www.ame.com.au/
KGHM Polska Miedz: http://www.kghm.pl/en/index.php

Paperloop: http://www.paperloop.com/
Pulp & Paper Week: http://www.pulpandpaperonline.com/

likely understate the correlation between a true w_e and s_{ev}, where the dollar is the vehicle currency. Alternatively, if some production inputs are imported from euro area countries and euro priced, the covariance between accession marginal costs and euro exchange rates may be understated.

Four destination markets d for accession country exports are introduced: the euro area, the non-euro area European Union, the United States, and Asia.[18] Destination market demand conditions, c_d, are constructed as quarter-to-quarter percent changes in real consumption expenditure for each of the four destination markets.[19] Thus, for each country, four values of m_{ed} are constructed, each corresponding to the relevant destination market and each construction assuming a value for α equal to 0.65.[20] Each series m_{ed} is then regressed against the accession country exchange rates with respect to the dollar and the euro, the two s_{ev} alternatives, according to the following regression:

$$m_{ed,t} = a_0 + a_1 \text{ } trend + a_2 \text{ } local \text{ } currency \text{ } per \text{ } dollar_t \tag{8}$$
$$+ a_3 \text{ } local \text{ } currency \text{ } per \text{ } euro_t + \varepsilon_t$$

where the exchange rate terms are in quarter-to-quarter percent changes and ε_t is a regression residual. According to the theory, a larger correlation with a specific currency will make that currency a better internal profit hedge and more appealing in international trade transactions with a particular destination market.

It is possible that currency choices based on hedging motives evolve over time, as the economic correlations evolve. For example, correlations may change as the accession countries draw closer to the euro area in international trade activity, economic policy, and exchange rate regime arrangements. To capture the possibility of changes over time in the attractiveness of the dollar versus the euro as invoicing currencies for smoothing exporter profits, we examine econometrically whether estimated a_2 and a_3 have changed over time. For this analysis a variable $dummy$ is defined as equal to 1 during and after 2000 and zero otherwise and is interacted with the exchange rate terms in the regression given by (9).

$$m_{ed,t} = a_0 + a_1 \text{ } trend + (a_2 + d_2\text{*}dummy) \text{ } local \text{ } currency \text{ } per \text{ } dollar_t \tag{9}$$
$$+ (a_3 + d_3\text{*}dummy) \text{ } local \text{ } currency \text{ } per \text{ } euro_t + \varepsilon_t.$$

Table 4 regressions have quarterly data, but the number of observations used is limited by the availability of wage data for the accession

Table 4
Dollar versus euro invoicing for stabilizing accession country export profits

	US as export destination Regression coefficient $\rho(m_{edus},s_{edollar})$ $-\rho(m_{edus},s_{e,euro})$	Euro area as destination Regression coefficient $\rho(m_{edeuroz},s_{edollar})$ $-\rho(m_{edeuroz},s_{e,euro})$	Other Europe as destination Regression coefficient $\rho(m_{edotherEU},s_{edollar})$ $-\rho(m_{edotherEU},s_{e,euro})$	Asia as export destination Regression coefficient $\rho(m_{edotherEU},s_{edollar})$ $-\rho(m_{edotherEU},s_{e,euro})$
		Early Period (1992–1999)†		
Bulgaria	−0.54	−0.49	−0.46	−1.24
Cyprus	0.71	0.66	0.67	0.68
Czech	−0.74	−0.71	−0.71	−0.98
Estonia	0.00	0.09	0.06	−0.67
Hungary	0.18	0.19	0.21	0.04
Latvia	−0.15	−0.06	−0.10	−0.30
Lithuania	1.57*	1.58*	1.52*	1.28
Malta	0.09	0.03	0.04	0.10
Poland	−0.28	−0.27	−0.25	−0.26
Slovakia	−1.10	−1.07	−1.04	−1.44
Slovenia	0.42	0.52	0.48	−0.22
		Late Period (2000–2005)		
Bulgaria	0.57	0.54	0.54	0.52
Cyprus	0.71	0.66	0.67	0.68
Czech	1.15	1.11	1.12	1.08
Estonia	1.05	1.02	1.02	0.96
Hungary	−0.90	−0.93	−0.92	−0.96*
Latvia	−1.14‡	−1.14‡	−1.14‡	−1.32‡
Lithuania	−0.11	−0.14	−0.14	−0.18
Malta	0.09	0.03	0.04	0.10
Poland	0.50	0.45	0.47	0.38
Slovakia	0.84	0.82	0.82	0.77
Slovenia	0.37	0.33	0.33	0.29

† Exact dates differ by country. Details in Appendix Table 4.
‡ The coefficients on one or both exchange rates are significant, although the difference between the two is not. Coefficients for each exchange rate are reported in Appendix Table 2.
Note: Regression coefficients on local currency per dollars versus local currency per euros.
*, **, and *** denote significance at 10, 5, and 1 percent levels, respectively.

countries. Since data for many countries is only available after 1992, the degrees of freedom are low: consequently, we consider the findings as indicative but not conclusive. The numerical entries in the table are the difference between estimated coefficients, a_2 minus a_3, on the dollar and euro exchange rates with local currencies in each period. A positive and significant coefficient would indicate whether the dollar would, as an invoicing currency, provide better stabilization of profits of the accession country exporter to a specific destination.[21] A negative and significant value on a_2 minus a_3 means that the invoicing decision by an accession country exporter export transaction should favor the euro.

The results reported in Table 4 show that, in general, the regression coefficients are statistically insignificant. This result indicates that accession country exporters generally should be indifferent to the dollar or euro as invoicing currencies on these transactions. One exception is Lithuania, which has a significant dollar preference in all markets during the early, pre-2000, period and an insignificant euro hedging preference since 2000. In the later period, Latvia has significant negative correlations between m_{ed} and both the euro and dollar exchange rates, suggesting that neither currency is a useful hedge. The difference between a_2 and a_3 favors the euro, but is insignificant. The final significant observation is Hungary's preference for the euro as a hedging currency in the later period for the Asian market only. In the other markets since 2000, Hungary also has a euro preference, but it is not significant.

As a broad pattern, the preponderance of negative coefficients (and recognizing that most of the coefficients are statistically insignificant) suggests that more accession countries have a euro preference prior to 2000 than after, but only Latvia has a euro preference in both periods. Bulgaria, the Czech Republic, Poland, and Slovakia have a euro preference early, then move to a dollar preference since 2000. Hungary and Lithuania have a dollar preference early moving to a euro preference later. Estonia and Slovenia prefer the dollar as a hedging currency throughout, with the exception of the early period in the Asian market. Cyprus and Malta have no data prior to 2000, but exhibit a dollar preference in the later period.[22]

3.4 The Role of Exchange Rate Regimes

The accession countries had a variety of currency arrangements since the early 1990s, the period covered by our correlation analysis. These shifting exchange rate regimes may contribute to the changing patterns of dollar and euro preferences as a hedging currency.

According to the exchange rate regime classifications of Reinhart and Rogoff (2004) and Levy Yeyati and Sturzenneger (2005), seven of the countries we examine have been closely aligned with the euro, or earlier the DM, throughout the period we examine. These countries, Bulgaria, Cyprus, Estonia, Hungary, Malta, Slovakia, and Slovenia, tied their currencies either exclusively to the DM or euro or to a basket of currencies dominated by the DM or euro. The Czech Republic pegged their currency to a DM-dominated basket until 1997 and has been floating since then. Poland first had a loose crawling peg to the dollar, and then to the DM and euro, and has been floating since 2000. Slovakia also began with a loose crawling peg to a DM/dollar basket, then began effectively pegging to the euro in 1999. Lithuania was the only country exclusively pegged to the dollar before switching to the euro in 2002 as part of the process of joining the euro zone. Latvia has also been primarily associated with the dollar, pegging to the SDR, a basket in which the dollar has the strongest weight, throughout the period.

In general, the countries that have experienced significant shifts in exchange rate policy between the early and late period are also the countries moved from one currency to the other as a preferred hedging currency (although these effects are typically statistically insignificant). Another reason for covariance changes could be if "other Europe," as a destination market for accession goods, had business cycles that covaried more directly with the rest of the euro area due to their increased use of the euro. Such effects could continue to be monitored over time.

3.5   Overall Empirics of Accession Country Invoicing

This final subsection pulls together the insights from the prior sections to generate suggestive conclusions on accession country export invoicing. Table 5 provides perspective on whether the use of dollars in export invoicing appears to be relatively high or low, while Table 6 provides similar intuitions concerning euro use in invoicing accession country exports.

The first data column of each table shows the observed shares of each currency in invoicing. The next columns address the "motives" for using the respective currencies in invoicing. The final column compares observed invoicing versus predictions from the theory. The second column presents the sum of reference priced and exchange-traded goods

Table 5
2003 dollar invoicing on exports higher or lower than predicted?

	Observed dollar invoicing share*	R+W share in exports	Dollar bloc share in exports	Hedging Consideration Favoring Dollar?+		@ Is dollar share in invoicing lower than theoretically optimal?
				On exports to euro zone and other Europe	On exports to Asia	
Bulgaria	44.5	35.1	9.0	no	no	no
Cyprus	44.7	38.3	3.7	no	no	no
Czech Republic	14.7	17.0	5.2	no	no	yes
Estonia	8.5	29.8	6.2	no	no	yes
Hungary	12.2	18.2	9.0	no	no	yes
Latvia	32.1	35.2	11.8	no	no	yes
Lithuania	—	31.8	7.4	no	no	—
Malta	—	—	29.0	no	no	—
Poland	29.9	24.5	5.2	no	no	no
Slovakia	11.6	18.0	6.1	no	no	yes
Slovenia	9.6	19.2	5.1	no	no	yes

* Dollar share data from 2002 instead of 2003; late sample Table 4 results used in the hedging columns.
— Data unavailable.
+ Only statistically significant results reported, as "favored" using "Late period" coefficients from Table 4.
@ Is [(R+W share in exports) plus (dollar bloc share in exports) (1−(R+W tradeshare)) plus "yes" in hedging considerations] in excess of the observed dollar invoicing share?
Source: Trade data from UN Comtrade, author's calculations; IMF, Direction of Trade Statistics; individual country sources (details in Appendix Table 2).

Table 6
2003 euro invoicing on exports higher or lower than predicted?

| | Observed euro invoicing share* | R+W share in exports | Exports to euro-zone countries, as share of total exports | Exports to all of Europe, as share of total exports | Hedging Consideration Favoring Euros?+ | | Is Euro Share in Invoicing Higher Than Predicted? Assumes Euros Used on All Exports to All of Europe | |
					On exports to euro zone and other Europe	On exports to Asia	Exports net of r+w share	Total Exports
Bulgaria	52.0	35.1	51.3	85.3	no	no	no	no
Cyprus	21.8	38.3	23.0	64.0	no	no	no	no
Czech Republic	68.8	17.0	62.9	93.2	no	no	no	no
Estonia	70.0	29.8	39.1	92.8	no	no	yes	no
Hungary	83.0	18.2	65.0	91.7	no	yes	yes	no
Latvia	47.7	35.2	29.7	92.3	no	no	no	no
Lithuania	22.0	31.8	27.0	94.5	no	no	no	no
Malta	—	—	23.9	39.8	no	no	—	—
Poland	60.0	24.5	57.8	93.2	no	no	no	no
Slovakia	73.9	18.0	59.3	92.7	no	no	no	no
Slovenia	87.0	19.2	54.5	92.3	no	no	yes	no

* Dollar share data from 2002 instead of 2003.
— Data unavailable.
+ Only statistically significant terms reported as favored, using "Late period" coefficients from Table 4. Hungary is the only country where the euro has a statistically significant hedge property, and only with respect to Asia. This consideration is precluded from computations in the last columns of the table. In the net column, predicted share equals (all Europe export share) (1-RW share).
Source: Trade data from UN Comtrade, author's calculations; IMF, *Direction of Trade Statistics*; individual country sources (details in Appendix Table 2).

in a country's exports, while the third data column shows the share of the dollar bloc countries in exports. The last column pulls together the R+W, dollar bloc, and hedging considerations, and asks whether the use of dollars in a country's export invoicing is lower than what might be expected under the presumption that (1) R+W goods are priced in dollars worldwide and (2) dollars are used in invoicing (non R+W) exports to dollar bloc countries. The share of dollars in export invoicing is lower than expected for the Czech Republic, Estonia, Hungary, Latvia, Slovakia, and Slovenia.

Table 6 presents similar considerations, this time addressing the question of whether the actual share of euros in accession country invoicing is higher than expected by the framework. The predicted level is the all Europe share in accession country exports. In the first prediction column, this is net of the share of goods that are reference priced and traded on organized exchanges (which embeds an the assumption that all these latter goods may be priced in dollars); in the next prediction column, the euro invoicing share is compared with the share of country exports to Europe, ignoring composition.

In three of the ten countries for which we can do a comparison, the euro share is higher than expected based on the generous assumption that the euro is used on all trade with European partners, except for products that are homogeneous (which are assumed to trade in dollars). Those countries are Estonia, Hungary, and Slovenia. These countries are not "overusing" the euro under the even more generous assumption that all trade with European partners, including in homogeneous commodities is in euros, with no euro use on trade with other countries.

On balance, we conclude that Estonia, Hungary, and Slovenia have a greater tendency towards invoicing in euros than might be expected on the basis of trade with Europe being completely in euros and on the basis of the theoretical considerations that we have presented. These same countries, plus three others have dollar share in invoicing that are lower than predicted.

4. Concluding Remarks

This paper has considered the issue of invoicing of trade transactions by accession countries. Many accession countries have moved sharply away from the U.S. dollar as a currency for invoicing trade, reaching levels that appear low compared with both the role of the United States as a trading partner and the composition of accession country trade. Suboptimal invoicing exposes producers to lower expected profits.

According to the theoretical exposition, whether or not an accession country is well suited to the euro in export invoicing should depend on the partners in trade, the composition of trade, and the structure of shocks facing that exporter. If accession countries turn more toward the euro area as a destination markets for exports, then the role of the euro in invoicing may increase. However, potentially more important for this consideration is the composition of these products and the norms in invoicing by competitors to accession countries. At least in the case of commodity exports and highly substitutable goods, dollar invoicing on some trade may continue to be desirable even within the euro area. If exchange rates between accession country currencies and the euro are stabilized or fixed, and if exchange rates with the dollar covary positively with local shocks (so that the accession country currency or euro depreciate against the dollar when the accession country exporter faces high marginal costs), the model predicts greater use of dollars in invoicing euro area trade even as exchange rates are fixed with respect to the euro area. Alternatively, if exchange rates with the dollar covary negatively with local shocks (so that the accession country currency or the euro appreciates against the dollar when the accession country exporter faces high marginal costs), the model predicts a further movement away from accession country invoicing in dollars on euro area trade when exchange rates are fixed with respect to the euro area.

A broader question for the suitability of the euro for the trade invoicing of accession countries stems directly from the force of herding in a particular currency in the destination market for goods sold. This paper has often used the presumption that the U.S. dollar is the vehicle currency on pricing many international trade transactions, especially in highly substitutable goods. Evidence from a range of countries and a range of markets has supported such an assumption. An important consideration, though, is that the theoretical arguments, made in a partial equilibrium analysis, do not pin down which single currency—for example, dollars or euros or an alternative—will be selected by market participants for such herding.

While this herding has in recent decades been via the U.S. dollar, the stability of this equilibrium is important to consider. In particular, it would be useful to determine what types of shocks could lead to an unseating of the dollar in its vehicle currency role. In theoretical work, the answer to this question depends on what modeling assumptions are made in order to move from our partial equilibrium solution to a general equilibrium solution. The role of transaction costs in trading in different currencies might be the drivers of the equilibrium choice. This point was exposited by Swoboda (1968, 1969), and then elegantly developed by Rey (2001) in a three-country general equilibrium model emphasizing that "thick market externalities" arise from a currency's large presence in global international trade and low transaction costs of exchange. Krugman (1980) importantly pointed to the presence of inertia in vehicle currency selection, arguing, as we have, that when a currency is established as the dominant one in a market, a particular firm has no incentive to invoice in an alternative currency as this would lead to higher transaction cost and more volatile sales because of movements in its price relative to its competitors'. Once a currency has acquired a prominent role, because of low transaction costs for instance, it may keep this role even if another currency with similarly low costs emerges.

The exclusive role of macroeconomic volatility considerations in invoicing have been emphasized in recent general equilibrium papers, as in by Bacchetta and vanWincoop (2005), Devereux, Engel, and Storegaard (2004), Oi, Otani, and Shirota (2004), and Engel (2005). Yet, once a currency has been established as dominant in invoicing or as a vehicle currency and has lower transaction costs, the thick market externalities may make the conditions for overcoming the inertia difficult to satisfy.

Future theoretical work could bring these insights on transaction cost and volatility considerations together to yield predictions for the future optimality of invoicing in dollars, euros, or other currencies for exporters worldwide. Future work could also consider the conditions for segmented markets to arise in herding, perhaps leading to multiple dominant currencies in different subsets of industries or locations.

Acknowledgements

Federal Reserve Bank of New York and NBER. Prepared for the International Seminar on Macroeconomics, National Bureau of Economic Research, Budapest June 2005. Roc Armenter, Charles Engel, Rebecca Hellerstein, Richard Portes, Cedric Tille, and participants at the ISOM meeting provided valuable comments. Eleanor Dillon provided excellent research support. The views expressed in this paper are those of the individual authors and do not necessarily reflect the position of the Federal Reserve Bank of New York or the Federal Reserve System. Address correspondences to Linda S. Goldberg, Federal Reserve Bank of NY, Research Department, 33 Liberty St, New York, N.Y. 10045. email: Linda.Goldberg@ny.frb.org.

Notes

1. While Bacchetta and van Wincoop discuss this herding motive in the case where the exchange rate is the only source of volatility, Goldberg and Tille also include volatility in wages and foreign demand. Campa and Goldberg (2005) and Campa, Goldberg, and Gonzalez-Minguez (2005) show that macroeconomic volatility is less important than industry features in determining exchange rate pass through into import prices.

2. Small countries typically have low use of their own currencies in international trade transactions, as reported in Goldberg and Tille (2005). The two accession countries that report this information, the Czech Republic and Latvia, use their home currency on invoicing less than 10 percent of their imports and exports.

3. Goldberg and Tille (2005) derive a similar set of intuitions for the case where the exporter is constrained to use a single currency, rather than a basket of currencies, in his optimal selection. The results are qualitatively the same.

4. If we were operating in an environment of increasing returns to scale, with α bounded by negative 1 and zero, the role of λ would be damped as the degree of scale economies in production rises. The effect of an increase in returns to scale, i.e., an α that is more negative, is an unambiguous reduction in the invoicing weight on herding.

5. This theoretical exposition has focused on invoice currency choice when prices are sticky over the invoicing interval. Of course, in some cases flexible prices may better match reality. In this case, our lessons still hold since there is a direct parallel between optimal invoice currency selection and observed levels of exchange rate pass through into traded goods prices (Goldberg and Tille 2005; and Engel 2005). There is a direct correspondence between models of optimal invoice currency selection under sticky prices and those of partial exchange rate pass through in the case of flexible prices.

6. *Review of the International Role of the Euro*, Jan 2005.

7. The data for the accession countries and Italy cover all exports, while the data for the other euro area countries cover extra-euro area exports only.

8. Appendix Table 1 provides the raw data on invoicing for euro area countries.

9. Another, more mundane explanation is that these results are purely due to translation effects from changes in the dollar-euro exchange rate between 2000 and 2002. The valuation effects due to the strong dollar during 2000 made the dollar value of exports disproportionately high for euro area countries. If the invoicing data are based on nominal values, not real quantities, the decline in the dollar against the euro through 2002 could reduce the measured dollar invoicing share, even if actual invoicing patterns were unchanged. The dollar appreciated by 3.1 percent from 2000 to 2001 and depreciated by 5.6 percent in 2002. The cumulative change from 2000 to 2002 was a dollar depreciation of

2.3 percent, much smaller than the total average declines in dollar invoicing of exports of 16 percent for accession countries, and 14 percent for euro area countries.

10. Indeed, for perhaps similar reasons that the accession countries choose to invoice trade largely in euros, many countries outside of Europe choose to invoice their exports largely in U.S. dollars. As an example of this, Goldberg and Tille (2005) show that among Australia, Japan, Korea, Malaysia, and Thailand dollar invoicing averages 73 percent for imports and 75 percent for exports.

11. Non-euro area European countries are Denmark, Sweden, the UK, and the ten accession countries. As documented in Padoa-Schioppa (2004), "Other euro bloc countries" are countries with an exchange rate policy of pegging to the euro specifically Bosnia-Herzegovina, Montenegro, Serbia, New Caledonia, Benin, Burkina Faso, Cameroon, Cape Verde, Central African Republic, Chad, Comoros, Côte d'Ivoire, Equatorial Guinea, Gabon, Guinea-Bissau, Mali, Niger, Republic of Congo, Senegal, and Togo.

12. Cambodia, China, Hong Kong, Indonesia, Korea, Malaysia, Philippines, Thailand, Vietnam.

13. We define "Other Dollar Bloc" as: Australia, New Zealand, Canada, Argentina, Bolivia, Brazil, Chile, Colombia, Costa Rica, Dominican Republic, Ecuador, El Salvador, Guatemala, Honduras, Mexico, Nicaragua, Panama, Paraguay, Peru, Uruguay, Venezuela.

14. The share of euro use in extra-euro area exports is constructed as: (share of total exports invoiced in euros – share of total exports sent to euro area) / (100-share of total exports sent to the euro area and the United States), where all shares are in percent.

15. Differentiated products comprise about three-quarters of 2003 imports.

16. Date ranges for individual countries vary, with data for the Accession countries generally only available after 1992. Details of data availability and sources are in the appendix.

17. Data from Eurostat cover all goods and services trade excluding public administration services (NACE industries C to K). Data from IFS vary somewhat in industries covered depending on available data from each country, but give preference to indices that cover salaried employees as well as wage earners.

18. "Asia" is a GDP-weighted average of China, Hong Kong, India, Indonesia, Japan, Malaysia, the Philippines, Singapore, South Korea, Taiwan, and Thailand.

19. Consumption data are from IFS, Eurostat, national sources, and the Federal Reserve Board. Consumption is either reported in real terms or reported in nominal terms and then deflated with a national CPI. Source data details are available on request.

20. The value $\alpha = 0.65$ correspondences to a markup of 20 percent over production costs.

21. We abstract from country-specific Ω, which is related to the shares of R+W goods in total exports.

22. The early period results for Bulgaria, Estonia, and Slovenia are particularly weak because they only have only a few years of data prior to 2000. For Bulgaria, the early period covers only 1998 and 1999; Estonia and Slovenia have data beginning in 1996. The other countries have data stretching back to at least 1993, and into the early 1980s for Hungary and Poland.

References

Bacchetta, Philippe, and van Wincoop, Eric. 2005. "A Theory of the Currency Denomination of International Trade." *Journal of International Economics* 67(2): 295–319.

Campa, José, and Goldberg, Linda. 2005. "Exchange Rate Pass-Through into Import Prices." *Review of Economics and Statistics* 87(4): 679–690.

Campa, José Manuel, Linda S. Goldberg, and José M. González-Mínguez. 2005. "Exchange Rate Pass-through to Import Prices in the Euro Area." NBER Working Paper no. 11632. Cambridge, MA: National Bureau of Economic Research.

Devereux, Michael, Charles Engel, and Peter Storegaard. 2004. "Endogenous Exchange Rate Pass-Through when Nominal Prices are set in Advance." *Journal of International Economics* 63(2): 263–291.

Engel, Charles. 2005. "Equivalence Results for Optimal Pass-Through, Optimal Indexing to Exchange Rates, and Optimal Choice of Currency for Export Pricing." NBER Working Paper no. 11209. Cambridge, MA: National Bureau of Economic Research.

European Central Bank. 2001, 2003, 2005. *Review of the International Role of the Euro*. Frankfurt am Main.

Giovannini, Alberto. 1988. "Exchange Rates and Traded Goods Prices." *Journal of International Economics* 24(1-2): 45–68.

Goldberg, Linda, and Cedric Tille. 2005. "Vehicle Currency Use in International Trade." NBER Working Paper no. 11127. Cambridge, MA: National Bureau of Economic Research.

Krugman, Paul. 1980. "Vehicle Currencies and the Structure of International Exchange." *Journal of Money, Credit and Banking* 12: 513–526.

Levy Yeyati, Eduardo, and Federico Sturzenegger. 2005. "Classifying Exchange Rate Regimes: Deeds vs. Words." *European Economic Review* 49(6): 1603–1635.

McKinnon, Ronald. 1979. *Money in International Exchange: The Convertible Currency System*. Oxford University Press.

Oi, Hiroyuki, Akira Otani, and Toyoichiro Shirota. 2004. "The Choice of Invoice Currency in International Trade: Implications for the Internationalization of the Yen." *Monetary and Economic Studies* 22(1): 27–63.

Padoa-Schioppa, Tommaso. 2004. *The Euro and Its Central Bank*. Cambridge, MA: MIT Press.

Portes, Richard, and Helene Rey. 1998. "The Emergence of the Euro as an International Currency." *Economic Policy* 13(26): 305–343.

Rauch, James. 1999. "Networks versus Markets in International Trade." *Journal of International Economics* 48(1): 7–35.

Reinhart, Carmen M., and Kenneth S. Rogoff. 2004. "The Modern History of Exchange Rate Arrangements: A Reinterpretation." *Quarterly Journal of Economics* 119(1): 1–48.

Rey, Helene. 2001. "International Trade and Currency Exchange." *Review of Economic Studies* 68(2): 443–464.

Swoboda, Alexander. 1969. "Vehicle Currencies and the Foreign Exchange Market: the Case of the Dollar." In Robert Z. Aliber, ed., *The International Market for Foreign Exchange.* Praeger Special Studies in International Economics and Development. New York: Frederick A. Praeger Publishers.

Swoboda, Alexander. 1968. "The Euro-Dollar Market: An Interpretation." *Essays in International Finance 64*, International Finance Section, Princeton University.

Appendix

Table A1
Dollar and euro shares of trade invoicing in euro zone countries

	Exports		Imports	
	Euro share	Dollar share	Euro share	Dollar share
Invoicing Patterns in 2000				
Average	**44.6**	**43.0**	**43.5**	**46.8**
Belgium*	46.7		46.6	
France	50.3	33.4	37.5	46.1
Greece*	15.6	76.9	25.4	65.3
Italy	66.2	24.8	59.8	34.3
Portugal	39.6	38.9	47.9	40.0
Spain	49.3	41.3	43.7	48.2
Invoicing Patterns in 2002				
Average	**50.7**	**36.0**	**49.5**	**38.8**
Belgium	53.9	31.9	54.4	33.5
France	55.8	34.2	48.6	43.3
Germany	49.0	31.6	48.0	34. 5
Greece	21.8	71.1	31.0	62.0
Italy†	74.9	17.5	70.2	24.9
Luxembourg	44.0	35.7	31.7	38.0
Portugal	48.1	33.4	57.8	34.5
Spain	58.1	32.8	54.7	39.5

*Data from 2001 instead of 2000, † data from 2003 instead of 2002.
Currency shares for euro zone countries are for extra-euro zone trade only except for Italy.
All shares are for invoicing of goods and services combined except for Germany (goods only).
Source: ECB report and individual country sources (details in Appendix Table 2).

Table A2
Documentation on currency invoicing data

Country	Euro share data source	Dollar share data source
Bulgaria	ECB publication, Review of the International Role of the Euro, Jan 2005	Bulgarian National Bank
Cyprus	from ECB, by special request	from ECB, by special request
Czech Republic	Czech Statistical Office	Czech Statistical Office
Estonia	ECB publication, Review of the International Role of the Euro, Jan 2005	from ECB, by special request
Hungary	ECB publication, Review of the International Role of the Euro, Jan 2005	from ECB, by special request
Latvia	Latvijas Banka (Latvian Central Bank)	Latvijas Banka (Latvian Central Bank)
Lithuania	ECB publication, Review of the International Role of the Euro, Jan 2005	
Malta	ECB publication, Review of the International Role of the Euro, Jan 2005	
Poland	ECB publication, Review of the International Role of the Euro, Jan 2005	from ECB, by special request
Slovakia	ECB publication, Review of the International Role of the Euro, Jan 2005	from ECB, by special request
Slovenia	ECB publication, Review of the International Role of the Euro, Jan 2005	from ECB, by special request
Belgium	ECB publication, Review of the International Role of the Euro, Jan 2005	from ECB, by special request
France	from ECB, by special request	from ECB, by special request
Germany	ECB publication, Review of the International Role of the Euro, Jan 2005	from ECB, by special request
Greece	ECB publication, Review of the International Role of the Euro, Jan 2005	from ECB, by special request
Italy	Ufficio Italiano dei Cambi, by special request	Ufficio Italiano dei Cambi, by special request
Luxembourg	ECB publication, Review of the International Role of the Euro, Jan 2005	from ECB, by special request
Portugal	from ECB, by special request	from ECB, by special request
Spain	from ECB, by special request	from ECB, by special request

Table A3
Documentation on data for covariance calculations
Series codes and data availability for exporter countries

NSA: Not Seasonally Adjusted; IFS: International Financial Statistics; Haver Analytics as
data feed for Eurostat information, with associated data codes provided.

Country	Available dates	Wages: index of wages in all non-government industries (all NSA)	Dollar exchange rate: local currency/ U.S. dollar (all IFS)
Bulgaria	1998 Q1 – 2005 Q3	Haver, L918WCMW@EUROSTAT	$Q91800RF
Cyprus	2000 Q1 – 2005 Q3	Haver, L423TCMW@EUROSTAT	$Q91800RF
Czech	1993 Q1 – 2005 Q1	IFS, $Q93565	$Q93500RF
Estonia	1996 Q1 – 2005 Q3	Haver, L939WCMW@EUROSTAT	$Q93900RF
Hungary	1979 Q1 – 2005 Q3	IFS, $Q94465	$Q94400RF
Latvia	1992 Q1 – 2005 Q3	IFS, $Q94165	$Q94100RF
Lithuania	1993 Q1 – 2005 Q3	IFS, $Q94665	$Q94600RF
Malta	2000 Q1 – 2005 Q3	Haver, L181TCMW@EUROSTAT	$Q18100RF
Poland	1982 Q1 – 2005 Q3	IFS, $Q96465	$Q96400RF
Slovakia	1993 Q1 – 2005 Q2	IFS, $Q93665	$Q93600RF
Slovenia	1996 Q1 – 2005 Q3	Haver, L961WCMW@EUROSTAT	$Q96100RF

Comment

Charles Engel, University of Wisconsin and NBER

1. Introduction

This paper explores an intuitive theory of invoicing for exporting firms, and then examines some new data on invoicing for the European Union accession countries. The paper makes a nice contribution to our understanding of invoicing practices. My comments are divided into two sections. In the first, I make some observations about the invoicing theory presented in the paper. In the second, I discuss the application of the theory to the data.

2. The Theory

The model presented in the paper is developed fully in Goldberg and Tille (2005) (hereinafter referred to as GT). The model builds on some work of my own (Devereux, Engel, and Storgaard 2004; Engel 2005), as well as work of Bacchetta and van Wincoop (2005), so my critique of the model applies to my work as well. All of these models are essentially static models that examine the price setting decision of a monopolistic firm that must set a price without knowledge of the realizations of various stochastic variables (exchange rates, and other variables that affect demand for its product). The expected discounted profits of the firm are affected by the currency in which prices are set. The goal of these papers is to examine the factors that determine which currency is optimal—the currency in which the firm incurs its costs, the currency of the importer, or some other currency.

The GT model assumes firms can index their export price to a basket of currencies, and determines the optimal weights on the firm's own currency, the importer's currency, and a vehicle currency. They refer to a "hedging" and a "herding" motive, which Goldberg nicely explains in this paper.

The terminology, however, may be a bit misleading. The firms in this model act as if they are risk neutral. That is, under the assumptions of the model, the decision of the firm is equivalent to maximizing expected profits. Firms do care how much their profits could fluctuate across states, but that is because the profit function is not linear in all variables. The desirability of having prices set in the producer's currency or some other currency depends on the shape of the profit function, as Giovannini (1988) and Bachetta and van Wincoop (2005) have explained. The model in this paper assumes that demand has constant elasticity, and costs are increasing, but the results do not carry over to more general settings.

A different set-up would allow firms to be genuinely risk averse. Firms in the model of this paper discount expected profits, but the discount factor is assumed to be exogenous to the firm. That is, the decisions of the firm do not affect the level of the discount factor in any state. As Engel (2005) explains: "Firm owners might be risk averse, so D [the discount factor] could be the marginal utility of an increment to profit denominated in the currency of the exporter." In short, this objective for the firm holds under a variety of possible assumptions about the objectives of the firm managers and the structure of asset markets and possibilities for hedging. The assumption that D is exogenous to the firm does rule out some possibilities, however. Suppose a single household owns the firm, and the owner-manager discounts profits by marginal utility. The outcome for the firm might directly affect the level of consumption of the owner, and thus the marginal utility. The assumption that D is exogenous to the firm would be violated. An exogenous discount factor is more sensible when, for example, there are many owners of the firm, and there are many other sources of income for each owner. Thus our assumption of an exogenous discount factor is violated in the models of Feenstra and Kendall (1997) and the model of risk-averse firm owners in Friberg (1998), who assume in essence that firm owners' only income is from profits (so that the firm maximizes the expected utility of profits). It may be that in modeling the decisions of many exporters in accession countries, the assumption of an exogenous discount factor is not the most plausible one. Modeling the price setting decision under genuine risk aversion may make more sense.

All of these models abstract, however, from what must be one of the most important determinants of the currency of pricing, which is the cost to the firms of setting prices in different currencies. The underlying assumption of modern models of price stickiness is that it is costly to set a price. The costs of price setting must increase if the firm sets the price in many different currencies. That is, local currency pricing might be costly if firms export to many markets.

From many casual conversations I have had with businesspeople, as well as from a little survey I did a couple of years ago of Wisconsin-based exporters, I believe that these cost considerations do weigh heavily in the decision of the currency of price setting. Many small U.S. firms price only in dollars because it is too costly to figure out how to set prices in other currencies. Often these firms sell their product to distributors who may set a price in a different currency for export.

Those firms that maintain non-dollar price lists may set prices in only one or two other currencies. Typically these firms price in a foreign currency if a foreign market represents a large part of their sales. I interpret this to mean that there are fixed costs to setting prices, so that firms maintain a foreign currency price list only for large export markets.

These cost considerations may help explain why markets settle on a vehicle currency for setting prices. And, it may explain why so many firms that export to the U.S. set prices in dollars—because the U.S. market is large.

3. Application of the Theory to the Data

This paper considers a model of a firm, but it examines aggregate data on the fraction of export prices from a number of countries invoiced in various currencies. The data do not allow us to ask how an individual firm's decision changes when it is faced with different states. The data can only be described with an equilibrium model.

Bacchetta and van Wincoop (2005) show that multiple equilibria are possible in a setting that is a special case of the model considered here. If multiple equilibria are possible, then without a mechanism to choose among equilibria, the model can only predict features of the data that are common to all of the equilibria. Is there a way for choosing among equilibria? The answer might be related to the cost considerations noted above. Future work in this area might fruitfully examine the costs of changing prices, rather than taking as given that prices must be set in some currency (or some basket of currencies).

The empirical section puts a lot of emphasis on the currency of invoicing for goods that are traded in exchange markets. But the model does not apply to those types of goods. The model is one in which firms set prices in advance of shocks to exchange rates, and then sell whatever is demanded at the price they set. That is not a good description of the pricing in organized exchanges. Those prices are just as flexible as exchange rates.

It is not even clear to me that the model applies to those goods that are "reference priced," although I do not know the details of these markets. If prices are published in catalogs, then it does seem like prices are sticky. But then do firms have price setting power, as the model assumes? Do these markets really work like the model, so that buyers accept the price that is listed and simply demand as much as they want at that price?

It would be helpful if the paper were explicit on exactly what "invoicing" means in the data. Do these statistical agencies actually look at invoices and write down what currency is used? The model determines what currency prices are set in. That is, in the model, the price is set in some currency and cannot change (presumably for some time) when there are shocks. Is this the same thing as the currency of invoicing? Can't a firm set its price in dollars but write its invoice in euros? Is there any evidence that this does not happen very much?

4. Conclusions

I view my comments here as suggestions for the direction of future research. I do not want to minimize the contribution of this paper, and the work it builds on by Goldberg and Tille (2005). I will close by emphasizing what I believe to be the main contribution of these papers: they take somewhat abstract theory of the currency of price setting, and rework it into a form that can be compared to data; the papers present unique data on invoicing from a large number of countries; and then they test some of the implications of the models against this data. All of this is novel, and a step forward.

Note

1. The revised version of Engel (2005) in turn benefited greatly from my reading of Goldberg and Tille (2005).

References

Bacchetta, Philippe, and Eric van Wincoop. 2005. "A Theory of the Currency Denomination of International Trade." *Journal of International Economics*, forthcoming.

Devereux, Michael B., Charles Engel, and Peter E. Storgaard. 2004. "Endogenous Exchange Rate Pass-Through when Nominal Prices are Set in Advance." *Journal of International Economics* 63: 263–291.

Engel, Charles. 2005. "Equivalence Results for Optimal Pass-Through, Optimal Indexing to Exchange Rates, and Optimal Choice of Currency for Export Pricing." University of Wisconsin, manuscript.

Feenstra, Robert C., and Jon D. Kendall. 1997. "Pass-through of Exchange Rates and Purchasing Power Parity." *Journal of International Economics* 43: 237–261.

Friberg, Richard. 1998. "In Which Currency Should Exporters Set Their Prices?" *Journal of International Economics* 45: 59–76.

Giovannini, Alberto. 1988. "Exchange Rates and Traded Goods Prices." *Journal of International Economics* 24: 45–68.

Goldberg, Linda S., and Cédric Tille. 2005. "Vehicle Currency Use in International Trade." Federal Reserve Bank of New York, manuscript.

Comment

Richard Portes, *London Business School, NBER, and CEPR*

1. Theory

The paper argues that the choice of a currency for invoicing will depend on: (1) hedging: macroeconomic volatility, in regard to differentiated products; and (2) herding: market structure, insofar as herding may be desirable in markets for "reference-prices" and "organized-exchange-traded" goods (collectively, "RW goods"). Note that despite the reference in the paper to network (thick-market) externalities, the model has no network externalities. Rather, the herding motive arises from strategic behavior with respect to competitors' pricing decisions, with the objective of limiting movements of the agent's relative price.

2. So Where Are Network Externalities?

There is no "vehicle" role in invoicing per se—invoicing refers to money as a unit of account, not medium of exchange. That is why I believe that in the international context, it is better to use "vehicle currency" for foreign exchange markets alone. And that is where we find network externalities, in the use of money as medium of exchange.

3. Role of Transaction Costs

In a wide range of asset markets, including foreign exchange, unit transaction costs fall with aggregate turnover. Thus a third currency, v, may be used as an intermediary in transaction between two others, e and d, because the volume of direct exchanges between e and d would be so low that transaction costs in that market would be higher than the sum of transaction costs in going from d to v and v to e. The direct d-e market disappears. Again, none of this has anything to do with invoicing.

4. Forex Market Vehicle Currency and Invoicing

Portes and Rey (1998) argued that network externalities in foreign exchange markets interact with transaction costs in securities markets (especially those for government bonds, which are used as short-term store of value for foreign currency holdings) to determine the choice of vehicle currency in the FX market and the choice of currency denomination of asset holdings. That suggests that choices in the financial (bond, foreign exchange) markets determine which is the vehicle currency; that this in turn strongly influences the choice of a peg (if any) for the domestic currency, hence the choice of intervention currency, and hence the currency of reserve holding (Papaioannou et al. 2006). Moreover, one of the key determinants of the choice of invoicing currency will be the role of the currency as a vehicle in foreign exchange markets and the currency peg (not the converse). The bottom line is that the invoicing decision is influenced by much broader considerations than the hedging and herding motives examined in the model and in the empirical work of the paper.

The dollar is still the dominant vehicle currency in the foreign exchange markets. It appeared on one side of 88.7 percent of all transactions in those markets in April 2004, whereas the euro appeared on one side of 37.2 percent of all transactions (Bank for International Settlements 2004). If the dollar were to give ground to the euro as a vehicle currency and an asset currency (the growing U.S. current account deficits and debt…), then European export invoicing would probably become almost entirely in euros.

5. Role of Exchange-rate Regimes

There is no direct role in the model for the exchange-rate regime—i.e., pegging, managed floating, etc. Of course this will affect cov (m_{ed}, s_{ed}) and cov (m_{ed}, s_{ev})—e.g., if s_{ed} or s_{ev} is constant. But surely the exchange-rate regime is more important than that—in the extreme, can we imagine Pemex invoicing any Mexican oil buyer in USD, or a Canadian producer of timber invoicing in USD to a buyer in another Canadian province? So we should expect the exchange-rate regime of accession countries to affect their invoicing choices. This point is discussed briefly in the paper, and some allowances are made for it in assessing whether countries invoice "excessively" in euros, but I believe it merits more extended treatment.

6. Empirics

Here we have extremely useful and informative work with the data, including the application of the Rauch framework to accession countries. Still, in Table 4, virtually all coefficients are insignificant, and I cannot even see the "preponderance of negative coefficients" that the author claims. Moreover, I am not convinced by the key Tables 5 and 6.

Going from the early 1990s through 2004 is necessary to get enough observations, but the exchange-rate regimes of several of the accession countries changed significantly during that period. The use of a post-1999 dummy variable cannot take account of these changes, which were spread out over the period (Poland 1996; Czech Republic 1997; Bulgaria 1997; Latvia, Lithuania, …). Moreover, the euro came into existence in the middle of the period—as an accounting and asset currency at the beginning of 1999, as a physical currency (notes and coins) not until 2002.

7. Tables 5 and 6: Are They Suited to the Euro?

In Table 5, several countries are likely now to show the hedging consideration not favoring the dollar for Europe trade—e.g., Estonia, Latvia, and Lithuania (now have euro pegs), Slovenia, Slovakia, Hungary (all with managed floats with respect to the euro). That might leave only CR as "yes" in the last column. In Table 6, even as it stands, there are very few cases in which the euro share in invoicing is higher than predicted. Of these, Hungary is now in the euro band system, Estonia is pegged (currency board) to the euro, and Slovenia has a managed float with respect to the euro, with the prospect of adopting the euro at the beginning of 2007.

8. Conclusions

This is a very nice application of theory to the data. The empirical work is careful and detailed. The results are suggestive but by no means conclusive. And in my own view, the answer to the title's question is "yes," without doubt. Slovenia will in fact enter the euro zone in January 2007, and at least two others should have joined it under any reasonable criteria (those applied by the European Commission and the European Central Bank are decidedly unreasonable). They and the others will, I expect, continue to show rising shares of euro invoicing for their trade both within the EU and outside it.

References

Bank for International Settlements. 2004. "Triennial Foreign Exchange Market Survey." Press release, September.

Papaioannou, E., R. Portes, and G. Siourounis. 2006. "Optimal Currency Shares in International Reserves: The Impact of the Euro and the Prospects for the Dollar." *Journal of the Japanese and International Economies*, forthcoming.

Portes, R., and H. Rey. 1998. "The Emergence of the Euro as an International Currency." *Economic Policy* 26: 305–343.

www.ingramcontent.com/pod-product-compliance
Lightning Source LLC
Chambersburg PA
CBHW060958280326
41935CB00009B/754